Advances in Computer Science Applications and Research

3

This outstanding new series publishes state-of-the-art research spanning the entire spectrum of informatics ranging from foundational topics in the theory of computing to information and communications science and technology. A broad variety of multidisciplinary and interdisciplinary topics are welcome, as well.

While the focus is on publication of peer-reviewed full papers presenting mature work, inclusion of reviewed short papers reporting on work in progress are welcome, too. Besides globally relevant meetings with internationally representative program committees guaranteeing a strict peer-reviewing and paper selection process, conferences run by societies or of high regional or national relevance are also considered for publication.

Publication in ACSAR is free of charge. No royalties are paid, however, we offer registered conference participants temporary free access to the online version of the conference proceedings on SpringerLink (http://link.springer.com) by means of an http referrer from the conference website and/or a number of complimentary printed copies, as specified in the official acceptance email of the event.

ACSAR proceedings can be published in time for distribution at conferences or as post-proceedings, and delivered in the form of printed books and/or electronically as USBs and/or e-content licenses for accessing proceedings at SpringerLink. Furthermore, ACSAR proceedings are included in the ACSAR electronic book series hosted in the SpringerLink digital library at http://link.springer.com/bookseries/7899. Conferences publishing in ACSAR are allowed to use our online conference service (Meteor) for managing the whole proceedings lifecycle (from submission and reviewing to preparing for publication) free of charge.

Publication process

The language of publication is exclusively English. Authors publishing in ACSAR have to sign the Springer ACSAR copyright transfer form, however, they are free to use their material published in ACSAR for substantially changed, more elaborate subsequent publications elsewhere. For the preparation of the camera-ready papers/files, authors have to strictly adhere to the Springer ACSAR Authors' Instructions and are strongly encouraged to use the ACSAR LaTeX style files or templates.

How to start

To start the evaluation of your proposal for inclusion in the ACSAR series, please send an e-mail to acsar@springer.com , or directly to the editor responsible for your region. For more information about the responsible editor for your region please check the **Editors** section.

Carolina Palma-Preciado ·
Magdalena Saldana-Perez ·
Yanil Contreras-Jimenez
Editors

Advances in Computing, AI, and ICT for Innovation, Sustainability, and Environmental Stewardship

International Congress of Computer Science, CORE 2025
Mexico City, Mexico, October 27–30, 2025
Proceedings

Springer

Editors
Carolina Palma-Preciado
Instituto Politécnico Nacional
Centro de Investigación en Computación
Mexico City, Mexico

Magdalena Saldana-Perez
Instituto Politécnico Nacional
Centro de Investigación en Computación
Mexico City, Mexico

Yanil Contreras-Jimenez
Instituto Politécnico Nacional
Centro de Investigación en Computación
Mexico City, Mexico

ISSN 3091-2954 ISSN 3091-2962 (electronic)
Advances in Computer Science Applications and Research
ISBN 978-3-032-08893-2 ISBN 978-3-032-08894-9 (eBook)
https://doi.org/10.1007/978-3-032-08894-9

This Springer imprint is published by the registered company Springer Nature Switzerland AG
The registered company address is: Gewerbestrasse 11, 6330 Cham, Switzerland

Preface

The CORE 2025 Conference marked the 23rd edition of this international forum for computer science research. This year, the conference highlighted sustainability and innovation, emphasizing how rapid technological advancements can be applied responsibly across diverse domains. This volume contains the proceedings of the CORE 2025 International Congress of Computer Science, held in Mexico City, Mexico, from October 27–30, 2025.

The conference organized submissions into three main tracks to reflect their contributions. The Information Science and Technology track covered data management, information retrieval, human-computer interaction, real-time processing on mobile devices, scalability, sensor data integration, and feature selection. The High-Performance Systems and Technologies track included works related to high-performance computing platforms and dynamical systems. Finally, the Artificial Intelligence and Scientific Computing track encompassed machine learning, deep learning, computer vision, natural language processing, quantum classification algorithms, neural networks, cryptography, transformer-based models, fuzzy inference systems, hybrid algorithm designs, audio signal processing, and associative memories.

The papers in this volume showcase research that combines innovation with sustainable practices. Across domains from digital healthcare and education to computational modeling, novel algorithms, hybrid AI models, and multimodal approaches were introduced, with many contributions emphasizing resource-efficient computation, real-time data analysis, and applications that enhance accessibility to support both societal and environmental sustainability. These works demonstrate how technological innovation can drive meaningful and responsible impact across sectors.

Regarding the review process, each paper received at least two independent reviews. Most reviews followed a double-blind protocol, although some second reviews were conducted single-blind due to practical constraints. Potential conflicts of interest were handled carefully: two papers with conflicts involving a PC chair and PC members were managed by other committee members. In all cases, decisions were made transparently and rigorously. Overall, 61 papers were reviewed; 16 were accepted in the first round, and 7 in the second round, with most acceptances reached by consensus.

We extend our sincere thanks to all PC committee members and external reviewers for their prompt and constructive evaluations. Their contributions were essential in building a strong program for CORE 2025 and ensuring the selection of high-quality papers.

October 2025 Carolina Palma-Preciado

Organization

General Chairs

Magdalen Saldana-Perez	Instituto Politécnico Nacional, Mexico
Juan Carlos Chimal-Eguia	Instituto Politécnico Nacional, Mexico

Program Committee Chairs

Carolina Palma-Preciado	Instituto Politécnico Nacional, Mexico
Yanil Contreras-Jimenez	Instituto Politécnico Nacional, Mexico
León S. Mora-Guerrero	Instituto Politécnico Nacional, Mexico

Program Committee

Jorge Emmanuel Zamora Zamora	Instituto Politécnico Nacional, Mexico
Rodolfo Salgado Rivera	Instituto Politécnico Nacional, Mexico
Norberto Carrillo-García	Instituto Politécnico Nacional, Mexico
Emanuel Saldana-Perez	Instituto Politécnico Nacional, Mexico
Erick Michel Ramírez Rodríguez	Instituto Politécnico Nacional, Mexico

Additional Reviewers

Abril Valeria Uriarte-Arcia
Alicia Martinez Rebollar
Axel Ernesto Moreno Cervantes
Christopher Morales Martínez
Francisco Alvarez Rodríguez
Gener Avilés Rodríguez
Giovanni Guzmán-Lugo
Jesús Alberto Verduzco Ramírez
Jonathan Jesus Lopez Armenta
Jose Antonio Xohua Chacon
Josué Padilla Cuevas
Maria del Carmen Heras Sanchez
Norberto Carrillo-Ramón
Odette Alejandra Pliego Martínez
Sandra Luz Canchola Magdaleno
Victor Manuel Palma Preciado
Abraham de Jesús Pablo-Sotelo
Alejandro Medina Santiago
Carlos Guzmán Sánchez Mejorada
Claudia Zendejas-Morales
Edgard Benítez-Guerrero
Enrique Alarcón Jiménez
Ernesto De la Cruz Nicolás
Francisco García Ugalde
Gabriela Sued
Gerardo Hernández Oregón
Gustavo Adolfo Alonso Silverio
Iclia Villordo-Jimenez

J. Alejandro Cornejo-Acosta
José Alejandro Reyes Ortiz
Jose Angel Gonzalez Fraga
José-Clemente Hernández-Hernández
Luis G. Montané-Jiménez
Luis Pellegrin
Luis Villaseñor Pineda
Marco Antonio Moreno Armendáriz
Miguel Torres-Ruiz
Miguel Morales-Sandoval
Noel García Díaz
Javier Hernández Gómez
Rolando Quintero Téllez
Salvador E. Venegas-Andraca
Samantha Acosta Ruiz
Valeria Karina Legaria-Santiago
Victor Gonzalez Huitron
Víctor Jimenez-Fernández
Yazmin Linares González
Zaic Rebolledo Nandi

Contents

High-Performance Systems and Technologies

U-Net Based Active Matter Time Evolution Prediction 3
Jorge Saavedra-Benavides, Emmanuel Martínez-Guerrero, Saulo Abraham Gante-Díaz, Jesús Yaljá Montiel-Pérez, and Guo-Hua Sun

Implementation and Comparison of FIR Digital Filters on DSP and FPGA 18
J. Brandon Mañón Juárez and Eusebio Ricárdez Vázquez

Information Science and Technology

Real-Time Sheet Alignment in Mobile Devices Using Reference Mark-Based Elements 35
Oscar A. Diaz-Sanguino, Beatriz A. González-Beltrán, and Josué Figueroa-González

Fine-Grained Insights Generation Based on Semantic Clustering from Online Reviews 48
Brenda I. Guzmán-Bonilla, María J. Merino-Pérez, Daniel Sánchez-Ruiz, Ricardo Ramos-Aguilar, and Eric Ramos-Aguilar

Rapid Upper Limb Assessment Based on Fuzzy Logic and a Bluetooth Low Energy Sensor Network 64
Juan Mora-Sánchez, Luis Sánchez-Fernández, José Carbajal-Hernández, Diana González-Baldovinos, and Cynthia Baeza-García

Understanding Functional Impairment in Rheumatoid Arthritis: A Data-Driven Approach Using HAQ-DI and Clinical Metrics 80
León S. Mora-Guerrero, Antonio Alarcón-Paredes, and Iris P. Guzmán-Guzmán

Data Lakehouse for Type 2 Diabetes Remission: Scoping Review and Architectural Proposal 97
Carlos Andrés Morales Rosales, Lisbeth Rodríguez Mazahua, Nidia Rodríguez Mazahua, Giner Alor Hernández, and José Luis Sánchez Cervantes

Artificial Intelligence and Scientific Computing

A Bio-Inspired Visual Cryptographic Architecture for Data Hiding in Binary Images Based on Spiking Neural P Systems Along with Structural Plasticity 121
Karen Alejandra Valerio-Trigueros, Luis Ángel Olvera-Martínez, Manuel Cedillo-Hernandez, Carlos Adolfo Díaz-Rodríguez, and Juan Carlos Sanchez-Garcia

Quantum Associative Classification Model Using Amplitude-Encoded Feature Similitude 136
Areli-Yesareth Guerrero-Estrada, L. F. Quezada, and Guo-Hua Sun

Physics-Informed Neural Networks for Approximating the Solution of the 1D Poisson Equation 149
Emmanuel Angel Cabrera Navarrete and Gabriela Berenice Díaz Cortès

Modeling the Diffusion Equation with Physics-Informed Neural Networks (PINNs) and Artificial Neural Networks (ANNs) 168
Zoila Sánchez López, Gabriela Berenice Díaz Cortés, Galileo Domínguez Zacarías, and Gorgonio Fuentes Cruz

Fuzzy Inference Systems with Evolutionary Optimization for Timely Harvest Prediction: A Case Study 187
Jesús Emmanuel Brizuela Ramírez, Omar Sánchez Alaniz, Miguel Ángel Vejar Cortes, Salvador Ávila Ramírez, and Abel Romero Ruíz

Impact of Binarization on the Performance of Associative Memories in Machine Learning 202
Jorge Emmanuel Zamora Zamora, Rodolfo Salgado Rivera, Cornelio Yañez Marquez, Elias Jesús Ventura Molina, and Antonio Alarcón-Paredes

An Integer Quadratically Constrained Program for the Firefighter Problem: an Empirical Evaluation 215
Lourdes Beatriz Cajica-Maceda, Zaida Adriana Gárate-Cahuantzi, and Jesús García-Díaz

BREX: *Blend of Ranked-Sequential Algorithms Executed* for Boosting-Based Classification Applied to Wine Dataset 226
Acevedo-Sánchez Gerardo, Alarcón-Paredes Antonio, Yáñez-Márquez Cornelio, and Camacho-Nieto Óscar

Impact of Data Augmentation Applied to Fundus Images Used in a Swin Transformer V2-Based Model for the Detection of Age-Related Macular Degeneration 245
Roberto Marquez Castro, Jorge Ernesto González Díaz, José Luis Sánchez Cervantes, Yara Anahí Jiménez Nieto, and Adolfo Rodríguez Parada

Development and Evaluation of a Classification Model for Parkinson's Disease Detection Based on Ensemble Learning and Comparative Feature Selection Strategies 258
J. A. Gómez-Acosta, J. F. Córdova-Manzo, J. A. Otero-Martínez, A. Rodríguez-Peña, A. Hernández-Jiménez, and A. Minor-Martínez

YOLO Meets Tlaxcala: Toward Real-Time Urban Object Detection for Assistive Technology 269
Emilio Márquez Martínez, Ernesto Mendieta Cuecuecha, Jesús García Ramírez, and Eric Ramos-Aguilar

EEG Conformer for Inner Speech: Limitations in Model Transferability and Mitigation Strategies 283
Luciana Espindola Ulibarri, Olga Kolesnikova, and Rolando Menchaca Méndez

Analysis of Conversations in Adults Using Multimodal Data Processing 301
Carolina Naomi Alvarez-Peralta, Janet Badillo-Tecuapacho, Eric Ramos-Aguilar, Daniel Sánchez-Ruiz, and Ricardo Ramos-Aguilar

Application of Natural Language Processing Techniques for the Classification and Recommendation of University-Level Mathematical Content 319
María Fernanda León-Pluma, Estefanía Fernanda Vázquez-Osorno, Daniel Sánchez-Ruiz, Eric Ramos-Aguilar, and Jesús García-Ramírez

Enhancing English–Urdu Machine Translation Using Transfer Learning 335
Fida Ullah, M. Tayyab Zamir, M. Ahmad, Irina Gelbukh, Grigori Sidorov, and Edgardo Manuel Felipe Riverón

Authorship Attribution in a Scientific Papers by Syntactic and Semantic Textual Representations 347
Carlos Pérez Guarneros, Cecilia Reyes-Peña, Jesús García-Ramírez, and Silvia Sánchez-Márquez

Author Index 359

High-Performance Systems and Technologies

U-Net Based Active Matter Time Evolution Prediction

Jorge Saavedra-Benavides(✉), Emmanuel Martínez-Guerrero, Saulo Abraham Gante-Díaz, Jesús Yaljá Montiel-Pérez, and Guo-Hua Sun

Centro de Investigación en Computación, Instituto Politécnico Nacional, UPALM, 07738 CDMX, Mexico
{jsaavedrab2024,emartinezg2025,sganted2023,jyalja,gsun}@cic.ipn.mx

Abstract. Complex dynamical systems, such as active matter composed of large populations of self-propelled particles interacting with each other, present significant challenges for traditional numerical simulations. Recent advances in machine learning offer a promising alternative to address the most computationally demanding problems. In this work, we evaluate the prediction performance of several state of the art neural networks on an active matter dataset from The Well benchmark, a collection of diverse physical simulations. Specifically, we replicate experiments using three benchmark models: CNextU net, classical U-net, and Fourier Neural Operator, all trained under identical conditions and compared using the Variance scaled Root Mean Squared Error (VRMSE) metric. To further improve efficiency, we introduce a U-net variant that replaces the traditional hyperbolic tangent activation functions with Rectified Linear Units. Within a fixed ten hour training budget, the ReLU-based variant completes substantially more epochs than its Tanh-based counterpart and achieves competitive VRMSE values surpassing previously reported results on the active matter dataset. Our findings demonstrate that modest architectural changes, combined with careful hyperparameter tuning, can yield high-accuracy prediction.

Keywords: Deep learning · Complex system · Prediction · Dynamics

1 Introduction

The study of complex physical systems, such as turbulence in fluid dynamics [1], spin glasses [2], disordered systems in statistical physics [3] and protein folding in molecular biology [4] has frequently served as a catalyst for the development of sophisticated computational techniques. These methods enable a detailed analysis of the time evolution of such systems, often modeled by partial differential equations (PDEs), that depend on initial conditions and external or internal stimuli [5]. However, this task becomes particularly challenging when the analytic solutions of PDEs cannot be found and the computational cost of numerical

C. Palma-Preciado et al. (Eds.): CORE 2025, ACSAR 3, pp. 3–17, 2026.
https://doi.org/10.1007/978-3-032-08894-9_1

methods becomes intractable. In such cases, simulations offer a practical means to explore system dynamics [6].

In recent years, deep learning has emerged as a promising alternative for modeling and solving problems traditionally approached through numerical methods and simulations. These approaches are notably valuable in high-dimensional and nonlinear systems where classical techniques often fail [7]. Nevertheless, the successful implementation of deep learning techniques depends heavily on the availability of high-quality datasets for training and evaluation [8,9]. In this context, *The Well* repository [10] has become as a valuable resource for the research community, offering a collection of 16 datasets that correspond to simulations of various physical phenomena. The dataset under consideration, which is the focal point of this study, is designated "*Active Matter*". This dataset encompasses the evolution of systems constituted of active biological matter.

To assess the effectiveness of neural networks in modeling such systems, we evaluated and compared the architectures proposed in previous studies [5] and introduced a U-Net ReLU-based variant architecture model adapted for temporal sequence prediction from image data. The aim of this work is to evaluate the efficacy of these models in predicting subsequent states of the system based on prior observations.

The remainder of this paper is structured as follows: Sect. 2 introduces the theoretical framework underlying the dynamics of active matter, provides a detailed description of the active matter dataset, and presents the U-net architecture as a prediction model. Section 3 describes the neural network architectures evaluated, including the proposed U-net variant with ReLU activations, along with the training protocols and evaluation metrics. Section 4 reports the experimental results, comparing prediction performance across models and discussing the effects of architectural modifications. Finally, Sect. 5 summarizes the main findings.

2 Background

Active matter systems exhibit complex collective behaviors that are computationally expensive to model using traditional numerical methods. In this section, we present the theoretical framework underlying active matter dynamics, describe the dataset from the Well repository used in this study, and introduce the U-Net architecture, which forms the core of our proposed model.

2.1 Active Matter Dynamics and Theoretical Framework

Active matter systems consist of self-driven particles that convert chemical energy into mechanical work, resulting in complex collective behaviors far from equilibrium. We focus on suspensions of N elongated active particles with length, ℓ, and thickness, b, characterized by a large aspect ratio, $\ell/b \gg 1$, immersed in a viscous Stokes fluid occupying a cubic domain, V [11]. A well-studied example of such systems is the bacterium E. Coli in water, where viscous forces dominate over inertial forces [12,13]. E. Coli cells are approximately 1.5 μm long and 0.5 μm wide, satisfying the slender-body assumption $\ell/b \gg 1$ [14].

In the large-particle limit, continuum kinetic theories effectively describe the evolution of the particle distribution function, $\Psi(\mathbf{x}, \mathbf{p}, t)$, which depends on spatial position, $\mathbf{x}$, orientation, $\mathbf{p}$, and time, t [11,15].

The Smoluchowski equation governs the time evolution of Ψ, ensuring conservation of particle number:

$$\frac{\partial \Psi}{\partial t} + \nabla_{\mathbf{x}} \cdot (\dot{\mathbf{x}}\Psi) + \nabla_{\mathbf{p}} \cdot (\dot{\mathbf{p}}\Psi) = 0, \tag{1}$$

where the translational and rotational fluxes, $\dot{\mathbf{x}} = \frac{d\mathbf{x}}{dt}$ and $\dot{\mathbf{p}} = \frac{d\mathbf{p}}{dt}$, arise from single-particle dynamics in the background fluid flow, $\mathbf{u}(\mathbf{x}, t)$.

Moments of Ψ define key physical fields: the particle local concentration, $c = \langle 1 \rangle$, and polarity, $\mathbf{n} = \langle \mathbf{p} \rangle / c$, where $\langle \cdot \rangle$ denotes surface integration over the unit orientation space [15].

For dense suspensions, the fluxes are modeled as:

$$\dot{\mathbf{x}} = \mathbf{u} - d_T \nabla_{\mathbf{x}} \log \Psi, \quad \dot{\mathbf{p}} = (\mathbf{I} - \mathbf{pp}) \cdot (\nabla \mathbf{u} + 2\zeta \mathbf{D}) \cdot \mathbf{p} - d_R \nabla_{\mathbf{p}} \log \Psi, \tag{2}$$

where d_T and d_R are dimensionless translational and rotational diffusion coefficients, ζ quantifies particle alignment strength, and $\mathbf{D} = \langle \mathbf{pp} \rangle$ is the second-moment tensor.

The Smoluchowski equation couples to the incompressible Stokes flow:

$$-\Delta \mathbf{u} + \nabla P = \nabla \cdot \mathbf{\Sigma}, \quad \nabla \cdot \mathbf{u} = 0, \tag{3}$$

with fluid pressure, $P(\mathbf{x}, t)$ and stress tensor, $\mathbf{\Sigma}$, incorporating active and passive contributions:

$$\mathbf{\Sigma} = \alpha \mathbf{D} + \beta \mathbf{S} : \mathbf{E} - 2\zeta\beta(\mathbf{D} \cdot \mathbf{D} - \mathbf{S} : \mathbf{D}), \tag{4}$$

where α is the dimensionless active dipole strength, β characterizes particle density, $\mathbf{E} = (\nabla \mathbf{u} + \nabla \mathbf{u}^\top)/2$ is the symmetric rate-of-strain tensor, and $\mathbf{S} = \langle \mathbf{pppp} \rangle$ is the fourth-moment tensor [11].

While this kinetic framework rigorously captures active matter physics, it is computationally expensive, especially for dense suspensions with strong alignment interactions (large ζ). Coarse-grained moment models reduce dimensionality but require phenomenological or learned closures to maintain accuracy [12,16,17].

Hence, there is a critical need for fast and data-efficient surrogate models that can accurately predict the evolution of low-order moments. Autoregressive surrogate models are promising candidates for efficiently exploring the complex parameter space of active matter systems and aiding the design of self-organizing materials with tunable dynamical states.

It is important to clarify that the equations presented in this section, which describe the theoretical framework of active matter systems, were not directly used to generate the results in this study. Instead, the simulation data used for training and evaluation were obtained from *The Well*, which employs numerical solvers based on continuum models. Furthermore, the theoretical background is included to provide context and motivation for the machine learning models evaluated. Accordingly, no direct comparisons are made between theoretical predictions from the kinetic framework and the surrogate model results obtained in this work.

2.2 The Active Matter Dataset

The Well is a large-scale collection of machine learning datasets containing 15TB of numerical simulations across 16 diverse physical systems, including biological processes, fluid dynamics, and magneto-hydrodynamics [5]. These datasets serve as benchmarks to advance machine learning and computational science research.

This work uses the *active matter* dataset from The Well repository [10], generated by solving the coupled Smoluchowski-Stokes equations on a 2D periodic square domain of length, $L = 10$. The domain is discretized into 256×256 spatial modes and 256 orientational modes, providing high-resolution spatiotemporal data.

Simulations employ a pseudo-spectral method with Fourier differentiation for spatial and orientational derivatives. Time integration uses a second-order implicit-explicit backward differentiation scheme (SBDF2), treating linear terms implicitly and nonlinear terms explicitly, with time step, $\Delta t = 0.0004\,s$. Physical parameters vary with active dipole strength, $\alpha \in \{-1, -2, -3, -4, -5\}$, particle density, $\beta = 0.8$, and alignment strength, $\zeta \in \{1, 3, 5, 7, 9, 11, 13, 15, 17\}$. The dataset consists of sequences of 256×256 images recorded at 81 time points spaced by $\Delta t = 0.25\,s$. Each data sample contains multiple fields as summarized in Table 1.

Table 1. Contents of each data sample in the active matter dataset

Field Name	Description
`input_fields`	Model input fields (spatiotemporal physical variables)
`output_fields`	Target output fields for prediction
`constant_scalars`	Physical constants used in the simulation
`boundary_conditions`	Boundary conditions applied to the domain
`space_grid`	Spatial grid coordinates
`input_time_grid`	Time points corresponding to input fields
`output_time_grid`	Time points corresponding to output fields

Our focus is on `input_fields` and `output_fields`, which serve as model inputs and targets. They have shapes (T_{in}, L_x, L_y, F) and (T_{out}, L_x, L_y, F) respectively, where T_{in} and T_{out} are input/output time steps, L_x and L_y are spatial dimensions, and $F = 11$ physical fields. These include particle concentration, velocity components, ($velocity_x$, $velocity_y$), second-moment tensor components, $(D_{xx}, D_{xy}, D_{yx}, D_{yy})$, and rate-of-strain tensor components, $(E_{xx}, E_{xy}, E_{yx}, E_{yy})$. Figure 1 illustrates example `input_fields`, comprising snapshots of the fields at four consecutive time steps from the dataset.

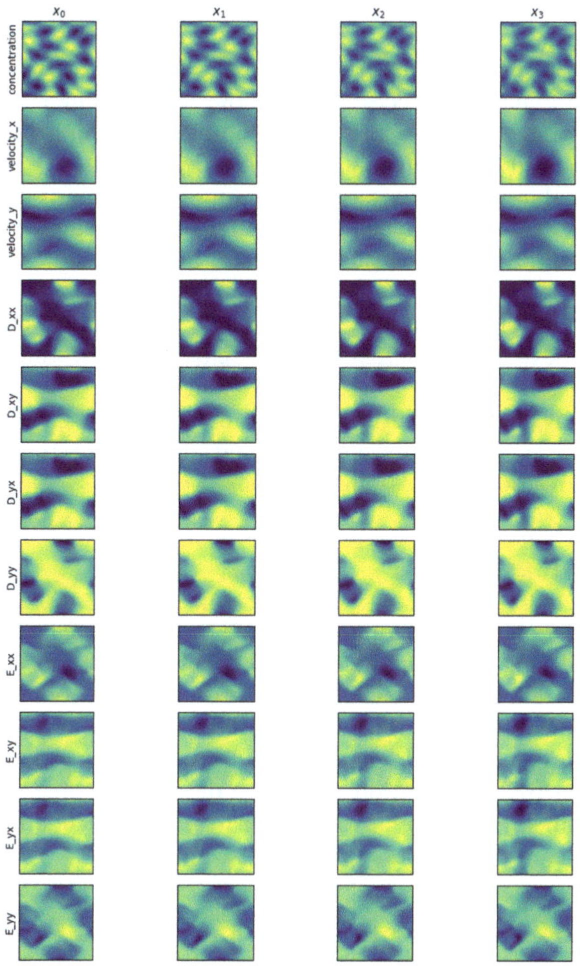

Fig. 1. Example input fields from the Active Matter dataset in *The Well* repository.

2.3 U-Net Architecture

The U-Net architecture is a type of fully convolutional neural network originally developed for biomedical image segmentation [18]. It is characterized by a distinctive U-shaped design composed of two main parts: a contracting path (encoder) and an expansive path (decoder).

The **contracting path** captures the context of the input by progressively downsampling the spatial dimensions while increasing the number of feature channels. This is typically achieved through repeated blocks of convolutional layers followed by pooling operations. Each convolutional block extracts increasingly abstract features, allowing the network to understand complex patterns at multiple scales.

The **expansive path** symmetrically upsamples these features to restore the spatial resolution, enabling precise localization. Upsampling is performed using transposed convolutions or other interpolation methods, and the number of feature channels is gradually reduced. Crucially, the expansive path incorporates *skip connections* that concatenate corresponding feature maps from the contracting path. These skip connections allow the network to combine high-resolution spatial information with the abstracted context, improving the accuracy of pixel-level predictions.

This encoder-decoder structure, with its skip connections, enables U-Net to effectively learn both global context and fine spatial details, which is essential for tasks requiring precise localization such as segmentation or spatial field prediction. Unlike traditional convolutional neural networks that often end with fully connected layers, U-Net is fully convolutional, allowing it to accept inputs of varying sizes and produce correspondingly sized outputs.

3 Methodology

In this section, we present the framework used to evaluate neural network architectures for predicting the temporal evolution of active matter systems. We begin by reviewing the benchmark U-NetâĂŞinspired models from the Well repository, which serve as baselines representing different architectural approaches to spatiotemporal prediction. Subsequently, we introduce our proposed U-Net variant incorporating ReLU activations. We then detail the experimental protocols, training procedures, and computational constraints, and finally, we define the evaluation metrics used to assess predictive accuracy.

3.1 Benchmark Architecture Models in The Well Framework

Within The Well framework, several U-Net-inspired architectures have been introduced and benchmarked for predicting the spatiotemporal dynamics of an active matter system. These models reflect a range of architectural choices balancing complexity, receptive field size, and computational efficiency, providing strong baselines for comparison.

Classical U-net serves as a baseline architecture closely following the original U-Net design [18]. It employs smaller 3x3 convolutional kernels, starts with a higher initial feature dimension of 48, and uses a single convolutional block per stage. The network maintains four downsampling and upsampling stages and a single bottleneck block. This simpler design emphasizes efficient feature extraction with fewer parameters and computational overhead, relying on skip connections to preserve spatial details.

CNextU-net is a modern U-Net variant designed to capture broader spatial context through larger convolutional filters and deeper feature extraction [5]. It uses spatial convolutional kernels of size 7, an initial feature dimension of 42, and two convolutional blocks per stage. The network comprises four downsampling and upsampling stages, connected by a single bottleneck block. This configuration increases the receptive field and feature richness, enabling the model to better represent complex spatial correlations. The larger kernel size and multiple blocks per stage aim to improve feature abstraction without excessively increasing depth.

Fourier Neural Operator (FNO) represents a distinct approach that operates in the spectral domain by learning mappings between function spaces using Fourier transforms [19]. The FNO model used here includes 16 spectral modes, a hidden dimension of 128, and four iterative blocks. While not a U-Net architecture, it is included in the benchmark due to its strong performance on PDE-related tasks and its ability to capture global dependencies efficiently through spectral convolutions.

3.2 Proposed U-Net Architecture

We propose a U-Net variant based on the classical encoder-decoder structure, designed to predict the time evolution of active matter fields with high spatial fidelity. The network consists of an encoder path that progressively downsamples the input through convolutional blocks and max-pooling, and a decoder path that upsamples and reconstructs the output while preserving spatial details via skip connections.

Each convolutional block in both encoder and decoder comprises a convolutional layer followed by batch normalization and the Rectified Linear Unit (ReLU) activation function [20,21]. The ReLU is mathematically defined as:

$$f(x) = \max(0, x) = \begin{cases} x & \text{if } x > 0, \\ 0 & \text{if } x \leq 0. \end{cases} \tag{5}$$

This piecewise linear function introduces essential nonlinearity into the network, allowing positive input signals to pass unchanged while zeroing out negative inputs. The derivative of ReLu is simple and constant (equal to 1) for positive inputs, and zero otherwise, which facilitates efficient gradient propagation during training.

For comparison, the hyperbolic tangent function, commonly used in earlier neural networks, is defined as:

$$\tanh(x) = \frac{e^x - e^{-x}}{e^x + e^{-x}}, \tag{6}$$

which smoothly maps real-valued inputs to outputs bounded between −1 and 1. It's derivative is given by:

$$\frac{d}{dx}\tanh(x) = 1 - \tanh^2(x), \tag{7}$$

which diminishes toward zero as the input magnitude grows large, causing the well-known vanishing gradient problem [22,23].

Unlike tanh, ReLU avoids this saturation issue because for positive inputs its gradient remains constant, thereby preserving stronger error signals during backpropagation. This property improves training stability and convergence speed, especially in deep networks. Furthermore, ReLU induces sparse activations by zeroing out all negative inputs, which can promote efficient feature representation and reduce overfitting. Computationally, ReLu is also more efficient since it requires only a simple threshold operation rather than exponential calculations involved in tanh, thus speeding up training and inference.

The encoder doubles the number of feature channels after each downsampling stage, enabling the network to learn increasingly abstract and complex features. The bottleneck layer operates at the lowest spatial resolution with the highest feature dimensionality, capturing global context before reconstruction.

In the decoder, transposed convolutions perform upsampling, and features from corresponding encoder layers are concatenated via skip connections. This fusion preserves fine-grained spatial information lost during downsampling, which is essential for accurate pixel-level predictions in physical fields.

Finally, a 1×1 convolution reduces the number of output channels to match the number of physical fields being predicted. This architecture balances depth and spatial resolution, leveraging ReLU activations to efficiently model the nonlinear, multiscale dynamics characteristic of active matter systems.

3.3 Experimental Setup

In this study, the model is designed to predict the subsequent state of the system based on four consecutive previous states, setting the input sequence length to $T_{in} = 4$ and the output horizon to $T_{out} = 1$. This means the network receives four sequential snapshots of the physical fields and forecasts the subsequent one. Figure 2 illustrates this temporal progression using the *concentration* field as an example.

Based on the architectural descriptions in The Well framework [5] and Sect. 3.1, we implemented the benchmark models CNextU-net, classical U-net and FNO to compare with our proposed U-net variant. The input to each model is a tensor of shape $(\text{batch size}, T_{in} \times F, L_x, L_y) = (64, 4 \times 11, 256, 256)$, where 11 denotes the number of physical fields. The corresponding output tensor has shape $(\text{batch size}, T_{out} \times F, L_x, L_y) = (64, 1 \times 11, 256, 256)$, representing the predicted next time step for all fields.

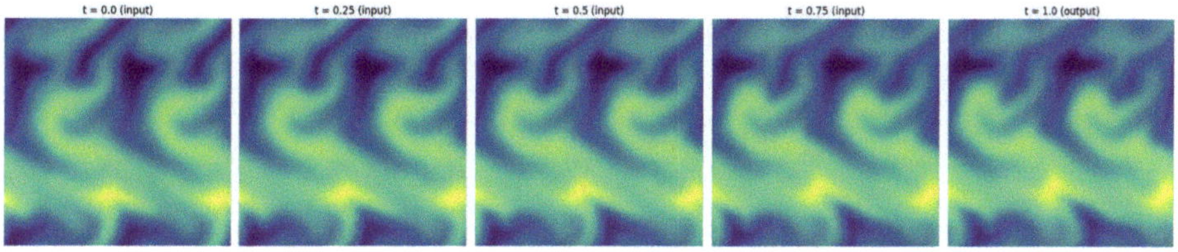

Fig. 2. Temporal evolution of the *concentration* field at times $t = 0$, $t = 0.25$, $t = 0.5$, and $t = 0.75$ (inputs), with the prediction target at $t = 1.0$ (output).

Our proposed U-net architecture features an encoder composed of convolutional blocks with kernel size 5, each followed by batch normalization and ReLU activation. A max-pooling layer is used to reduce spatial dimensions while increasing feature channels. The bottleneck operates at the smallest spatial scale, applying convolutional transformations to capture abstract features. The decoder reconstructs the spatial resolution through transposed convolutions, concatenates corresponding encoder features via skip connections to preserve spatial details, and applies convolutional blocks to refine the reconstructed features. A final 1×1 convolutional layer maps the output to the required number of physical fields.

All models were trained using the Mean Square Error (MSE) as the loss function and the AdamW optimizer [24] with a weight decay coefficient of 0.1. The selection criterion for learning rates (lr) was to maintain alignment with the original benchmark setup, and thus we conducted a search over three values: 5×10^{-4}, 1×10^{-3}, and 5×10^{-3}, where the lr remains constant over training time. This approach maintains methodological consistency and facilitates direct performance comparison.

Throughout training, convolutional layers employed zero padding to maintain spatial dimensions. Regarding the activation functions, the classical U-net utilized the hyperbolic tangent (tanh), the proposed U-net variation incorporated ReLU function and the CNextU-net employed the GeLu function. The batch size was fixed at 64 for all experiments. Training was conducted under computational constraints, with each run limited to 10 h on an NVIDIA L4 GPU.

3.4 Evaluation Metric

To assess the predictive performance of the models, we employ the Variance Scaled Root Mean Squared Error (VRMSE), a metric particularly suited for physical fields whose mean values often deviate significantly from zero, such as pressure or density [5]. VRMSE normalizes the prediction error by the spatial variance of the target field, providing a scale-invariant measure that facilitates fair comparison across different fields and conditions.

The VRMSE between a predicted field v and the ground truth u is defined as:

$$\mathrm{VRMSE}(u, v) = \sqrt{\frac{\langle |u - v|^2 \rangle}{\langle |u - \bar{u}|^2 \rangle + \epsilon}}, \tag{8}$$

where $\langle \cdot \rangle$ denotes spatial averaging, $\bar{u}$ is the spatial mean of the target field u, and $\epsilon = 10^{-7}$ is a small constant added to avoid division by zero in cases where the variance is negligible.

This formulation ensures that a naïve prediction equal to the spatial mean $\bar{u}$ yields a VRMSE close to 1. Consequently, VRMSE values greater than or equal to 1 indicate predictions no better than simply estimating the mean, while values less than 1 reflect increasingly accurate predictions.

4 Results

The training loss values for the different neural networks architectures analyzed in this work were recorded every 10 epochs and are presented in Fig. 3.

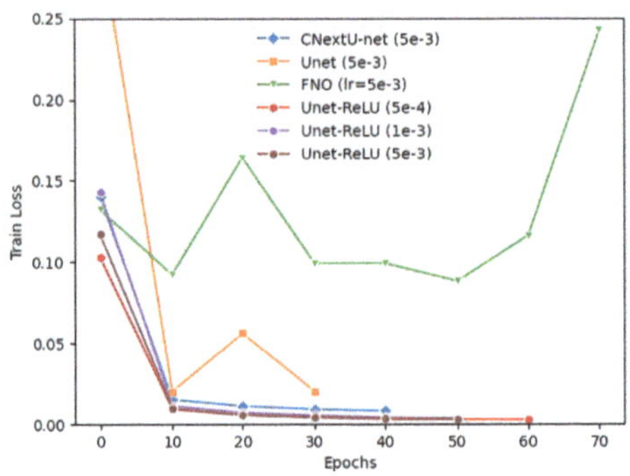

Fig. 3. Train Loss of the analyzed state-of-the-art models and the Unet-ReLU variation with different learning rates.

As shown in Fig. 3, the models exhibiting the fastest convergence during training were the CNextU-net and the U-net-ReLU variant, each evaluated using various learning rates. In particular, the U-net-ReLU configuration with a learning rate of 5×10^{-4} achieved notably rapid convergence. Furthermore, this configuration completed more epochs within the fixed 10-hour training window, likely due to the computational efficiency of the ReLU activation function relative to the tanh function employed in the classical U-net. The ReLU's simpler, non-saturating computation reduces per-epoch processing time, allowing more optimization steps to be performed within the same computational budget. This increased training throughput, combined with the favorable gradient properties of ReLU, contributed to the superior overall performance of the U-net-ReLU model compared to the classical U-net.

A comparison between the VRMSE values reported in [5] and those obtained here for the different neural network models (CNextU-net, classical U-net, and FNO) is presented in Table 2, along with the VRMSE values obtained for the proposed U-net-ReLU variant. Bold VRMSE values indicate the best results in each comparison, with lower values signifying better performance.

Table 2. VRMSE values (reported and obtained) in the validation set for the different neural network architectures analyzed, using various learning rates.

Models		LR (epochs)	VRMSE
CNextU-net	Reported	5×10^{-3} (156)	0.0953
	Obtained	5×10^{-3} (41)	**0.0678**
U-net	Reported	5×10^{-3} (239)	0.2609
	Obtained	5×10^{-3} (35)	**0.2332**
FNO	Reported	5×10^{-3} (239)	0.3157
	Obtained	5×10^{-3} (75)	**0.2407**
U-net-ReLU	Obtained	5×10^{-4}(60)	**0.0756**
		1×10^{-3} (61)	**0.0756**
		5×10^{-3} (60)	0.0804

Table 2 shows that the values obtained by replicating the neural network models are consistent with those reported in [5] on the active matter dataset, particularly in that the lowest VRMSE values correspond to the CNextU-net. This holds true even though fewer epochs were completed, suggesting greater training efficiency. In general, the VRMSE values obtained here are lower than the reported values, despite the models being trained for fewer epochs. The architecture exhibiting the largest difference between the reported and obtained values was FNO, with a difference of 0.0750, compared to 0.0275 for the CNextU-net.

Regarding the proposed U-net-ReLU variant, the best results were achieved using the learning rates of 5×10^{-4} and 1×10^{-3}, both yielding a VRMSE of 0.0756 after 60 and 61 epochs, respectively. The nearly identical performance and similar training duration suggest that the model is robust and relatively insensitive to the precise learning rate within this range, reflecting a stable optimization process and efficient use of the available training budget. Compared to the CNextU-net, which achieved a lower VRMSE of 0.0678 using the same learning rate (5×10^{-3}) but after only 41 epochs, architectural differences likely influence convergence speed and final accuracy. Specifically, the CNextU-net uses a larger convolution kernels and multiple convolutional blocks per stage, while our U-net-ReLU adopts a classical encoder-decoder structure with an initial feature dimension of 48, a spatial filter size of 3, and a single convolutional block per stage. This simpler and more modular design balances model complexity and computational efficiency, employing ReLu activations that facilitate faster convergence and effective feature learning. Although the U-net-ReLU requires more epochs to achieve competitive results, the architectural configuration provides a straightforward and computationally efficient framework.

An important consideration in interpreting the training efficiency of the reported experiments is the difference in computational resources. The models in *The Well* were trained for up to 12 h using an NVIDIA H100 GPU that delivers approximately 67 TFLOPS in FP32 and 3.35 TB/s of HBM3 bandwidth [25]. In contrast, our experiments were conducted on an NVIDIA L4, offering only 30.3 TFLOPS in FP32 and 300 GB/s of GDDR6 bandwidth [26]. These hardware limitations explain the substantial difference between the reported and the registered number of epochs during our training. Despite this, the combinations of efficient architecture design and the use of ReLU activation function allowed our models to train more rapidly and generalize competitively.

Figures 4, 5, and 6 present a visual comparison of the expected images and the images obtained by the CNextU-net, FNO and U-net architectures, respectively, for a random selection of physical fields. Additionally, Figs. 7, 8, and 9 present a visual comparison of the expected and the obtained images by the Unet-ReLU variant architecture at different learning rate values for a random selection of physical fields.

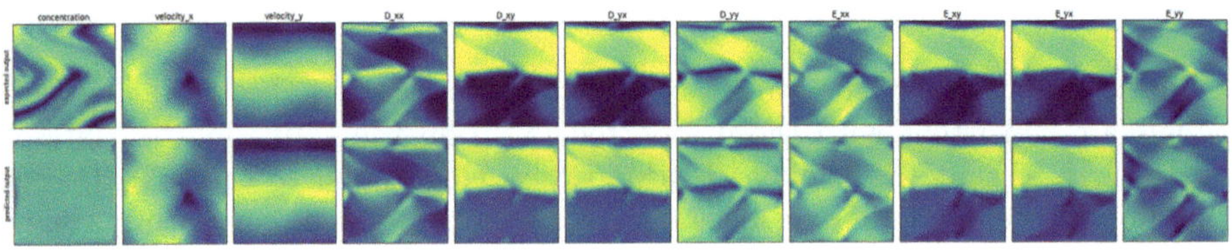

Fig. 4. Expected output images (first row) and images obtained with the state-of-the-art CNextU-net neural network architecture (second row) for various physical fields.

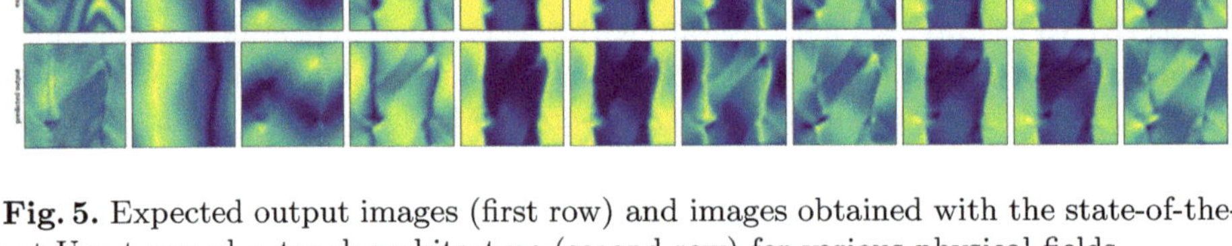

Fig. 5. Expected output images (first row) and images obtained with the state-of-the-art U-net neural network architecture (second row) for various physical fields

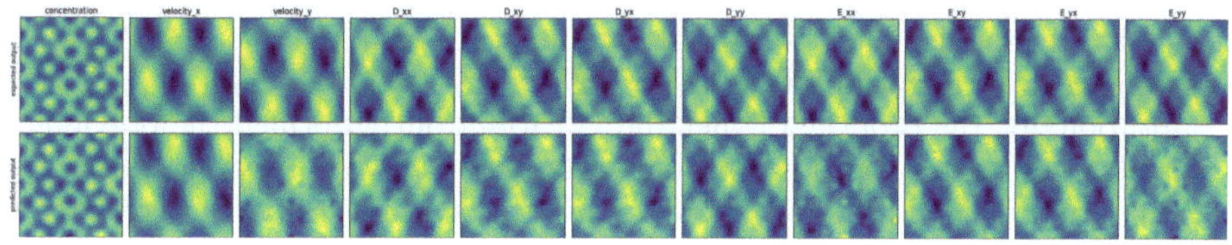

Fig. 6. Expected output images (first row) and images obtained with the state-of-the-art FNO neural network architecture (second row) for various physical fields

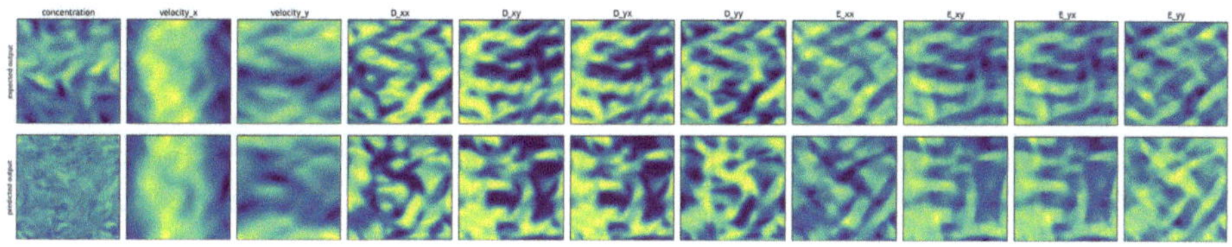

Fig. 7. Expected images (first row) and images obtained with the U-net-ReLU variant neural network architecture at $lr = 5 \times 10^{-4}$ (second row) for various input physical fields.

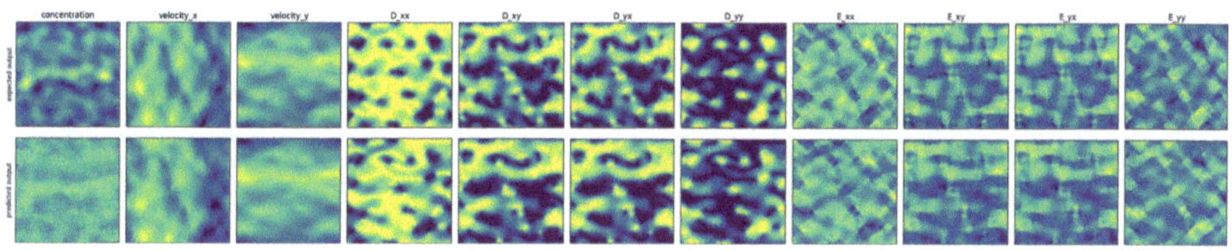

Fig. 8. Expected images (first row) and images obtained with the U-net-ReLU variant neural network architecture at $lr = 1 \times 10^{-3}$ (second row) for various input physical fields.

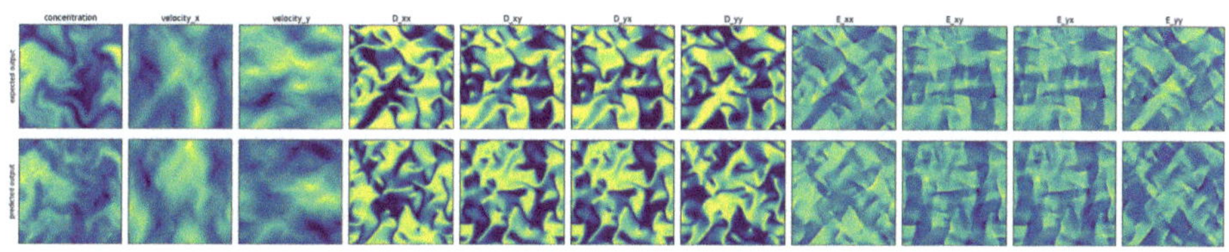

Fig. 9. Expected images (first row) and images obtained with U-net-ReLU variant neural network architecture with $lr = 5 \times 10^{-3}$ (second row) for various input physical fields.

5 Conclusions

This work reinforces the study of the effectiveness of neural networks as surrogates for modeling the complex dynamical evolution of active matter systems, offering an alternative to traditional continuum-based simulations. Despite the difference in computational resources, the results obtained form replicating the state-of-the-art architectures were consistent with the reported findings. Among the analyzed models, the CNextU-net architecture achieved the best VRMSE performance with a learning rate of 5×10^{-3}.

Additionally, the proposed U-net-ReLU variant outperformed the previously reported architectures used to evaluate the *active matter* data set from *The well* in terms of VRMSE. We showed that the learning rates that registered the best VRMSE values were 5×10^{-4} and 1×10^{-3}, corresponding to a 20.7% improvement over the best-reported VRMSE. Further experiments are needed to systematically evaluate the sensitivity of the U-net-ReLU architecture to learning rate variations, as preliminary results suggest almost identical performance. The key factor contributing of this performance was the use of ReLU activation function, which is computationally simpler and faster compared with the Tanh used in the classical U-net of the state-of-the-art. This reduced the per-epoch training time, allowing more epochs in same 10-hours budget, without compromising the model's ability to generalize to complex dynamical forecasting tasks.

Acknowledgments. The authors acknowledge the financial support provided by the Secretaría de Ciencia, Humanidades, Tecnología e Innovación (SECIHTI). Additional thanks are extended to the Instituto Politécnico Nacional, Secretaría de Investigación y Posgrado (SIP-IPN) for their valuable support of this research through projects SIP-20251087 and SIP-20251109.

Disclosure of Interests. The authors declare no conflicts of interest regarding this article.

References

1. Frisch, U.: Turbulence: The Legacy of A. N. Kolmogorov. Cambridge University Press (1995)
2. Mézard, M.: Spin glass theory and its new challenge: structured disorder. Indian J. Phys. **98**(11), 3757–3768 (2024). https://doi.org/10.1007/s12648-023-03029-8
3. Mézard, M., Parisi, G., Virasoro, M.A.: Spin Glass Theory and Beyond, vol. 9. World Scientific Publishing Company (1987)
4. Dill, K.A., Chan, H.S.: Levinthal's paradox: how protein folding avoids the exponential explosion of states. Nat. Struct. Biol. **4**(1), 10–19 (1997)
5. Ohana, R., et al.: The well: a large-scale collection of diverse physics simulations for machine learning. arXiv:2412.00568 (2024). https://doi.org/10.48550/arXiv.2412.00568
6. Vlachas, P.R., Arampatzis, G., Uhler, C., Koumoutsakos, P.: Multiscale simulations of complex systems by learning their effective dynamics. Nat. Mach. Intell. **4**(4), 359–366 (2022). https://doi.org/10.1038/s42256-022-00464-w. https://www.nature.com/articles/s42256-022-00464-w
7. Raissi, M., Perdikaris, P., Karniadakis, G.: Physics-informed neural networks: a deep learning framework for solving forward and inverse problems involving nonlinear partial differential equations. J. Comput. Phys. **378**, 686–707 (2019). https://doi.org/10.1016/j.jcp.2018.10.045. https://www.sciencedirect.com/science/article/pii/S0021999118307125
8. LeCun, Y., Bengio, Y., Hinton, G.: Deep learning. Nature **521**(7553), 436–444 (2015). https://doi.org/10.1038/nature14539. https://www.nature.com/articles/nature14539

9. Sun, C., Shrivastava, A., Singh, S., Gupta, A.: Revisiting unreasonable effectiveness of data in deep learning era. In: 2017 IEEE International Conference on Computer Vision (ICCV), pp. 843–852. IEEE, Venice (2017). https://doi.org/10.1109/ICCV.2017.97. http://ieeexplore.ieee.org/document/8237359/
10. PolymathicAI/the_well (2024). https://github.com/PolymathicAI/the_well, gitHub repository
11. Gao, T., Betterton, M.D., Jhang, A.S., Shelley, M.J.: Analytical structure, dynamics, and coarse graining of a kinetic model of an active fluid. Phys. Rev. Fluids **2**(9), 093302 (2017)
12. Saintillan, D., Shelley, M.J.: Theory of active suspensions. In: Complex Fluids in Biological Systems: Experiment, Theory, and Computation, pp. 319–355 (2015)
13. Gentile, L., Kurzthaler, C., Stone, H.A.: What is 'active matter'? In: Out-of-Equilibrium Soft Matter. The Royal Society of Chemistry (2023). https://doi.org/10.1039/9781839169465-00001
14. Shiomi, D., Mori, H., Niki, H.: Genetic mechanism regulating bacterial cell shape and metabolism. Commun. Integr. Biol. **2**(3), 219–220 (2009)
15. Ezhilan, B., Shelley, M.J., Saintillan, D.: Instabilities and nonlinear dynamics of concentrated active suspensions. Phys. Fluids **25**(7) (2013)
16. Weady, S., Stein, D.B., Shelley, M.J.: Thermodynamically consistent coarse-graining of polar active fluids. Phys. Rev. Fluids **7**(6), 063301 (2022)
17. Maddu, S., Weady, S., Shelley, M.J.: Learning fast, accurate, and stable closures of a kinetic theory of an active fluid. J. Comput. Phys. 112869 (2024)
18. Ronneberger, O., Fischer, P., Brox, T.: U-Net: convolutional networks for biomedical image segmentation. In: Navab, N., Hornegger, J., Wells, W.M., Frangi, A.F. (eds.) MICCAI 2015. LNCS, vol. 9351, pp. 234–241. Springer, Cham (2015). https://doi.org/10.1007/978-3-319-24574-4_28 Springer (2015)
19. Li, K., Ye, W.: D-FNO: a decomposed fourier neural operator for large-scale parametric partial differential equations. Comput. Methods Appl. Mech. Eng. **436**, 117732 (2025). https://doi.org/10.1016/j.cma.2025.117732
20. Bai, Y.: RELU-function and derived function review. SHS Web Conf. **144**, 02006 (2022). https://doi.org/10.1051/shsconf/202214402006
21. Hosseini, A., Guay, M., Li, X.: On RELU neural networks as piecewise linear surrogate models. Comput. Chem. Eng. **201**, 109208 (2025). https://doi.org/10.1016/j.compchemeng.2025.109208
22. Tan, H.H., Lim, K.H.: Vanishing gradient mitigation with deep learning neural network optimization. In: 2019 7th International Conference on Smart Computing & Communications (ICSCC), pp. 1–4 (2019). https://doi.org/10.1109/ICSCC.2019.8843652
23. Haroon-Sulyman, S.O., Kamaruddin, S.S., Ahmad, F.K., Abdul-Rahman, S., Aziz, N.I.: Techniques for mitigating the vanishing gradient problem in deep neural networks. In: Mat Aji, Z., Romli, R., Packeer Mohamed, S.F., Saip, M.A., Herawan, T. (eds.) KMICe 2024, pp. 428–438. Springer, Cham (2025). https://doi.org/10.1007/978-3-031-91485-0_33
24. Loshchilov, I., Hutter, F.: Decoupled weight decay regularization. In: International Conference on Learning Representations (2017). https://api.semanticscholar.org/CorpusID:53592270
25. Nvidia: GPU NVIDIA H100 con núcleo Tensor. https://www.nvidia.com/es-es/data-center/h100/
26. Nvidia: GPU NVIDIA L4 con núcleo Tensor. https://www.nvidia.com/es-es/data-center/l4/

Implementation and Comparison of FIR Digital Filters on DSP and FPGA

J. Brandon Mañón Juárez(✉) and Eusebio Ricárdez Vázquez

Centro de Investigación en Computación, Instituto Politécnico Nacional, 07738 Ciudad de México, Mexico
{jmanonj2023,ericardez}@cic.ipn.mx

Abstract. This paper presents the design, implementation, and comparative evaluation of a finite impulse response (FIR) digital filter on two distinct hardware platforms: a digital signal processor (DSP) board, specifically the Texas Instruments DSK6713, and a field-programmable gate array (FPGA). FIR filters represent a fundamental building block in digital signal processing, with widespread applications in communications, audio and speech enhancement, biomedical instrumentation, and real-time control. The hardware realization of such filters remains an important area of study, since performance strongly depends on factors such as processing speed, computational efficiency, and hardware resource utilization. For the FPGA-based implementation, two alternative architectures are explored: a parallel structure, designed to maximize throughput, and a serial structure, intended to minimize hardware consumption while maintaining satisfactory accuracy and speed. These approaches allow a systematic examination of the trade-offs between performance and complexity, which is essential for embedded and resource-constrained applications. In contrast, the DSP-based implementation provides a conventional reference, reflecting the continued relevance of programmable DSPs in real-time signal processing due to their optimized instruction sets and design flexibility. The three implementations are assessed in terms of execution speed, efficiency, and hardware requirements. The results demonstrate that while the DSP achieves adequate filter performance, the FPGA-based implementations significantly improve speed and scalability. Furthermore, the serial FPGA architecture highlights remarkable optimization in resource usage, underscoring its suitability for compact, cost-sensitive, and performance-driven embedded systems.

Keywords: Digital Signal Processing · FIR Filters · FPGA · DSP · ADC · DAC

1 Introduction

Digital signal processing refers to the set of techniques by which mathematical operations and calculations are applied through computational tools to the

C. Palma-Preciado et al. (Eds.): CORE 2025, ACSAR 3, pp. 18–31, 2026.
https://doi.org/10.1007/978-3-032-08894-9_2

values obtained from real world variable information converted to the discrete domain either by implementing a computational algorithm or physically using digital hardware for this processing. It is present in various real-world applications in everyday life, from the quality of sound in audio devices to the clarity of images in visualization systems.

An important stage of digital signal processing is digital filters, which attenuate unwanted components of the signal or improve its quality, intensity, and resolution. A digital filter is a process by which certain signal characteristics are modified in the frequency domain.

The application of digital filters is becoming increasingly relevant in various everyday situations. For example, in biomedical signal measurement devices [8], digital filters are used to improve signal quality and reduce ambient noise. In audio systems, digital filters are used to equalize, amplify, and improve audio quality.

There are devices dedicated to digital signal processing that enable the implementation of digital filters, such as development boards based on DSP processors with specific architectures. The capacity of these devices allows for precision and speed in processing results. However, currently, many digital signal processing devices, due to their application, require a reduction in the hardware in which they are implemented in order to use less space and make the system more efficient in terms of energy and resource consumption. It is also important to consider that processing speed has an impact. As a sequential device, a DSP can have a very noticeable delay despite the clock frequency at which it operates. A widely used solution today is the implementation and application of DSP algorithms in FPGAs [6] due to their flexibility, scalability, and reconfiguration according to needs.

2 Literature Review

There are several papers on the implementation of FIR filters using both DSP and FPGA development boards. However, only a few get to the physical implementation, and many stop at the simulation phase. One such work using a DSP development board is that of [9], who designs and implements a digital filter on a dsPIC microcontroller by coding digital processing algorithms in the C language for these microcontrollers. The design shows adequate performance in operation.

Prototypes that perform digital signal processing using FPGAs employ a variety of techniques. For example, [2] proposes two finite impulse response (FIR) digital filter architectures, one in series and one in parallel. It is noted that the parallel architecture, despite using more FPGA resources, offers better processing speed and filtering time than the serial architecture.

In [7], the design and implementation of FIR filters are done by hardware description with high-level synthesis, which allows optimizing resource management in the FPGA.

The work of [4] consists of the design of digital filters using the MATLAB tool FDA, from which the hardware description code of the filter is obtained and synthesized in Vivado. Additionally, modules are generated for simulation tests with Simulink, although no physical implementation is performed.

In [1] a sequential architecture FIR filter is implemented in a development board with FPGA, however, this board has an external codec which is read through an I2C interface and then a serial to parallel controller module is described to read the ADC values and then process them in the FIR. In that work, the number of coefficients used is 8.

Finally, a comparison between the FIR filter implementation between the DSK6713 and a Xilinx FPGA is made in[3]. The number of coefficients for the FIR filter is 40, the ADC readout in both cases is from an external codec device and only the implementation of the parallel FIR architecture is done from the Matlab FDA tool.

None of the FPGA-based cases involves the implementation of a microcontroller for additional processes. However, this decision is appropriate considering the optimal performance characteristics expected for each case.

It is necessary to explore the implementation of the FIR digital filter using both devices to analyze the behavior with real signals and improve the performance.

3 Materials and Method

From the stages of digital signal processing, it is necessary to mention that, for this work, it is considered from the analog to digital conversion for data acquisition to the digital to analog conversion to obtain the processed information. Figure 1 shows a block diagram that summarizes the main stages of digital signal processing. The digital processing block is where FIR type digital filtering is implemented.

Fig. 1. Block diagram of digital signal processing

From the analog to digital conversion of a signal, the sampled and quantized value is sent to a digital signal processing device, this device is responsible for performing the calculations and operations corresponding to the FIR digital filter with which components at unwanted frequencies of the signal will be attenuated. At the end of the process, the result for each sample is sent to the digital to analog converter to obtain the processed signal in the continuous time domain.

There are several techniques and devices to perform each of the processing stages, it is necessary to consider the characteristics of each one, among the most important ones are the conversion resolution, sampling frequency, operating frequency, storage resources, etc.

In this work, for practical purposes, a bandpass FIR type filter between 100 and 800 Hz is proposed in the digital processing stage.

The Texas Instruments DSK6713 development board is used to implement the FIR digital filter by means of software with DSP programming in C language. Likewise, a development board with FPGA Terasic DE-10 Lite is used for the implementation of the filter in hardware.

3.1 FIR Digital Filter Design

Due to the characteristics of the signal of many systems that require digital filtering of signals, it is necessary the use of band-pass filters so for the development of the work is taken as a base example the implementation of a band-pass filter, likewise, the method of application of windows in the design of filters allows the impulse response of a digital filter becomes finite resulting in the type of FIR filter. The windowing method allows the approximation of the ideal frequency response of the filter but with a level of ripple in both the pass band and the rejection band and also a transition band with a slow slope. The Hamming window is proposed for its characteristics since it is one of the windows with the highest attenuation in the rejection band, approximately -41dB, a transition band a little slow compared to other filters. It is important to note that the analysis and comparison with other types of windows, as well as with other cut-off and rejection frequencies depending on the application must be performed to find a suitable and optimal filter in terms of implementation resources and performance. The following characteristics are taken into account for the design of the filter:

- Passing band: 100–800 Hz
- Sample rate: 8 KHz
- Number of coefficients: 223

Although there are mathematical models to design from specific characteristics of the FIR digital filter and obtain the optimal number of coefficients and their values, there are now computational tools to optimize the process, however, the mathematical procedure of the entire design of an example of a FIR filter can be consulted in [5].

The computational tool employed to compute the coefficient values is MATLAB, using a dedicated script that exports the data to a .txt file formatted specifically for compatibility with the corresponding implementation IDEs, such as those used for the DSK6713 and FPGA platforms.

3.2 Implementation in C Language for the DSK6713 Board

For the software implementation, a Texas Instruments DSK C6713 development board is used, which has a TMS320C6713 DSP chip running at 225 MHZ with

264 kB of internal memory (8 kB as L1P and L1D cache, and 256 kB as L2 shared memory between program space and data space). The board also includes devices and integrated circuits necessary for different tasks such as connection to a computer, peripheral extension, LED indicators, switches, etc. One of the important devices is the AIC23 Audio Codec which is an analog to digital converter and digital to analog converter for audio signal. The inputs and outputs for the codec are conditioned.

For signal processing, it is necessary that, starting from the reading obtained from the AIC23 codec, each of the samples is processed in the algorithm implemented in the FIR filter. At the end, the result is sent back to the codec for digital to analog conversion. Figure 2 shows a block representation of the system and the appropriate process. Since different tasks can be executed in the DSP, it is important that the reading of the codec and the calculation of the output signal are executed without interrupting the other possible tasks, so the codec reading scheme must be interrupted so that it will only be processed each time the codec indicates that a value is available.

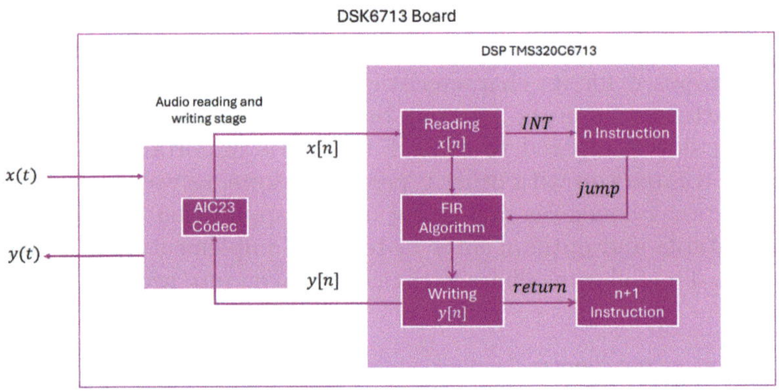

Fig. 2. FIR filter implementation on the DSK6713 card

For the implementation of the FIR filter, the mathematical model in Eq. 1 is considered.

$$y[n] = \sum_{k=0}^{N-1} h[n]x[n-k] \tag{1}$$

where $y[n]$ is the output value of the FIR at time n, $x[n-k]$ is the sample at time $n-k$ i.e., a previous sample, and $h[n]$ is the $n-th$ coefficient previously calculated.

Based on the above, a first approximation for the implementation of the algorithm is shown below:

Since $x[n-k]$ indicates that it is a previous value k samples before, then it is necessary to store those values, but in turn to traverse them as a function of

Algorithm 1. General FIR filter algorithm

Require: N, $x[n]$, $h[n], x_n$
  $y_n := 0$
  $x[0] := x_n$
  for $k = 0$ to N **do**
    $y_n := y_n + h[k] * x[n-k]$
  end for
  return y_n

time, that is, to define and update an array of $x[n-k]$ values that are traversed as a function of k. Therefore, we define a new version of the algorithm.

Algorithm 2. Modified FIR filter algorithm

Require: N, $x[n]$, $h[n], x_n$
  $y_n := 0$
  for $k = 1$ to N **do**
    $x[i] := x[i-1]$
  end for
  $x[0] := x_i$
  $y := 0$
  for $k = 0$ to $N-1$ **do**
    $y_n := y_n + h[k] * x[k]$
  end for
  return y_n

With the above modification, the values of x_n representing the sample at time n are stored for later use in the $n-k$ cases, so that values for earlier samples are available at the same time as they are accommodated for later samples.

The algorithm is coded in C language for the DSK6713 and compiled in the Code Composer Studio environment of Texas Instruments. For the coding and implementation of the algorithm, it is necessary to have the coefficients previously calculated and stored in an array and saved in a header file (.h), in the program code each of the values of the array is read as required. Once y_n is calculated, it is sent to the card codec to obtain a reading of the signal and verify its behavior. In this case, the sampling frequency for the codec is defined as 8 KHz.

3.3 FPGA Implementation

The hardware implementation uses reconfigurable logic from an FPGA through the Terasic DE10-Lite development board that has an FPGA chip of the MAX 10 family of Intel Altera, the FPGA has approximately 50 thousand logic elements, 1,638 Kbit of M9K block memory and 144 multipliers of 18 × 18. One of the important features of the FPGA chip of the board is that it has an ADC embedded in the chip to which can be added configurable logic depending on the needs for its implementation or even an IP core for its use recommended by Intel.

For the FPGA implementation, the block diagram of the FIR filter model in Fig. 3 is taken as a reference. From this, the FIR can be conceptualized to be encoded by means of hardware description language in the logic elements of the FPGA.

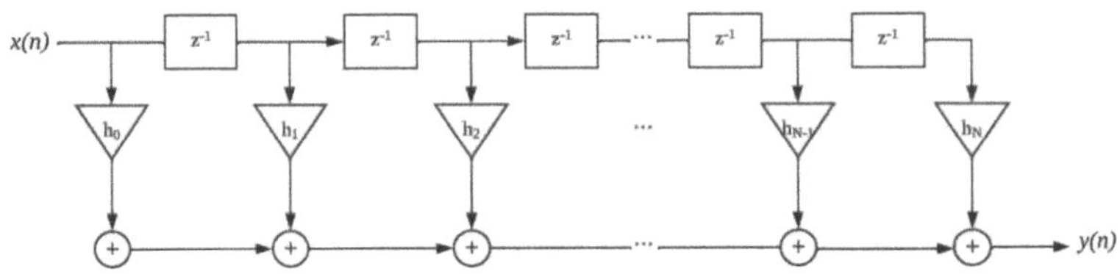

Fig. 3. FIR filter diagram block model

Parallel Implementation: From Fig. 3 the concept of FIR blocks is abstracted, in this case, an analogy can be made of the FIR elements as logic elements, in Fig. 4 it is observed that the data retention and delay elements are implemented as flip-flops, the gain elements (multiplication of coefficients) are implemented with multipliers and the addition operation with its corresponding adder element in FPGA. In this case where the implementation is in parallel is due to the fact that no addition and multiplication operation is required to finish before the next one can be executed, that is, all the additions and multiplications are executed at the same time.

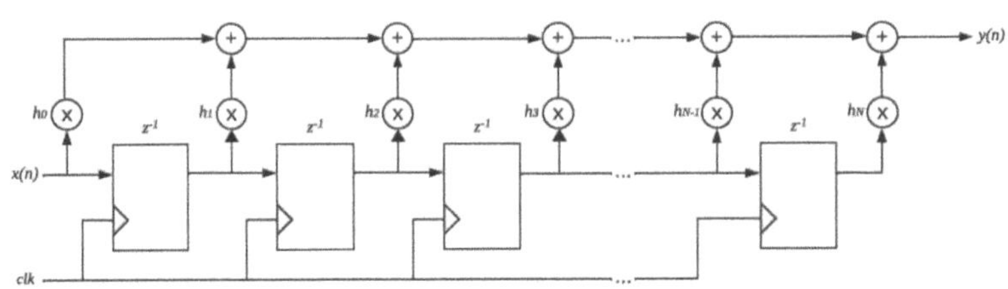

Fig. 4. FIR filter implementation in digital hardware

For the use of the coefficients in the FPGA implementation, due to the complexity of the implementation of operations with floating point or even fixed values, it is possible and efficient to perform the operations with integer values. However, the coefficients previously obtained must be scaled by a constant and optimal value, that is, multiplying each of the coefficients by a value whose implementation is not costly in logic elements, for example, a bit shift (multiplication by a multiple of 2). Likewise, the scaling value must adjust the significant figures of the coefficients without losing information (avoid null values). The new values must be adjusted to the word width with which the multiplications are worked and avoid overflow errors. The coefficients are stored in hexadecimal format in a text file. The generated file is used as an initialization file for registers in the development environment.

From the logic diagram, the design is simplified in the hardware description with Verilog because some elements of such languages are similar to some operations and instructions of other languages. For cycles, however, these allow generating concurrent hardware, that is, hardware that interacts at the same time without having to depend on the execution time or wait for previous results.

Because of this, part of Algorithm 2 must be followed for the hardware design, considering that the values produced by the operations are concurrent.

As mentioned above, the FPGA has an internal ADC to which previously has been developed a control stage for reading at a variable sampling frequency from 500 KHz, however for this design a sampling frequency of 7.8125 KHz is used. Each sample obtained generates an interrupt signal which enables the displacement of the previous samples between registers, updating as each sample is received. Due to the short propagation time, the result y_n is immediately present at the FPGA output and is then taken to a physical R-2R DAC circuit for readout.

It is observed that no additional time is required other than the maximum propagation time of the signal in the FPGA through the logic elements, which is negligible since it is a synchronous circuit.

Figure 5 shows the block diagram of the hardware structure of the FIR filter implemented in parallel for the Terasic DE10-Lite development board.

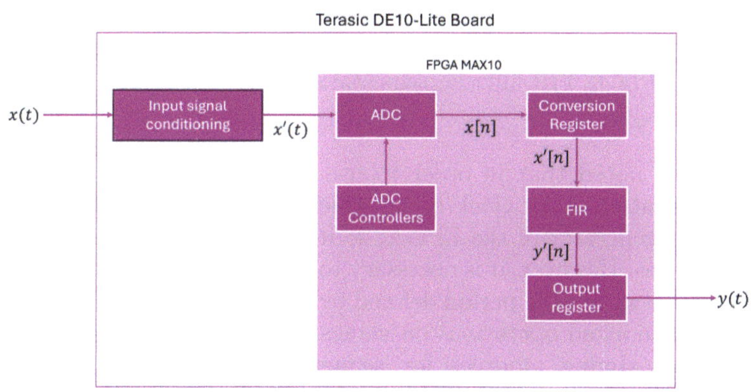

Fig. 5. FIR filter implementation on the Terasic DE10-Lite card

Sequential Implementation (Accumulator): For a complete comparison, the FIR is also implemented in sequential form, that is, some operations are done one at a time and for that cumulative storage of the sum of multiplications is required.

Because sequential instructions cannot be implemented in the FPGA as if it were a microcontroller, units are described that allow the elements to interact with each other every few clock cycles to achieve the effect of sequential execution between operations. The description in Fig. 4 is modified to result in the use of a single register, a single adder, and a single multiplier as shown in Fig. 6. In this case, the FIR module in Fig. 5 now consists of a counter that accesses the coefficient memory addresses and buffer register for sample $x[n-k]$ and coefficient $h[k]$ respectively. These values are subsequently multiplied and summed with the previous value in the accumulator. In this case, the coefficient memory is synthesized with elements from FPGA memory blocks, so again the .txt file previously generated with the MATLAB script can be used to initialize the memory with the coefficient values.

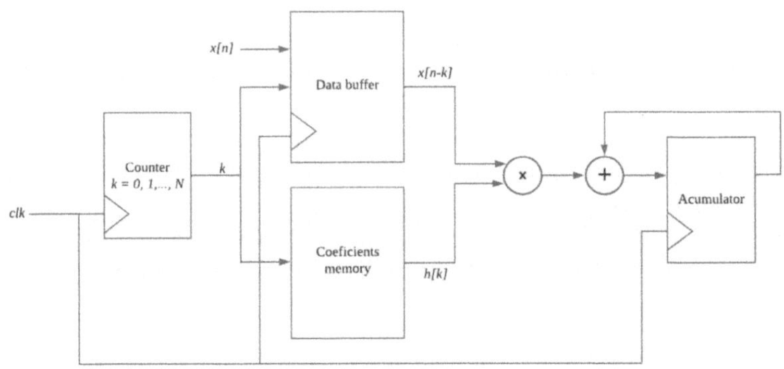

Fig. 6. FIR filter implementation with accumulator

It should be noted that in order to use an accumulator it is necessary to update the operation every clock cycle, which is received from the input of the 100 MHz clock generator of the FPGA, so it is possible to execute at least 100 million operations. However, it is necessary to adjust to the number of operations that can be done within the period defined by the ADC sampling frequency since it is important to avoid operations on values at non-corresponding times.

Control and timing modules for sequential execution of operations are described. The operation of the FIR implemented sequentially varies in that now, after the ADC conversion is finished when an interruption is generated, a counter is triggered indicating the number of operations to be performed and then stops when the N operations corresponding to the total number of coefficients are fulfilled, at the end the result is displayed at the output and the process starts again.

4 Results

Mainly it is important to perform tests with both filter implementations for comparison, i.e., using a function generator to create a sinusoidal signal sweep, connect the devices and observe using the oscilloscope. The behavior of the signal at the cutoff and pass frequencies is analyzed, as well as the amplitude in the output signal.

In the case of implementation on the DSK6713 development board, the program compiles and loads correctly. In general terms, the memory space used to store 223 coefficients is approximately 3568 bytes, as they are defined as double-word values, i.e., two 32-byte words, or 8 bytes per word or 16 bytes per double word. Similarly, to use the above $x[n]$ value storage array, an array of 223 double-byte elements is used, so the space used by this variable is 446 bytes.

When the FIR filter was implemented in the board and tested with a signal generator with a signal of 2 Vpp and a sweep between 40 Hz and 1 KHz, the correct attenuation of components in the rejection band and an adequate behavior in the pass band was observed. At 40 Hz the attenuation had good performance approaching to zero the signal at that frequency. Between 50 and 80 Hz the attenuation still performed well, however the signal shape could be appreciated in a few millivolts. At 100 Hz and above the signal was clearer but a little attenuated compared to the original signal. From 200 Hz to 600 Hz the signal is observed correctly. Again at 800 Hz the signal begins to attenuate until it approaches 0 again at almost 1 KHz. In Fig. 7 the comparison of the original signal with the resulting signal at 100 Hz is observed, it is observed by means of oscilloscope cursors that there is a phase shift in the signal of approximately 7.5 ms.

In the FPGA implementation in parallel structure, it is observed that the consumption of FPGA logic elements amounts to approximately 15828 of the almost 50 thousand logic elements that the FPGA has. In this case, a signal generator conditioned to receive only positive voltages is used for testing. At the output of the already processed 12-bit values, an R-2R digital-to-analog conversion circuit is connected to display the result. Similar to the DSK6713 implementation, the sweep between 40 Hz and 1 KHz shows correct performance in the rejection band and adequate behavior in the pass band. In this case, at 40 Hz the values are close to zero but not as close as in the previous case, this is due to the precision of the scaling of the coefficients with the scale factor, as well as to the resolution of the ADC. Between 50 and 80 Hz the signal display is also very faint. Again at 100 Hz a slight attenuation is observed, between 200 and 600 Hz the signal is displayed correctly, attenuating again at 800 Hz so that at 1 KHz the values again approach zero. Figure 8 shows that there is a signal offset of approximately 5 ms.

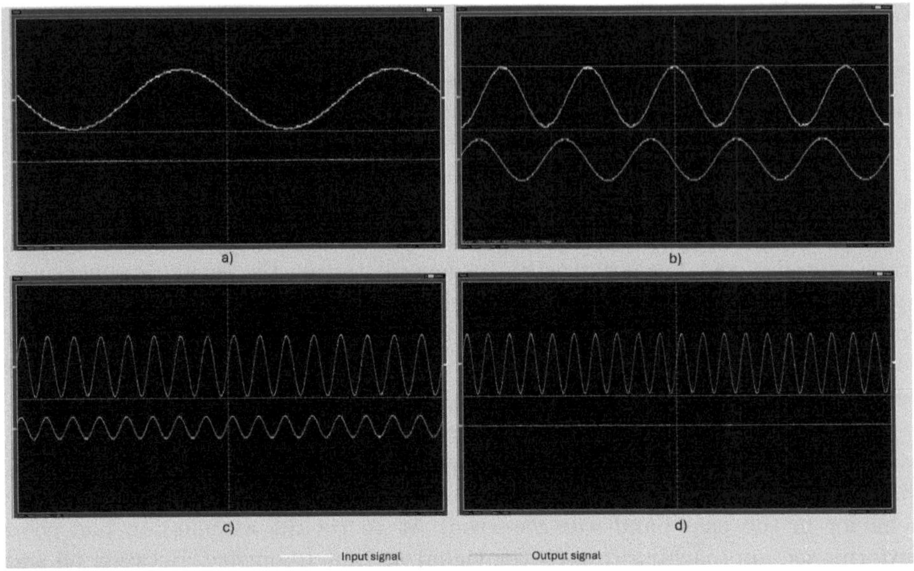

Fig. 7. Physical test oscilloscope signal with signal at a) 60 Hz, b) 100 Hz, c) 800 Hz and d) 1 KHz on DSK6713

Finally, in the sequential hardware implementation, the FPGA resource consumption was 3331 logic elements, 4096 bits of dedicated embedded memory, and two dedicated multipliers were also used. The behavior in the rejection and pass bands is similar to the previous cases however, the signal offset is still close to 5 ms. Figure 9 shows the input and output signal at 100 Hz, and the interval between the cursors indicates the signal offset time.

From the tests performed in the three cases, it is identified that the FIR filter implementation works properly in all cases at the cut-off frequencies, attenuating them in amplitude, while the pass band does not present irregularities in its operation. In addition, the filter is not unstable in any case. However, the FPGA implementation has a lower phase delay compared with the DSK6713 board, which affects both the response time and the time it takes to handle the interrupt routine in the DSK6713. This implies that the main program remains in an extended wait, reducing the performance and speed of the program in the DSP. If in a specific case more samples are required to be processed, this time is further affected.

From the resource consumption between the two FPGA cases, the parallel method consumes many logic elements limiting the implementation to both the FPGA model and the number of modules that can be implemented together. However, the serial method looks optimal by using much less resources and taking advantage of dedicated elements such as memory blocks and multipliers. Also, it is observed that the difference of both phase shift times is not significant compared to the phase shift time in the DSK6713.

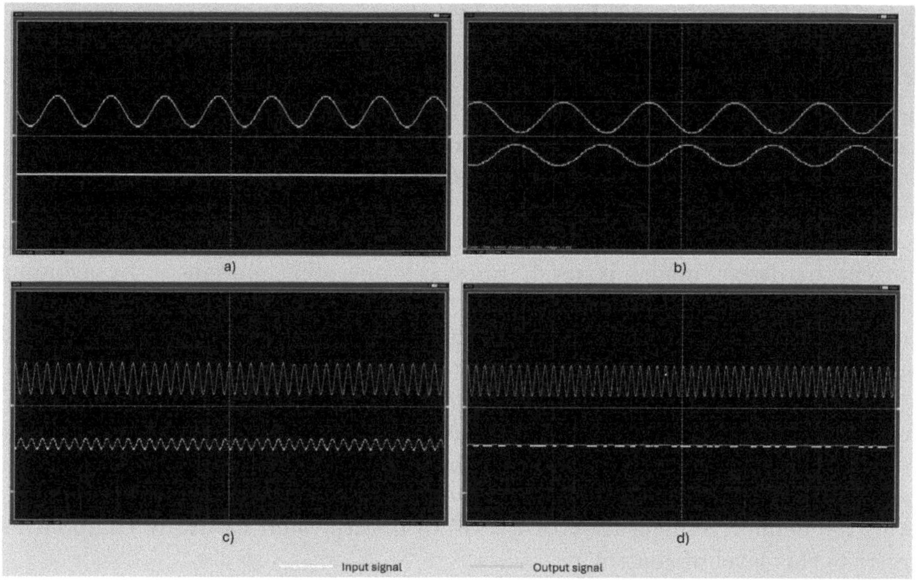

Fig. 8. Oscilloscope test signal at a) 40 Hz, b) 100 Hz, c) 800 Hz and d) 1 KHz on FPGA parallel method

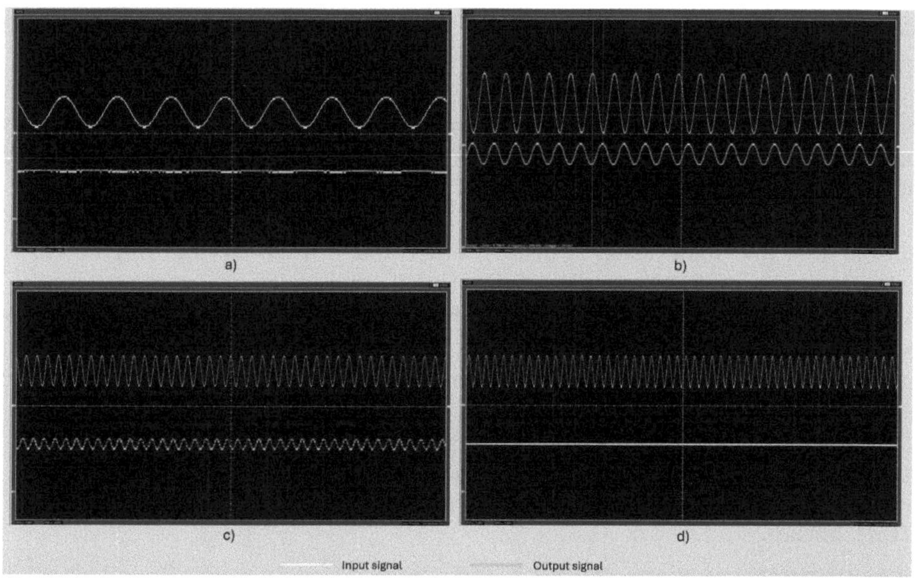

Fig. 9. Oscilloscope test signal at a) 40 Hz, b) 100 Hz, c) 800 Hz and d) 1 KHz on FPGA serial method

5 Conclusions and Future Work

If the application requires compact devices with limited resources such as memory or clock speed, optimizing the FIR filter design enables efficient implementation of window-based FIR digital filters in both software and embedded hardware. These implementations perform adequately depending on the design constraints.

When the filter algorithm is abstracted for Verilog implementation, a concurrent hardware model is used, resources operate simultaneously, avoiding delays caused by sequential execution. This allows greater control over hardware resources, in contrast to DSPs, which depend heavily on their predefined architecture, execution cycles, interrupt routines, and peripheral communication.

For embedded software implementations, several parameters must be carefully adjusted. Notably, the sampling rate must match the execution time of the FIR algorithm, from ADC sampling to output computation. This timing affects how often new samples can be acquired while the main program runs. However, the default configuration of DSK6713 libraries and hardware components restricts this level of control.

Compared to earlier FPGA-based implementations, improvements are observed by increasing the number of coefficients, storing them in dedicated memory, and leveraging integrated ADCs to boost speed and reduce resource usage. While DSPs are designed for signal processing, their sequential execution and multitasking limitations lead to increased cycle usage and degraded performance, as reflected in signal delays in the DSK6713 tests.

Coefficient rescaling has minimal impact on filter performance in both FPGA cases. However, comparing different scaling factors remains important, especially near-zero outputs, where accuracy can be compromised if coefficients are treated as zero.

Exploring optimal scaling values can improve accuracy while minimizing execution time and logic usage. Future work could involve testing different filter types to assess performance as computational complexity increases.

For optimizing FIR filters on the DSK6713, techniques like circular buffering could reduce coefficient execution time. Additionally, using loop bounds that exploit filter symmetry can lower the number of required computations when calculating the $y[n]$ terms.

Acknowledgement. This work was carried out in the Digital Signal Processing Laboratory of the Computing Research Centre (CIC) at Instituto Politécnico Nacional (IPN), México.

Declaration of Conflict of Interest. The authors declare that there is no conflict of interest regarding the publication of this paper.

References

1. Al-Dulaimi, M.A., Wahhab, H., Abdulhussein, A.: Design and implementation of communication digital FIR filter for audio signals on the FPGA platform. J. Commun. **18**(2) (2023)
2. Artetxe, Q.I.: Procesado digital de señales mediante circuitos integrados reconfigurables. filtros de respuesta impulso finita (fir) (2014)
3. Douri, O., Gaga, A., et al.: Comparison study of hardware architectures performance between FPGA and DSP processors for implementing digital signal processing algorithms: application of fir digital filter. Results Eng. **16**(1) (2022)
4. Ferenc-Emil, M., Germán-Salló, Z.: Implementation of digital filters in FPGA structures (2024)
5. Mañón, J.B., Ricárdez, E.: Analysis of digital signal processing algorithms and their implementation in hardware and embedded software. In: Telematics and Computing. WITCOM. Communications in Computer and Information Science, vol. 2250, pp. 49–56 (2024)
6. Pérez, A., Portillo, G., et al.: Implementación de un filtro pasobajas digital en fpga. In: Memorias del XVII Concurso Lasallista de Investigación, Desarrollo e Innovación (CLIDi) (2015)
7. Reddy, G.R.K.: Design of digital filters in FPGA using high level synthesis. Lecture notes/report, assistant Professor
8. Reyes, L.D.: Implementación en fpga de un clasificador de movimientos de la mano usando señales emg. Redes de Ingeniería **6**(1), 85–94 (2015)
9. Vazquez, R., Mariguetti, J., Burgos, A., Canali, L.: Implementación de un algoritmo de filtrado en microcontroladores dspic y pic32

Information Science and Technology

Real-Time Sheet Alignment in Mobile Devices Using Reference Mark-Based Elements

Oscar A. Diaz-Sanguino(✉), Beatriz A. González-Beltrán, and Josué Figueroa-González

Universidad Autónoma Metropolitana, México City 02128, Mexico
{al2233804916,bgonzalez,jfgo}@azc.uam.mx

Abstract. This paper presents an innovative mobile device-based system for digitizing and automatic alignment of Optical Mark Recognition sheets. The system uses image processing techniques, including grayscale conversion, contrast enhancement, and edge detection, to ensure high-quality alignment of captured images. By employing template-based automatic alignment and perspective warping, the system compensates for distortions such as tilts and rotations, enhancing the accuracy of subsequent analysis. The system was tested in real-world conditions using live image capture, demonstrating its ability to process diverse, unlabeled data in real time without relying on pre-existing datasets or prior training. Experimental results validate the system's effectiveness in real-time auto-alignment, compensating for rotational offsets of up to 12° with an average execution time of 1.24 s, this, even under the limited processing capabilities of mobile devices.

Keywords: Automatic alignment · template matching · optical mark recognition · mobile devices · perspective warping · edge detection

1 Introduction

Optical Mark Recognition (OMR) techniques are vital for the automatic evaluation of student assessments, enabling efficient and accurate processing of large amounts of data. By converting physical answer sheets into digital formats, OMR allows for the swift collection and analysis of responses, significantly reducing manual effort and the risk of human error. With the integration of advanced image processing and artificial intelligence, these techniques not only streamline the evaluation process but also enhance the quality of results [10], ensuring accurate interpretation of the marked answers.

To illustrate the proposed solution, consider a college teacher who needs to assess the learning of 400 students. The evaluation includes a test with both closed and open-ended questions. Manual grading of these tests can be a laborious task and is prone to errors. Imagine there is a mobile application, though limited in processing capabilities, that can automatically evaluate the responses.

C. Palma-Preciado et al. (Eds.): CORE 2025, ACSAR 3, pp. 35–47, 2026.
https://doi.org/10.1007/978-3-032-08894-9_3

This app allows the teacher to capture images of his/her response sheets along with the students' answers. The first stage of this system involves real-time alignment of the sheets using the mobile device, and this paper presents an innovative solution.

Current solutions for real-time alignment face challenges, particularly when it comes to image capture and alignment. Mobile devices used for scanning answer sheets may produce images that suffer from misalignment, varying quality, or poor lighting conditions, which can hinder the effectiveness of automatic evaluation systems. This can lead to inaccurate results and necessitate additional correction steps. To resolve these issues, a new proposed solution focuses on improving the alignment and processing of captured images, leveraging more sophisticated algorithms to ensure better accuracy and reliability during the evaluation process [6,8,9].

The correct alignment of the sheet is crucial in this process, as it significantly affects the following steps. This alignment is particularly necessary when using tools that are challenging to stabilize, such as mobile devices. To address this issue, we present a mobile device-based system that simplifies real-time image capture and alignment. This system utilizes the device's camera and employs reference marks on the page to assist in aligning the images effectively. The experiments were conducted in real-world settings, where a mobile device captured images of the sheets at a rate of four frames per second, simulating typical usage conditions. Importantly, no pre-compiled datasets were used; instead, all images were collected on-site using sheets of various formats. This approach ensures that the evaluation genuinely represents the system's performance in practical environments.

The remaining sections of this paper are as follows. In Sect. 2, we briefly describe previous works concerning automatic alignment. Our methodology is presented in Sect. 3. Later, in Sect. 3.1, we explain image preprocessing such as grayscale conversion, contrast adjustment, and edge enhancement for automatic alignment. Section 3.2 presents our approach to automatic alignment. Finally, in Sects. 5 and 6 we expose our conclusions and future work.

2 Related Work

An approach proposed in [1] introduces a vertical bar in the sheet design for OMR. This addition facilitates the use of principal component analysis (PCA) for faster and more accurate skew correction of OMR sheets captured via mobile phone cameras. The challenge of accurately evaluating OMR sheets captured under conditions like tilt and rotation is addressed by leveraging the PCA's property to identify the direction of maximum data variance . This is achieved by analyzing the captured image to correct its orientation prior to evaluation. The approach guarantees 100% accuracy and boasts an average processing time of just 1.15 s, demonstrating a substantial improvement over current methods.

Otherwise, Kommey, Keelson, Samuel, Twum-Asare & Akuffo propose the creation of an automated grading system for multiple-choice exams that surpasses traditional grading methods in terms of both efficiency and cost-effectiveness. By employing advanced image processing and OMR techniques, the system will scan and grade answer sheets with precision. The system is designed to function across a variety of devices, including smartphones and tablets, ensuring accessibility. The challenge of automating the grading of multiple-choice tests is addressed by developing a system capable of precisely scanning and interpreting OMR sheets. To achieve this, the system utilizes an array of image processing and pattern recognition methodologies, including contour detection, template matching, and the Hough transform. Contour detection is employed to delineate the edges of the OMR sheet and identify the individual answer bubbles. Template matching compares the student's marked responses to the pre-set correct answers, ensuring alignment [2]. Meanwhile, the Hough transform is leveraged to detect the specific marks made by the student, effectively identifying selected answers. The experimental results indicate that the proposed grading system delivers high accuracy in evaluating multiple-choice exams.

De Elias Paulo & Hirata's article emphasizes the critical role of automatic alignment in OMR systems, which ensures accurate detection of marks on scanned sheets despite potential misalignments. Automatic alignment addresses challenges such as slight document rotations or distortions during scanning, which can lead to errors in mark identification [3]. Techniques like image preprocessing, feature extraction, and geometric transformations are used to adjust and align scanned sheets, ensuring marks are detected accurately. While these methods have improved OMR performance, issues like paper quality variability and uneven scanning still present challenges, although advancements in image processing and machine learning continue to enhance alignment accuracy in large-scale assessments.

In the work presented by Mahmud et al., automatic rotation is used to align an answer sheet within an automatic multiple-choice question evaluation system. In this case, the evaluation process is carried out using an existing function in the Python programming language, specifically image_to_osd() from the pytesseract package [11]. This function is based on a concept known as Orientation and Script Detection (OSD), which, as implemented in pytesseract, enables the detection of text orientation by returning the rotation angle (in degrees) of the text in an image. To achieve this, the function attempts to identify a character in the image and, based on its orientation, determines the degree of inclination of the text—essentially assessing how much a character is tilted relative to its expected upright position.

In the work presented in [16], an automatic evaluation of written responses is carried out. The process begins by capturing an image, followed by a preprocessing stage that involves various transformations. These include noise reduction, grayscale conversion, and alignment using techniques such as skew correction, which involves rotating a digitized image to align the contained text based on the scanner's coordinate system. The importance of this process is emphasized in optical character recognition and other analysis tasks.

In Table 1, we summarize related works based on the method used, execution time, maximum angle, and device computation.

Table 1. Related Work Comparison

Author	Method	Execution Time (s)	Max Angle (°)	Device Computation
Rachchh & Gopi [1]	PCA	0.91	12	Desktop
Kommey et al. [2]	Hough Detection	0.8	15	Desktop
De Elias et al. [3]	Hough Detection	2.76	2	Desktop
Mahmud [11]	OSD Tesseract	2.8	10	Mobile
Jayapandian [16]	Hough Detection	-	-	Desktop
This work	Template Matching	1.24	12	Mobile

3 Methodology

The document digitization process goes beyond simply capturing a high-quality image; it includes transformations to ensure accurate and efficient data extraction using OpenCV, compiled with WebAssembly for a WebView environment. In this context, image preprocessing plays a crucial role in preparing the captures for further analysis. This stage involves multiple steps (see Fig. 1) that enhance image quality and highlight key elements while minimizing imperfections or noise present in the original image. In Sect. 3.1 and 3.2, the steps shown in Fig. 1 are explained in detail. The preprocessing stage enhances image clarity, while the alignment step ensures proper positioning and orientation of the image.

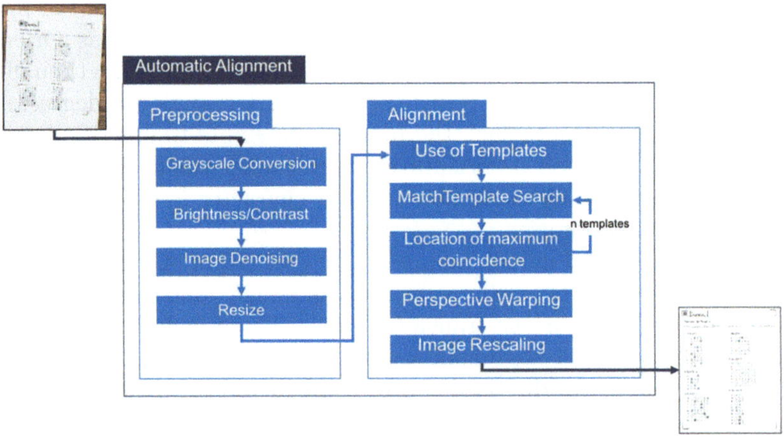

Fig. 1. Automatic alignment process

3.1 Preprocessing

This section describes essential preprocessing steps in image analysis, starting with grayscale conversion. Contrast enhancement follows to amplify important details, while image denoising and refinement are applied through convolution filters to sharpen edges and suppress noise. These transformations optimize the image for subsequent feature detection and analysis, improving processing accuracy.

Grayscale Conversion. One of the initial transformations applied to the captured image is the conversion to grayscale. This simplification reduces the visual data's complexity by eliminating color variations that could interfere with the detection of important elements [4,6]. The conversion uses a standard formula, which incorporates the red (R), green (G), and blue (B) components of the original image, as expressed in Eq. 1:

$$Y = 0.299 \times R + 0.587 \times G + 0.114 \times B \tag{1}$$

Equation 1, defined by the ITU-R BT.601 standard, weights the colors according to their perception by the human eye, so that the contrast and visibility of the most relevant elements in the image are maximized [4,5].

Brightness/Contrast. After converting the image to grayscale, the next step is to enhance its contrast. This adjustment is essential for making important details and elements in the image more visible. Without adequate contrast, some features may remain obscure or poorly defined, complicating their subsequent analysis. In this step, a custom brightness and contrast filter is applied, using Eq. 2.

$$A_{res}(x, y) = \alpha \left[A(x, y) - \beta \right] \tag{2}$$

where $\alpha = 1.5$ is the contrast factor and $\beta = 30$ is the brightness offset. These parameters were determined experimentally: α was selected after iteratively testing values in a linear range from 0 to 100, evaluating the visibility and clarity of image features at each step. In the case of β, whose influence on brightness is more sensitive, the base value was set to 1.0 and adjusted incrementally. Larger changes (e.g., to 2.0 or beyond) produced excessive distortion. The selected values highlight key image details while reducing the impact of noise [7], facilitating the identification of features in subsequent processing steps.

Image Denoising. Image convolution involves applying a filter or kernel to the original image to modify its features, such as contrast, smoothness, or edge detection. After converting the image to grayscale and adjusting the contrast, convolution helps to extract features by applying appropriate filters that emphasize key details [4,6].

Noise, which can be generated by suboptimal lighting conditions or imperfections in the device's camera, is a common challenge in image processing. To resolve this issue, an additional filter K is applied, expressed in Eq. 3, which sharpens the edges of the image, further improving the visibility of the relevant elements [7,12].

$$K = \begin{bmatrix} 0 & -1 & 0 \\ -1 & 5 & -1 \\ 0 & -1 & 0 \end{bmatrix} \tag{3}$$

This kernel K is derived from the unsharp masking technique, a form of high-boost filtering where the original image is combined with a scaled version of the difference between itself and a blurred version. The result is a kernel that emphasizes the center pixel while suppressing its neighbors, enhancing edges and fine details [12].

Together with the contrast adjustment, the custom filter helps reduce the interference of unwanted elements, ensuring that the most important details are the most prominent in the processed image.

3.2 Alignment

A crucial step in the image digitization process is to ensure that the captured photos are accurately aligned and free from distortions. Because images taken with mobile devices can be affected by tilts, rotations, or warping due to the angle of the camera, it is essential to use an automatic alignment technique to correct these issues before proceeding with image analysis.

Automatic alignment aims to detect any tilt or distortion in the original image and correct it efficiently without direct intervention. It is a process composed of a series of steps, illustrated in Fig. 1. The process starts with the identification of key points in the image, such as corners or edges, which act as reference points for alignment. These points are essential for calculating the transformation needed to straighten and rectify the image.

The system uses auxiliary patterns (templates) positioned near the edges of the image, given as visual guides to locate the area of interest. These patterns are created to be easily identifiable, even when the image is tilted or distorted. By identifying the most accurate matching points with these patterns, the system can determine how the image should be transformed to properly align the edges and ensure that the region of interest is correctly centered.

Use of Templates. To perform the alignment, the system uses alignment templates presented in the sheet, which are small images representing the corners or edges of the image. These templates are placed at key locations within the image. The idea is to use these templates to locate the edges of the image, ensuring that the area of interest remains centered and free from distortions. The Fig. 2 shows the four corners: (2a)top left, (2b) top right, (2c) lower left, and (2d) lower right.

(a) Top left corner (b) Top right corner

(c) Lower left corner (d) Lower right corner

Fig. 2. Templates used for automatic alignment

MatchTemplate Search and Location of Maximum Coincidence. The search utilizing normalized convolution is conducted through the *MatchTemplate* method from OpenCV, which compares templates against the captured image to identify locations with the highest match. This process employs multiple template sizes (14, 16, and 20 pixels square) to enhance accuracy and detect the most precise matches by selecting the highest matching points. This approach ensures that even with slight rotations or shifts in the image, the algorithm can accurately identify key points, as illustrated in Fig. 3.

The mathematical formulation used by the *MatchTemplate* function when the method is set to `TM_CCOEFF_NORMED` is given by Eq. 4.

$$R(x,y) = \frac{\sum_{x',y'} (T'(x',y') \cdot I'(x+x',y+y'))}{\sqrt{\sum_{x',y'} T'(x',y')^2 \cdot \sum_{x',y'} I'(x+x',y+y')^2}} \tag{4}$$

where,

$$T'(x',y') = T(x',y') - \frac{1}{w \cdot h} \sum_{x'',y''} T(x'',y'') \tag{5}$$

$$I'(x+x',y+y') = I(x+x',y+y') - \frac{1}{w \cdot h} \sum_{x'',y''} I(x+x'',y+y'') \tag{6}$$

Equation 4 computes the *Normalized Cross-Correlation* between the template T and the sub-region of the image I located at position (x, y). Here:

- $T'(x', y')$ is the zero-mean version of the template, i.e., the mean value of the template has been subtracted, shown as Eq. 5.
- $I'(x + x', y + y')$ is the corresponding patch of the input image subtracting the mean value of patch (see Eq. 6).
- The numerator calculates the cross-correlation between the template and the image patch.
- The denominator normalizes the result by Euclidean norm of both the template and the image patch.

The result $R(x, y)$ ranges from -1 to 1, where 1 indicates a perfect match. This normalization makes the algorithm invariant to local changes in brightness and contrast, which is crucial for robust template matching in varying image conditions [13].

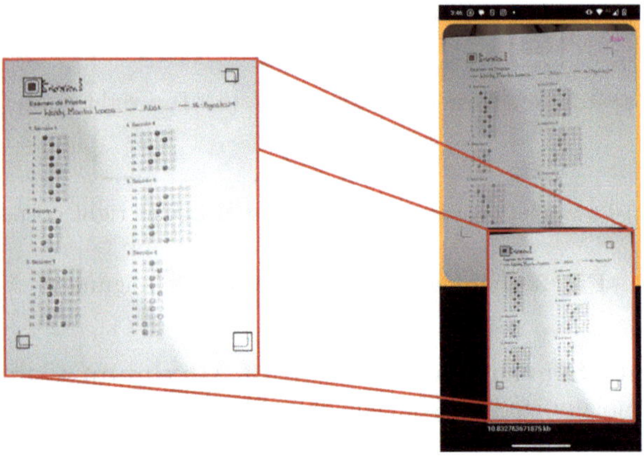

Fig. 3. Edges detection

Perspective Warping. After identifying the key markers, perspective correction is performed using the *WarpPerspective* method. This method applies a transformation matrix that adjusts the original image based on the reference points found in the previous step with the reduced image. The matrix determines how the pixels in the image should be transformed to align properly, correcting any distortions or tilts.

To estimate the transformation matrix M, we first compute a homography matrix using the *findHomography* function [14]. This method finds the best transformation between matched keypoints from the source and destination planes, often using the RANSAC (Random Sample Consensus) algorithm to increase robustness against outliers [14]. The result is a 3×3 homography matrix M that encapsulates the projective transformation.

$$\mathrm{dst}(x, y) = \mathrm{src}\left(\frac{M_{11}x + M_{12}y + M_{13}}{M_{31}x + M_{32}y + M_{33}}, \frac{M_{21}x + M_{22}y + M_{23}}{M_{31}x + M_{32}y + M_{33}}\right) \tag{7}$$

Equation 7 explains how each pixel (x, y) in the output image is computed using the source image and transformation matrix M, with coordinates normalized to Cartesian form. If the flag `WARP_INVERSE_MAP` is set, M is used directly; otherwise, it's inverted. The transformation is applied using the matrix M from *findHomography* and linear interpolation, with constant border handling [15].

By combining *findHomography* with **RANSAC** and *warpPerspective*, a robust and geometrically accurate alignment is ensured, even in the presence of partial occlusions or erroneous point matches. Linear interpolation with a constant border mode is recommended for smooth results. This perspective-warping step is crucial because it not only straightens the image but also ensures that the proportions and geometry are accurate. The result is an aligned image with the area of interest centered and ready for the subsequent stages of analysis.

Image Rescaling. Finally, by using the location information of the markers from the reduced image obtained in Sect. 3.2, this data is proportionally scaled according to the scaling ratio (between the sizes of the original image and the reduced image). By applying this scaled data in the perspective warping on the original image, the image acquires, in its original size, the alignment properties of the reduced image.

Effect of Automated Alignment. The automatic alignment process is essential for ensuring the accuracy of automated systems in subsequent stages. Without correcting distortions, detection algorithms may struggle to identify key elements, which could degrade the quality of the automated analysis. Accurate alignment also improves computational efficiency, as the system can focus only on the relevant regions, decreasing the processing loads on other parts of the image.

Computational Optimization. Computational efficiency is crucial in image processing systems, especially on mobile devices with limited resources. To optimize performance, techniques such as reducing the image resolution before performing computationally intensive tasks—like convolutions and geometric transformations—are commonly used. This approach reduces pixel processing, speeding up calculations while maintaining quality for tasks like edge detection and alignment. Afterward, the image is adjusted to match the original resolution.

4 Results

The automatic alignment process has shown the ability to correct rotational discrepancies within specific margins as well as certain distortions in images. During experimentation, the system's effectiveness was assessed in compensating for images with relative rotational angles of up to 12°. The tests utilized a variety of images captured with mobile devices, where perfect alignment is not always guaranteed.

The results indicated that even with *relative parallel rotations* of up to 12°, the system successfully restored the images to a better position, significantly enhancing their quality for subsequent analytical processing (see Table 2).

The system was evaluated under different conditions, including images with varying rotation angles and different levels of distortion, as illustrated in Fig. 4. The effectiveness of the correction capability was assessed based on acceptance criteria, specifically whether the image was properly aligned. This evaluation was conducted in real-time and took into account the processing limitations of the mobile device used, namely the Motorola G30 running on the Android 12 operating system.

The proposed method allows automatic alignment without invasive markers. While the inclusion of a vertical bar for PCA-based alignment offers fast processing (avg, 1.15 s) [1], it imposes significant constraints on the design flexibility of

Table 2. Correction based on rotation angle measured in degrees

Rotation Angle (°)	N° Correct	N° Incorrect	N° Unrecognized	Average Computation Time (s)
-14	0	0	100	0.00
-12	77	4	19	1.26
-10	87	4	9	1.25
-8	97	2	1	1.23
-6	99	1	0	1.25
-4	100	0	0	1.24
-2	100	0	0	1.23
0	100	0	0	1.25
2	100	0	0	1.24
4	99	1	0	1.24
6	100	0	0	1.27
8	97	3	0	1.25
10	88	5	7	1.23
12	74	5	21	1.24
14	0	0	100	0.00

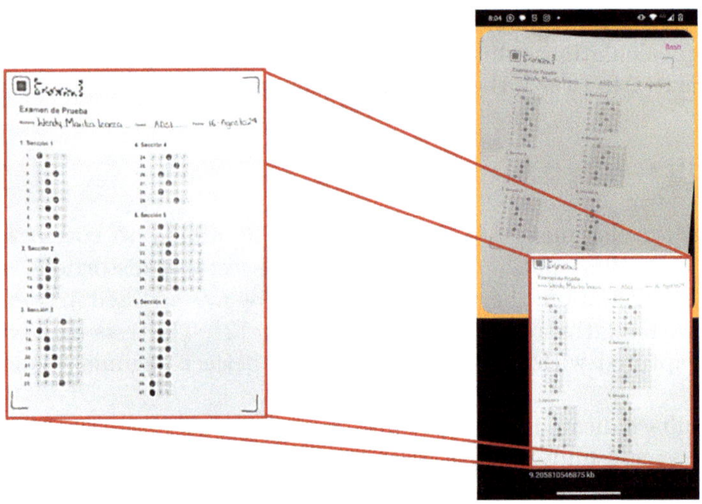

Fig. 4. Automatic alignment

the sheet. The current approach introduces a cleaner solution with more discreet markers while maintaining a similar processing time (avg, 1.24 s). The method proposed demonstrates better handling of perspective warping and blur, leading to more accurate content alignment in various situations (see Fig. 5).

On the other hand, the edge detection method implemented via OpenCV in the *'edge_detection'* Flutter plugin [2] exhibits several challenges. It is com-

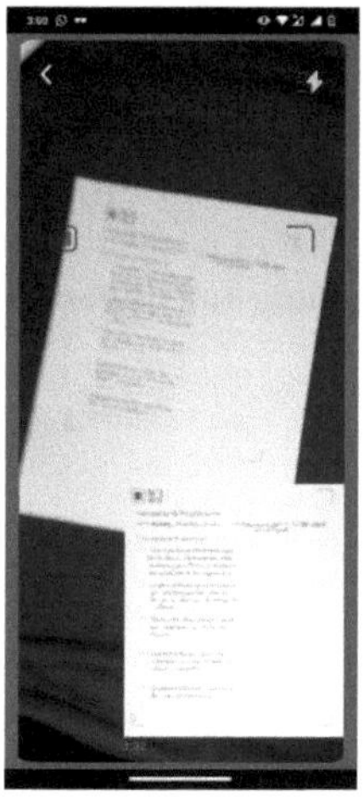

Fig. 5. Blurred and distorted image auto-alignment

Fig. 6. White background detection and auto-alignment

putationally expensive and yields relatively low precision in edge delineation. Moreover, the method requires the sheet to be placed on a high-contrast surface, with potential interfering effects stemming from the sheet's content itself. The proposed solution offers greater flexibility by allowing the sheet to be placed on any surface, eliminating these limitations (see Fig. 6).

5 Conclusions

In this work, we present an alternative mobile device-based system for digitalization and automatic alignment of OMR sheets. Our proposal efficiently manages several images preprocessing stages, including grayscale conversion, contrast adjustment, and edge enhancement for automatic alignment. By utilizing a pre-compiled and WebAssembly-optimized library like OpenCV at each stage, the system executes these operations efficiently and natively. This accelerates calculations, ensures faster processing, and prepares the images for subsequent content analysis.

A key component of the optimization process is the automatic alignment of images, which utilizes templates to identify the image edges. To enhance efficiency, smaller templates are employed, and the search for matches is limited to the most relevant areas of the image, reducing unnecessary calculations. Only the points with the highest matching scores are selected, ensuring precise alignment without performing exhaustive searches that could lead to system overload.

During testing, the system's performance was evaluated on sheets with slight variations in rotation angles, successfully aligning them in **real-time** using physical sheets of the same format. These tests were carried out under real-world conditions, where the sheets were captured automatically four times per second with a mobile device, as in typical use scenarios. Notably, no pre-existing datasets were utilized; all images were taken on-site with different format sheets, ensuring that the results accurately reflect the system's capabilities in practical applications. This method also emphasizes the system's ability to operate without the need for pre-labeled data, relying exclusively on **real-time** image processing.

6 Future Work

While the current system is effective at correcting rotations of up to 12°, there are plans to improve its tolerance to greater distortions, such as more pronounced tilts or more complex deformations. In this regard, additional alignment techniques will be explored, including the definition of other templates and transformations based on local features, which could enable more robust correction in the presence of severe distortions. The templates considered for future use should be shapes that are invariant to rotational transformations, ensuring that the template looks identical from any angle and allowing reliable detection. Circles are the best candidates for this purpose.

Furthermore, efforts will focus on improving the accuracy of templates and optimizing the matching search process to ensure the system can handle a wider variety of scenarios without increasing computational load. Another consideration for future work is enhancing the system's capability to handle images with variable lighting or poor-quality conditions, as these factors may affect the alignment accuracy.

Acknowledgements. The authors acknowledge the support of the Universidad Autonóma Metropolitana and SECIHTI through the award of a postgraduate scholarship, which enabled the development of the project encompassing the work presented. We also express our gratitude to the students who completed the assessments employed in the automatic alignment process.

Disclosure of Interests. The authors declare that they have no conflicts of interest related to the work and the results presented.

References

1. Rachchh, K., Gopi, E.S.: Inclusion of Vertical Bar in the OMR Sheet for Image-Based Robust and Fast OMR Evaluation Technique Using Mobile Phone Camera. (2023)
2. Kommey, B., Keelson, E., Samuel, F., Twum-Asare, S., Akuffo, K.K.: Automatic Multiple Choice Examination Questions Marking and Grade Generator Software. IPTEK The J. Technol. Sci. **33**(3) (2022)
3. de Elias, E.M., Tasinaffo, P.M., Hirata, R.: Optical mark recognition: advances, difficulties, and limitations. SN Comput. Sci. **2**(5), 1–13 (2021). https://doi.org/10.1007/s42979-021-00760-z

4. Bradski, G., Kaehler, A.: Learning OpenCV: Computer Vision with the OpenCV Library. O'Reilly Media (2008)
5. Forsyth, D.A., Ponce, J.: Computer Vision: A Modern Approach. Prentice Hall (2002)
6. Szeliski, R.: Computer Vision: Algorithms and Applications. Springer (2010)
7. OpenCV Documentation: OpenCV: Open Source Computer Vision Library (2025).https://opencv.org/
8. Liu, X., Zhang, Y.: Deep Learning for Computer Vision. Springer (2017)
9. Nair, V., Hinton, G.E.: Rectified Linear Units Improve Restricted Boltzmann Machines. In: Proceedings of the 27th International Conference on Machine Learning (ICML) (2010)
10. Rajagopal, R., Saha, B.: Optical mark recognition (OMR) automated grading using OpenCV. AIP Conference Proceedings (2024)
11. Mahmud, S., Biswas, K., Alam, A., Rudro, R.A.M., Anannya, N.J., Mouri, I.J., Nur, K.: Automatic multiple choice question evaluation using Tesseract OCR and YOLOv8. In: Proceedings of the 2024 IEEE Conference on Artificial Intelligence (CAI), pp. 246–252. IEEE (2024)
12. Jerod Weinman, CSC 161 Homework: Convolution Kernels, Grinnell College (2021)
13. OpenCV, *Template Matching — OpenCV Documentation*, version 3.4. Available at: https://docs.opencv.org/3.4/df/dfb/group_imgproc_object.html#gga3a7850640f1fe1f58fe91a2d7583695dac6677e2af5e0fae82cc5339bfaef5038
14. OpenCV, Feature Matching and Homography Estimation, https://docs.opencv.org/4.x/d1/de0/tutorial_py_feature_homography.html. Accessed: 2025-07-14
15. OpenCV, Image Processing: Geometric Transformations of Images, https://docs.opencv.org/4.x/da/d54/group_imgproc_transform.html. Accessed: 2025-07-14
16. Jayapandian, N and Kavya, A and Keneshia, A and others: Machine learning based automatic answer script evaluation using artificial neural network. In: 2024 IEEE 4th International Conference on ICT in Business Industry & Government (ICTBIG), pp. 1–7. IEEE (2024)

Fine-Grained Insights Generation Based on Semantic Clustering from Online Reviews

Brenda I. Guzmán-Bonilla, María J. Merino-Pérez, Daniel Sánchez-Ruiz(✉), Ricardo Ramos-Aguilar, and Eric Ramos-Aguilar

Unidad Profesional Interdisciplinaria de Ingeniería Campus Tlaxcala - IPN, Tlaxcala, Mexico
{bguzmanb2101,mmerinop2100}@alumno.ipn.mx, {dsanchezro,rramosa,eramosa}@ipn.mx

Abstract. This paper presents a scalable methodology for extracting actionable insights from skincare product reviews by combining topic modeling, semantic clustering, and generative language models. Using a dataset of more than one million reviews from Sephora's catalog, trigram-based TF-IDF vectorization with Latent Dirichlet Allocation (LDA) uncovered latent topics, while HDBSCAN clustering identified coherent subgroups reflecting concerns such as hydration performance, packaging usability, scent, and texture. To synthesize these findings, Google's Flan-T5 Large model generated structured recommendations classified as strengths, areas for improvement, and best practices. Quantitative evaluation included pseudo-perplexity scores obtained with RoBERTa, achieving a mean of 14.33 (SD = 14.77) and a median of 8.01, indicating high syntactic fluency and semantic coherence in most outputs. Additional metrics, such as lexical diversity and redundancy, confirmed the quality of the generated insights. Results demonstrate that the trigram + HDBSCAN configuration produced the most coherent and diverse clusters, outperforming alternative setups. In conclusion, the proposed framework effectively transforms large-scale unstructured feedback into fine-grained, interpretable recommendations, supporting decision-making in product development, marketing, and customer experience design within the skincare industry.

Keywords: Natural Language Processing · Text Mining · Semantic Clustering · Generative Models

1 Introduction

The exponential growth of customer review data presents both unprecedented opportunities and significant analytical challenges for businesses. While approximately 97% of consumers consult reviews before making purchases, affecting over $3.2 trillion in annual consumer spending, the vast majority of this feedback

C. Palma-Preciado et al. (Eds.): CORE 2025, ACSAR 3, pp. 48–63, 2026.
https://doi.org/10.1007/978-3-032-08894-9_4

remains unanalyzed—an estimated 95% of customer feedback in unstructured text format goes unexplored [16]. This represents a critical gap in our ability to transform raw customer opinions into actionable business intelligence.

In the beauty and personal care industry, which are strongly driven by subjective perceptions and individual experiences, online product reviews have emerged as a vital resource for businesses [16]. These reviews can be used as detailed repositories of product feedback that can guide innovation, customer service strategies, and brand positioning [10,16].

Unlike structured surveys or focus groups, online reviews are unmoderated, spontaneous, and massive in scale. As they are written in natural language, these reviews are inherently noisy, often containing slang, abbreviations, inconsistent grammar, and ambiguous references. Although this complexity presents challenges, it also has the potential to uncover nuanced patterns and unmet needs when analyzed with appropriate computational techniques [7].

The central problem addressed by this research is the absence of scalable, interpretable methodologies that can systematically transform large volumes of unstructured customer reviews into actionable insights.

Current approaches suffer from three fundamental limitations: traditional sentiment analysis fails to capture the granular, feature-specific feedback patterns essential for product development decisions [17]; existing text mining frameworks lack the semantic coherence necessary to generate contextually relevant business recommendations [1,19]; and there is no unified approach that combines topic discovery, semantic clustering, and natural language generation to produce interpretable, actionable outputs at scale.

In order to approach these limitations, this work proposes the following research questions: (1) How can topic modeling, semantic clustering, and generative language models be integrated to extract coherent, actionable insights from customer review data? (2) What combination of text preprocessing, vectorization, and clustering techniques yields the most semantically meaningful product-specific recommendations? (3) To what extent can automated insight generation from review clustering achieve both syntactic fluency and practical business relevance?

This study aims to: develop a scalable methodology that transforms unstructured customer reviews into structured, interpretable insights; optimize the combination of LDA topic modeling, HDBSCAN clustering, and generative language models for maximum semantic coherence; and demonstrate the practical applicability of the framework for generating actionable product improvement recommendations in the skincare industry.

The rest of this document is structured as follows. The Related Work section discusses prior work in the areas of topic modeling, semantic clustering, and the use of NLP in marketing and customer review analysis. Section Methodology presents the proposed approach, first in general terms and then through detailed descriptions of each component. The Results section includes the experimental design and the results obtained. Finally, Section Conclusions offers the conclusions of the study and outlines future research directions.

2 Literature Review

Recent years have witnessed a surge in research focused on extracting value from user-generated content using natural language processing and machine learning techniques. Among the most notable contributions is the work of Zhang et al. [22], who developed models to mine innovation ideas directly from online product reviews. They demonstrated how deep learning architectures could detect subtle patterns in consumer feedback, providing direction for new product features.

Similarly, Zhang et al. [23] introduced a machine learning framework to assess synergy and dysergy in product reviews, revealing how combinations of product attributes contribute to consumer satisfaction or dissatisfaction.

In the context of crowdfunding and early-stage product feedback, Boye et al. [1] implemented a clustering-based text mining approach to identify emergent consumer needs from project comments. Their results showed that even short, informal user-generated texts could be grouped into coherent clusters representing functional or emotional expectations.

In a corporate setting, Nusch et al. [15] focused on integrating text mining into knowledge management systems to support internal innovation processes. Their approach demonstrated the potential for unstructured data to enrich formal decision-making frameworks.

Goldberg and Abrahams [5] extended this idea by proposing a pipeline to mine innovation intelligence directly from customer reviews, emphasizing the importance of extracting actionable signals from noisy input. Their work forms a foundation for the interpretability aspect addressed in our approach.

Similarly, Park et al. [6] explored customer satisfaction using TF-IDF models on reviews from global cosmetic brands. Their results illustrated the feasibility of extracting key indicators of satisfaction from review corpora, though they did not pursue clustering or synthesis of recommendations.

Advanced methodologies were also explored by Qin et al. [17] and Zhang and Song [21], who proposed multi-stage models combining sentiment analysis, semantic similarity, and decision-making frameworks for product redesign. These works emphasize the value of incorporating multiple analytic layers to derive design insights. Additionally, Zatonatska et al. [20] and Kumar [9] contributed to strategic marketing and decision support system design through hybrid data mining models, while Kokkodis and Lappas [8] highlighted the biases in consumer feedback on reputation platforms.

Despite these advancements, few studies offer a holistic, interpretable, and scalable solution that integrates topic modeling, semantic clustering, and natural language generation in a single pipeline.

2.1 NLP in Marketing and Customer Review Analysis

Recent advances in NLP have had a significant impact on how businesses analyze customer opinions for marketing insights. Liu et al. [11] proposed a model that integrates explainable AI with ingredient-based product attributes to provide personalized beauty recommendations. Their work demonstrates how customer language can be mapped to structured product attributes, providing both transparency and actionable insight.

Mahdi et al. [12] used transformation-based NLP tasks to identify product improvement opportunities in online reviews, highlighting the role of syntactic and semantic transformations in extracting deeper meaning from user expressions. Chen [2] explored strategic marketing initiatives in the beauty industry and how data analytics is central to customer relationship management.

The emergence of benchmarking practices in marketing has also benefited from NLP. Rumbo [18] illustrated early frameworks for comparative analysis, now increasingly automated through sentiment and topic-based systems. These advancements show a clear trend toward integrating NLP, clustering, and interpretability into marketing pipelines that directly impact product refinement, branding, and consumer engagement strategies.

3 Methodology

This section presents the methodology used to analyze and extract actionable insights from skincare product reviews. The proposed pipeline consists of several sequential stages, starting from raw text preprocessing, followed by feature extraction, topic modeling, semantic clustering, and finally, the generation of consumer-driven suggestions. Figure 1 illustrates the overall workflow, which is then detailed in the subsequent subsections.

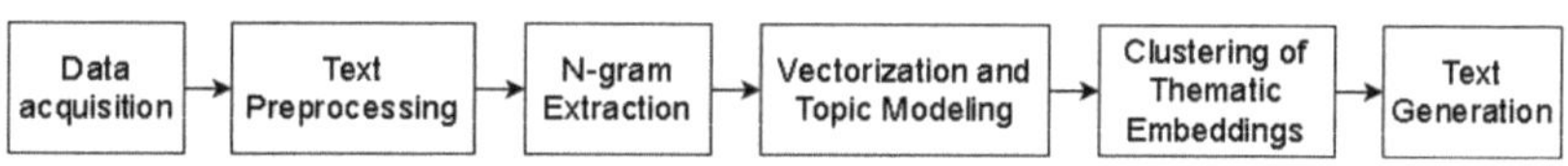

Fig. 1. Pipeline of the proposed methodology.

3.1 Dataset Description

The dataset used in this study was collected via Python-based web scraper in March 2023 and comprises reviews and detailed attributes of beauty products, specifically from the online catalog of Sephora. This dataset is publicly available for academic and research purposes [14].

The dataset consists of information on over 8,000 beauty products listed in the Sephora online store, including variables such as product and brand names, regular and discounted prices, ingredients, average user ratings, and various product-specific attributes. In addition, it contains approximately one million user reviews covering more than 2,000 skincare products. These reviews are enriched with metadata on the reviewing users, such as skin type, skin tone, hair color, and eye color, as well as feedback metrics like usefulness ratings from other users.

While the dataset provides substantial coverage of skincare product reviews, several methodological considerations must be acknowledged regarding data representativeness and bias mitigation. The dataset's focus on Sephora customers may introduce demographic and socioeconomic sampling bias, as this platform primarily serves higher-income consumers. To address potential coverage bias, we implemented stratified sampling techniques to ensure proportional representation across product categories, price ranges, and rating distributions.

3.2 Data Preprocessing

The preprocessing phase included the cleaning, structuring, and preparation of both product attributes and textual reviews for further analysis. Categorical Encoding, Text Cleaning and Normalization were applied. User reviews were normalized using a series of NLP preprocessing steps such as: conversion to lowercase, expansion of contractions (e.g.,"don't" → "do not"), removal of special characters, punctuation, and numeric digits, tokenization and stopword removal, lemmatization and spelling correction.

Given the substantial volume of textual data, the `Dask` [4] library was employed instead of `pandas` [13] to enable parallelized and memory-efficient processing. This decision helped prevent memory saturation and facilitated scalable computations.

3.3 N-Gram Extraction and Sampling

Due to computational constraints, n-gram frequency analysis was performed on a stratified sample of 200,000 reviews. This subset was used exclusively for frequency visualizations. To validate the representativeness of the sample, the distribution of review lengths was compared between the sample and the full dataset. As shown in Fig. 2, the similarity in distributions confirms that the sample adequately preserves the structural characteristics of the original dataset without introducing sampling bias.

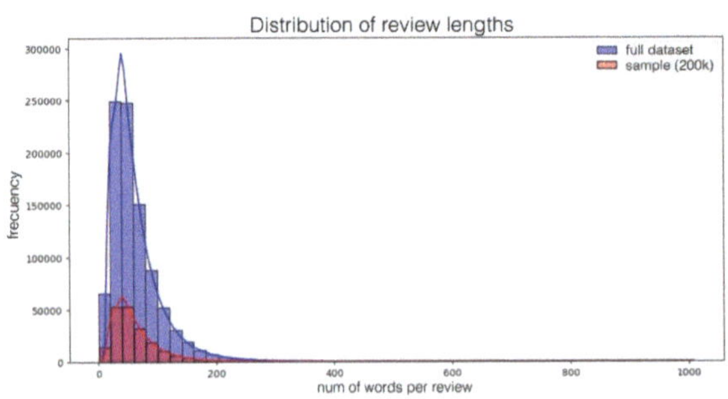

Fig. 2. Comparison of review length distributions between the full corpus and the 200,000-review sample.

To gain an initial understanding of the most frequent terms used by consumers, word clouds were generated from the sample. These visualizations highlight common expressions and facilitate a more intuitive grasp of recurring themes. Figure 3 presents two word clouds: (a) one generated from the entire corpus. In the general corpus, prominent terms include *skin*, *face*, *used*, *love*, *moisturizer*, *feel*, *smooth*, and *leave*, indicating emphasis on product use, skin effects, and user experience. In contrast, the word cloud derived from negative reviews highlights terms such as *dry*, *sensitive*, *smell*, *oily*, *did not*, and *tried*, which reflect more critical or unsatisfactory experiences.

(a) All reviews (b) Negative reviews

Fig. 3. Word clouds generated from online reviews.

Selection of Relevant N-Grams

To identify the most relevant n grams, frequency plots (e.g. rank frequency plots and histograms) were generated. For bigrams, a total of 69 combinations were selected based on a frequency threshold of 14,348. This threshold was determined using the derivative of the logarithmic frequency function to identify an optimal inflection point:

$$\text{optimal frecuency} = \text{frecuency}\left[\arg\max\left(\Delta \log(\text{frecuency})\right)\right] \quad (1)$$

This data-driven approach was preferred over manual or purely statistical cut-offs, as it better aligned with the actual frequency distribution, balancing coverage and specificity.

For trigrams, the inflection point in the frequency distribution was located near rank 54, corresponding to a frequency of 2,760. Trigrams above this threshold were retained, resulting in 105 selected trigrams from a total of 39,556 unique candidates. This ensured that only the most semantically meaningful and commonly used sequences were preserved.

3.4 Text Vectorization and Topic Modeling

To extract meaningful linguistic patterns from the corpus, the text was vectorized using Term Frequency–Inverse Document Frequency (TF-IDF) applied to trigrams. This configuration was selected after empirically comparing several alternatives, including different n-gram sizes (bigrams and trigrams) and vectorization methods (TF-IDF and Bag-of-Words). Among these, the TF-IDF trigram representation yielded the most semantically coherent and thematically distinct topics in downstream modeling.

As an initial step, the most frequent trigrams were identified in the corpus to gain a general understanding of recurrent expressions in user reviews. Table 1 presents the ten most common trigrams, which capture typical consumer discourse related to product effectiveness, skin conditions, and overall sentiment.

Table 1. Top 10 most frequent trigrams in the corpus.

Trigram	Frequency
i do not	59,208
i have been	53,797
i received this	41,419
it doe not	39,492
have been using	38,797
it is a	37,238
my skin is	36,615
my skin feel	35,616
i love this	33,218
i did not	29,624

Subsequently, Latent Dirichlet Allocation (LDA) was applied to the TF-IDF trigram matrix to discover latent semantic structures in the reviews. The number of topics was optimized using coherence score maximization, with the optimal value found at $k = 3$ (see Fig. 4).

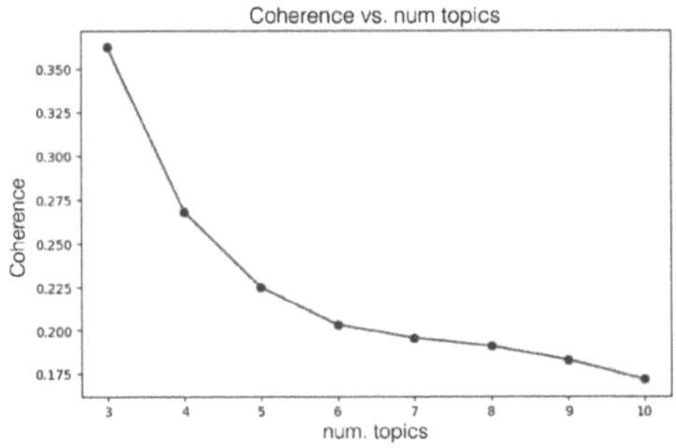

Fig. 4. Coherence plot for TF-IDF trigram matrix.

The three resulting topics are summarized in Table 2, each represented by its most significant trigrams. These topics reflect recurring patterns in user reviews, capturing negative or ambiguous product experiences, positive effects on skin feel and appearance, and highly enthusiastic endorsements, often associated with promotional samples.

Table 2. Summary of LDA topics using TF-IDF trigrams

Topic	Representative Trigrams	Interpretation
1	*i have been, i do not, have been using, on my face, it is not*	Negative experiences or lack of clear results, mostly regarding facial product use
2	*my skin feel, make my skin, it does not, i love it, my skin look*	Positive descriptions of product effects on skin feel and appearance
3	*love this product, i received this, i love this, my skin is, i absolutely love*	Strong enthusiasm and positive recommendations, often in the context of received samples

To further validate the quality of the topic modeling, a two-dimensional projection of the document embeddings was generated using t-Distributed Stochastic Neighbor Embedding (t-SNE). Figure 5 displays this projection, with each point representing a review and colored according to its dominant topic. The visual separation among clusters indicates that the identified topics correspond to meaningful differences in user language and content.

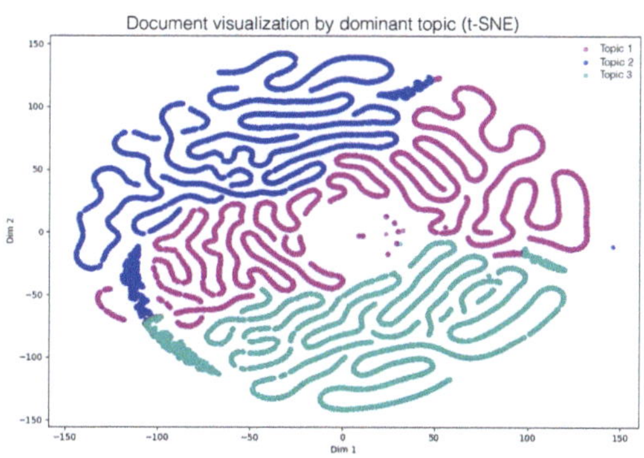

Fig. 5. t-SNE projection of document embeddings, colored by dominant topic.

These results demonstrate that TF-IDF with trigrams provides a semantically rich and thematically distinct basis for downstream tasks such as clustering and text generation. Other configurations were tested during development but ultimately discarded due to lower coherence and relevance.

3.5 Clustering of Thematic Embeddings

To identify latent semantic structures within the textual reviews, we performed unsupervised clustering on the vector representations of trigram-based embeddings. These embeddings were grouped by dominant topic, as previously obtained from the LDA-based topic modeling over the TF-IDF matrix. For each topic, the set of review embeddings was independently clustered using HDBSCAN, a density-based algorithm that automatically determines the optimal number of clusters without requiring manual specification of k.

This approach allowed to capture fine-grained subgroups of reviews within each topic, enabling the discovery of recurrent linguistic patterns and semantically coherent segments. HDBSCAN also identifies outliers as noise points (labeled as cluster -1), which were excluded from subsequent interpretation and generation tasks.

As an example, Table 3 illustrates the clustering structure obtained for Topic 1. Three meaningful clusters were identified, along with a small group of noise points. Similar patterns were observed across other topics.

Table 3. Example of clustering results for Topic 1 using HDBSCAN

Cluster ID	Review Count	Label
0	43,317	Main cluster
1	128	Minor cluster
2	61	Minor cluster
-1	307	Noise (outliers)

Although K-means was initially explored as a baseline clustering method—guided by silhouette scores and Davies–Bouldin indices indicating $k = 7$ as a plausible choice—the results were less granular and harder to interpret. HDBSCAN was ultimately preferred due to its ability to identify clusters of arbitrary shape and its robustness to noise, which proved essential for revealing nuanced subtopics and stylistic variations within each theme.

3.6 Text Generation Strategy

To synthesize actionable insights from user reviews, implemented a text generation strategy using Google's Flan-T5 Large [3], a state-of-the-art language model based on the T5 architecture. The objective was to produce structured summaries that describe three key aspects for each product: (i) its perceived strengths, (ii) specific areas for improvement, and (iii) best practices observed in competing products.

The model's input consisted of clusters of reviews, which were generated using HDBSCAN on contextual embeddings of review n-grams. Each cluster captured a distinct aspect of the product—such as packaging, ingredients, or user experience—while topic modeling was used to identify the thematic orientation of the reviews, e.g., dissatisfaction, positive feedback, or comparative judgments.

Using this structure, clusters within negative-oriented topics were used to generate suggestions for improvement, while clusters in neutral or positive topics served to identify strengths and best practices. This allowed the model to generate targeted outputs for each product rather than general summaries across all reviews.

The generated texts were evaluated based on linguistic metrics including average sequence length, lexical diversity (ratio of unique words to total words), and redundancy (repetition of terms or phrases). These metrics allowed us to compare different configurations and assess the expressive quality of the generated content. Table 4 illustrates these metrics by text category.

Table 4. Linguistic quality metrics for generated text by category

Text Category	Avg. Length	Lexical Diversity	Redundancy
Strengths	15.67	0.713	0.096
Suggestions	14.75	0.814	0.119
Best Practices	13.62	0.706	0.046

An example of the model's outputs includes suggestions such as: *"Ensure the product stays on a long time without smudges or residue"* and *"The applicator is too small"*, reflecting specific improvement opportunities derived from clusters about product durability and packaging, respectively.

This approach demonstrates the effectiveness of combining contextual embeddings, clustering, and generative modeling to translate dispersed customer feedback into actionable product insights.

3.7 Experimental Protocol

To evaluate the effectiveness of the text generation strategy, conducted a series of experiments combining different preprocessing and clustering configurations. We explored both bigrams and trigrams as n-gram representations, applied to either the complete corpus of reviews or a subset containing only negative reviews. Each of these configurations was vectorized using both Term Frequency–Inverse Document Frequency (TF-IDF) and Bag of Words (BoW). After preliminary evaluations, BoW was discarded due to inferior performance in topic modeling.

TF-IDF vectors were subsequently embedded and clustered using two unsupervised methods: KMeans (with 3, 5, and 7 clusters) and HDBSCAN (with `min_cluster_size` set to 30 and 50). Based on topic coherence and interpretability, the best-performing configurations involved clustering all reviews (not just negative ones) using TF-IDF, with both bigram and trigram features.

Quantitative evaluation included the analysis of average text length, lexical diversity, redundancy (repetition of terms), and perplexity—used as a proxy for syntactic fluency. Additionally, qualitative assessment was conducted through manual inspection, focusing on thematic coherence, relevance, and the overall clarity of generated content.

The optimal configuration was selected by jointly considering the quantitative metrics and the qualitative evaluation. Finally, this configuration was used to generate text-based insights for individual products. Each output was accompanied by its corresponding evaluation metrics.

4 Experiments and Results

This section presents the experimental results of our pipeline for extracting and synthesizing user feedback from skincare product reviews. We evaluate different configurations combining n-gram tokenization and clustering algorithms by examining the linguistic characteristics of the generated outputs. Subsequently, we illustrate the qualitative performance of the selected configuration (trigrams + HDBSCAN) through generated insights—strengths, improvement suggestions, and best practices—across multiple products.

4.1 Quantitative Evaluation

These clustered review sets were then input into the Flan-T5 text generation model using specific prompts tailored for each type of insight: strengths, improvement suggestions, and competitor best practices. The prompts remained fixed during generation, with cluster-specific review content appended for context.

Table 5 summarizes the average length, lexical diversity, and redundancy scores for the generated texts grouped by the type of suggestion (strengths, improvements, best practices) across different configurations.

Table 5. Linguistic Evaluation of Generated Suggestions Across Configurations

Configuration	Strengths			Improvements			Best Practices		
	Length	Diversity	Redundancy	Length	Diversity	Redundancy	Length	Diversity	Redundancy
Trigrams + KMeans	11.00	0.618	0.255	8.17	0.837	0.102	28.50	0.392	0.497
Trigrams + HDBSCAN	**15.67**	**0.713**	**0.096**	**14.75**	**0.814**	0.119	**13.62**	**0.706**	**0.046**
Bigrams + KMeans	15.67	0.532	0.277	9.50	0.754	**0.018**	38.67	0.341	0.621
Bigrams + HDBSCAN	19.25	0.662	0.234	5.33	**1.000**	**0.000**	36.00	0.403	0.514

As shown, the configuration using trigrams with HDBSCAN clustering offers a balanced trade-off across the three categories, yielding outputs with high lexical diversity and low redundancy. This configuration was therefore selected for subsequent qualitative evaluations.

4.2 Qualitative Examples on Selected Products

We present selected outputs generated for different products using the optimal configuration (trigrams + HDBSCAN), illustrating the variety and relevance of the insights generated.

As an illustration of the generated insights, Table 6 presents the outputs obtained for the LANEIGE Lip Sleeping Mask, where clusters capture both positive evaluations and specific improvement opportunities.

Table 6. Generated Insights for *Lip Sleeping Mask Intense Hydration with Vitamin C (LANEIGE)* by Cluster

Type	Examples	Perplexity
Strengths	• This mask is worth the price.	7.87
	• Hydrating and moisturizing with subtle scent.	5.74
Improvements	• Better packaging and larger applicator suggested.	57.23
	• Product not as hydrating as expected.	9.83
Best Practices	• Highly rated for soothing effects and vitamin E content.	7.29
	• Contains nourishing blend of essential oils.	1.75

Similarly, Table 7 summarizes the insights generated for the GENIUS Liquid Collagen Serum (Algenist), highlighting strengths such as effectiveness on fine lines and areas of improvement including packaging usability.

Table 7. Generated Insights for *GENIUS Liquid Collagen Serum (Algenist)*

Type	Examples	Perplexity
Strengths	• Effective at reducing fine lines and wrinkles.	2.33
	• Hydrating and leaves skin feeling smoother.	21.31
Improvements	• Pump bottle difficult to open.	14.74
	• UI and product interface can be improved.	21.75
Best Practices	• Absorbs quickly; suitable for oily skin; affordable.	8.01
	• Good consistency and effective hydration.	14.33

Table 8 shows the case of the Alpha Beta Extra Strength Daily Peel Pads (Dr. Dennis Gross), where recommendations emphasize acne treatment effectiveness but also point to issues of price and product consistency.

Table 8. Generated Insights for *Alpha Beta Extra Strength Daily Peel Pads (Dr. Dennis Gross)*

Type	Examples	Perplexity
Strengths	• Best acne-fighting product for sensitive skin.	4.13
	• Provides anti-aging and moisturizing benefits.	1.86
Improvements	• Product is very expensive; customer service issues.	40.14
	• Lacks sufficient thickness and consistency.	24.12
Best Practices	• Moisturizer suitable for all skin types.	2.07
	• Pleasant texture and long-lasting effect.	8.01

4.3 Discussion

The insights generated using the most optimal configuration—trigrams combined with HDBSCAN clustering—demonstrate the effectiveness of our approach in synthesizing customer reviews into coherent and actionable summaries. The tripartite structure of *strengths*, *improvements*, and *best practices* provided a consistent framework for organizing the extracted information, yielding outputs that reflect meaningful user concerns.

Qualitative analysis of the examples revealed that the generated statements were generally concise, diverse, and closely aligned with the original review content. Clusters captured thematically coherent information, such as positive sentiments toward product texture, issues with packaging, or recommended usage patterns.

To further assess the linguistic quality of the generated insights, computed pseudo-perplexity scores using the RoBERTa-base masked language model. This metric estimates the fluency and plausibility of sentences based on the model's internal probability predictions. Most statements achieved scores below 10, which generally indicates high syntactic and semantic fluency. Statements involving complex or less conventional constructions—often associated with suggested improvements–tended to receive higher scores. Notably, these higher-perplexity outputs were still interpretable and contextually appropriate.

It is worth noting that no domain-specific fine-tuning was performed on the language model. While this choice avoids the additional training overhead and maintains general applicability, it may lead to slight underestimation of fluency for context-specific expressions typical of product reviews. Nonetheless, the perplexity values remain useful for comparative analysis across sentence types and product clusters.

The framework's performance across different product categories suggests good generalizability within the cosmetics domain. However, adaptation to other product categories would require validation of the topic modeling parameters and potential adjustment of the semantic clustering approach to accommodate different vocabulary patterns and consumer expression styles.

5 Conclusions

This study addresses the critical gap between the abundance of user-generated feedback and the actionable insights required for product improvement. Through a robust and modular pipeline, we demonstrate how advanced natural language processing techniques can be harnessed to process, cluster, and synthesize large volumes of cosmetic product reviews. Using data from Sephora, we applied Latent Dirichlet Allocation (LDA) to uncover latent topics across positive and negative reviews. This was followed by semantic clustering using vector-based representations (e.g., sentence embeddings), and finally, text generation to articulate consumer-driven suggestions.

The proposed methodology can effectively differentiate between high-level sentiment and product-specific concerns, producing recommendations that are both detailed and interpretable. For example, clustering revealed themes such as hydration performance, packaging usability, scent preferences, and texture-related satisfaction. The generative model enabled the formulation of actionable suggestions like 'consider developing a fragrance-free version' or 'redesign the pump for better precision,' all derived from authentic user expressions.

6 Future Work

This integrative approach offers several advantages. It enables scalable benchmarking across competing products, supports strategic marketing efforts, and informs research and development with concrete, user-grounded evidence. Additionally, by incorporating generative modeling, the pipeline goes beyond analytics into recommendation generation, making it practical for real-world decision-making.

The current implementation using general-purpose language models (Flan-T5) without domain-specific fine-tuning represents a conservative approach that prioritizes broad applicability over domain optimization. However, implementing LoRA (Low-Rank Adaptation) techniques could help to adapt the base model to cosmetics domain vocabulary and expression patterns while maintaining general language capabilities.

The acknowledged limitation of potential fluency underestimation for context-specific utterances can be addressed through: domain-specific vocabulary expansion in the model's tokenizer or implementing context-aware evaluation metrics that account for domain-specific language use.

Finally, niche products often have insufficient review data for reliable analysis, it could be implemented several strategies to address small sample size challenges, such as: establish minimum thresholds for reliable analysis and implement bootstrap sampling to estimate confidence intervals for generated insights or employ domain adaptation techniques.

Acknowledgments. The authors thank the Unidad Profesional Interdisciplinaria de Ingeniería Campus Tlaxcala of the Instituto Politécnico Nacional for its support in the preparation of this work.

Disclosure of Interests. The authors declare that they have no competing interests to declare that are relevant to the content of this article.

References

1. Boye, D., Ozcan, S., Fajana, O.: Text mining approach for identifying product ideas and trends based on crowdfunding projects. IEEE Trans. Eng. Manage. **71**, 7112–7127 (2023)
2. Chen, J.: Development of sephora's marketing strategies. Adv. Econ. Manag. Polit. Sci. **14**, 217–223 (2023)
3. Chung, H.W., et al.: Scaling instruction-finetuned language models. arXiv preprint arXiv:2210.11416 (2022)
4. Dask Development Team: Dask: Flexible parallel computing for analytic computing (2016). https://dask.org. Accessed 03 Mar 2025
5. Goldberg, D.M., Abrahams, A.S.: Sourcing product innovation intelligence from online reviews. Elsevier (2022)
6. Park, J., Kim, Y.R., Kang, S.B.: Customer satisfaction analysis for global cosmetic brands: text-mining based online review analysis. J. Korean Soc. Qual. Manag. **49**(4), 595–607 (2021)
7. Jain, P.K., Pamula, R., Srivastava, G.: A systematic literature review on machine learning applications for consumer sentiment analysis using online reviews. Comput. Sci. Rev. (2021)
8. Kokkodis, M., Lappas, T.: Your hometown matters: popularity-difference bias in online reputation platforms. Prod. Oper. Manag. (2020)
9. Kumar, S.: Data mining based marketing decision support system using hybrid machine learning algorithm. Artif. Intell. (2020)
10. LinkedIn: Las últimas tendencias en ventas en línea para el 2024. n.d. (2024)
11. Liu, S., Suresh, R., Banitalebi-Dehkordi, A.: Beauty beyond words: explainable beauty product recommendations using ingredient-based product attributes. arXiv preprint arXiv:2409.13628 (2024)
12. Mahdi, H.F., Gupta, L.K., Choudhury, T., Bansal, N.: Idea mining from online reviews using transformation-based natural language processing tasks. In: International Symposium on Multidisciplinary Studies and Innovative Technologies (2022)
13. McKinney, W.: pandas: a high-performance Python library for data analysis and modeling. In: Proceedings of the 9th Python in Science Conference, vol. 445, no. 1, pp. 51–56 (2010)
14. Nadyinky: Sephora products and skincare reviews 2023 (2023). https://www.kaggle.com/datasets/nadyinky/sephora-products-and-skincare-reviews
15. Nusch, C.J.: Breve introducción a la mineríÂŋa de textos (2024). https://sedici.unlp.edu.ar/handle/10915/171646, dirección PREBI-SEDICI
16. Orús, A.: Comercio electrónico en el mundo - datos estadíÂŋsticos. Statista (2024)
17. Qin, J., Zheng, P., Wang, X.: Product redesign and innovation based on online reviews: a multistage combined search method. INFORMS J. Comput. (2024)
18. Rumbo García, N.: Análisis web y redes sociales en el sector de la cosmética en francia. yves rocher, sephora, bourjois y bioderma (2022)
19. Rumbo GarcíÂŋa, N.: Análisis web y redes sociales en el sector de la cosmética en francia. yves rocher, sephora, bourjois y bioderma (2022)
20. Zatonatska, T., Hubska, M., Shpyrko, V.: Marketing strategies in the banking services sector with the help of data science. Marketing i menedžment innovacij (2022)

21. Zhang, F., Song, W.: Product improvement in a big data environment: a novel method based on text mining and large group decision making. Expert Syst. Appl. (2023)
22. Zhang, M., Fan, B., Zhang, N., Wang, W., Fan, W.: Mining product innovation ideas from online reviews. Elsevier (2020)
23. Zhang, Z., Yang, K., Zhang, J.Z., Palmatier, R.W.: Uncovering synergy and dysergy in consumer reviews: a machine learning approach. Manag. Sci. (2022)

Rapid Upper Limb Assessment Based on Fuzzy Logic and a Bluetooth Low Energy Sensor Network

Juan Mora-Sánchez, Luis Sánchez-Fernández(✉), José Carbajal-Hernández, Diana González-Baldovinos, and Cynthia Baeza-García

Centro de Investigación en Computación, Instituto Politécnico Nacional, Ciudad de México, Mexico

jmoras1400@alumno.ipn.mx, {lsanchez,jcarbajalh,d.gonzalezb, cbaezag2023}@cic.ipn.mx

Abstract. Postural assessment in occupational and sports contexts faces challenges due to the subjectivity of the observational methods like the Rapid Upper Limb Assessment (RULA), which helps identify and prevent injuries. Given the potential of inertial sensors for motion capture, integrating them with the RULA method offers an alternative for obtaining quantitative and repeatable assessments. This article proposes a fuzzy logic system based on three inference models using data acquired by a Bluetooth Low Energy (BLE) 5.0 network of six Inertial Measurement Units (IMUs) at a sampling frequency of 50 Hz. To validate the system, 25 participants were assessed on both sides simultaneously while performing three postures involving prolonged sitting in front of a computer. A total of 150 risk injury assessments were conducted. Results obtained by three experts using the traditional method were compared with those obtained using the Fuzzy Inference System (FIS). Agreement between the experts and the FIS was evaluated using Fleiss' Kappa coefficient, showing good agreement (ranging from 0.57 to 0.63) in four of the six evaluated cases and excellent agreement (ranging from 0.75 to 0.78) in the remaining two cases.

Keywords: Postural assessment · RULA · Fuzzy Inference System · IMU

1 Introduction

In 2019, a data analysis from the Global Burden of Disease study revealed that approximately 1.71 billion people worldwide suffered from musculoskeletal disorders, with low back pain being the most common, affecting 570 million individuals [1]. The shift to teleworking during the COVID-19 pandemic has further contributed to poor posture and an increase in such disorders [2].

Trauma and musculoskeletal risks related to workplace posture and movement are analyzed using observational methods, such as the Rapid Upper Limb Assessment (RULA), the Rapid Entire Body Assessment (REBA), and the Ovako Working Posture Analysis System (OWAS) [3]. Clinical tools such as goniometers, inclinometers, laser trackers, and optical technologies have been used to quantify movement [4].

C. Palma-Preciado et al. (Eds.): CORE 2025, ACSAR 3, pp. 64–79, 2026.
https://doi.org/10.1007/978-3-032-08894-9_5

RULA method helps prevent upper limb injuries; however, one of its limitations, as noted by its authors, is that it can only evaluate the right or left side at a time. Its reliability was validated through tests involving 120 physiotherapists [5]. Other methods, such as the Mallet scale, although reliable, exhibit shortcomings by not accounting for inter-joint coordination during movement tasks [6].

The objective of this work is to develop and validate a quantitative system for assessing upper limb posture using fuzzy logic and wearable sensors. The system enables dynamic, bilateral and postural risk assessment, thereby overcoming key constraints of conventional observational approaches.

1.1 Literature Review

The use of motion capture devices facilitates conducting biomechanical assessments, with Inertial Measurement Units (IMUs) being one of the most prominent options [7]. Currently, the use of motion capture technologies has significantly increased, particularly in the field of rehabilitation [8]. There is no standard for placing IMU sensors on the human body to assess the upper limb, but promising results have been achieved by placing them on both arms, both shoulders, the sacrum, and the cervical region [9].

Particularly, RULA is popular and widely used for assessing sitting posture [12], but a key limitation of RULA method is its reliance on classical set theory which creates rigid boundaries within body segment's range or motion. To address this issue, alternative approaches such as fuzzy logic systems have been proposed [12]. Furthermore, these models can be considered a form of explainable artificial intelligence, which is accepted by medical professionals, and it has become integral to healthcare, particularly in rehabilitation [10, 14]. Fuzzy models are effective for modeling the severity and states of a variable due to their high level of interpretability, as they utilize high-level linguistic descriptors [11], and are well-suited for processing and reasoning with imprecise information, making them reliable tools for motion analysis evaluations, as they address the subjectivity inherent in observational assessment methods [13].

Several related studies have conducted biomechanical signal evaluations with IMUs using fewer than 150 measurements [8, 13, 17]. Therefore, the 150 assessments used in this study are considered sufficient to support the validity of the results. These 150 assessments were obtained by conducting three different postures with 25 participants, evaluating both the right and left sides bilaterally. Meanwhile, other studies focused on RULA combined with fuzzy logic have evaluated no more than 15 participants performing a single task in a single posture [12].

2 Materials and Methods

Figure 1 shows a diagram of the procedure followed by the designed system to assess injury risk level based on posture. The signals acquired by each sensor are post-processed to obtain the variables of interest that describe the posture of the upper limb, which are then input into the fuzzy inference models to obtain a qualitative assessment.

Biomechanical Model and Sensor Location. To assess the risk associated with prolonged sitting in daily occupational activities, the biomechanical model shown in Fig. 1 is proposed with six sensors that are placed at the locations suggested by [9].

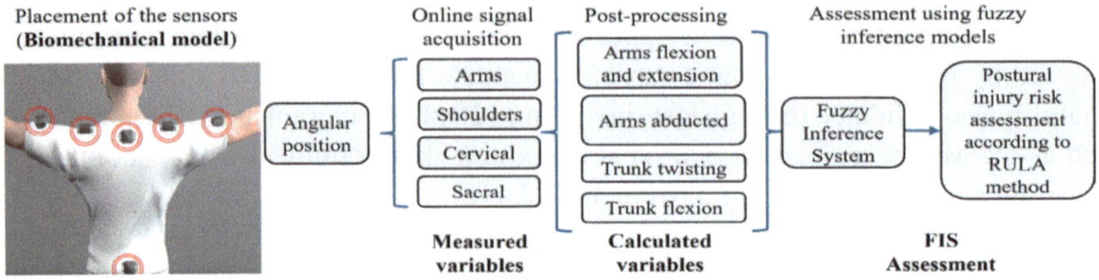

Fig. 1. Procedure diagram of the designed system.

Data Acquisition. A network of six IMUs (model WT901BLECL), manufactured by WitMotion Shenzhen Co., Ltd., was integrated into the system. These sensors incorporate the Madgwick Attitude and Heading Reference System (AHRS) algorithm and support Bluetooth Low Energy 5.0 communication. Each IMU transmits data at 8Kbps, with each packet consisting of a 20-byte hexadecimal string. A sampling frequency of 50 Hz is used, and an interface was designed in LabVIEW to monitor real-time data acquisition and store the collected data.

Human movement, particularly in postural tasks or slow upper limb motions as assessed by RULA, typically contains relevant frequency components below 10–15 Hz. A sampling frequency of 50 Hz is sufficient to accurately capture such movements without aliasing as previous studies in biomechanics have been successfully using wireless IMU sensors at similar sampling rates, confirming its adequacy for ergonomic assessments [13, 17–19].

Post-processing. With online processing, the displacement angles of upper limb segments where the sensors are placed, relative to Earth's vertical axis, are obtained and stored. However, each inertial sensor uses a right-handed coordinate system, where the X-axis points forward, Y-axis to the left, and Z-axis upward when placed on a flat surface. Sensors were placed on the body following anatomical landmarks, and their orientation was standardized through an initial calibration in a neutral posture. The biomechanical variables needed must be derived through analysis, as shown in Fig. 2.

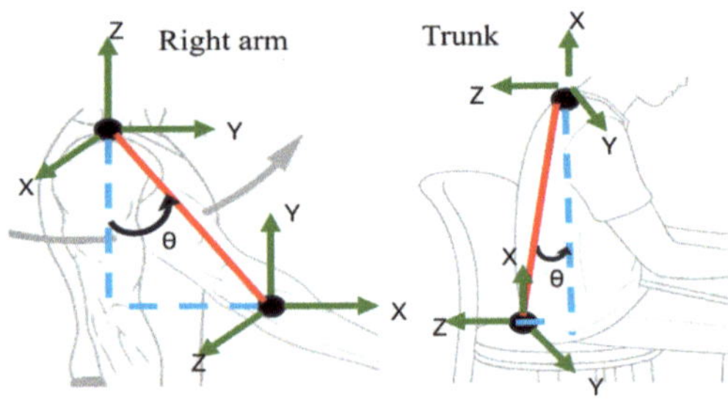

Fig. 2. Obtaining the resultant angle of the arms and trunk.

For the right side of the upper limb (1) is established, and for the left side (2) is used.

$$-\alpha + \beta = \theta \tag{1}$$

where α is the shoulder tilt (X-axis), β is the arm's flexion/extension (Y-axis), and θ is the resulting angle between the arm and the trunk.

$$\alpha + \beta = \theta \tag{2}$$

For the trunk (3) is applied where α and β are the Y-axis inclination angles measured by sensors placed near the cervical region and sacrum, respectively. Their values are adjusted based on each sensor's measurement range (from –88° or –87.8° to 0°), which reflects their individual drift. According to the datasheet, the expected value should be close to 90°. θ represents the resulting angle between these two body segments and indicates the trunk's inclination when a person leans forward or backward.

$$(\alpha + 88) - (\beta + 87.8) = \theta \tag{3}$$

RULA Analysis. The Rapid Upper Limb Assessment (RULA) method was chosen to evaluate tasks involving prolonged sitting. This approach analyzes body postures, the amount of force used, and the frequency of movements required for each task. Scores are determined based on how much a posture deviates from a neutral position. The assessment generates two separate scores: one for the arms and wrists, and another for the neck, trunk, and legs. These are the combined to produce a final RULA score ranging from 1 to 7. Scores of 1–2 are considered acceptable, 3–4 suggest further evaluation and possible modifications, 5–6 indicates that changes should be made soon, and a score of 7 signals the need for immediate investigation and corrective action [5].

Design of the Fuzzy Inference System (FIS). The FIS consists of three fuzzy inference models: one for group A, another for group B, and a third to obtain the overall assessment. Table 1 separates the variables that make up the system (measured, calculated, and entered by the rater), with the calculated variables serving as inputs for the inference models. The three models were designed using the Mamdani inference method and the centroid defuzzification method due to their ease of implementation and effectiveness. Measured variables are the processed data acquired from the sensors, while the calculated variables are the post-processed data that provide information about the participant's posture. This allows for determining whether the arms are flexed, extended, or in abduction, and whether the trunk is upright, inclined, or rotated. The variables entered by the rater have a lesser impact and can be set according to the specific case study. The models for group A and group B are created following the structure shown in Fig. 3, which describes the computational model for both groups.

Group A. The Membership Functions (MFs) for the input variables were defined by analyzing RULA scores presented in [5], where each MF corresponds to the different angle ranges proposed by the methodology. For example, the Arm Flexion/Extension variable is assessed across five defined ranges, each corresponding to a specific arm position. For arm abduction, when the arm is close to the trunk, the angle is near 90°, while at shoulder height, the angle approaches 0°. Thus, a medium abduction is defined as a decrease of less than 75° from the horizontal shoulder axis. In both cases—medium and high abduction—one point is added to the final risk level score for group A.

Trapezoidal functions were chosen because human movements are often abrupt and rapid, rather than gradual or slow. These functions are more suitable since they provide

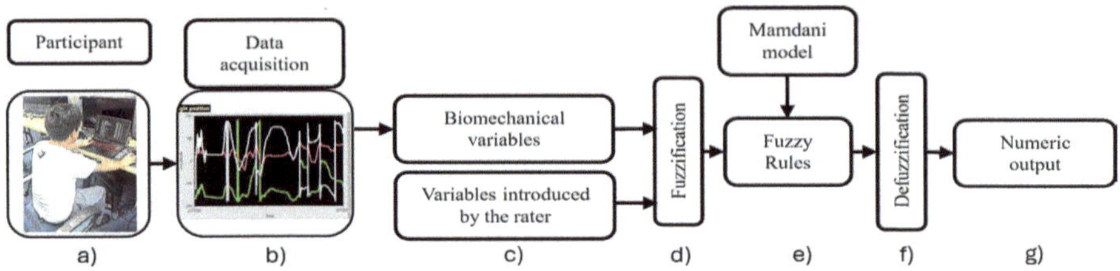

Fig. 3. Overview of the computational model for the fuzzy inference model of groups A and B. (a) The network consists of six IMUs. (b) Angular position data is acquired. (c) Post-processing of the data to obtain the biomechanical variables of interest. (d) Fuzzification. (e) Fuzzy rules based on RULA assessment in [5]. (f) Defuzzification using the centroid method. (g) Numeric output from both inference models.

Table 1. Variables measured, calculated, and introduced by the rater.

Group	Variables		
	Measured	Calculated	Entered by the rater
A (Both sides)	1. Arm angle 2. Shoulder angle	1. Arm flexion and extension 3. Arm abduction	4. Supported arms 5. Lower arms movement 6. Wrist position (Neutral or flexion/extension) 7. Wrist twist (Pronation or supination)
B	1. Cervical angle 8. Sacrum angle	1. Trunk flexion 9. Trunk twisting	10. Neck twisting 11. Legs supported

well-defined value ranges and a full membership plateau, unlike triangular or Gaussian ones. The functions for the two calculated biomechanical variables of group A are shown in Fig. 4 and Fig. 5, the remaining four functions corresponding to the variables entered by the rater were proposed using numerical values tailored to the case study and are available upon request from the article's author.

The fuzzy inference rules were developed based on expert knowledge, considering the possible scores the participant can receive for each variable in group A.

Table 2 presents two representative rules. The MFs for the four variables entered by the rater were defined as follows for the case study of sitting in front of a computer: If arms are supported on the chair, desk, or body, the value is 1, 0 if not. For the forearm, since the forearms move inward and outward from the trunk while using the mouse and keyboard, this value is always 3. For wrist position, due to the constant movement, this value can be selected between 1 (neutral) or 2 (flexed/extended). For wrist twist, it is assumed that the wrist always remains in pronation, so this value will always be 2.

Regarding the created inference rules, rule 4 is used as an example, and is explained as follows: If the arm flexion or extension angle is less than $-20°$, the arm abduction is low, the arms are supported, the forearm is in motion, the wrist is neutral, and in

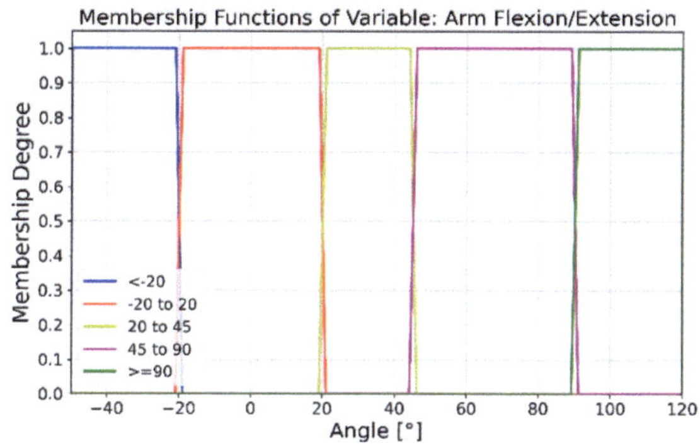

Fig. 4. Input MFs for the arm flexion/extension variable.

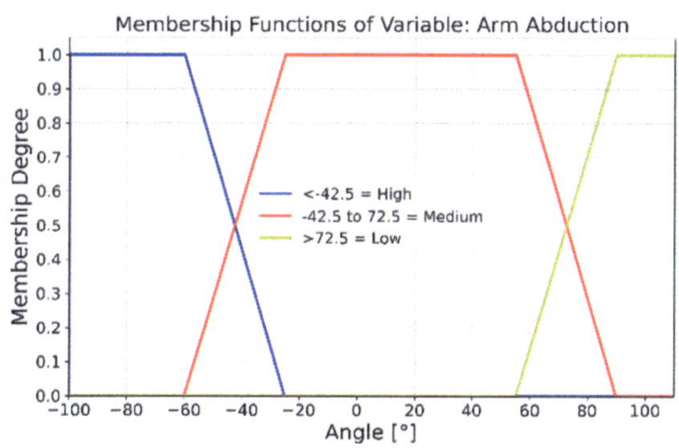

Fig. 5. Input MFs for the arm abduction variable.

Table 2. Two representative rules of the fuzzy inference model for group A.

Rule	Description
4	If Arm Flexion/Extension is < **-20** and Arm Abduction is **Low** and Supported arms is **yes** and Lower arm movement is **yes** and Wrist position is **Neutral** and Wrist twist is **Pronation** then Numerical output for group A is **3**
54	If Arm Flexion/Extension is > **+ 90** and Arm Abduction is **Medium** and Supported arms is **no** and Lower arm movement is **yes** and Wrist position is **Flexion/Extension** and Wrist twist is **Pronation** then Numerical output for group A is **7**

pronation, then the total numerical output for group A is 3. This value is obtained using Table A in [5].

The outputs, ranging from 3 to 7, use triangular MFs (see Fig. 6). These MFs do not encompass wide ranges of values, ensuring a logical transition between each expected numerical value efficiently, without high computational complexity, and establishing a clear boundary between each category.

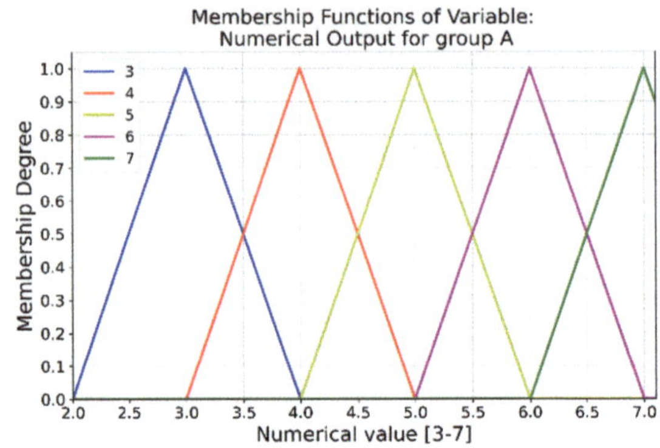

Fig. 6. Output MFs for group A.

Group B. As in group A, the Membership Functions (MFs) for the input variables were created by analyzing the scores according to the case study using the RULA method, trapezoidal MFs were also used for this group. The functions for the two calculated biomechanical variables of group B are shown in Fig. 7 and Fig. 8, while the remaining two functions corresponding to the variables entered by the rater were proposed using numerical values tailored to the case study and are available upon request from the article's author. For trunk flexion, four MFs were created, each covering specific angular ranges, as outlined in step 10 in [5]. Trunk twisting is considered when the angle between the sacrum and cervical is greater than 6 degrees or less than −6 degrees. If the angle between the sacrum and cervical remains within the range of 6 to −6 degrees, then trunk twisting is not considered.

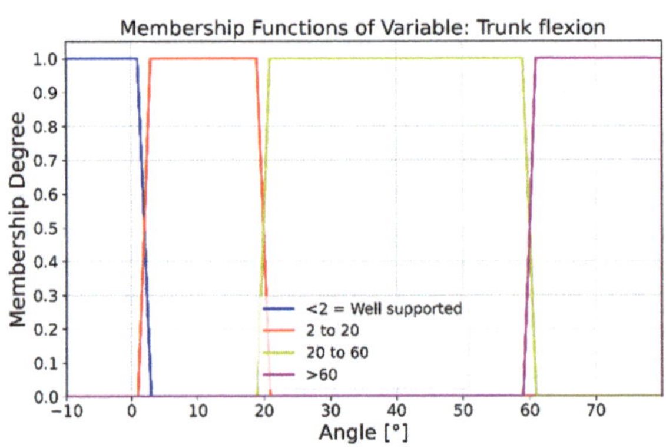

Fig. 7. Input MFs for trunk flexion variable.

Table 3 presents two representative rules for group B where rule 9 is used as an example and is explained as follows: If the neck is upright, the trunk flexion is well supported and right twist, and legs position is sitting, then the total numerical output for the group B is 2. This value is obtained using Table B in [5]. The two variables entered by

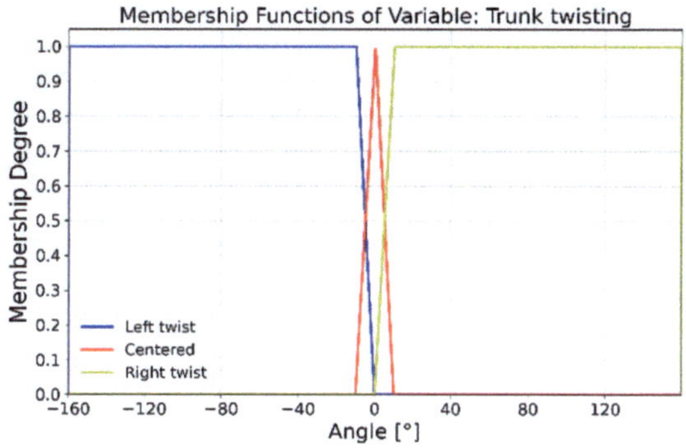

Fig. 8. Input MFs for trunk twisting variable

the rater were defined as follows for the case study: For neck position, if the participant's neck is upright, the value is 1; if it is downward, the value is 2. For legs, since the case study involves sitting, the value is always 1.

Table 3. Two representative rules of the fuzzy inference model for group B.

Rule	Description
9	If Neck is **Upright** and Trunk flexion is **Well supported**, and Trunk twisting is **Right twist** and Legs is **Sitting,** then Numerical output for group B is **2**
18	If Neck is **Downward** and Trunk flexion is **2 to 20** and Trunk **twisting** is Left twist and Legs is **Sitting,** then Numerical output for group B is **4**

The outputs, ranging from 1 to 6, use triangular MFs (See Fig. 9). These MFs do not encompass wide ranges of values, ensuring a logical transition between each expected numerical value efficiently, without high computational complexity, and establishing a clear boundary between each category.

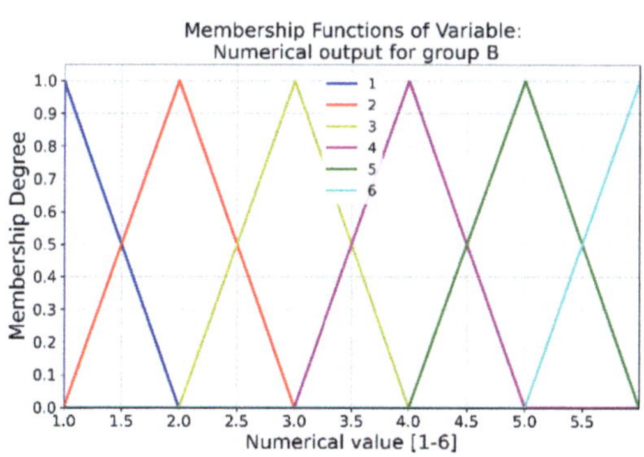

Fig. 9. Output MFs for group B.

Overall Assessment. Figure 10 illustrates the computational model to obtain the participant's final assessment based on Table C of the RULA method [5], using the numerical values from groups A and B as inputs. Since this assessment involves static activity, one unit must be added to each value before assessment. Analyzing Table C, where group A scores are on the vertical axis and group B scores are on the horizontal axis, it is observed that, after adjustment, the minimum possible scores are 4 for group A and 2 for group B. Thus, only medium, high, and severe risk levels (values from 3 to 7) will be obtained, with no "acceptable" risk levels (values 1 and 2).

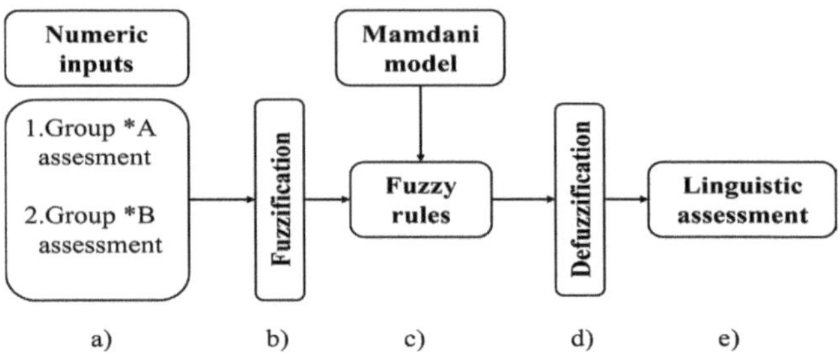

Fig. 10. Overview of the computational model. (a) A and B scores are modified, indicated as A*, B*. (b) The scores are fuzzified. (c) Fuzzy rules based on RULA assessment [5]. (d) Defuzzification using the centroid method. (e) Linguistic output values (medium, high, severe).

Table 4 presents two representative rules, with outputs corresponding to the injury risk level. Since there are two values for the medium-risk level (3–4), as well as for the high-risk level (5–6), trapezoidal membership functions were used, and a triangular function was employed for the severe-risk level, which involves the number value 7 (Fig. 11).

Table 4. Two representative rules of the fuzzy inference model 3.

Rule	Description
1	If Total score for group **A is 4** and Total score for group **B is 4** then Final injury **risk assessment is Medium**
15	If Total score for group **A is 7** and Total score for group **B is 7** then Final injury **risk assessment is Severe**

Designing three independent fuzzy inference models and defining the corresponding rules enabled a more efficient and accurate generation of scores. Otherwise, a single model covering all biomechanical variables from groups A and B would have required 1440 rules to replicate the RULA assessment. By contrast, the approach in this study required only 58 rules for group A, 24 for group B, and 24 for the final model, totaling 106 fuzzy inference rules.

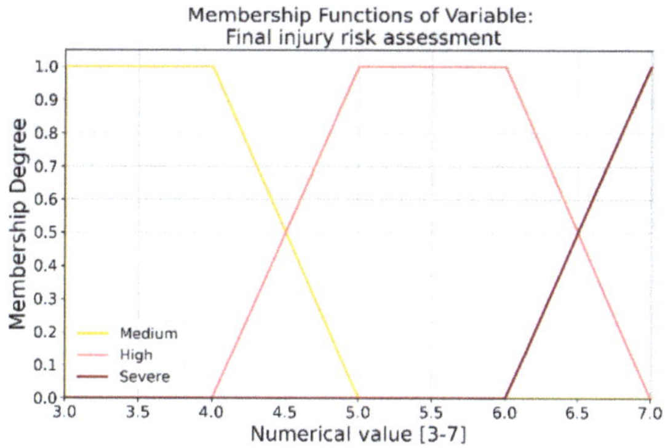

Fig. 11. Output membership functions for the total RULA assessment.

Validation. To validate the designed FIS, 25 participants were evaluated in three different postures (Fig. 12). The first one involves sitting with an erect back, relaxed shoulders, and arms as close to the trunk as possible, as suggested by the WHO [14], the second one represents a typical curved posture after an extended period, with a slouched back, and the third one is a resting position, where the person is leaning backward.

The 5-min evaluation duration was based on the ISO 11226:2000 – Ergonomics – Evaluation of static working postures [16], which defines maximum acceptable holding times for trunk inclination, head posture, and upper arm elevation. Figures 4, 7, and 10 in the standard relate joint angles to recommended holding durations. Thus, the selected 5-min period enables the observation of relevant sustained postures without surpassing safe exposure limits.

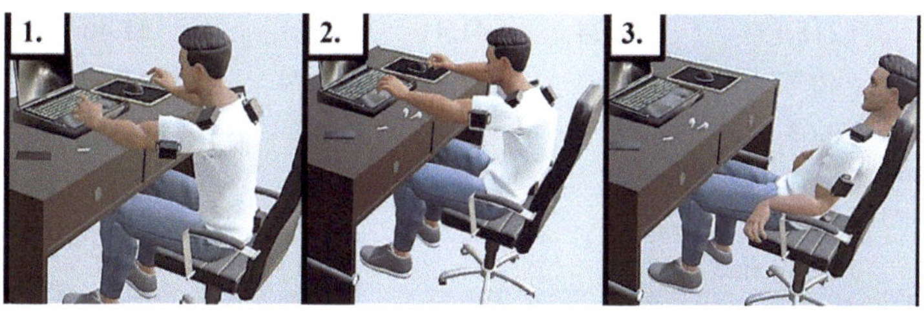

Fig. 12. Postures for experiments 1, 2 and 3.

Three experts evaluated the participants using the traditional RULA method, while signals were acquired through the IMU network, one of the advantages of using a sensor network is that both sides of the upper limb could be simultaneously evaluated.

Using the experts' assessment table and the FIS results, the concordance among raters was calculated using the Fleiss Kappa coefficient. According to Landis and Koch, Kappa values greater than 0.75 indicate excellent agreement, values below 0.4 indicate poor agreement, and values between 0.4 and 0.75 indicate good agreement [15].

3 Results

Table 5 presents the results of the three experiments according to Fig. 12, including the average time spent on each injury risk level for the 25 participants, as well as the concordance coefficient between the three raters and the FIS. Additionally, a statistical evaluation was carried out using the Root Mean Square Error (RMSE) and the Mean Absolute Error (MAE), which allowed for a quantitative comparison.

Table 5. Average time in each risk level, concordance coefficient, RMSE, and MAE results.

Experiment 1						
Risk level	Right side			Left side		
	Average time [s]	RMSE [s]	MAE [s]	Average time [s]	RMSE [s]	MAE [s]
Medium	187.51	81.41	69.45	153.60	79.36	68.10
High	111.70	81.21	69.08	137.20	70	57.49
Severe	0.80	1.59	1.13	9.21	29.02	15.32
Concordance coefficient K	**0.58**			**0.6**		
Experiment 2						
Risk level	Right side			Left side		
	Average time [s]	RMSE [s]	MAE [s]	Average time [s]	RMSE [s]	MAE [s]
Medium	40.42	52.37	38.35	36.19	30.41	24.24
High	218.73	52.24	41.41	211.1	51.46	42.28
Severe	40.77	42.63	32.81	52.74	53.69	42.36
Concordance coefficient K	**0.63**			**0.57**		
Experiment 3						
Risk level	Right side			Left side		
	Average time [s]	RMSE [s]	MAE [s]	Average time [s]	RMSE [s]	MAE [s]
Medium	5.23	5.75	4.63	3.1	4.13	3.03
High	284.59	21.86	15.14	288.65	17.42	12.78
Severe	10.2	20.26	13.89	8.19	16.70	11.73
Concordance coefficient K	**0.75**			**0.78**		

The lowest—yet still good ($k = 0.57$)—level of agreement was found in Experiment 2 for the left side (Figs. 13, 14 and 15), where the high data dispersion, as indicated by

RMSE and MAE, reflects the difficulty raters face in reaching consensus when postural assessments vary widely over time due to the individual Range of Motion (ROM) allowed by each participant's posture in this experiment.

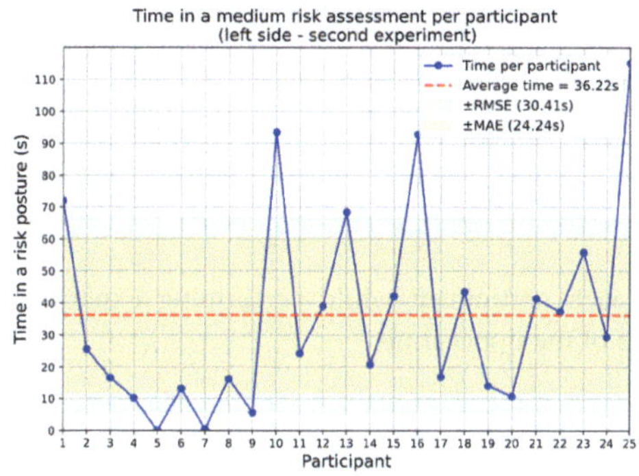

Fig. 13. Time spent by each participant while performing experiment 2 with a medium risk assessment on the left side of the upper limb.

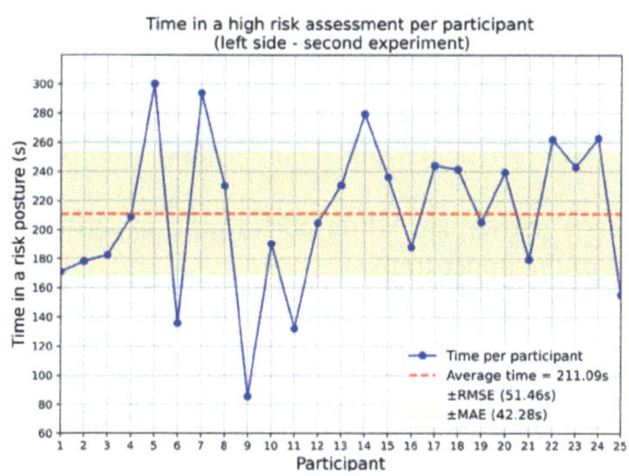

Fig. 14. Time spent by each participant while performing experiment 2 with a high-risk assessment on the left side of the upper limb.

In contrast, the excellent level of agreement observed in Experiment 3—particularly for the left side (k = 0.78)—is reflected in Figs. 16, 17 and 18, where the low data dispersion, shown by RMSE and MAE, suggests that raters found it easier to reach consensus when postural variations over time were minimal due to a more constrained range of movement (ROM) in the participants' posture for this experiment.

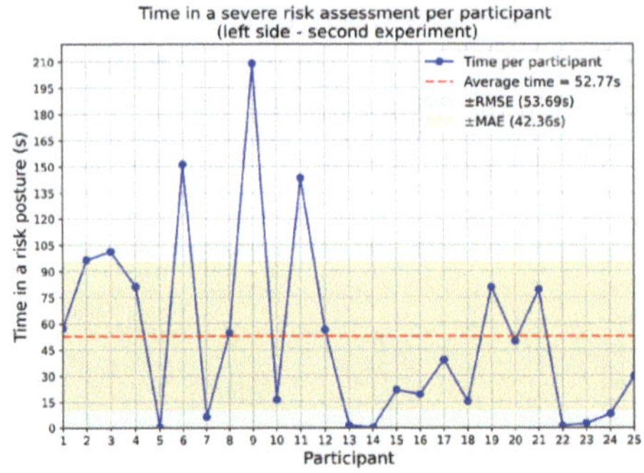

Fig. 15. Time spent by each participant while performing experiment 2 with a severe risk assessment on the left side of the upper limb.

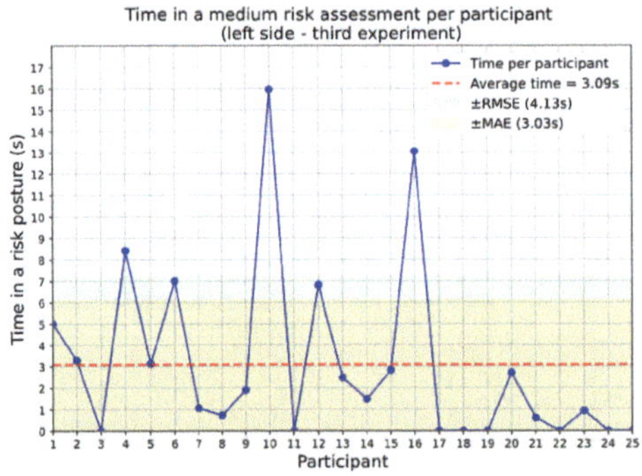

Fig. 16. Time spent by each participant while performing experiment 3 with a medium risk assessment on the left side of the upper limb.

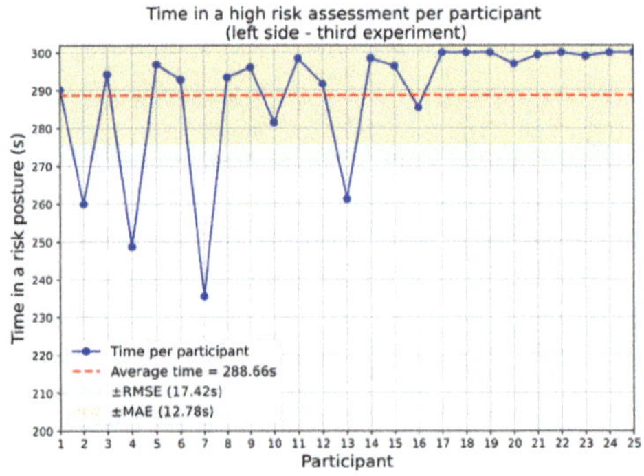

Fig. 17. Time spent by each participant while performing experiment 3 with a high-risk assessment on the left side of the upper limb.

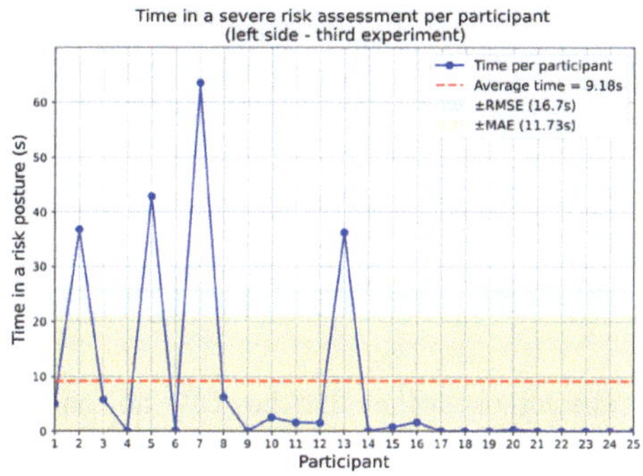

Fig. 18. Time spent by each participant while performing experiment 3 with a severe risk assessment on the left side of the upper limb.

4 Discussion

Despite the promising results, this study has some limitations. First, the sample size of 25 participants may limit the statistical power and generalization of the findings to broader populations or different occupational settings. Additionally, the experiments were conducted under controlled postural scenarios. Future work should aim to validate the system in diverse and dynamic work contexts where RULA methodology applies and can be replaced by the computational system designed.

However, recent studies have shown—through correlation tests and Bland-Altman analyses—that the scores obtained using fuzzy inference models exhibit high reliability compared to the standard method [12]. Other RULA-based evaluations using sensors have reported results primarily for arm abduction movements only [9]. Moreover, a few studies have investigated how sensor placement affects the measurement of kinematic variables during upper limb movement [6].

5 Conclusions

The good and excellent level of agreement between the raters and the FIS confirms the reliability and accuracy of using a quantitative computational tool for postural risk assessment. Complementary statistical analyses were conducted using the Root Mean Square Error (RMSE) and the Mean Absolute Error (MAE) to evaluate the dispersion of the time values recorded by the system. Cases with high variability relative to the average time suggest that certain individuals maintained medium, high, or severe risk postures for significantly longer or shorter periods than the group mean. This high dispersion highlights the need for individualized ergonomic interventions.

This approach overcomes the limitations of the traditional RULA method by enabling dynamic evaluations, eliminating the dependence on single high-risk postures as a reference, and simultaneously assessing both sides of the upper limb. The integration of a BLE IMU sensor network with fuzzy inference models allowed precise identification of ergonomic preventive measures, yielding quantitative outcomes based on expert knowledge.

We recommend following WHO-aligned ergonomic practices for prolonged sitting, such as keeping the trunk upright, shoulders relaxed, arms close to the body, changing posture regularly, and avoiding static or repetitive tasks.

Acknowledgments. We thank the Instituto Politécnico Nacional, México, for their academic support and for allowing us to use their laboratories. We also thank the National Council of Humanities, Science and Technology (CONAHCYT) of Mexico for supporting this research.

Disclosure of Interests. The authors declare that they have no conflicts of interest.

References

1. World Health Organization (WHO) and International Labour Organization (ILO). Musculoskeletal health. https://www.who.int/news-room/fact-sheets/detail/musculoskeletal-conditions. Accessed 07 Jan 2025
2. World Health Organization (WHO) and International Labour Organization (ILO). Crucial changes needed to protect workers' health while teleworking (2022). https://www.who.int/news/item/02-02-2022-crucial-changes-needed-to-protect-workers-health-while-teleworking. Accessed 07 Jan 2025
3. Villacís Jara, H., Zambrano Orejuela, I., Baydal-Bertomeu, J.M.: Study of the ergonomic risk in operators of an assembly line using the RULA method in real working conditions through the application of a commercial sensor. Mater. Today: Proc. **49**, 122–128 (2022). https://doi.org/10.1016/j.matpr.2021.07.482
4. Ager, A.L., Roy, J.-S., Hébert, L.J., Roos, M., Borms, D., Cools, A.M.: Measuring upper limb active joint position sense: Introducing a new clinical tool - the upper limb proprioception reaching test. Musculoskelet. Sci. Pract. **66**, 102829 (2023). https://doi.org/10.1016/j.msksp.2023.102829
5. McAtamney, L., Nigel Corlett, E.: RULA: a survey method for the investigation of work-related upper limb disorders. Appl. Ergon. **24**(2), 91–99 (1993). https://doi.org/10.1016/0003-6870(93)90080-S
6. Höglund, G., Grip, H., Öhberg, F.: The importance of inertial measurement unit placement in assessing upper limb motion. Med. Eng. Phys. **92**, 1–9 (2021). https://doi.org/10.1016/j.medengphy.2021.03.010
7. Wang, S., et al.: Recognizing wearable upper-limb rehabilitation gestures by a hybrid multi-feature neural network. Eng. Appl. Artif. Intell. **127**, 107424 (2024). https://doi.org/10.1016/j.engappai.2023.107424
8. Gu, C., Lin, W., He, X., Zhang, L., Zhang, M.: IMU-based motion capture system for rehabilitation applications: a systematic review. Biomimet. Intell. Robot. **3**(2), 100097 (2023). https://doi.org/10.1016/j.birob.2023.100097
9. Dias, P., Matta, A., Pilastri, A., Matos, L.M., Cortez, P.: RTSIMU: real-time simulation tool for IMU sensors. Softw. Impacts **17**, 100522 (2023). https://doi.org/10.1016/j.simpa.2023.100522
10. Lai, Y.-C., Chiang, S.-Y., Kan, Y.-C., Lin, H.-C.: Coupling analysis of multiple machine learning models for human activity recognition. Comput. Mater. Continua **79**(3), 3783–3803 (2024). https://doi.org/10.32604/cmc.2024.050376
11. Legaria-Santiago, V.K., Sánchez-Fernández, L.P., Sánchez-Pérez, L.A., Garza-Rodríguez, A.: Computer models evaluating hand tremors in Parkinson's disease patients. Comput. Biol. Med. **140**, 105059 (2022). https://doi.org/10.1016/j.compbiomed.2021.105059

12. Kar, M.B., Aruna, M., Kunar, B.M.: Fuzzy logic-based rapid upper limb assessment: a novel approach to evaluate the postural risk of dumper operators. J. Inst. Eng. (India): Ser. C **104**(5), 1047–1055 (2023). https://doi.org/10.1007/s40032-023-00986-1
13. Sánchez-Fernández, L.P., Sánchez-Pérez, L.A., Concha-Gómez, P.D., Shaout, A.: Kinetic tremor analysis using wearable sensors and fuzzy inference systems in Parkinson's disease. Biomed. Signal Process. Control **84**, 104748 (2023). https://doi.org/10.1016/j.bspc.2023.104748
14. Luttmann, A., Jager, M., Griefahn, B., Caffier, G., Liebers, F.: Preventing musculoskeletal disorders in the workplace. Berlín (2004). https://iris.who.int/handle/10665/42803. Accessed 07 Jan 2025
15. Fleiss, J., Levin, B., Cho Paik, M.: Statistical Methods for Rates and Proportions, 3rd edn. Wiley, New Jersey (2003)
16. ISO 11226:2000 – Ergonomics – Evaluation of static working postures, International Organization for Standardization, Geneva, Switzerland (2000)
17. Sanchez-Perez, L.A., Sanchez-Fernandez, L.P., Shaout, A., Martinez-Hernandez, J.M., Alvarez-Noriega, M.J.: Rest tremor quantification based on fuzzy inference systems and wearable sensors. Int. J. Med. Inform. **114**, 6–17 (2018). https://doi.org/10.1016/j.ijmedinf.2018.03.002
18. Ornelas-Vences, C., Sánchez-Fernández, L.P., Sánchez-Pérez, L.A., Martínez-Hernández, J.M.: Computer model for leg agility quantification and assessment for Parkinson's disease patients. Med. Biol. Eng. Comput. **57**(2), 463–476 (2019). https://doi.org/10.1007/s11517-018-1894-0
19. Sánchez-Fernández, L.P.: Biomechanics of Parkinson's disease with systems based on expert knowledge and machine learning: a scoping review. Computation **12**(11), 230 (2024). https://doi.org/10.3390/computation12110230

Understanding Functional Impairment in Rheumatoid Arthritis: A Data-Driven Approach Using HAQ-DI and Clinical Metrics

León S. Mora-Guerrero[1(✉)], Antonio Alarcón-Paredes[1], and Iris P. Guzmán-Guzmán[2]

[1] Centro de Investigación en Computación, Instituto Politécnico Nacional, Mexico City, Mexico
{lmorag2024,aalarcon}@cic.ipn.mx

[2] Laboratorio de Investigación Multidisciplinaria e Innovación Biomédica, Facultad de Ciencias Químico Biológicas, Universidad Autónoma de Guerrero, Chilpancingo, Mexico

Abstract. Rheumatoid arthritis presents considerable diagnostic challenges, particularly in its early stages. This study analyzes clinical variables and results from the DAS-28 and HAQ-DI instruments to identify which factors most effectively distinguish between levels of functional impairment in RA patients. Using a dataset of 124 patients from a Mexican hospital, we applied a comprehensive set of statistical methods including ANOVA, Kruskal-Wallis, mutual information analysis and mean decrease in impurity assessment, to evaluate the discriminatory power of individual features. Two dataset variants were compared: one with HAQ-DI category scores and another with responses to each individual question. Results show that certain HAQ-DI components and specific questions offer greater predictive value than general clinical variables. Notably, strength in the right hand, and HAQ-DI categories such as "Reaching" and "Other," stand out as informative. These findings may support simplified and more accurate machine learning models for future RA diagnosis by guiding dimensionality reduction and feature selection strategies.

Keywords: Rheumatoid arthritis · Statistical analysis · Model simplification · Feature selection

1 Introduction

Rheumatoid arthritis (RA) is a chronic degenerative disease that causes inflammation in the lining of the joints, resulting in numbness, stiffness, pain (in many cases severe) and, without proper treatment, deformity and inability to perform even simple, everyday tasks [1]. It affects approximately 0.3% to 1.2% of the world population and 1.5% of the Mexican population, which is equivalent to

C. Palma-Preciado et al. (Eds.): CORE 2025, ACSAR 3, pp. 80–96, 2026.
https://doi.org/10.1007/978-3-032-08894-9_6

approximately 2 million people [2]. Due to the age range in which symptoms usually appear, between 25 and 55 years of old, it is also considered a generator of socioeconomic affectation, due to the fact that the main affected people in this group are those in the stage of greatest working capacity.

It is especially difficult to diagnose, particularly in the early stages, because its initial symptoms are similar to those of many other diseases and conditions, including simple reactive joint inflammation. In addition, there are no tests, either laboratory or radiology, that by themselves allow an accurate diagnosis, so it depends on the combination of a large number of studies and medical evaluations to reach its determination [3].

Among other clinical criteria, a specialist's evaluation usually includes the count of inflamed and painful joints using the DAS-28 index, calculated by analyzing the status of 28 joints frequently affected by RA. This score has been established as a reliable tool to indicate the level of disease activity [4].

On the other hand, the HAQ-DI questionnaire is an instrument in which the patient is asked to rate the difficulty with which they perform 20 day-to-day tasks, such as getting dressed, opening a door or opening a container. It is divided into 8 categories grouping tasks belonging to categories such as "Hygiene" or "Eating". To obtain the final score, the criterion with the highest value in each category is taken, added together and averaged. The result obtained, between 0 and 3, will categorize the patient in a spectrum that varies between an unaffected RA patient and a disabled patient [5].

It is notorious that the diagnosis of AR is an extremely complex task and that is why, given the encouraging advances that Machine Learning (ML) has allowed in the medical area, the objective of this study is to analyze through various statistical techniques, the predictive power contained in different clinical variables and results of the DAS-28 and HAQ-DI mechanisms in determining the level of functional disability of the patient, all in anticipation of their future implementation in classifiers, focusing on those metrics that can make a difference in the search for a simpler and more accurate diagnosis, while imposing a lower complexity necessary in ML models given the decrease in the dimensionality of the input vectors.

2 Literature Review

The pure evaluation of clinical variables not derived from laboratory or radiological studies from a statistical perspective and with a view to measuring the predictive power of the level of functional impairment is a topic that is not widely discussed in the literature concerning RA. Most efforts tend to focus on finding the best way to diagnose the disease, the stage it is at, the damage caused to various body systems, or related issues such as its remission capacity or the effectiveness of certain drugs. all of the above, using as much information as possible, often favoring novel and sophisticated data obtained from tests that, although sometimes highly effective, are often inaccessible to a large part of the population.

The works most directly related to the approach of this paper could be considered classics, due to the time that has passed since their publication, but also because they could be considered foundational.

In the study by Aletaha et al. (2010), the classification criteria for RA developed by the American College of Rheumatology (ACR) and the European League Against Rheumatism (EULAR) were proposed. To this end, the study integrated an explicit statistical analysis of different clinical and laboratory variables in order to generate a scoring system capable of discriminating between patients with a high probability of developing persistent RA and those with more nonspecific presentations. The main conclusion was that the combination of several clinical and serological parameters allows for more accurate classification of patients in the early stages. In other words, a large number of variables that may be obtained about a patient during their complete clinical evaluation were analyzed, resulting in a set that, while capable of achieving a reliable diagnosis, requires multiple tests, evaluations, and studies [4].

Bruce and Fries (2003) conducted a key study on the HAQ-DI, focusing on exploring its applicability in assessing quality of life. Rather than considering only the overall score, the authors analyzed each of the categories that make up the questionnaire in detail, which allowed them to identify differential patterns in the way different functional limitations impact daily life. This approach revealed that certain domains, such as those related to mobility and hand strength, provide particularly valuable clinical information beyond the composite score. This paper can be considered the most direct predecessor to the present study; however, its focus is on evaluating the components of the HAQ-DI for comprehensive patient assessment rather than on classifying them according to a grade of disability. Furthermore, the only data considered was that provided by the questionnaire [5].

On the other hand, given the difficulty of the technical problems related to this disease, in most cases, attempts are made to use all available data, in the hope that this will lead to an improvement in the performance of the mechanisms in use. The preceding, without paying special previous attention to the individual contribution of each characteristic, performing if any, a retrospective analysis of the markers involved. This leading to the generation of highly complex predictive models. This approach has been exploited far more extensively, and some recent examples that illustrate this are as follows.

The work of Salehi et al. sought to predict remission after six months of treatment with biological agents, using data from routine clinical practice. The models compared included Random Forest, XGBoost, SVM, and AdaBoost. They also applied SHAP to interpret the contribution of each variable, highlighting DAS28 and patient assessment as key predictors [6].

In a subsequent study, Salehi extended his analysis to predicting disease activity at 12 months. They used longitudinal data from patients treated with biologics and compared penalized regression models, support vector machines, and ensemble methods. No feature selection mechanism was applied [7].

The group led by Fujii et al. worked with patients with seronegative undifferentiated arthritis, with the aim of predicting which patients would develop RA. They trained a simple neural network using clinical and laboratory data, incorporating biomarkers such as the MMP-3 protein. To explain the prediction, they used SHAP, which indicated that MMP-3 was the most decisive variable [8].

The article by Wang et al. focused on predicting the progression of bone erosion in rheumatoid arthritis by combining clinical data with metabolic profiles. The proposal was a probabilistic model based on Naive Bayes. The approach included a comparative analysis to show the gain provided by metabolites compared to conventional clinical variables, although no formal attribute selection process was proposed [9].

None of the studies mentioned above address the problem from the same perspective as this article, focusing either on the direct creation of an ML model without the use of prior statistical tests or on the analysis of general RA markers to establish diagnostic criteria for clinical practice.

The novelty and contribution of this work lies in the review of the predictive capacity of clinical variables from questionnaires and first-contact assessments through rigorous and exhaustive statistical screening, using a pipeline of tests, with a focus on their subsequent use in ML to create simpler and easier-to-train models, both due to their reduced complexity and the greater ease with which the data required can be obtained. This contrasts with the currently widely used methodology, which first addresses the creation of classifiers and then performs subsequent analyses of the impact of each variable, not with a view to simplifying the mechanism, but for interpretation purposes. In addition, a granular study of the HAQ-DI components is included, both by category and by individual question, to elucidate whether, in opposition to clinical practice, a different assignment of scores could be more beneficial for predictive models.

3 Materials and Methods

This section details the data used, as well as the statistical tests performed on them, their functioning, calculation methodology, and purposes.

3.1 Dataset

The dataset used consists of the clinical history, DAS-28 test results and HAQ-DI questionnaire responses, in addition to the calculated score, of 124 patients with AR from the "Dr. Raymundo Abarca Alarcón" General Hospital of Chilpancingo in the state of Guerrero, Mexico. It contains records of 28 patients who do not present any complication in the performance of daily tasks derived from AR, 64 who begin to present difficulties, 15 who present high levels of complication and 4 who are close to being or are disabled.

Specifically, the data considered are sex, age, dominant hand, strength in the left and right hand, years with the disease, BMI and height; in addition, the variables of count of inflamed, painful and limited joints collected by the

DAS-28 are available. The responses obtained to each of the 20 questions of the standard HAQ-DI questionnaire are available, as well as the scores by category and overall calculated from these.

3.2 Related Statistical Concepts

Covariance. Covariance measures how two random variables vary with respect to their means, thus quantifying the linear relationship that exists between them, as well as the direction of such relationship. Thus, if two variables increase or decrease together, they will have positive covariance, while if they have opposite behaviors, they will exhibit negative ones. Variables with no apparent linear relationship will exhibit a covariance close to zero [10].

It is calculated as:

$$\text{Cov}(X, Y) = \mathbb{E}[(X - \mathbb{E}[X])(Y - \mathbb{E}[Y])] \tag{1}$$

Correlation Matrix. It is a symmetric matrix showing the degree of linear relationship between all pairs of features in the dataset, where each cell (i, j) contains the correlation value of feature i with feature j; this can be a number between -1 and 1, indicating these extremes, negative or positive linear correlation, respectively. A 0 will indicate that no correlation exists [11].

These values are calculated using Pearson's correlation coefficient between two variables X and Y:

$$\rho_{X,Y} = \frac{\text{Cov}(X, Y)}{\sigma_X \cdot \sigma_Y} \tag{2}$$

P-Value. The probability value or p-value is the probability of obtaining a result equal to or more extreme than the one obtained under the assumption that the null hypothesis of a statistical test is true.

That is, it is not the probability that the question to be answered with the test is true nor the probability that the hypothesis is true, but a measure of compatibility between the data under evaluation and the hypothesis proposed.

A sufficiently large p value for this hypothesis not to be rejected is 0.05, while something smaller is said not to provide sufficient evidence to support it [12].

Shapiro-Wilk Test. It is a statistical test used to verify whether a sample of data comes from a normal distribution, and is especially accurate for medium and small data sets.

It starts with an ordering of the data to conform the order statistics of the sample.

It then constructs a vector of weights $a = (a_1, ..., a_n)$ using the mean and covariance of the theoretical order statistics that a standard normal distribution possesses. With m being its vector of means and V its covariance matrix, these are computed as:

$$\mathbf{a} = \frac{V^{-1}\mathbf{m}}{\|\mathbf{V}^{-1}\mathbf{m}\|} \tag{3}$$

With these data, the Shapiro-Wilk statistic W is calculated as:

$$W = \frac{\left(\sum_{i=1}^{n} a_i x_{(i)}\right)^2}{\sum_{i=1}^{n} \left(x_i - \bar{x}\right)^2} \tag{4}$$

Being closer to 1 the more the data approximates a normal distribution [13].

ANOVA Test: The Analysis of Variance test is used to evaluate whether there are significant differences between the means of independent groups of values and is usually used to answer questions related to the possibility that values of a certain characteristic change according to the class to which a pattern belongs.

Thus, its null hypothesis is that all the population means of the groups are statistically equal.

It is based on the analysis of the variability of the group means and the internal variability of each group and requires that the observations are independent, each group follows a normal distribution and that the variances are homogeneous [14].

Obtaining it requires the calculation of several quantities, starting with the size n_i of each group and the sum N of all observations. The calculation of means per group and the global mean. The SST:

$$SST = \sum \left(x_{ij} - \bar{X}_{\text{global}}\right)^2 \tag{5}$$

The SSB:

$$SSB = \sum_{i=1}^{k} n_i \left(\bar{X}_i - \bar{X}_{\text{global}}\right)^2 \tag{6}$$

The SSW:

$$SSW = SST - SSB \tag{7}$$

The degrees of freedom:

$$df_b = k - 1 \tag{8}$$

$$df_w = N - k \tag{9}$$

The Mean Square Between groups:

$$MSB = \frac{SSB}{df_b} \tag{10}$$

The Mean Square Within groups:

$$MSW = \frac{SSW}{df_w} \tag{11}$$

And finally the statistic F:

$$F = \frac{MSB}{MSW} \tag{12}$$

Levene Test: This test is the most commonly used to verify the homogeneity of variances, that is, whether the variances of different population groups are equal. To do this, it calculates the difference of each value with respect to the median of its respective group and then, using the ANOVA test, evaluates whether these differences have a similar variance between groups.

The test process is as follows:

1. Groups the data by their respective category.
2. Calculates a central value, mean or median, per group.
3. For each pattern in each group, it calculates its absolute difference with respect to the central value.

$$Z_{ij} = \left| X_{ij} - \tilde{X}_i \right| \tag{13}$$

4. Having all the Z_{ij} grouped by category, performs an ANOVA test on them to verify if the means of the differences are equal [15].

Tukey HDS Test: The Tukey Honestly Significant Difference test is a post-hoc test that allows, once the ANOVA test has confirmed that there is a difference between the means of the groups, to make a comparison between all of them to indicate which are exactly the pairs of groups whose distribution differs.

It is based on the calculation of the critical difference HDS, above which the difference between two means is considered to be significant. It has the additional advantage that it controls for type I error arising from multiple comparisons [16].

For the calculation of the HDS, the critical value q_alpha obtained from Tukey's table, the number of groups k, the number of samples per group n, the degrees of freedom d_f calculated in ANOVA and the mean square of the ANOVA error MS_{error} are used:

$$\text{HSD} = q_{\alpha,k,df} \cdot \sqrt{\frac{MS_{\text{error}}}{n}} \tag{14}$$

The following comparison is then made between each possible pair of groups:

$$\left| \bar{X}_i - \bar{X}_j \right| > \text{HSD} \tag{15}$$

Kruskal-Wallis: It is a non-parametric test that compares independent groups to verify whether their medians are statistically different. Similar to ANOVA, it provides information on the behavior of a specific characteristic among different patterns of different classes, assuming as null hypothesis that all related distributions are equal.

To calculate it, it is assumed that there are k groups with sizes n_i with N being their sum and the totality of the patterns. All the data are combined into a single vector and sorted in ascending order, assigning them ranks from 1 to N, averaging the ranks where there is a tie. For each group, its respective sum of ranks R_i is calculated.

Finally, the H statistic is computed:

$$H = \frac{12}{N(N+1)} \sum_{i=1}^{k} \frac{R_i^2}{n_i} - 3(N+1) \tag{16}$$

It only provides information about the difference between distributions, not about which of the groups are the ones that differ [17].

Dunn Test: It is a nonparametric post-hoc statistical test used after finding global differences between groups of samples of the same characteristic by means of the Kruskal-Wallis test, with the objective of identifying which are the specific pairs of groups whose distribution differs significantly.

That is, this test compares all possible combinations of pairs of groups, given different values of the group variable, to indicate precisely which are the groups between which the distribution of the variable differs.

The calculation of its statistic requires the total number of observations N, the cardinality n_i of each of the groups and the average $\bar{R}_i$ of the ranks, assigned as in the Kruskal-Wallis test, for each group. Its equation is:

$$Z_{ij} = \frac{\bar{R}_i - \bar{R}_j}{\sqrt{\frac{N(N+1)}{12}\left(\frac{1}{n_i} + \frac{1}{n_j}\right)}} \tag{17}$$

An error correction derived from the application of multiple comparisons must be applied to the p-values obtained. Typically, the Bonferroni or Holm methods are the ones used [18].

Mutual Information: It is a measure of dependence between two characteristics, so it is used to quantify how much information the knowledge of one variable gives about the possible value of the other or, in other words, the reduction of uncertainty with respect to a variable obtained by knowing the value of another.

It is not limited to linear relationships, so it is very useful for the selection of variables for classification, measuring how much the uncertainty about the value with respect to the class is reduced by knowing the value of a certain characteristic [19].

Its calculation is performed by using probabilities:

$$I(X;Y) = \sum_{x \in X} \sum_{y \in Y} P(x,y) \cdot \log\left(\frac{P(x,y)}{P(x)P(y)}\right) \tag{18}$$

In order to improve its interpretation, establish appropriate comparisons and normalize its values between 0 and 1, the value obtained is usually normalized by the entropy of the variable representing the class, which is calculated as follows:

$$H(Y) = -\sum_{i=1}^{k} P(y_i) \cdot \log_b P(y_i) \tag{19}$$

And so, the normalized mutual information is computed as:

$$\text{NMI} = \frac{I(X;Y)}{H(Y)} \tag{20}$$

3.3 Model-Based Attribute Selection

Mean Decrease in Impurity: It is a metric that estimates how much each attribute contributes to reduce the impurity in a decision tree or an ensemble of trees, based on criteria such as entropy or Gini. An attribute that is frequently used and whose splits result in large prediction improvements will be considered important.

Empirical evidence has positioned it as an effective tool as a preliminary filter for the initial selection of variables in predictive models, as it enables the capture of nonlinear interactions without requiring assumptions about the distribution of the data, all at a low computational cost [20].

It was originally proposed in ensembles, specifically in Randon Forest, where the way to calculate it is to sum up all the impurity reductions that each variable makes across all the trees involved, finally normalizing those sums [21].

Thus, considering $\Delta i(s)$ as the impurity decrease at node s, T being the total number of trees and S_t the nodes where the attribute X_j is used in tree t, the calculation of the importance of X_j is performed as:

$$\text{Importance}\,(X_j) = \sum_{t=1}^{T} \sum_{s}^{S_t} \Delta i(s) \tag{21}$$

4 Results

To determine the relevance of each of the variables, the pipeline of statistical deterministic (except from the last one) tests shown in Fig. 1 was carried out. These were applied to two variants of the dataset, one containing all the available clinical data of the patient and the scores of each HAQ-DI category and the other in which the HAQ-DI scores are not general, but the answers given by the patient to each individual question are shown. In this way, it will be possible to evaluate the weight in the classification provided by each response separately and to contrast it with the generalization used in current clinical practice.

4.1 Filtering Irrelevant Variables

The first group of tests focused on locating variables that, due to their statistical characteristics, would not be directly relevant for classification.

The first test applied was an analysis of variance, to find out if any of the variables did not present any variance (directly cero) across classes, because if so, it would present very similar data for all of them, making it useless for discrimination between possible classes. None of the variables reported this characteristic.

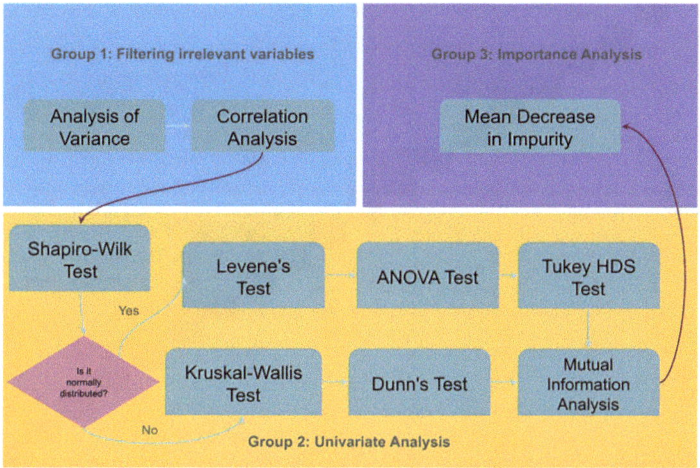

Fig. 1. Statistic tests pipeline flowchart.

The next test was a correlation analysis, which sought to find variables that were strongly linearly correlated with some other variable, so that their inclusion in the characteristics used for classification would be redundant since they did not provide information that the other variable was not already providing. For this purpose, use was made of the correlation matrix between variables per dataset, as shown in Figs. 2 and 3, and of a threshold of 0.85, which, when reached or exceeded, marked the variables as correlated. As a result of this test, it was found that left hand strength was redundant with respect to the information provided by right hand strength and that pain was completely linked to inflammation. Given this evidence, the variables of left hand strength and inflammation were dropped from consideration for further analysis.

4.2 Univariate Analysis

The second group focused on understanding the behavior of each of the remaining variables on the categories, evaluating their distribution and statistical indicators. In all these tests the p-value used to indicate the presence of evidence of statistical significance was 0.05.

The first test used in this group was the Shapiro-Wilk test to analyze whether the data of a characteristic, regardless of which class they belong to, follow a normal distribution. It was found that the only data that followed it were the patients' age, height and BMI.

Subsequently, Levene's test was applied to these three characteristics to verify whether they exhibited homogeneity of variances, i.e., whether their variance was homogeneous when their values were considered grouped this time by class. The result was that all of them also complied with this characteristic.

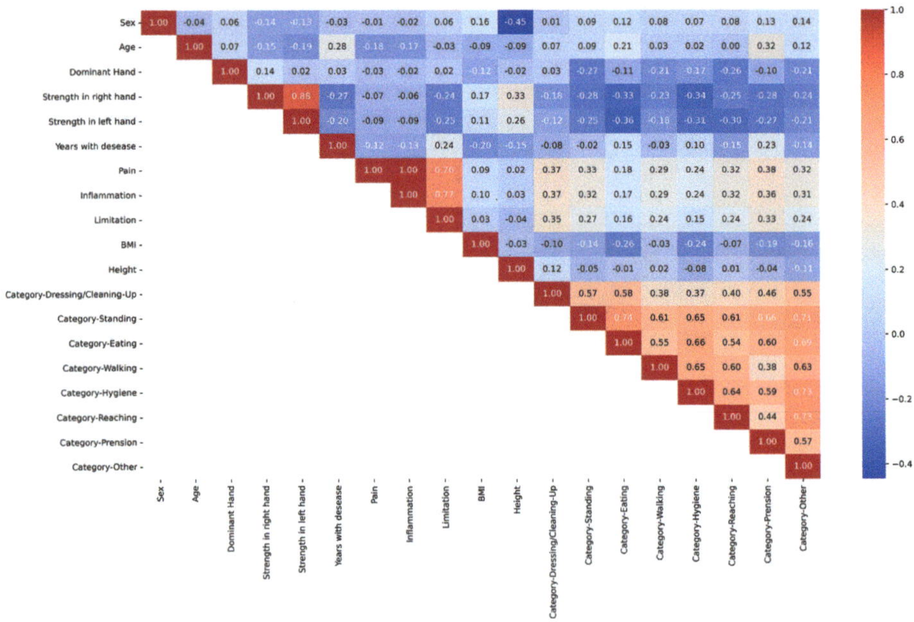

Fig. 2. Correlation matrix for dataset with HAQ-DI reported by category.

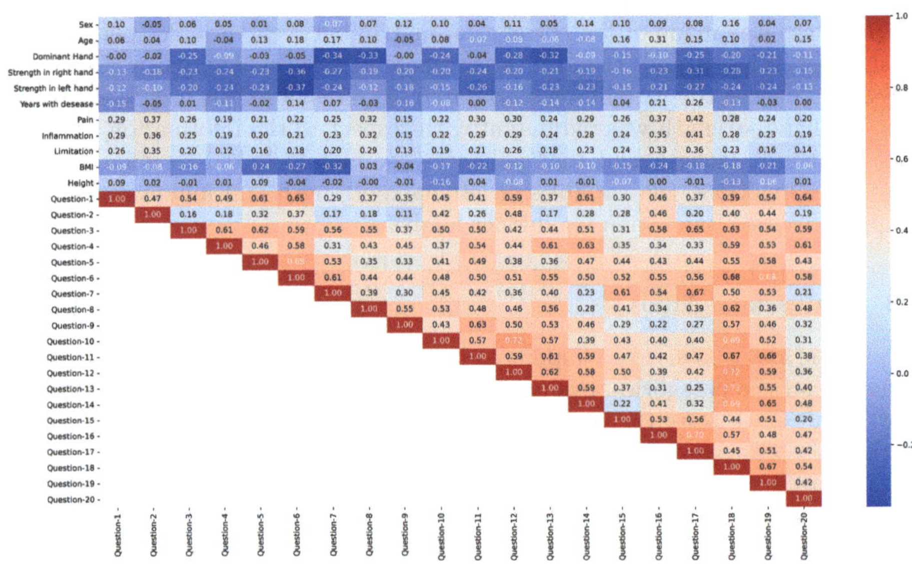

Fig. 3. Correlation matrix for dataset with HAQ-DI reported by question.

Given that these two conditions were met for all these attributes, the ANOVA test was then used to interpret the similarities of their distributions among the degrees of disability and, more explicitly, to determine whether the means of these characteristics in their different groupings by class are significantly similar, because if so, it would imply that they are not so relevant for separating between categories, since they would be behaving similarly in all of them. With a p-value greater than 0.5, height showed similarities between its means, while BMI did so with only a p-value of 0.058. On the other hand, age was shown to be a variable with certain differences in behavior between the groups.

In order to determine which groups showed different age distributions, a Tukey HDS test was performed. The results showed that in reality, age behaved similarly in almost all groups, showing significant differences only between the group with no affectation in their functions and the group with affectation close to disability.

With respect to the variables for which the conditions of normality of distribution and homogeneity of variances were not verified, the Kruskal-Wallis test was carried out to observe the similarity in the behavior of their distributions across classes, in order to evaluate their effectiveness as discriminatory measures between categories. With a p-value of 0.69, the sex characteristic showed similar means between groups, as did the dominant hand attribute, with a p-value of 0.20, and surprisingly, the number of years the patient has suffered from the disease, which is not a very suitable marker for discerning between classifications with a very high p-value of 0.85.

Dunn's post-hoc test was used to understand which groups showed different distributions for each of the variables that did show differences. The results are shown in Table 1, indicating which characteristics exhibit significantly different medians between each specific pair of groups.

Based on the preceding results, the boxplots shown in Fig. 4 were generated, illustrating the distribution of characteristics with remarkably different behaviors between the different levels of RA.

To finalize this set of tests, a mutual information analysis was carried out between all the remaining characteristics with the class label, to obtain information on how much the uncertainty of the categorization was reduced given the assumption that information is available for a certain attribute, hoping to obtain those attributes with greater power of discernment between groups. Table 2 shows an ordered sample of the results (indicating as *Rank* the position reached by the feature), considering that they are normalized between 0 and 1.

Table 1. Features with different behaviors displayed by pairs of groups.

Pair of groups	Features (2-column layout)	
(1, 2)	Strength in right hand	Limitation/Pain
	8 Categories	Questions-1-20
(1, 3)	Limitation/Pain	Category-Dressing/Cleaning-Up
	Questions 1-4, 7-8, 10 12, 15, 17	
(1, 4)	Strength in right hand	Category-Dressing/Cleaning-Up
	Category-Hygiene	Questions 1-3, 5, 7, 9-12, 14-15 and 19
(2, 3)	Limitation/Pain	Category-Prension
	Category-Dressing/Cleaning-Up	Category-Standing
	Category-Walking	Category-Reaching
	Questions 1-5, 7-10, 12-13, 15-17, 20	
(2, 4)	Strength in right hand	Limitation
	Questions 1-20	8 Categories
(3, 4)	Strength in right hand	Limitation/Pain
	8 Categories	Question 1-20

4.3 Importance Analysis

Finally, following the search for which variables may be more relevant for classification, an importance analysis based on the model-based approach with the mean decrease in impurity, that is, the use of the features in a Random Forest classifier, was carried out. It was decided to use Random Forest to follow the original methodology proposed for calculating this metric [21], since, as mentioned previously, it has delivered remarkable results.

The reported importance of the 15 attributes with the highest mean decrease in impurity can be visualized in Table 3 and Fig. 5. The last two columns correspond to the limits of the confidence intervals for a confidence level of 95%.

5 Discussion

The first variables shown to be not useful for classification are left hand strength and inflammation, due to their redundancy with other characteristics. It is, however, interesting to note how, in general, the deterioration in the strength of both hands occurs equally and how, as might be intuitive, inflammation is completely related to pain levels.

The three normally distributed variables, height, BMI and age do not appear to be good discriminants either, maintaining in almost all cases the same probability distribution across all classes. While age, the only one in this group that shows any difference between groups, seems to have an interesting significance value in the Random Forest test, it also scores rather discouragingly poorly in the mutual information test.

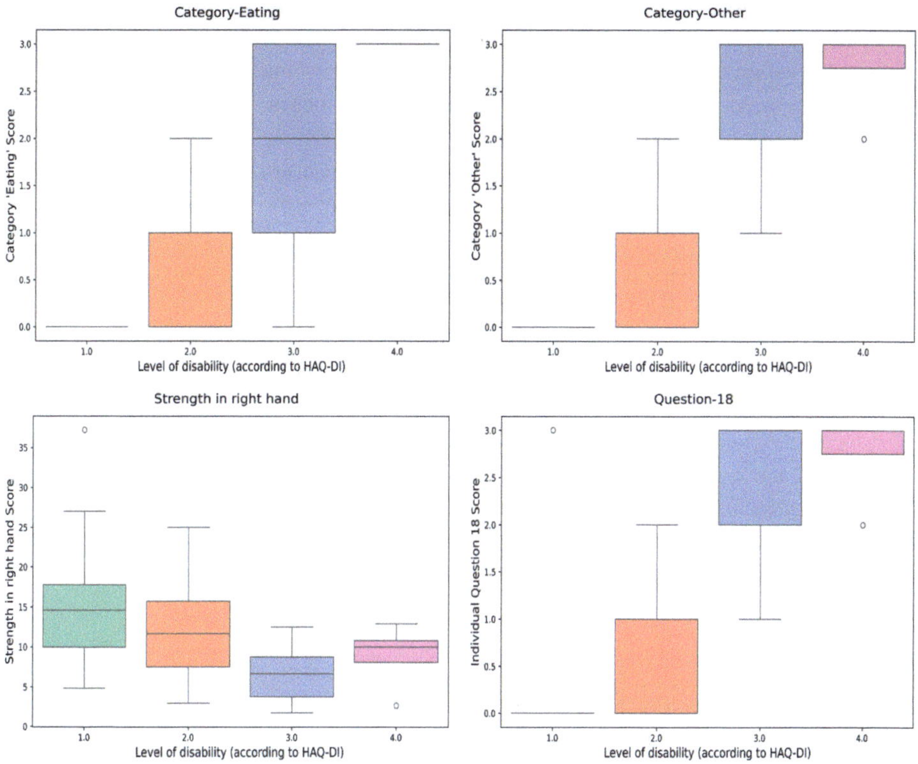

Fig. 4. Boxplots regarding the RA level for significant variables.

Table 2. Mutual information test results.

Rank	Feature	Mutual information measure
1	Question-6	0.2695
2	Question-19	0.2572
3	Category-Eating	0.2395
4	Question-11	0.2377
5	Category-Other	0.2320
6	Question-18	0.2292
7	Category-Reaching	0.2273
8	Category-Prension	0.1881
9	Category-Walking	0.1787
10	Category-Hygiene	0.1523
16	Sex	0.1016
25	BMI	0.0400
26	Strength in right hand	0.0354
30	Pain	0.0189
36	Years with desease	0.0000
37	Question-15	0.0000

Table 3. Features importance based on mean decrease in impurity.

Feature	Mean MDI	Std MDI	Low bound	High bound
Strength in right hand	0.118269	0.065408	0.105449	0.131089
Category-Other	0.113127	0.080811	0.097289	0.128966
Age	0.098316	0.070088	0.084580	0.112052
Category-Walking	0.089448	0.075630	0.074624	0.104271
Height	0.087925	0.064060	0.075369	0.100481
Category-Prension	0.087201	0.067340	0.074003	0.100400
Category-Eating	0.084801	0.075497	0.070004	0.099599
BMI	0.073088	0.055669	0.062177	0.083999
Category-Reaching	0.067410	0.063773	0.054911	0.079910
Years with desease	0.060491	0.047604	0.051161	0.069821
Question-18	0.060246	0.075415	0.045465	0.075028
Question-16	0.058113	0.053901	0.047548	0.068677
Question-13	0.043443	0.045690	0.034487	0.052398
Limitation	0.037372	0.036069	0.030302	0.044441
Question-9	0.032931	0.036695	0.025739	0.040123

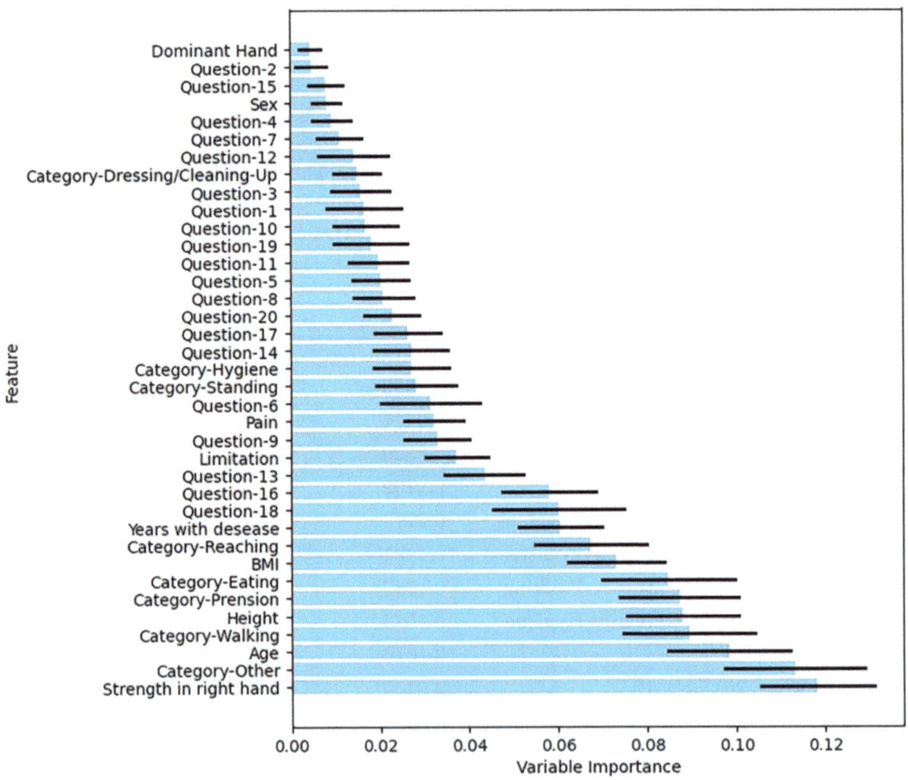

Fig. 5. Features importance.

Given the results of the Kruskall-Wallis test, sex, dominant hand and years with the disease can be directly ruled out as good predictors, conclusions that are supported by their scores in the mutual information and significance analysis tests.

The rest of the variables seem to have a moderately different behavior across the different groups, as reflected by Dunn's test. However, among those exhibiting the greatest divergence between their distributions are Category-Dressing/Cleaning-Up and Question 1–3, 7, 10, 12 and 15.

Finally, based on the results of the mutual information and importance tests, it can be observed that strength in the right hand is the best of all the clinical history characteristics, with the others in almost independent mutual information ranges and weakly relvant levels of importance. As for the HAQ-Di categories, those with the greatest predictive power are Category-Other, Category-Reaching, Category-Eating and Category-Walking. Finally, as for the questions, those with the greatest potential for discernment appear to be Question-18 and Question-16, although on their own they exhibit considerably worse markers than their category counterparts, which is consistent with current clinical practice.

6 Conclusions

The present work clearly reveals that not all clinical data collected from patients with rheumatoid arthritis provide the same diagnostic value. Through various statistical tests, characteristics were identified whose influence on the classification of disability levels is marginal or even null. Variables such as sex, dominant hand and, surprisingly, years with the disease did not show significant differences between groups, suggesting their low potential as reliable predictors.

In contrast, certain items of the HAQ-DI questionnaire, especially those associated with the "Reaching", 'Other' and "Walking" categories, as well as some specific questions, demonstrated clear differential behavior between patient groups.

In addition, right hand strength was found to have a higher discriminant value than other more traditional clinical measures. This observation highlights the importance of assessing functionality in a direct and quantifiable way, rather than relying solely on perceptions or indirect variables.

In sum, the results invite us to rethink what data are really useful when constructing automatic models for diagnostic support. By focusing the analysis on the most informative variables, more accurate and less complex tools could be developed, thus facilitating early detection and monitoring of the disease.

Disclosure of Interests. The authors have no competing interests to declare that are relevant to the content of this article.

References

1. García, D.G.: Rheumatoid arthritis: epidemiology, pathophysiology, diagnostic criteria and treatment. J. Med. Res. Auton. Univ. State Mexico **6**(2), 53–61 (2018)
2. Institute of Hygiene and Public Health (Mexico): World Arthritis and Rheumatic Diseases Day, October 12, Mexico City (2022)
3. Mexican Institute of Social Security: Diagnosis and treatment of rheumatoid arthritis in adults, Mexico City (2010)
4. Aletaha, D., et al.: 2010 Rheumatoid arthritis classification criteria: an American College of Rheumatology/European League Against Rheumatism collaborative initiative. Arthritis Rheum. **62**(9), 2569–2581 (2010)
5. Bruce, B., Fries, J.F.: The Stanford health assessment questionnaire: dimensions and practical applications. Health Qual. Life Outcomes (2003)
6. Salehi, F., et al.: A robust machine learning approach to predicting remission and stratifying risk in rheumatoid arthritis patients treated with bDMARDs. Sci. Rep. **15** (2025)
7. Salehi, F., et al.: Predicting disease activity score in rheumatoid arthritis patients treated with biologic disease-modifying antirheumatic drugs using machine learning models. Technologies **13** (2025)
8. Fujii, T., et al.: Predicting rheumatoid arthritis progression from seronegative undifferentiated arthritis using machine learning: a deep learning model trained on the KURAMA cohort and externally validated with the ANSWER cohort. Arthritis Res. Therapy **27** (2025)
9. Wang, Z., et al.: Early prediction of bone destruction in rheumatoid arthritis through machine learning analysis of plasma metabolites. Arthritis Res. Therapy **27** (2025)
10. Wasserman, L.: All of Statistics: A Concise Course in Statistical Inference. Springer, New York (2004)
11. Montgomery, D.C., Runger, G.C.: Applied Statistics and Probability for Engineers, 5th edn. Wiley, Hoboken (2010)
12. Devore, J.L.: Probability and Statistics for Engineering and the Sciences, 8th edn. Cengage Learning, Boston (2011)
13. Shapiro, S.S., Wilk, M.B.: An analysis of variance test for normality (complete samples). Biometrika **52**(3/4), 591–611 (1965)
14. Fisher, R.A.: Statistical Methods for Research Workers. Oliver and Boyd, Edinburgh (1925)
15. Levene, H.: Robust tests for equality of variances. In: Olkin, I. (ed.) Contributions to Probability and Statistics: Essays in Honor of Harold Hotelling, pp. 278–292. Stanford University Press (1960)
16. Tukey, J.W.: Comparing individual means in the analysis of variance. Biometrics **5**(2), 99–114 (1949)
17. Kruskal, W.H., Wallis, W.A.: Use of ranks in one-criterion variance analysis. J. Am. Stat. Assoc. **47**(260), 583–621 (1952)
18. Dunn, O.J.: Multiple comparisons using rank sums. Technometrics **6**(3), 241–252 (1964)
19. Cover, T.M., Thomas, J.A.: Elements of Information Theory, 2nd edn. Wiley-Interscience, Hoboken (2006)
20. Toloşi, L., Lengauer, T.: Classification with correlated features: unreliability of feature ranking and solutions. Bioinformatics **27**(14), 1986–1994 (2011)
21. Breiman, L.: Random forests. Mach. Learn. **45**(1), 5–32 (2001)

Data Lakehouse for Type 2 Diabetes Remission: Scoping Review and Architectural Proposal

Carlos Andrés Morales Rosales(✉), Lisbeth Rodríguez Mazahua, Nidia Rodríguez Mazahua, Giner Alor Hernández, and José Luis Sánchez Cervantes

Tecnológico Nacional de México/I.T. Orizaba, 94320 Orizaba, Veracruz, Mexico
{M18011260,lisbeth.rm2,d16010227,giner.ah, jose.sc}@orizaba.tecnm.mx

Abstract. Type 2 diabetes, one of the most prevalent chronic diseases worldwide, represents a critical challenge for healthcare systems due to its progressive course and the need for continuous management to prevent long-term complications. Although previous research has demonstrated the possibility of remission under specific conditions, a more comprehensive understanding of the underlying determinants remains essential. This study presents a scoping review on data repository technologies and proposes a Data Lakehouse-based architecture for the analysis of factors associated with type 2 diabetes remission. The proposed framework enables the ingestion, integration, storage, and advanced analysis of large-scale, heterogeneous, and multi-format data sets, facilitating the identification of patterns, correlations, and key variables linked to remission. To assess feasibility, a functional prototype was implemented, incorporating a large language model to semantically classify scientific articles, with outputs integrated into a Lakehouse infrastructure using Apache Kafka, Spark, and Iceberg. Furthermore, a relational data model is designed to enable longitudinal monitoring of clinical variables such as dietary habits, pharmacological treatments, physical activity, and medical interventions. By leveraging structured, interoperable, and traceable data, the proposed approach aims to enhance clinical decision-making, support personalized therapeutic strategies, and ultimately contribute to more effective disease management and improved patient outcomes.

Keywords: Data Analysis · Data Lakehouse · Data Repository · Diabetes · Machine Learning · Remission

1 Introduction

Type 2 diabetes, one of the most prevalent chronic diseases worldwide, represents a significant challenge for healthcare systems due to its progressive nature and the need for continuous management to prevent severe complications. According to the study [1], this disease can enter a state of remission under certain conditions. Subsequent research made in [2, 3] identified several contributing factors, such as weight loss, reduced caloric intake, blood glucose monitoring, and physical exercise.

C. Palma-Preciado et al. (Eds.): CORE 2025, ACSAR 3, pp. 97–117, 2026.
https://doi.org/10.1007/978-3-032-08894-9_7

Among these investigations, a wide range of treatment approaches and strategies has been proposed, spanning from surgical interventions [4–6] to dietary modifications [7–9], and physical activity programs [10, 11]. Each of these perspectives focuses independently on supporting the remission process of diabetes. However, there remains a critical need for a comprehensive framework that integrates these diverse factors to optimize both the duration and quality of the remission process. Identifying and controlling these key factors could significantly improve patients' quality of life and reduce the burden this disease places on healthcare systems.

While no prior specific proposals of Data Lakehouse architectures applied to type 2 diabetes were identified, this disease presents unique challenges that justify the development of a dedicated data management infrastructure. Its multifactorial nature requires integrating highly heterogeneous data sources, including clinical records, lifestyle patterns, laboratory results, imaging studies, and even patient-reported outcomes. Traditional data warehouses often lack the flexibility to efficiently handle unstructured or semi-structured data, whereas data lakes may not ensure the governance and analytical consistency needed for clinical research [12–14]. A Data Lakehouse approach bridges these limitations by combining scalability and schema enforcement with advanced analytical capabilities, enabling longitudinal tracking and multi-domain correlation analysis. In the context of type 2 diabetes, this infrastructure is essential to uncover complex interactions among remission-related factors and to support both research and precision medicine.

To address this knowledge gap, this article presents the results of a scoping review of 50 studies related to the development of data repositories across various domains. It also introduces the design of a technological platform architecture capable of analyzing large volumes of multi-source and multi-format data, with the goal of identifying the factors that enable type 2 diabetes patients to achieve remission. To this end, the study adopts an innovative approach based on Data Lakehouse technology, which combines the strengths of both Data Warehouses and Data Lakes, as described in [15]. This architecture will support the ingestion, storage, and efficient processing of large-scale data, enabling insights into type 2 diabetes remission from structured, semi-structured, and unstructured data.

The implementation of technologies such as Apache NiFi [16], Kafka [17], Flink [18], and Spark [19], among others, will not only provide a robust platform for managing big data, but also offer enhanced flexibility in data analysis and interpretation. This combination of tools is essential to ensure that the proposed solution can adapt to the complexity of the problem and generate valuable outcomes for both the scientific and medical communities.

This research article is structured as follows: Sect. 2 offers a comprehensive review of the state of the art, including a comparative analysis of current studies on type 2 diabetes remission and the data processing technologies employed. Section 3 details the architecture of the proposed Data Lakehouse-based platform. Finally, Sect. 4 presents the conclusions and acknowledgments.

2 Literature Review

To design a Data Lakehouse focused on type 2 diabetes remission, it was necessary to examine existing data repository technologies and their use in medical and industrial contexts. This section presents a scoping review aimed at identifying trends, technological gaps, and insights to guide the proposed architecture. The following subsections outline the selection methodology and key findings, including comparisons of repository types, technologies, and their relevance to the research objective.

The criteria used for comparing the selected articles included the year of publication, the type of repository implemented, the domain of application, and the technologies used for development—categorized into data integration, storage, processing, analysis, and visualization.

Table 1 compares the analyzed articles across the three main types of repositories: Data Warehouse, Data Lakehouse, and Data Lake. In addition, it evaluates whether each work belongs to the medical domain and, if so, whether it specifically focuses on type 2 diabetes. This comparative view provides insight into the technological orientation and thematic focus of the selected literature.

This research is highly relevant as it addresses a critical gap in current data infrastructure applied to chronic disease management. While various studies have explored isolated technological components such as storage or processing in general medical contexts, few—if any—have proposed a comprehensive architecture specifically tailored to analyzing the remission of type 2 diabetes. By designing a Data Lakehouse architecture focused on this purpose, the study enables the integration and analysis of large-scale, multi-source data to uncover key factors influencing remission. This focused approach has the potential to support clinical decision-making, improve treatment personalization, and ultimately enhance patient outcomes, making it a significant contribution to both the fields of data engineering and healthcare.

Table 1. Comparison of articles

Article	Repository	Medical domain	Diabetes focused
Fleuren *et al.* [20]	*Data Warehouse*	Yes	No
Pressat-Laffouilhère *et al.* [21]	*Data Warehouse*	Yes	No
Lamer *et al.* [22]	*Data Warehouse*	Yes	No
Ansoborlo *et al.* [23]	*Data Warehouse*	Yes	No
Kaspar *et al.*[24]	*Data Warehouse*	Yes	No
Baum *et al.* [25]	*Data Warehouse*	Yes	No
Ndisha *et al.* [26]	*Data Warehouse*	Yes	No
Cheng-Zarate *et al.* [27]	*Data Warehouse*	Yes	No
Turcan *et al.* [28]	*Data Warehouse*	Yes	No
Arnold *et al.* [29]	*Data Warehouse*	Yes	No

(*continued*)

Table 1. (*continued*)

Article	Repository	Medical domain	Diabetes focused
Windsor *et al.* [30]	*Data Warehouse*	Yes	No
Shae *et al.* [31]	*Data Lake*	Yes	No
Melchor-Uceda *et al.* [32]	*Data Lake*	Yes	No
Babu *et al.* [33]	*Data Lake*	Yes	No
Mabel Rani *et al.* [34]	*Data Warehouse*	Yes	No
Amara *et al.* [35]	*Data Warehouse*	Yes	No
Kumar *et al.* [36]	*Data Lakehouse*	No	No
Hernandez Cruz *et al.* [37]	*Data Warehouse*	Yes	No
Spengler *et al.* [38]	*Data Warehouse*	Yes	No
Divya *et al.* [39]	*Data Warehouse*	Yes	No
Setiadi *et al.* [40]	*Data Warehouse*	Yes	No
Neamah *et al.* [41]	*Data Warehouse*	Yes	No
Yeng *et al.* [42]	*Data Lake*	Yes	No
Ramesh *et al.* [43]	*Data Lake*	Yes	No
Kumar *et al.* [44]	*Big Data*	Yes	No
Patil *et al.* [45]	*Data Lakehouse*	Yes	No
Abdelhedi *et al.* [46]	*Data Lake*	Yes	No
Babu *et al.* [47]	*Data Lake*	Yes	No
González-Velázquez *et al.* [48]	*Big Data*	No	No
Oliveira *et al.* [49]	*Data Catalog*	No	No
Harby *et al.* [50]	*Data Lakehouse*	No	No
Bindal *et al.* [51]	*Big Data*	No	No
Edara *et al.* [52]	*Data Warehouse*	No	No
Batalla *et al.* [53]	*Data Warehouse*	No	No
Hoseini *et al.* [54]	*Data Lake*	No	No
Siddiqi *et al.* [55]	*Big Data*	Yes	No
Wang *et al.* [56]	*Data Lakehouse*	No	No
Begoli *et al.* [57]	*Data Lakehouse*	Yes	No
Li *et al.* [58]	*Data Lakehouse*	Yes	No
Park *et al.* [59]	*Data Lakehouse*	No	No
Zhang *et al.* [60]	*Data Lake*	Yes	No
Tripathi *et al.*[61]	*Datasets*	Yes	No
Bellandi *et al.* [62]	*Big Data*	Yes	No
Schneider *et al.* [63]	*Data Lakehouse*	No	No

(*continued*)

Table 1. (*continued*)

Article	Repository	Medical domain	Diabetes focused
Vox *et al.* [64]	*Data Lakehouse*	No	No
Zhao *et al.* [65]	*Data Lake*	Yes	No
Harby *et al.* [66]	*Data Lakehouse*	Yes	No
Ren *et al.* [67]	*Data Lake*	Yes	No
Xiao *et al.* [68]	*Data Lakehouse*	Yes	No
Sheng *et al.* [69]	*Data Lakehouse*	Yes	No
This work	*Data Lakehouse*	Yes	Yes

3 Methodology

To analyze and select the articles for the state-of-the-art review, the PRISMA methodology (Preferred Reporting Items for Systematic Reviews and Meta-Analyses), in its updated 2020 version [70], was applied. PRISMA is a widely adopted framework in scoping reviews that ensures transparency and reproducibility throughout the literature selection process. Following this methodology, the review was conducted in several phases: identification, screening, eligibility, and inclusion.

In the identification phase, a comprehensive search was carried out across digital databases to gather relevant articles, the following search string was used: ("data warehouse" OR "data lake" OR "data lakehouse"). During the screening phase, duplicate entries and publications older than four years were removed. Thematic filters related to Data Lakehouse, Data Warehouse, and Data Lake were applied. In the eligibility phase, the full texts of the remaining articles were examined to verify their alignment with the study's objectives and methodological rigor. Finally, in the inclusion phase, a total of 50 articles were consolidated, meeting the criteria of recency (published within the last four years), thematic relevance, and pertinence to the medical or industrial domains.

The application of the PRISMA methodology enabled a systematic structure for the analysis, ensuring that the findings were grounded in a solid base of scientific evidence.

Figure 1 illustrates the article selection process. The review began with a search in major digital libraries, filtering results related to Data Lakehouse, Data Warehouse, and Data Lake. A total of 1652 articles were retrieved from the following sources: IEEE Xplore (312), ACM Digital Library (41), ScienceDirect (26), SpringerLink (96), Wiley Online Library (11), MDPI (174), and Google Scholar (992).

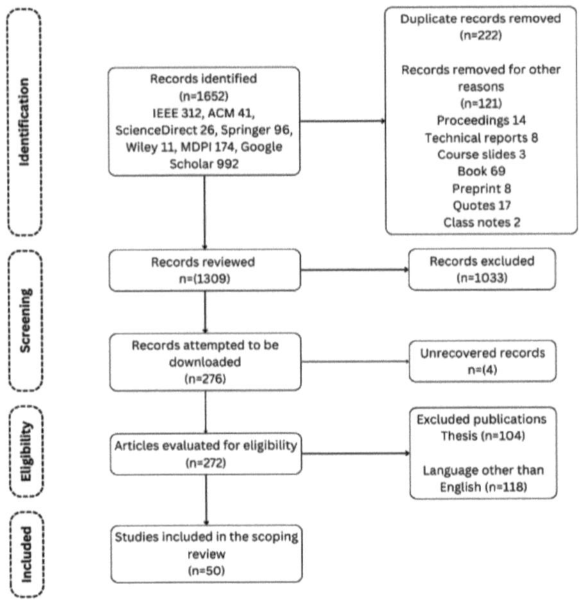

Fig. 1. PRISMA flowchart

Additionally, Fig. 2 illustrates the classification process of the analyzed articles. As a starting point, the selected articles were categorized based on the type of repository used and the domain in which they were applied (medical or industrial). Lastly, the technologies employed in their development were classified according to their function in data ingestion, processing, storage, analysis, and visualization.

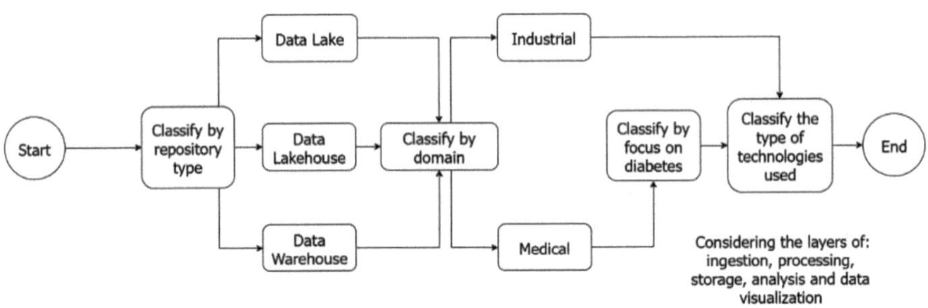

Fig. 2. Classification flowchart

To properly guide the research and focus on the desired outcomes, several questions were formulated:

- Which type of repository demonstrates the greatest versatility across the medical and industrial domains?
- How has the use of different repository types evolved in recent years?
- Which technologies lead data integration in the analyzed studies?

- Which technology dominates data processing, and in what proportion?
- What is the most frequently mentioned storage technology, and why is it considered so widely used?
- Which vendor dominates each stage of the data pipeline?

4 Results

This section presents the main findings of the literature review and introduces the proposed architecture, the analysis highlights trends in repository usage and supporting technologies, while also identifies gaps in current approaches. Building on these insights, we propose a Data Lakehouse architecture designed to address such limitations and provide a scalable, flexible framework for studying type 2 diabetes remission.

4.1 Literature Review Results

Figure 3 illustrates how different types of repositories are used across each domain. Notably, Data Lakehouse leads the chart, showing a most near equal usage in both medical and industrial settings—highlighting its broad range of applications. In contrast, Data Warehouse and Data Lake are predominantly applied within the medical domain.

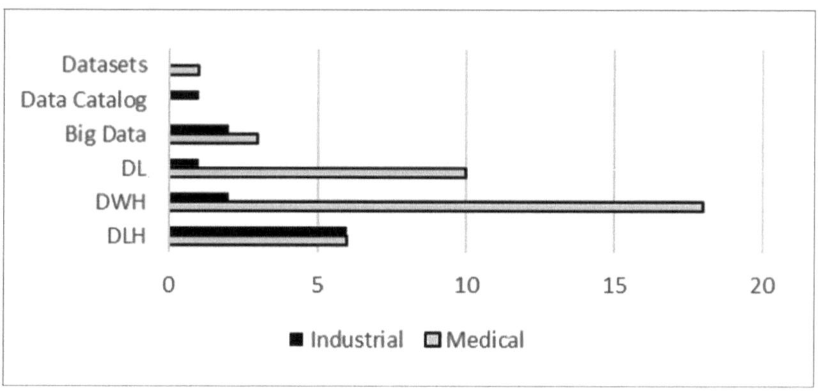

Fig. 3. Repositories by domain

Regarding the information presented in Fig. 4, the horizontal axis displays the years, while the chart categorizes the different types of repositories—DLH (Data Lakehouse), DWH (Data Warehouse), and DL (Data Lake)—by domain. The data reveals an upward trend in the use of all three repository types beginning in 2022. Data Warehouses focused on the medical domain were the most widely used during 2022 [21, 24, 28, 30, 37, 40] and 2023 [22, 26, 29, 39]. By 2024, the usage of Data Lakehouse [45, 63, 66, 69] and Data Warehouse [23, 25, 27, 34, 52, 53] became more balanced, with Data Lake falling entirely out of use.

Figure 5 shows the technologies used for data integration. Apache Kafka [44, 55, 63, 68] is one of the most widely used alternatives for this task, often in combination with

Apache NiFi [42, 50]. Beyond these two, a variety of other tools appear, depending on the origin and nature of the data involved in each study [32, 36, 52, 53, 63, 68].

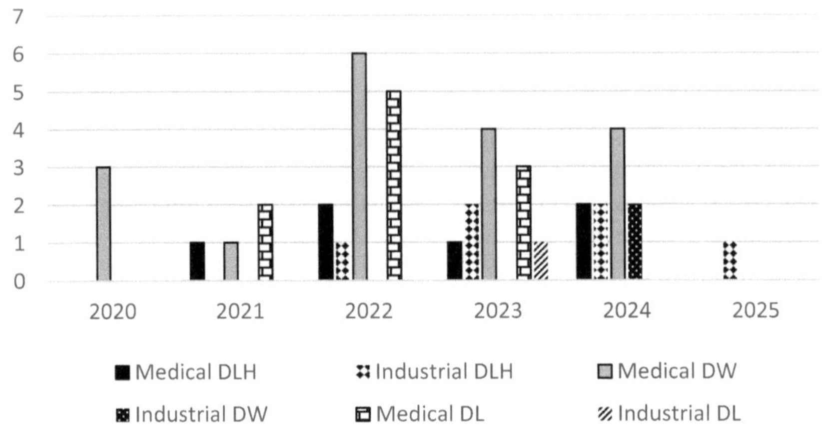

Fig. 4. Years of article publication by repository type and domain

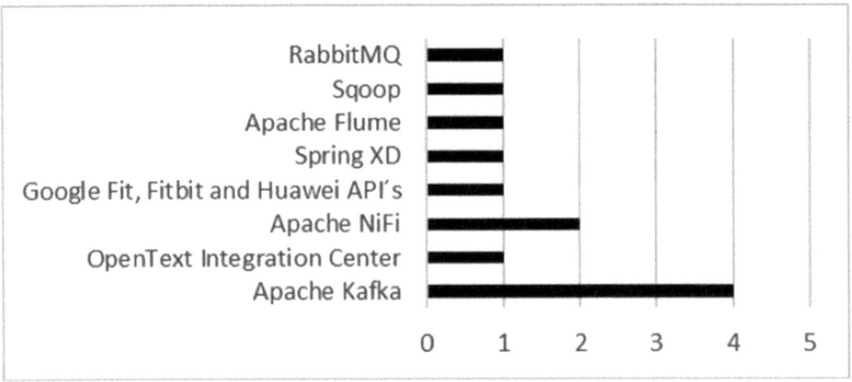

Fig. 5. Data integration technologies

Figure 6 illustrates the distribution of data processing technologies used in the reviewed studies, where Apache Spark stands out significantly ahead of its competitors [36, 42, 44, 45, 48, 54–56, 59, 60, 64–66, 68]. It serves as the core processing technology in 56% of the articles that mention specific processing tools—25 out of the total 50 studies. In some cases, such as [53, 54], and [63], Spark was used in combination with other technologies like Apache Flink or Apache Hudi, which are also among the most frequently adopted.

Figure 7 presents the storage technologies identified across the analyzed studies. Delta Lake [36, 44, 58, 63, 66–68] emerged as the most used solution, favored for its versatility and compatibility with various architectures. HDFS (Hadoop Distributed File System) [47, 54, 59, 68] and Amazon S3 [36, 50, 56, 58] are also widely adopted due to their scalability and ability to integrate with big data processing environments. Additionally, a group of less frequently mentioned technologies was classified under the "Others" category. This includes a diverse range of storage solutions such as Google Sheets, Sybase, HBase, InfluxDB, Kudu, IPFS (InterPlanetary File System), Microsoft Azure Data Lake, SQLite3, i2b2, Oracle 11G, MIMIC-III (Medical Information Mart for Intensive Care), Apache Cassandra, and Colossus, which were used in specific contexts depending on the nature of the data and the objectives of each study.

Also, a clear dominance of specific software vendors was observed across different stages of the data pipeline. Figure 8 shows the distribution of technologies employed in the processes of data ingestion, processing, and storage, highlighting those developed by the Apache Software Foundation versus those offered by other vendors. Among the most notable competitors are Amazon Web Services (AWS), which provides services such as AWS Glue and Amazon S3; Microsoft Azure, with tools like Azure Data Factory and Azure Synapse; and Databricks, known for its unified platform built around Apache Spark and Delta Lake.

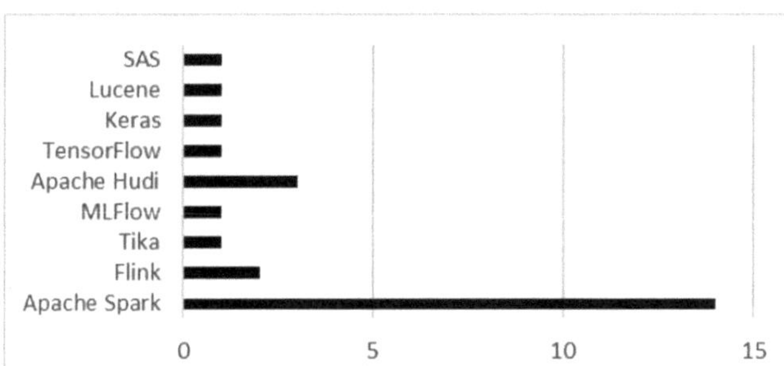

Fig. 6. Data processing technologies

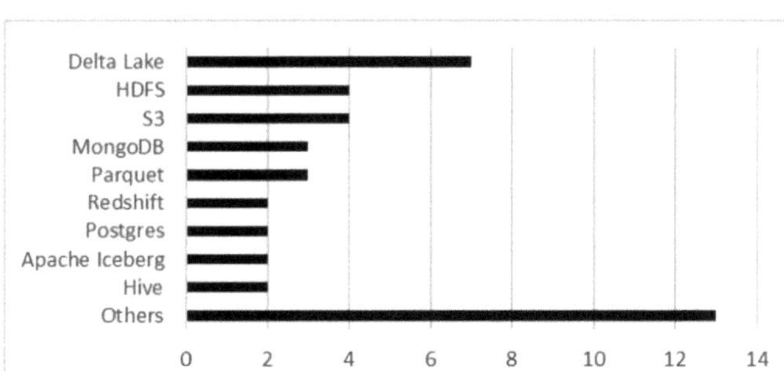

Fig. 7. Data storage technologies

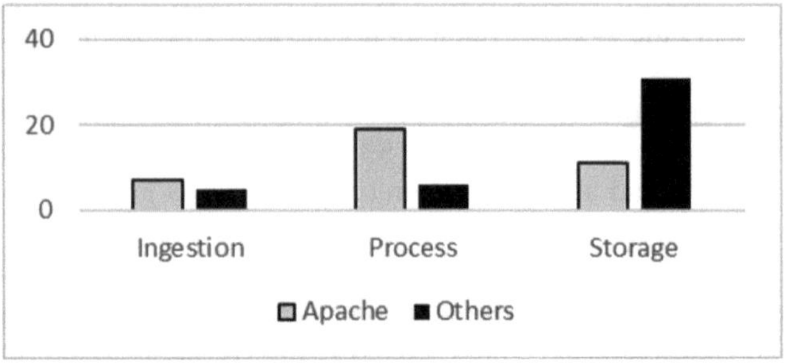

Fig. 8. Distribution of technologies by manufacturer

In the analysis and visualization stages, a wide range of technologies were identified across the reviewed studies. Due to the diversity of the works analyzed, the use of these tools was distributed heterogeneously, adapting to the specific needs of each study. This highlights the absence of a single, standardized approach for analysis and visualization; instead, the selected solutions vary according to the requirements of each domain and the available technological infrastructure.

Following a thorough review of 50 articles, none were found to explicitly integrate the approach proposed in this study. While some works address individual components such as storage, processing, or visualization within Data Lakehouse environments, none propose a comprehensive solution that combines these elements with a focus on discovering factors that enable type 2 diabetes remission within a unified framework. This reveals a gap in the current literature and underscores the importance of the present research. Accordingly, the architecture of the proposed Data Lakehouse is described below, developed in alignment with the findings and identified needs.

4.2 Data Lakehouse Architecture

To enable the development of the Data Lakehouse, a layered architecture is proposed, as illustrated in Fig. 9.

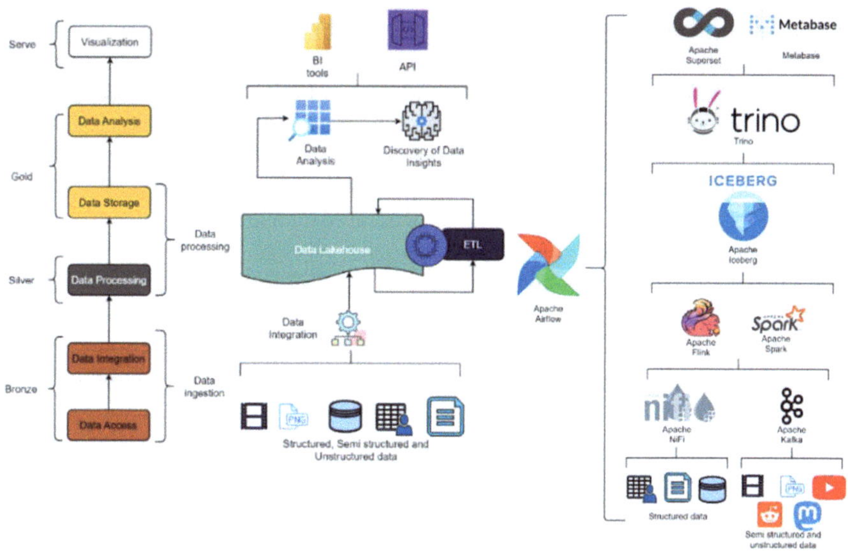

Fig. 9. Data Lakehouse architecture proposal

The selection of tools for this architecture was based on a comparative analysis with solutions from AWS and Azure. Open-source technologies were chosen due to their ability to deliver performance and scalability comparable to those of commercial providers, while offering the added advantages of greater flexibility and control over infrastructure customization. This decision also avoids licensing costs and benefits from an active developer community, allowing for continuous improvement and tailored adaptations without vendor lock-in.

The architecture consists of seven core components, described below:

1. Data Access: This represents the outermost layer of the Data Lakehouse, where data is sourced from a wide variety of origins, including traditional databases, genomic databases, files in various formats, scientific publications, and social media platforms (such as Facebook, TikTok, YouTube, among others). This layer enables the system to ingest structured, semi-structured, and unstructured information about type 2 diabetes remission.
2. Data Integration: The data integration layer employs technologies such as Apache NiFi and Apache Kafka to unify data from various sources into a centralized repository. Using icons and workflows that represent ETL (Extract, Transform, Load) processes, this layer illustrates the connectors and data paths that enable information to flow into the Data Lakehouse. ETL tools and processes play a critical role in preparing data for storage, ensuring it is in the proper format for subsequent stages.
3. Data Processing: This layer leverages Big Data technologies such as Apache Flink and Apache Spark to optimize data processing. These tools support both real-time and batch processing, ensuring efficient data handling and enabling the extraction of valuable insights aligned with the project's objectives. Flink and Spark are essential

for managing large volumes of data and supporting scalable processing within this architecture.

4. Data Storage: The Data Lakehouse architecture is built upon a storage system that combines the capabilities of both a Data Lake and a Data Warehouse. Technologies such as Apache Iceberg [71] is used to manage data transactions and versioning, ensuring consistency and high availability of the repository. These technologies enable the Lakehouse to handle structured and unstructured data in a unified manner, adapting to the project's storage and querying needs.
5. Data Analysis: The analysis layer includes Trino [72] to explore and query the data stored in the Lakehouse. These technologies provide a robust foundation for large-scale data analysis and deliver results that are accessible to visualization tools. Trino improves the speed and efficiency of queries, ensuring that users can obtain accurate and timely insights.
6. Data Visualization: Finally, the visualization layer is implemented using tools such as Apache Superset [73] and Metabase [74]. These dashboard applications allow for the creation of visual reports and interactive charts that help users interpret and understand the outcomes of data analysis. Effective visualization supports informed decision-making by offering a clear and accessible representation of the processed data.
7. Workflow Orchestration: To coordinate, monitor, and automate the execution of data workflows across the architecture, Apache Airflow [75] is employed. Airflow enables the scheduling of data ingestion, processing, and analysis tasks through Directed Acyclic Graphs (DAGs), ensuring that dependent processes are executed in the correct sequence. This orchestration layer allows for the implementation of event-driven triggers, enabling the system to react to specific conditions such as the arrival of new data or the completion of a processing stage without manual intervention. Additionally, Airflow's monitoring capabilities provide detailed logs and alerts, facilitating operational oversight and ensuring the reliability and reproducibility of analytical pipelines.

4.3 Implementation Prototype

To validate the feasibility of the proposed architecture, an initial functional prototype was developed. This prototype focuses on the ingestion and semantic classification of scientific literature related to type 2 diabetes remission, facilitating the early identification and structuring of remission-associated factors.

The ingestion pipeline was implemented using Apache Airflow, which orchestrates a sequence of tasks executed every five minutes. The pipeline scans a designated folder for new scientific articles in PDF format. Upon detection, each file is processed using PyMuPDF to extract its full textual content.

Subsequently, a language model (DeepSeek 32B [76]) deployed locally via Ollama [77] semantically classifies the extracted text. The model assigns each article to a clinical category (e.g., diet, physical activity, medication, or surgical intervention) and determines its likely impact on diabetes remission (positive, neutral, or negative). The classification result is returned as a structured JSON response.

Once classified, the metadata and a summary of the text are published to the Apache Kafka topic *pdf-articulos*, while the original PDF is stored in MinIO [78] for traceability and further reference. This approach enables downstream processing and analytics without loss of source context.

To complete the end-to-end ingestion and processing flow, a second Airflow DAG (directed acyclic graph), named *kafka_to_iceberg_dag*, was implemented. This DAG triggers a Spark job via a BashOperator inside the spark-iceberg container. The job consumes messages from the Kafka topic, deserializes the JSON payload, and performs schema validation and transformation using Apache Spark.

The processed records are then persisted into Apache Iceberg tables, which serve as the structured and query layer of the platform. Each entry is stored in the appropriate table—such as Nutrition, Medication, or Activity—based on the clinical category inferred by the language model.

This prototype demonstrates the platform's ability to integrate heterogeneous data sources, perform early semantic annotation, and distribute results across the Lakehouse infrastructure to support scalable, data-driven clinical analysis.

The flow of this prototype is illustrated in Fig. 10.

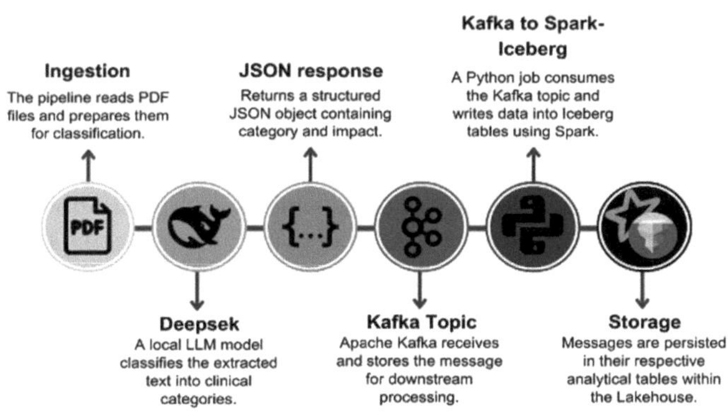

Fig. 10. Prototype flow

4.4 Infrastructure Details

The prototype and the overall Lakehouse platform have been fully containerized using Docker Compose to ensure modularity, scalability, and reproducibility. The deployed environment includes the following components:

Data ingestion and orchestration:

- Apache Airflow 2.7.3 orchestrates DAGs for ingestion, classification, and dispatch.
- PyMuPDF for PDF parsing and text extraction.
- Ollama serving DeepSeek 32B for local, offline LLM inference.
- Apache Kafka for message streaming and decoupled processing.

Data storage and Lakehouse layer:

- MinIO emulates an S3-compatible object store for raw file storage.

- Apache Iceberg serves as the Lakehouse catalog for structured and versioned data.
- Apache Spark 3.3.2 handles batch and streaming processing tasks, with built-in support for Iceberg.

Query and visualization:

- Trino provides distributed SQL querying across Iceberg tables.
- Apache Superset enables dashboard creation and data exploration.

Orchestration support services:

- Apache Zookeeper and Kafka-UI for Kafka management.
- PostgreSQL as backend for Airflow metadata.
- Custom Python scripts and notebooks mounted as volumes for exploratory and development tasks.

This stack enables end-to-end data flow: from ingestion and classification to persistent storage, querying, and dashboard-based exploration—all with open-source tools that support extensibility and deployment in resource-constrained environments.

4.5 Clinical Data Model

The data model was designed to support the capture and analysis of clinical and behavioral factors associated with type 2 diabetes remission. It focuses on storing events or interventions—dietary, pharmacological, physical, or surgical—linked to individual patients, along with associated metadata and derived indicators.

At the core of the model is the Factors table, which serves as a central hub connecting various types of clinical data through foreign keys to domain-specific tables:

- Nutrition (dietary patterns)
- Medication (prescribed drugs and dosages)
- Physical_Activity (type, frequency, and energy expenditure)
- Surgical_Interventions (clinical or surgical procedures)
- Sentiment (classification sentiment derived from source content)
- File_Metadata (information about document origin, upload date, category, and classification)

Each entry in the Factors table is also associated with a specific patient record from the Patient table, enabling the longitudinal analysis of changes over time—such as BMI and age progression—and their possible connection to remission outcomes.

This schema is depicted in Fig. 11.

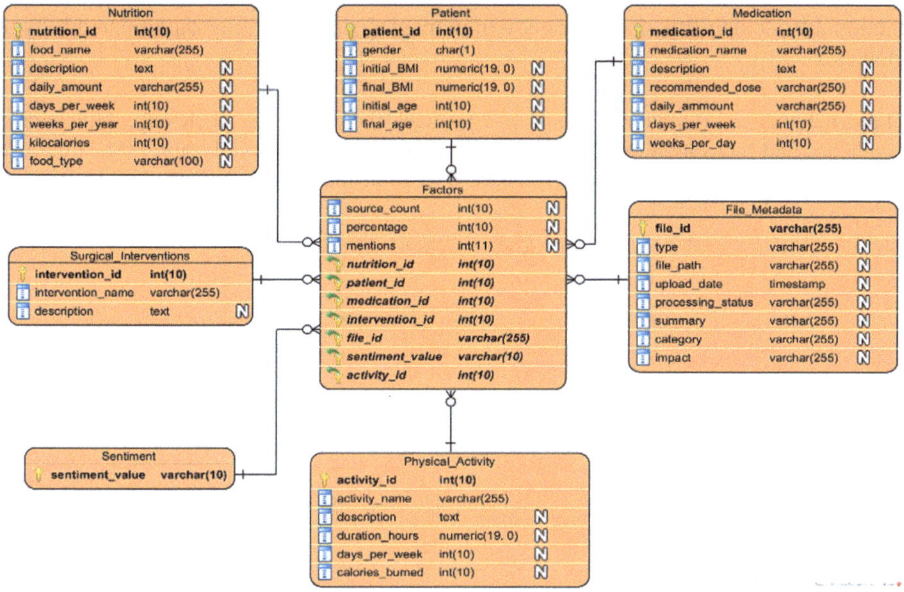

Fig. 11. Entity Relationship diagram

Additionally, the model records key contextual attributes, such as initial and final BMI, age range, and text summary, providing the foundation for longitudinal analysis. The Factors table is designed to support time-partitioned storage, allowing efficient tracking of remission-related variables over time and across diverse data sources.

This relational structure balances clinical expressiveness with analytical tractability, enabling both descriptive and predictive analysis in future stages of development.

5 Conclusions

The development of a Data Lakehouse represents an innovative and effective solution to address the challenges associated with managing complex data related to type 2 diabetes. Through the research and literature review, it was possible to identify how previous studies have been developed in similar environments by analyzing their approaches, technologies used, and areas of application. This review revealed the absence of a comprehensive solution specifically aimed at identifying the factors that influence disease remission, reinforcing the need to create a specialized Data Lakehouse for this domain.

The implementation of this technology enables the integration and analysis of large volumes of multi-source data, optimizing the efficiency of data storage and processing. Additionally, it provides an advanced analytical environment that facilitates the generation of more accurate insights, thus enhancing personalized medical decision-making and improving clinical outcomes and patients' quality of life.

As future work, the full development of the Data Lakehouse will be carried out using the technologies identified in this study. Subsequently, extensive testing will be performed to ensure that the solution meets the defined objectives, guaranteeing its functionality, scalability, and efficiency in managing and analyzing data related to type 2 diabetes.

Acknowledgments. The authors would like to thank the Secretariat of Science, Humanities, Technology, and Innovation (SECIHTI) and the Secretariat of Public Education (SEP) through the PRODEP program for funding this project. Special thanks are also extended to the Instituto Tecnológico de Orizaba for serving as the home institution of the first author and the workplace of the co-authors, as well as for providing the necessary support to carry out this research.

Conflicts of Interest/Competing Interest. The authors declare no competing interests.

References

1. Lim, E.L., Hollingsworth, K.G., Aribisala, B.S., Chen, M.J., Mathers, J.C., Taylor, R.: Reversal of type 2 diabetes: normalisation of beta cell function in association with decreased pancreas and liver triacylglycerol. Diabetologia **54**, 2506–2514 (2011). https://doi.org/10.1007/s00125-011-2204-7
2. Shamanna, P., et al.: Reducing HbA1c in type 2 diabetes using digital twin technology-enabled precision nutrition: a retrospective analysis. Diabetes Ther. **11**, 2703–2714 (2020). https://doi.org/10.1007/s13300-020-00931-w
3. Ricci, M., et al.: Remission of type 2 diabetes: a critical appraisal. Front. Endocrinol. (Lausanne) **14** (2023). https://doi.org/10.3389/fendo.2023.1125961
4. Lafarge, J.-C., et al.: French National Authority for Health assessment of metabolic surgery for type 2 diabetes remission—a meta-analysis in patients with class I to III obesity. Diabetes Metab. **50**, 101495 (2024). https://doi.org/10.1016/j.diabet.2023.101495
5. Mirghani, H., Altedlawi Albalawi, I.: Metabolic surgery versus usual care effects on diabetes remission: a systematic review and meta-analysis. Diabetol. Metab. Syndr. **15**, 31 (2023). https://doi.org/10.1186/s13098-023-01001-4
6. Zhou, X., Zeng, C.: Diabetes remission of bariatric surgery and nonsurgical treatments in type 2 diabetes patients who failure to meet the criteria for surgery: a systematic review and meta-analysis. BMC Endocr. Disord. **23**, 46 (2023). https://doi.org/10.1186/s12902-023-01283-9
7. Lean, M.E., et al.: 5-year follow-up of the randomised diabetes remission clinical trial (DiRECT) of continued support for weight loss maintenance in the UK: an extension study. Lancet Diabetes Endocrinol. **12**, 233–246 (2024). https://doi.org/10.1016/S2213-8587(23)00385-6
8. Mozaffari, H., et al.: The impact of food-based dietary strategies on achieving type 2 diabetes remission: a systematic review. Diabetes Metab. Syndr.: Clin. Res. Rev. **18**, 103096 (2024). https://doi.org/10.1016/j.dsx.2024.103096
9. Churuangsuk, C., Hall, J., Reynolds, A., Griffin, S.J., Combet, E., Lean, M.E.J.: Diets for weight management in adults with type 2 diabetes: an umbrella review of published meta-analyses and systematic review of trials of diets for diabetes remission. Diabetologia **65**, 14–36 (2022). https://doi.org/10.1007/s00125-021-05577-2
10. Corbin, L.J., et al.: The metabolomic signature of weight loss and remission in the diabetes remission clinical trial (DiRECT). Diabetologia **67**, 74–87 (2024). https://doi.org/10.1007/s00125-023-06019-x
11. Gregg, E.W., et al.: Impact of remission from type 2 diabetes on long-term health outcomes: findings from the Look AHEAD study. Diabetologia **67**, 459–469 (2024). https://doi.org/10.1007/s00125-023-06048-6

12. Harby, A.A., Zulkernine, F.: From data warehouse to lakehouse: a comparative review. In: 2022 IEEE International Conference on Big Data (Big Data), pp. 389–395. IEEE (2022). https://doi.org/10.1109/BigData55660.2022.10020719
13. Clevertech Partners, L.: Data lakes vs data warehouses. https://lumenalta.com/insights/data-lakes-vs-data-warehouses. Accessed 14 Aug 2025
14. Hart, inc.: Using data lakes and warehouses to unlock enterprise-wide insights. https://hart.com/blog/using-data-lakes-and-warehouses-to-unlock-enterprise-wide-insights. Accessed 14 Aug 2025
15. Reis Joe, H.M.: Fundamentals of Data Engineering. O'Reilly Media, Inc. (2022)
16. Apache NiFi Team: Apache NiFi Documentation, https://nifi.apache.org/documentation/v2/. Accessed 26 Aug 2024
17. The Apache Software Foundation: Apache Kafka Documentation. https://kafka.apache.org/documentation/. Accessed 26 Aug 2024
18. The Apache Software Foundation: Apache Flink. https://flink.apache.org/. Accessed 26 Aug 2024
19. The Apache Software Foundation: Apache Spark, https://spark.apache.org/. Accessed 26 Aug 2024
20. Fleuren, L.M., et al.: The dutch data warehouse, a multicenter and full-admission electronic health records database for critically ill COVID-19 patients. Crit. Care **25**, 304 (2021). https://doi.org/10.1186/s13054-021-03733-z
21. Pressat-Laffouilhère, T., et al.: Evaluation of Doc'EDS: a French semantic search tool to query health documents from a clinical data warehouse. BMC Med. Inform. Decis. Mak. **22**, 34 (2022). https://doi.org/10.1186/s12911-022-01762-4
22. Lamer, A., Moussa, M.D., Marcilly, R., Logier, R., Vallet, B., Tavernier, B.: Development and usage of an anesthesia data warehouse: lessons learnt from a 10-year project. J. Clin. Monit. Comput. **37**, 461–472 (2023). https://doi.org/10.1007/s10877-022-00898-y
23. Ansoborlo, M., et al.: Feasibility of automated surveillance of implantable devices in orthopaedics via clinical data warehouse: the Studio study. BMC Med. Inform. Decis. Mak. **24**, 324 (2024). https://doi.org/10.1186/s12911-024-02697-8
24. Kaspar, M., et al.: Querying a clinical data warehouse for combinations of clinical and imaging data. J. Digit. Imaging **36**, 715–724 (2022). https://doi.org/10.1007/s10278-022-00727-3
25. Baum, L., et al.: An interactive dashboard for analyzing user interaction patterns in the i2b2 clinical data warehouse. BMC Med. Inform. Decis. Mak. **24**, 333 (2024). https://doi.org/10.1186/s12911-024-02748-0
26. Ndisha, M., et al.: Leveraging electronic medical records for HIV testing, care, and treatment programming in Kenya—the national data warehouse project. BMC Med. Inform. Decis. Mak. **23**, 183 (2023). https://doi.org/10.1186/s12911-023-02265-6
27. Cheng-Zarate, D., et al.: Creating a data warehouse to support monitoring of NSQHS blood management standard from EMR data. BMC Med. Inform. Decis. Mak. **24**, 353 (2024). https://doi.org/10.1186/s12911-024-02732-8
28. Turcan, G., Peker, S.: A multidimensional data warehouse design to combat the health pandemics. J. Data Inf. Manage. **4**, 371–386 (2022). https://doi.org/10.1007/s42488-022-00082-6
29. Arnold, C.G., et al.: Accessing and utilizing clinical and genomic data from an electronic health record data warehouse. Transl. Med. Commun. **8**, 7 (2023). https://doi.org/10.1186/s41231-023-00140-0
30. Windsor, C., et al.: Healthcare trajectory of critically ill patients with necrotizing soft tissue infections: a multicenter retrospective cohort study using the clinical data warehouse of Greater Paris University Hospitals. Ann. Intensive Care **12**, 115 (2022). https://doi.org/10.1186/s13613-022-01087-5

31. Shae, Z.-Y., Tsai, J.J.P.: On the design of medical data ecosystem for improving healthcare research and commercial incentive. In: 2021 IEEE Third International Conference on Cognitive Machine Intelligence (CogMI), pp. 124–131. IEEE (2021). https://doi.org/10.1109/CogMI52975.2021.00024
32. Melchor-Uceda, I.A., Olivares-Rojas, J.C., Gutierrez-Gnecchi, J.A., Garcia-Ramirez, M.C., Reyes-Archundia, E., Tellez-Anguiano, A.C.: Data ingestion system for interoperability and integration of hospital data online and in real time. In: 2021 Mexican International Conference on Computer Science (ENC), pp. 1–5. IEEE (2021). https://doi.org/10.1109/ENC53357.2021.9534795
33. Babu, D., Girimadesh, S., Karthick, K., Manivannan, P. T., Prabhu, S.: Retrieval of large data from medical lake repository-heart note. In: 2022 1st International Conference on Computational Science and Technology (ICCST), pp. 518–522. IEEE (2022). https://doi.org/10.1109/ICCST55948.2022.10040351
34. Gayathri, S., Rani, A.J.M., Ravi, C.N., Jeyalaxmi, M., Pandi, V.S.: A novel approach to design secured and privacy enabled health data linkage system based on cyber security principles. In: 2024 IEEE International Conference on Big Data & Machine Learning (ICBDML), pp. 14–20. IEEE (2024). https://doi.org/10.1109/ICBDML60909.2024.10577373
35. Amara, N., Lamouchi, O., Gattoufi, S.: Design of a breast image data warehouse framework. In: 2020 International Multi-Conference on: "Organization of Knowledge and Advanced Technologies" (OCTA), pp. 1–13. IEEE (2020). https://doi.org/10.1109/OCTA49274.2020.9151855
36. Kumar, D., Li, S.: Separating storage and compute with the databricks lakehouse platform. In: 2022 IEEE 9th International Conference on Data Science and Advanced Analytics (DSAA), pp. 1–2. IEEE (2022). https://doi.org/10.1109/DSAA54385.2022.10032386
37. Maria Hernandez Cruz, L., et al.: Use of the Hefesto v2.0 methodology to implement a data warehouse: case applied COVID-19. In: 2022 17th Iberian Conference on Information Systems and Technologies (CISTI), pp. 1–6. IEEE (2022). https://doi.org/10.23919/CISTI54924.2022.9820132
38. Spengler, H., Gatz, I., Kohlmayer, F., Kuhn, K.A., Prasser, F.: Improving data quality in medical research: a monitoring architecture for clinical and translational data warehouses. In: 2020 IEEE 33rd International Symposium on Computer-Based Medical Systems (CBMS), pp. 415–420. IEEE (2020). https://doi.org/10.1109/CBMS49503.2020.00085
39. Sudharson, D., Divya, P., Saranya, K., Dubey, A.K., Vijay, S., Mayuri, G.: A novel AI framework for assuring data sustainability in health care dataset. In: 2023 Third International Conference on Ubiquitous Computing and Intelligent Information Systems (ICUIS), pp. 161–166. IEEE (2023). https://doi.org/10.1109/ICUIS60567.2023.00035
40. Setiadi, T.F., Rahutomo, R.: A data warehouse schema for monitoring regional COVID-19 case registration. In: 2022 International Conference on Information Management and Technology (ICIMTech), pp. 144–148. IEEE (2022). https://doi.org/10.1109/ICIMTech55957.2022.9915222
41. Neamah, A.F.: Flexible data warehouse: towards building an integrated electronic health record architecture. In: 2020 International Conference on Smart Electronics and Communication (ICOSEC), pp. 1038–1042. IEEE (2020). https://doi.org/10.1109/ICOSEC49089.2020.9215433
42. Yeng, P.K., et al.: HEALER2: a framework for secure data lake towards healthcare digital transformation efforts in low and middle-income countries. In: 2023 International Conference on Emerging Trends in Networks and Computer Communications (ETNCC), pp. 1–9. IEEE (2023). https://doi.org/10.1109/ETNCC59188.2023.10284959

43. Dilli Babu, M., Ramesh, K., Renjith, P.N., Prabha, B.: A risk model based heart disease prediction using data lake architecture. In: 2022 First International Conference on Electrical, Electronics, Information and Communication Technologies (ICEEICT), pp. 1–6. IEEE (2022). https://doi.org/10.1109/ICEEICT53079.2022.9768452
44. Kumar, M., Lee, S., Hoon Park, B., Blum, J., Ward, M., Nebeker, J.R.: Advanced health information technology analytic framework and application to hazard detection. In: 2020 IEEE International Conference on Big Data (Big Data), pp. 1–4. IEEE (2020). https://doi.org/10.1109/BigData50022.2020.9442793
45. Patil, S., Belloum, A.S.Z.A.: Processing FHIR in modern data lakehouse. In: 2024 IEEE 20th International Conference on e-Science (e-Science), pp. 1–7. IEEE (2024). https://doi.org/10.1109/e-Science62913.2024.10678734
46. Abdelhedi, F., Jemmali, R., Zurfluh, G.: Medical data lake query assistance. In: 2023 20th ACS/IEEE International Conference on Computer Systems and Applications (AICCSA), pp. 1–8. IEEE (2023). https://doi.org/10.1109/AICCSA59173.2023.10479336
47. Babu M.D., Ramesh, K., Renjith, P.N., Prabha, B.: An efficient healthcare medication system with clustering algorithm using euclidean distance adjoining data lake. In: 2022 International Conference on Advances in Computing, Communication and Applied Informatics (ACCAI), pp. 1–5. IEEE (2022). https://doi.org/10.1109/ACCAI53970.2022.9752473
48. González-Velázquez, R., et al.: Smart factory hub – towards a data mesh in smart manufacturing. Procedia Comput. Sci. **232**, 2709–2719 (2024). https://doi.org/10.1016/j.procs.2024.02.088
49. Oliveira, B., Duarte, A., Oliveira, Ó.: Towards a data catalog for data analytics. Procedia Comput. Sci. **237**, 691–700 (2024). https://doi.org/10.1016/j.procs.2024.05.155
50. Harby, A.A., Zulkernine, F.: Data lakehouse: a survey and experimental study. Inf. Syst. **127**, 102460 (2025). https://doi.org/10.1016/j.is.2024.102460
51. Bindal, P., Madan, K.: Quantum flow: enterprise data orchestration and processing suite. In: Proceedings of the 2024 Sixteenth International Conference on Contemporary Computing, pp. 577–584. ACM, New York (2024). https://doi.org/10.1145/3675888.3676116
52. Edara, P., Forbesj, J., Li, B.: Vortex: a stream-oriented storage engine for big data analytics. In: Companion of the 2024 International Conference on Management of Data, pp. 175–187. ACM, New York (2024). https://doi.org/10.1145/3626246.3653396
53. Batalla, S.: From data to value: turn unstructured data into a dimensional data model using data warehouse (SAP BW/4HANA) and business intelligence (SAP Lumira designer) visualizations. In: Proceedings of the 2024 10th International Conference on Computer Technology Applications, pp. 103–108. ACM, New York (2024). https://doi.org/10.1145/3674558.3674572
54. Hoseini, S., Ali, A., Shaker, H., Quix, C.: SEDAR: a semantic data reservoir for heterogeneous datasets. In: Proceedings of the 32nd ACM International Conference on Information and Knowledge Management, pp. 5056–5060. ACM, New York (2023). https://doi.org/10.1145/3583780.3614753
55. Siddiqi, M.H., Idris, M., Alruwaili, M.: FAIR health informatics: a health informatics framework for verifiable and explainable data analysis. Healthcare **11**, 1713 (2023). https://doi.org/10.3390/healthcare11121713
56. Wang, P., et al.: A construction system of lake-warehouse integration in the electricity industry based on hudi. In: Proceedings of the 3rd International Conference on Public Management and Big Data Analysis, PMBDA 2023, 15–17 December 2023, Nanjing, China. EAI (2024). https://doi.org/10.4108/eai.15-12-2023.2345365
57. Begoli, E., Goethert, I., Knight, K.: A Lakehouse architecture for the management and analysis of heterogeneous data for biomedical research and mega-biobanks. In: 2021 IEEE International Conference on Big Data (Big Data), pp. 4643–4651. IEEE (2021). https://doi.org/10.1109/BigData52589.2021.9671534

58. Li, R., Choy, M., Laik, M.N.: A cloud data lakehouse-based AI diagnostic solution for small and medium-sized health facilities. In: Proceedings of the International Conference on Industrial Engineering and Operations Management, pp. 945–956. IEOM Society International, Michigan (2022). https://doi.org/10.46254/AP03.20220190
59. Park, S., Yang, C.-S., Kim, J.: Design of vessel data lakehouse with big data and AI analysis technology for vessel monitoring system. Electron. (Basel) **12**, 1943 (2023). https://doi.org/10.3390/electronics12081943
60. Zhang, Y., et al.: A heterogeneous multi-modal medical data fusion framework supporting hybrid data exploration. Health Inf. Sci. Syst. **10**, 22 (2022). https://doi.org/10.1007/s13755-022-00183-x
61. Tripathi, A., Waqas, A., Venkatesan, K., Yilmaz, Y., Rasool, G.: Building flexible, scalable, and machine learning-ready multimodal oncology datasets. Sensors. **24**, 1634 (2024). https://doi.org/10.3390/s24051634
62. Bellandi, V., Ceravolo, P., Maggesi, J., Maghool, S.: Data management for continuous learning in EHR systems. ACM Trans. Internet Technol. (2024). https://doi.org/10.1145/3660634
63. Schneider, J., Lutsch, A., Gröger, C., Schwarz, H., Mitschang, B.: First experiences on the application of lakehouses in industrial practice. In: 35th GI-Workshop on Foundations of Databases (2024)
64. Vox, C., Broneske, D., Piewek, J., Feigel, J., Saake, G.: Investigating lakehouse-backbones for vehicle sensor data. Presented at the (2023). https://doi.org/10.1007/978-3-031-39847-6_17
65. Zhao, T., et al.: Multi-modal medical data exploration based on data lake. In: Health Information Science: 12th International Conference, Melbourne, pp. 213–222 (2023). https://doi.org/10.1007/978-981-99-7108-4_18
66. Harby, A., Al-Yateem, N., Zulkernine, F.H.: Revolutionizing healthcare management: architecture of a web-based medical triage service. Presented at the July (2024). https://doi.org/10.1109/COMPSAC61105.2024.00299
67. Ren, P., et al.: A hybrid medical causal inference platform based on data lake. In: Health Information Science: 11th International Conference, pp. 136–144 (2022). https://doi.org/10.1007/978-3-031-20627-6_13
68. Xiao, Q., et al.: MHDML: construction of a medical lakehouse for multi-source heterogeneous data. In: Health Information Science Lecture Notes in Computer Science, pp. 127–135 (2022). https://doi.org/10.1007/978-3-031-20627-6_12
69. Sheng, M., et al.: A multi-source heterogeneous medical data enhancement framework based on lakehouse. Health Inf. Sci. Syst. **12**, 37 (2024). https://doi.org/10.1007/s13755-024-00295-6
70. Page, M.J., et al.: Declaración PRISMA 2020: una guía actualizada para la publicación de revisiones sistemáticas. Rev. Esp. Cardiol. **74**, 790–799 (2021). https://doi.org/10.1016/j.recesp.2021.06.016
71. The Apache Software Foundation: Apache Iceberg. https://iceberg.apache.org/. Accessed 12 May 2025
72. Trino Software Foundation: Trino. https://trino.io/. Accessed 27 Aug 2024
73. The Apache Software Foundation: Apache Superset. https://superset.apache.org/. Accessed 26 Aug 2024
74. Metabase: A tour of Metabase. https://www.metabase.com/learn/metabase-basics/getting-started/tour-of-metabase. Accessed 08 Sept 2024
75. The Apache Software Foundation: Apache Airflow. https://airflow.apache.org/. Accessed 12 May 2025
76. DeepSeek: DeepSeek R1. https://www.deepseek.com/en. Accessed 14 Aug 2025
77. Ollama: Ollama Chat & build with open models. https://ollama.com/. Accessed 14 Aug 2025

78. MinIO, Inc.: MinIO Exascale Object Store for AI Data, Agentic Computing, and Analytics. https://www.min.io/. Accessed 14 Aug 2025

Artificial Intelligence and Scientific Computing

A Bio-Inspired SN P-Based Visual Cryptographic for Binary Data Hiding in Digital Images

Karen Alejandra Valerio-Trigueros(✉), Luis Ángel Olvera-Martínez, Manuel Cedillo-Hernandez, Carlos Adolfo Díaz-Rodríguez, and Juan Carlos Sanchez-Garcia

Instituto Politecnico Nacional, Escuela Superior de Ingenieria Mecanica y Electrica, Unidad Culhuacán, Avenida Santa Ana 1000, San Francisco Culhuacan, Culhuacan CTM V, Coyoacán, 04440 Ciudad de México, Mexico
{kvaleriot2100,lolveram1500}@alumno.ipn.mx, {mcedilloh,jcsanche}@ipn.mx

Abstract. This proposal introduces a novel system for data hiding in binary images, integrating visual cryptography with Spiking Neural P (SN P) systems incorporating astrocyte-controlled structural plasticity. The SN P system automatically generates the cryptographic shares required for the visual encryption process. A secret message is split into 5-bit groups: the first 3 bits are embedded in the first share, and the remaining 2 bits in the second, using predefined and visually imperceptible patterns to preserve image appearance. This embedding strategy ensures that the visual content of the shares remains practically unchanged, thus maintaining discretion and security. Experimental results show the shares do not display significant visual changes post-embedding. To assess the effectiveness of the proposed method, quantitative metrics such as entropy and the Structural Similarity Index (SSIM) were employed, ensuring objective and reproducible evaluation. The average SSIM value obtained was 0.44885, reflecting a moderate degree of structural similarity between the original and the resulting images after data hiding. The results indicate high structural preservation with only minor variations in entropy. These findings objectively demonstrate the low perceptual impact of the hiding process and the high level of discretion achieved by the method.

Keywords: Information security · Data embedding · Spiking Neural P System (SN P) · Astrocyte Controlled Plasticity · Visual content protection

1 Introduction

In an era where digital communication is present in every aspect of modern life, ensuring the secure transmission and storage of information has become a critical challenge across diverse domains, including personal messaging, financial systems, healthcare, and national security. As the exchange of sensitive data over open networks increases, so too does the risk of interception, unauthorized access, and manipulation [1,2].

C. Palma-Preciado et al. (Eds.): CORE 2025, ACSAR 3, pp. 121–135, 2026.
https://doi.org/10.1007/978-3-032-08894-9_8

Among various forms of digital content, images have emerged as a dominant medium due to their ability to rapidly convey complex information and their widespread use in fields such as social media, health, surveillance, and biometrics [2]. To address the growing demand for secure visual data exchange, cryptography and data hiding have become essential technologies. While cryptography transforms data into unintelligible formats to ensure confidentiality, data hiding conceals the very presence of sensitive information often by embedding it imperceptibly within images. However, conventional encryption methods, though effective for textual data, face limitations when applied to images, such as high computational complexity and visible artifacts that degrade visual quality [3,4].

To overcome these limitations, visual cryptography and data hiding have emerged as complementary techniques for protecting visual information. Visual cryptography encrypts an image by dividing it into multiple shares, each appearing as random noise, which can only reveal the original image when correctly superimposed [5–7]. Data hiding enhances this by embedding secret content into the shares, reinforcing security through both obfuscation and redundancy [8]. The combination of these techniques offers the dual advantages of encryption (confidentiality) and steganography (invisibility), particularly effective when the resulting shares resemble visual noise to external observers.

This paper introduces a novel framework that integrates visual cryptography with data hiding, implemented through Spiking Neural P systems (SN P) enhanced by astrocyte-controlled structural plasticity. SN P systems, inspired by biological neural networks, offer intrinsic parallelism and distributed computation. The integration of astrocyte-regulated plasticity allows the system to dynamically adapt its internal structure based on activity patterns, introducing biologically plausible variability and non-determinism into the share generation process. This dynamic behavior significantly reduces the predictability of traditional visual cryptography schemes and enhances security.

The remainder of this paper is organized as follows. Section 2 introduces the theoretical foundations of visual cryptography, binary image data hiding, and Spiking Neural P systems. Section 3 describes the proposed methodology, including the design of the SN P-based circuit and the data hiding scheme. Section 4 presents the experimental results, including visual comparisons, quantitative assessments, and performance benchmarks. Finally, Sect. 5 discusses the findings and outlines directions for future research.

2 Background

Visual Cryptography (VC). The first formal method of visual cryptography was proposed by Naor and Shamir (1994) [5]. Visual cryptography is an image encoding technique, initially based on binary images, but it has also been extended to work with color images [9–11]. This technique allows an image to be shared among several users by dividing it into parts called shares. Each share, by itself, reveals nothing about the original image. The goal is for the original image to be recoverable only by properly superimposing these parts, as the hidden information in the shares is only revealed when they are correctly aligned. This method is based on visual encryption, in such a way that decoding does not require high computational power, but rather relies on human visual perception. When the shares are superimposed, the image is visually reconstructed without the need for complex processing. In the field of security, visual cryptography has found applications in various areas, such as the protection of sensitive data, document authentication, and personal identification systems [5,6,12].

To generate the shares, basis matrices composed of binary values are used, which define how each pixel of the original image will be encoded. These matrices vary depending on the visual cryptography scheme used: whether it is the traditional threshold scheme (k,n)-CV, the general access structure scheme, or the extended scheme.

Once the matrices are constructed, the share generation process is identical for all variants. Therefore, it is sufficient to properly define these matrices to ensure correct encoding [6].

The two fundamental matrices used are show in Eq. (1)

- S^0, employed when the pixel in the secret image is black.
- S^1, used when the pixel is white.

Both matrices have dimensions $n \times m$, where:

- n is the total number of participants (and therefore, the number of generated shares),
- m is the number of subpixels per original pixel (expansion factor).

$$\mathbf{S}^0 = \begin{bmatrix} s^0_{1,1} & s^0_{1,2} & \cdots & s^0_{1,m} \\ s^0_{2,1} & s^0_{2,2} & \cdots & s^0_{2,m} \\ \vdots & \vdots & \ddots & \vdots \\ s^0_{n,1} & s^0_{n,2} & \cdots & s^0_{n,m} \end{bmatrix}, \quad \mathbf{S}^1 = \begin{bmatrix} s^1_{1,1} & s^1_{1,2} & \cdots & s^1_{1,m} \\ s^1_{2,1} & s^1_{2,2} & \cdots & s^1_{2,m} \\ \vdots & \vdots & \ddots & \vdots \\ s^1_{n,1} & s^1_{n,2} & \cdots & s^1_{n,m} \end{bmatrix} \tag{1}$$

In both cases, the elements $s^b_{i,j} \in \{0,1\}$, with $b \in \{0,1\}$, represent the binary subpixels assigned to each participant.

Figure 1 shows the block diagram of the generic encryption algorithm in visual cryptography.

Before assigning the basis matrices, a column permutation is applied using an optional key. This introduces variability to enhance security without affecting decoding.

Given a permutation vector $\mathbf{v_p} = [2,1,4,3]$ and matrices of size $m = 4$, the process rearranges the columns of each matrix accordingly to Eq. (2)

$$\mathbf{S}^b = \begin{bmatrix} s^b_{1,1} & s^b_{1,2} & s^b_{1,3} & s^b_{1,4} \\ s^b_{2,1} & s^b_{2,2} & s^b_{2,3} & s^b_{2,4} \\ \vdots & \vdots & \vdots & \vdots \\ s^b_{n,1} & s^b_{n,2} & s^b_{n,3} & s^b_{n,4} \end{bmatrix} \xrightarrow{\mathbf{v_p}} \hat{\mathbf{S}}^b = \begin{bmatrix} s^b_{1,2} & s^b_{1,1} & s^b_{1,4} & s^b_{1,3} \\ s^b_{2,2} & s^b_{2,1} & s^b_{2,4} & s^b_{2,3} \\ \vdots & \vdots & \vdots & \vdots \\ s^b_{n,2} & s^b_{n,1} & s^b_{n,4} & s^b_{n,3} \end{bmatrix} \tag{2}$$

Now consider the following example show in Eq. (3)

$$\mathbf{S}^0 = \begin{bmatrix} 1\,1\,0\,0 \\ 1\,1\,0\,0 \end{bmatrix}, \quad \mathbf{S}^1 = \begin{bmatrix} 1\,1\,0\,0 \\ 0\,0\,1\,1 \end{bmatrix} \tag{3}$$

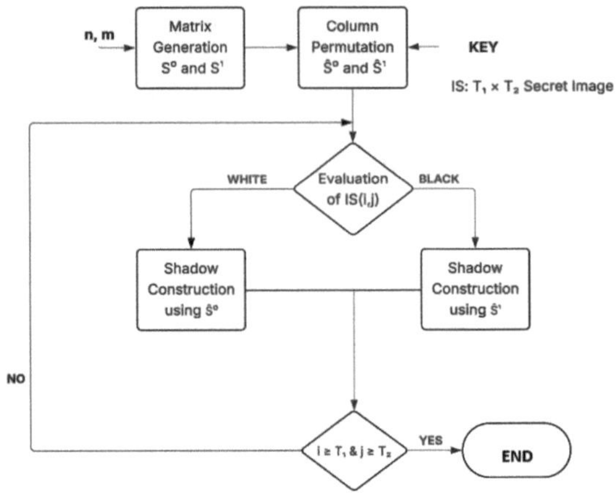

Fig. 1. Block diagram of the generic encryption algorithm in visual cryptography.

Applying the permutation vector ($\mathbf{v_p} = [2, 4, 3, 1]$), we obtain in the Eq. (4)

$$\hat{\mathbf{S}}^0 = \begin{bmatrix} 1\,0\,0\,1 \\ 1\,0\,0\,1 \end{bmatrix}, \quad \hat{\mathbf{S}}^1 = \begin{bmatrix} 1\,0\,0\,1 \\ 0\,1\,1\,0 \end{bmatrix} \tag{4}$$

Each row of the permuted matrix is translated into a shadow for a participant. To preserve the visual appearance, the resulting vectors are transformed into (2×2) subpixel blocks,as shown in Eq. (5)

$$V_1 = [1\ 1\ 0\ 0] \Rightarrow \begin{bmatrix} 1\,1 \\ 0\,0 \end{bmatrix}, \quad V_2 = [0\ 0\ 1\ 1] \Rightarrow \begin{bmatrix} 0\,0 \\ 1\,1 \end{bmatrix} \tag{5}$$

To reconstruct the image, it is sufficient to superimpose the shadows of at least k participants. This is done using a bitwise logical **OR** operation at each subpixel position,as shown in Eq. 6

$$\begin{bmatrix} 1\,1 \\ 0\,0 \end{bmatrix} \vee \begin{bmatrix} 0\,0 \\ 1\,1 \end{bmatrix} = \begin{bmatrix} 1\,1 \\ 1\,1 \end{bmatrix} \tag{6}$$

The result is a completely black block, corresponding to a black pixel of the original image.

This operation can be performed either digitally (using matrices) or physically (using transparencies).

Data Hiding (DH). Data hiding (DH) is a discipline that has been defined in various ways in the scientific literature. According to Petitcolas et al. [13], DH refers to techniques that allow information to be inserted into digital media in an imperceptible way to the observer, maintaining the quality of the original content. Cox et al. [14] says that data hiding seeks to ensure the confidentiality, authentication, or integrity of the content by embedding data in digital files without affecting their visual or auditory perception.

Bender et al. [15] state that data hiding (DH) is the process of hiding information in digital media in such a way that it is not perceptible to the human eye and is resistant to common transformations. In addition, Kundur and Hatzinakos [16] emphasize that DH not only hides data but must also ensure the recovery of the information even after the content has been subjected to compression or moderate manipulation.

Based on the method proposed by Chang et al. [8] in the article Data Hiding in Binary Image with High Payload, a data hiding system was developed specifically designed for binary images. Unlike conventional methods that work with color images, where modifications are usually imperceptible, in binary images any alteration can cause noticeable visual distortions. Therefore, it is essential to consider the limitations imposed by the Human Visual System (HVS). The HVS presents greater tolerance to changes that do not substantially modify the global density of black and white pixels, nor affect the dominant orientations (mainly horizontal and vertical). Under this premise, modifying a small number of pixels within strategically selected blocks allows information to be inserted imperceptibly.

The technique of this method consists of dividing the binary image into 2×2 pixel blocks. Each block is classified according to the number of black pixels it contains:

- Blocks with **0 or 4 black pixels** are omitted, avoiding perceptible visual alterations.
- Blocks with **2 black pixels** are used to hide **3 bits** of information.
- Blocks with **1 or 3 black pixels** are used to hide **2 bits**.

For data insertion, the following rules and encoding tables are used:

Rule 1: If a block has **2 black pixels**, **3 bits** of information can be inserted, as shown in Table 1.

Table 1. Three bits of information hiding

3 bits info.	New values for 4 pixels in block
000	0001
001	0010
010	0100
011	0111
100	1000
101	1011
110	1101
111	1110

Rule 2: If a 2×2 block has 1 or 3 black pixels, it is possible to insert 2 bits of information, as shown in Table 2.

These rules allow data to be inserted efficiently without significantly compromising the visual quality of the image.

The proposed approach, which uses 2×2 pixel blocks for adaptive data insertion, has proven to be highly effective. This methodology offers a higher hiding capacity

Table 2. Two bits of information hiding

2 bits info.	New values for 4 pixels in block
00	0011
01	0101
10	1001
11	1100

compared to existing techniques, and also enables information recovery without requiring the original image (blind extraction). Its low computational cost makes it an ideal solution for steganographic applications that demand speed and efficiency.

Spiking Neural P Systems (SN P) and Astrocyte Control. Spiking Neural P Systems (SN P) are bio-inspired computational models, formally defined by [17–19], which simulate the behavior of biological neural networks by using spikes as the basic unit of communication. In these systems, each neuron processes and transmits information by applying evolution rules that operate in discrete time steps.

Spiking Neural P Systems (SN P) operate through two fundamental types of rules: activation rules and inhibition rules.

1) Spiking or Activation Rules. Spiking or activation rules, also called *spiking rules*, have the form as shown in Eq. (7).

$$E/a^c \rightarrow a; d \tag{7}$$

where:

- E is a regular expression over the symbol a, which specifies when the rule can be applied (i.e., under which configurations of *spikes* in the neuron).
- a^c indicates that c *spikes* are consumed from the neuron if the total number of *spikes* satisfies the expression E.
- a represents the production of one *spike* that will be sent to all connected target neurons.
- d is the time delay, indicating after how many time steps the *spike* will be emitted.

2) Forgetting Rules. Forgetting rules, which have the following form in the Eq. (8).

$$a^s \rightarrow \lambda \tag{8}$$

where:

- a^s indicates that if there are exactly s *spikes* in the neuron, they are removed.
- λ represents that no output is produced (no *spike* is fired).

These rules allow the dynamic simulation of how neurons behave. The spiking rule represents the moment when a neuron sends a signal (a spike), while the forgetting rule acts as a cleaning mechanism: it removes certain accumulated spikes when they are no longer needed or do not meet the conditions to emit a signal. This helps prevent the network from becoming saturated and contributes to maintaining its stability.

Thanks to this rule structure, SN P systems have proven capable of solving complex problems with great efficiency, even reaching universal computing capabilities [17].

In a proposal of this model, the use of astrocytes is incorporated. Astrocytes are a type of glial cell present in the brain. These cells act as controllers in neuronal communication and play an important role in functions such as learning, memory, and the organization of brain circuits [20,21].

3 Methodology

This work presents a system that uses visual cryptography data hiding techniques in binary images. Its innovation lies in the use of a bioinspired cryptographic circuit based on Spiking Neural P Systems (SN P), which is responsible for the dynamic generation of *shares* with structural regulation through astrocytes. The method combines elements from the classical visual cryptography scheme proposed by Naor and Shamir [5], adapted to 2×2 blocks, with high-capacity data hiding techniques proposed in [8], and implements cryptographic logic with synaptic control following the model of [7].

The process can be divided into three main stages: (1) visual encoding through the dynamic generation of *shares* by an SN P circuit, (2) hiding of binary information within the generated *shares*, and (3) optical and digital recovery of both the original image and the hidden message. This process can be observed in Fig. 2.

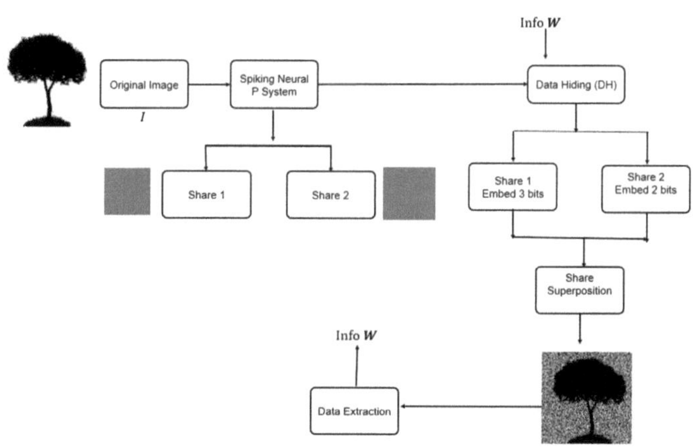

Fig. 2. General Diagram of the Proposed Method..

3.1 SN P Visual Cryptography

The first stage of the proposed system consists of transforming each pixel of an original binary image into two blocks of subpixels using a visual cryptography scheme that is dynamically controlled by a bio-inspired circuit based on Spiking Neural P systems (SN P). This procedure enables the generation of two encrypted images, referred to as *shares*, whose subsequent superimposition allows for visual recovery of the original content without requiring complex computational operations.

Let $I \in \{0,1\}^{M \times N}$ be a binary image such that:

- $I(i,j) = 0$ represents a black pixel,
- $I(i,j) = 1$ represents a white pixel.

Each pixel $I(i,j)$ is expanded into two 2×2 blocks, resulting in the shares S_1 and S_2, both of size $2M \times 2N$. This expansion is defined by the Eq. (9).

$$\phi_1, \phi_2 : \{0,1\} \rightarrow \{0,1\}^{2\times 2} \tag{9}$$

such that:

$$S_1(2i-1:2i,\ 2j-1:2j) = \phi_1(I(i,j)), \quad S_2(2i-1:2i,\ 2j-1:2j) = \phi_2(I(i,j)) \tag{10}$$

Unlike traditional schemes that rely on predefined lookup tables, in this proposal the functions ϕ_1 and ϕ_2 are dynamically generated by an SN P circuit that simulates spatiotemporal neural networks with astrocyte-regulated synaptic control.

The SN P system used, denoted by $\mathscr{P}_{VC}$, is modeled as shown in the Eq. (11).

$$\mathscr{P}_{VC} = \{O, \sigma_p, \sigma_i, \sigma_j, \sigma_k, \sigma_l, ast_1, ast_2, out_{i1}, out_{i2}, out_{j1}, out_{j2}, out_{k1}, out_{k2}, out_{l1}, out_{l2}\} \tag{11}$$

where:

- $O = \{a\}$ is the spike alphabet.
- $\sigma_p = (0, R_{p1}, R_{p2})$:is the input neuron, with rule set: $\Rightarrow R_{p1} = \{a^2 \rightarrow \pm 2(a^2, \sigma_p, \{\sigma_i, \sigma_j, \sigma_k, \sigma_l\}), R_{p2} = \{a \rightarrow \pm 4(a, \sigma_p, \{\sigma_i, \sigma_j, \sigma_k, \sigma_l\})\}$
- $\sigma_i = (0, R_{i1}, R_{i2}) \Rightarrow R_{i1} = \{a^2 \rightarrow \pm 2(a, \sigma_i, \{o_{i1}, o_{i2}\}), R_{i2} = \{a \rightarrow \pm 1(a, \sigma_i, \{o_{i1}, o_{i2})\}$
- $\sigma_j = (0, R_{j1}, R_{j2}) \Rightarrow R_{j1} = \{a^2 \rightarrow \pm 2(a, \sigma_j, \{o_{j1}, o_{j2}\}), R_{j2} = \{a \rightarrow \pm 1(a, \sigma_j, \{o_{j1}, o_{j2})\}$
- $\sigma_k = (0, R_{k1}, R_{k2}) \Rightarrow R_{k1} = \{a^2 \rightarrow \pm 2(a, \sigma_k, \{o_{k1}, o_{k2}\}), R_{k2} = \{a \rightarrow \pm 1(a, \sigma_k, \{o_{k1}, o_{k2})\}$
- $\sigma_l = (0, R_{l1}, R_{l2}) \Rightarrow R_{l1} = \{a^2 \rightarrow \pm 2(a, \sigma_l, \{o_{l1}, o_{l2}\}), R_{l2} = \{a \rightarrow \pm 1(a, \sigma_l, \{o_{l1}, o_{l2})\}$
- $ast_i \subseteq syn$ of the form $ast_i = (syn_{ast_x},\ 2)$, where 2 is the threshold representing the maximum number of dendritic connections allowed by the astrocyte. Here, $i \in \{1,2\}$ denotes the astrocyte identifier, and $x \in \{i, jk, l\}$ represents the possible dendritic connections that may be formed based on the spike firing rules.

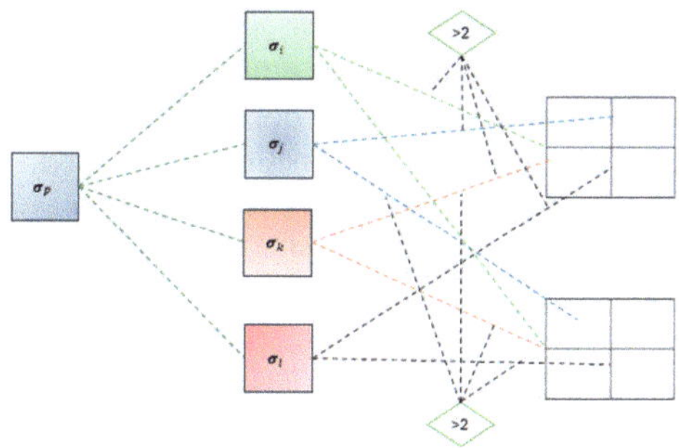

Fig. 3. VCSN P circuit with astrocyte-controlled plasticity. The neuron σ_p regulates the activation of output neurons σ_i, σ_j, σ_k, σ_l and the assignment of subpixel patterns to 2×2 blocks.

As shown in Fig. 3, the bio-inspired neural circuit governs the generation of synaptic connections toward the outputs that form the *shares*. Its behavior depends on the number of spikes received by the input neuron σ_p:

- If $I(i, j) = 1$ (white), 2 spikes are injected, generating:

$$\phi_1(1) = \phi_2(1) \tag{12}$$

- If $I(i, j) = 0$ (black), 1 spike is injected, generating:

$$\phi_2(0) = \overline{\phi_1(0)} \tag{13}$$

In addition, the circuit implements advanced structural plasticity mechanisms. Astrocytes associated with the output neurons continuously monitor the synaptic connections directed toward each 2×2 block. If the number of connections toward a single block exceeds a predefined maximum threshold τ, the corresponding astrocyte triggers a non-deterministic pruning process that eliminates some of these synapses. This pruning prevents the spike from being transmitted, which in turn reactivates the plasticity rule of the sending neuron. Consequently, a new connection is formed toward another region of the block, ensuring controlled and balanced structural growth. This reconfiguration is subsequently supervised by a second astrocyte.

This behavior, inspired by biological synaptic regulation phenomena, enhances the spatial distribution of connections and prevents visual oversaturation in the *shares*. For further technical details about the neural architecture and astrocytic pruning mechanism, the reader is referred to the original proposal in [7].

3.2 Hiding of Binary Information

Once the encrypted images S_1 and S_2 are generated via the SN P circuit, a secret binary message is incorporated into both *shares* using a hiding scheme. Unlike conventional steganographic techniques, this method encodes information through visual patterns distributed in 2×2 blocks, preserving the appearance of visual noise and ensuring faithful reconstruction of the original image upon superposition.

During the hiding process, the binary message is sequentially traversed. For each pair of selected blocks in the *shares*, 3 bits are embedded into a block of S_1 by applying Table 1, followed by 2 bits embedded into the corresponding block of S_2 using Table 2. This process is repeated until the entire data string is processed.

Rule 1 is exclusively applied to blocks in S_1 that contain exactly two black pixels, allowing 3 bits to be represented using a table of 8 predefined visual patterns. Subsequently, Rule 2 modifies the corresponding block in S_2, choosing a complementary pattern that enables the insertion of 2 additional bits without altering the visibility or distorting the optical reconstruction of the original image.

This procedure can be represented using the following encoding functions,as shown in Eq. (14).

$$\psi_1 : \{0,1\}^3 \rightarrow \mathscr{P}_{S_1}, \quad \psi_2 : \{0,1\}^2 \times \mathscr{P}_{S_1} \rightarrow \mathscr{P}_{S_2} \tag{14}$$

where:

- ψ_1 selects a valid visual pattern for the block of S_1, based on the first 3 bits,
- ψ_2 selects the corresponding pattern in S_2, considering the last 2 bits and the pattern already applied in S_1.

The result of the process is the two *shares* modified with embedded information,as shown in Eq. (15).

$$S_1^* = \text{Embed}_{\psi_1}(m_1, S_1), \quad S_2^* = \text{Embed}_{\psi_2}(m_2, S_2) \tag{15}$$

where m_1 and m_2 represent the partial sequences of the binary message hidden in each *share*.

4 Results

This section aims to validate the effectiveness of our approach by demonstrating its ability to securely embed and accurately recover secret messages while preserving the visual quality of the cover images. The experiments were designed to test the system's performance across a diverse set of binary images, evaluate its security through entropy analysis and SSIM measurements. The implementation of the proposed method was carried out on a personal computer equipped with the Microsoft Windows 11© operating system, an Intel© Core i7 processor, and 16 GB of RAM. MATLAB R2024a was used as the simulation environment. The experimental tests were conducted using a set of binary images with varying visual characteristics, aiming to evaluate the robustness and adaptability of the system under different structural complexities in the input data.

The experimental tests were conducted on representative binary images selected for their visual diversity, including human silhouettes, institutional logos, and natural patterns. Each image was processed using the proposed system, generating two pairs of shares: the first using classical visual cryptography, implemented through the VCSNP circuit; and the second incorporating the data hiding scheme based on 2×2 blocks. In this configuration, binary messages equivalent to text strings of up to 375 bits—corresponding to approximately 46 alphanumeric characters—were embedded directly into selected blocks of the encrypted image. This data embedding operation was performed without perceptibly compromising the visual quality of the resulting shares. This setup allowed for the evaluation of the system's visual, structural, and statistical stability when embedding secret data, considering both human perception and objective quality metrics.

Figure 4 shows the visual results of the superimposed *shares*, comparing the cases without data hiding (left) and with data hiding (right). At a glance, both versions are visually similar, preserving the recognizable structure of the original images, which indicates that the data hiding method does not perceptibly affect the visual reconstruction.

To quantify the impact of the data hiding process, two metrics were used. The Structural Similarity Index (SSIM) evaluates visual perception by comparing luminance, contrast, and structure between two images. Its value ranges from 0 to 1, where a value of 1 indicates perfect similarity. On the other hand, Shannon entropy measures the level of randomness or uncertainty in the distribution of pixel values; in binary images, values close to 1 indicate greater unpredictability, which is desirable in visual cryptography schemes. A minimal change in entropy suggests that the hiding process has not significantly altered the statistical distribution of pixels, thus helping to prevent detection by statistical analysis. In the context of visual cryptography and data hiding, the main objective is not to assess the exact visual fidelity between two images, but rather to ensure that:

The pixel distribution does not reveal hidden information, and that the generated image is indistinguishable from a random or natural image. Therefore, Shannon entropy was selected as the evaluation metric for the present proposal, as it measures the randomness and statistical distribution of the pixels, which are the key factors to ensure undetectability and cryptographic security. [22]

Mathematically, these metrics are defined as follows, as shown in Eq. (16):

$$\mathrm{SSIM}(x,y) = \frac{(2\mu_x\mu_y + C_1)(2\sigma_{xy} + C_2)}{(\mu_x^2 + \mu_y^2 + C_1)(\sigma_x^2 + \sigma_y^2 + C_2)} \tag{16}$$

where μ_x and μ_y are the means of images x and y, σ_x^2 and σ_y^2 are their variances, and σ_{xy} is the covariance. The constants C_1 and C_2 are used to stabilize the expression and avoid division by zero. The entropy is calculated according to Eq. (17):

$$H = -\sum_{i=1}^{n} p_i \log_2(p_i) \tag{17}$$

where p_i denotes the probability of occurrence of pixel value i in the image. In the case of binary images, the possible values are 0 and 1, and the maximum entropy ($H = 1$) is reached when both values have equal probability.

As shown in Table 3, the entropy difference in all cases was minimal, with absolute values lower than 0.0011. This indicates that embedding the hidden message does not significantly affect the statistical structure of the images. Even when the difference was negative (as in the case of the logo or the tree), the impact was negligible and did not influence visual perception. Additionally, the SSIM values reflect a high structural sim-

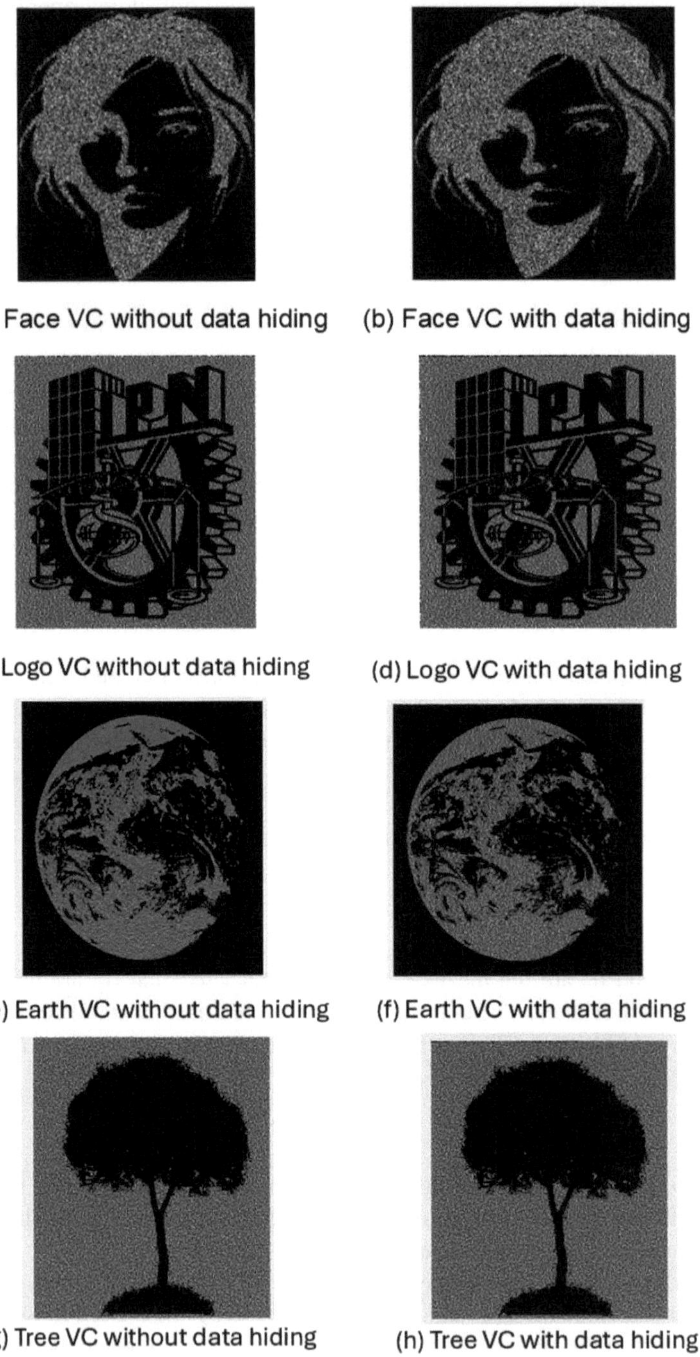

(a) Face VC without data hiding (b) Face VC with data hiding

(c) Logo VC without data hiding (d) Logo VC with data hiding

(e) Earth VC without data hiding (f) Earth VC with data hiding

(g) Tree VC without data hiding (h) Tree VC with data hiding

Fig. 4. Visual comparison between the superimposed shares without data hiding (left) and with data hiding (right).

Table 3. Comparison between pure visual cryptography (VC) and VC with data hiding (VC+DH).

Image	SSIM	Entropy without hiding	Entropy with hiding	Δ Entropy
Face	0.5762	0.7039	0.7040	+0.0001
Logo	0.3444	0.8280	0.8269	−0.0011
Tree	0.3131	0.9098	0.9090	−0.0008
Earth	0.5617	0.6706	0.6714	+0.0008

ilarity in visually complex images such as the face (0.5762) and Earth (0.5617), which confirms that the method preserves perceptual integrity after message embedding.

Overall, these results demonstrate that the proposed system is capable of securely and reversibly hiding binary information, maintaining.

5 Conclusions

In this work, a novel system for data hiding in binary images is proposed, integrating visual cryptography with Spiking Neural P systems (SN P) enhanced by astrocyte-controlled structural plasticity. The experiments demonstrated the effectiveness and security of the proposed method. Results showed that the generated shares exhibited no significant visual alterations after the injection of hidden data, maintaining their appearance as random noise. This aspect is crucial for ensuring the covertness of the hidden information and preventing potential attackers from detecting the presence of embedded data.

Moreover, entropy measurements revealed that the changes introduced by the data hiding process were minimal, with variations not exceeding 0.0011 in the worst case. The secret message could also be reliably extracted from the shares, demonstrating the practicality and effectiveness of the proposed approach.

Additionally, the method offers enhanced security through the dynamic and adaptive capabilities of the SN P systems with astrocyte-regulated structural plasticity. This integration not only strengthens the system's robustness against potential attacks but also ensures efficient and secure data sharing—particularly in scenarios where images are used as carriers of sensitive information.

However, since the visual cryptography scheme in this proposal relies entirely on the direct superimposition of the generated shares to reconstruct the original image, the system may lack robustness against external disturbances such as noise, compression, or degradation during transmission. Even minor alterations in the shares may prevent accurate visual recovery, as the decoding process does not include error correction mechanisms. Therefore, the system's tolerance to distortions represents a key limitation and an important direction for future improvement.

Future Work. As future work, a key direction involves enhancing the SN P circuit used in the visual cryptography process to more seamlessly integrate the data hiding mechanism into the SN P framework. This may involve refining the algorithms that govern the splitting and embedding of secret messages, as well as improving the computational performance of the system to handle more complex operations with fewer resource requirements. Furthermore, extending the system's capabilities to support color images represents a promising area for exploration.

Acknowledgments. This document is the result of the research project supported by Secretaria de Ciencia, Humanidades, Tecnologia e Innovacion (SECIHTI) scholarship and grant number 161591, and the Secretaria de Investigacion y Posgrado (SIP) of Instituto Politecnico Nacional (IPN).

References

1. Filkins, B.L., Kim, J.Y., Roberts, B., Armstrong, W., Miller, M.A., Hultner, M.L., et al.: Privacy and security in the era of digital health: what should translational researchers know and do about it? Am. J. Trans. Res. **8**(3), 1560 (2016)
2. Abu-Faraj, M., et al.: Protecting digital images using keys enhanced by 2d chaotic logistic maps. Cryptography **7**(1), 1–18 (2023)
3. Islam, M.A., et al.: Enhancing security of image steganography using visual cryptography. In: Proceedings of the 2021 International Conference on Robotics, Electrical and Signal Processing Techniques (ICREST), pp. 70–5. IEEE (2021)
4. Himthani, V., et al.: Comparative performance assessment of deep learning based image steganography techniques. Sci. Rep. **12**(1), 1–12 (2022)
5. Naor, M., Shamir, A.: Visual cryptography. In: Advances in Cryptology—EUROCRYPT'94: Workshop on the Theory and Application of Cryptographic Techniques Perugia, pp. 1–12, Italy, May 9–12, 1994 Proceedings 13. Springer (1995)
6. Nakano, M., Escamilla, E., Pérez, H., Iwamoto, M.: Criptografía Visual basada en el esquema de umbral: una revisión tutorial. Inf. Tecnol. **22**(5), 107–20 (2011)
7. Olvera-Martinez, L., et al.: First SN P visual cryptographic circuit with astrocyte control of structural plasticity for security applications. Neurocomputing **457**, 67–73 (2021)
8. Ding, W., Wang, Y.: Data hiding in binary image with high payload. Arab. J. Sci. Eng. **43**(12), 7737–45 (2018)
9. Hou, Y.C.: Visual cryptography for color images. Pattern Recogn. **36**(7), 1619–29 (2003)
10. Pan, J.S., Liu, T., Yang, H.M., Yan, B., Chu, S.C., Zhu, T.: Visual cryptography scheme for secret color images with color QR codes. J. Vis. Commun. Image Represent. **82**, 103405 (2022)
11. Leung, B.W., Ng, F.Y., Wong, D.S.: On the security of a visual cryptography scheme for color images. Pattern Recogn. **42**(5), 929–40 (2009)
12. Ateniese, G., Blundo, C., De Santis, A., Stinson, D.R.: Visual cryptography for general access structures. Inf. Comput. **129**(2), 86–106 (1996)
13. Petitcolas, F.A., Anderson, R.J., Kuhn, M.G.: Information hiding-a survey. Proc. IEEE **87**(7), 1062–78 (2002)
14. Cox, I., Miller, M., Bloom, J., Fridrich, J., Kalker, T.: Digital watermarking and steganography. Morgan Kaufmann (2007)
15. Bender, W., Gruhl, D., Morimoto, N., Lu, A.: Techniques for data hiding. IBM Syst. J. **35**(3.4), 313–36 (1996). https://doi.org/10.1147/sj.353.0313
16. Kundur, D., Hatzinakos, D.: Digital watermarking using multiresolution wavelet decomposition. In: Proceedings of the 1998 IEEE International Conference on Acoustics, Speech and Signal Processing, ICASSP'98 (Cat. No. 98CH36181). vol. 5, pp. 2969–72. IEEE (1998)

17. Ionescu, M., Păun, G., Yokomori, T.: Spiking neural p systems. Fundamenta Inform. **71**(2-3), 279-308 (2006)
18. Chen, H., Ionescu, M., Ishdorj, T.O., P0103un, A., P 0103un, G., P0103un, M.J.: Spiking neural P systems with extended rules: universality and languages. Nat. Comput. **7**, 147–66 (2008)
19. Yang, Q., Li, B., Huang, Y., Peng, H., Wang, J.: Spiking neural P systems with structural plasticity and anti-spikes. Theoret. Comput. Sci. **801**, 143–56 (2020)
20. Santaeufemia FAC. Desarrollo de nuevos algoritmos neurogliales que modelizan la interacción astrocito-neurona en sistemas de altas prestaciones [Tesis doctoral]. Universidade da Coruña; 2019. http://hdl.handle.net/2183/22634
21. Leporati, A., Mauri, G., Zandron, C.: Spiking neural P systems: main ideas and results. Nat. Comput. **21**(4), 629–49 (2022)
22. Alghamdi, Y., Munir, A.: Image encryption algorithms: a survey of design and evaluation metrics. J. Cybersecur. Privacy. **4**(1), 126–52 (2024)

Quantum Associative Classification Model Using Amplitude-Encoded Feature Similitude

Areli-Yesareth Guerrero-Estrada[1], L. F. Quezada[2](✉), and Guo-Hua Sun[1]

[1] Computing Research Center, National Polytechnic Institute, 07700 Mexico City, Mexico
[2] Research Center for Quantum Physics, Huzhou University, Huzhou 313000, People's Republic of China
lf_quezada@outlook.com

Abstract. This work introduces a novel quantum associative classification model that employs amplitude-encoded distance, which requires fewer qubits for data encoding and therefore uses a real value feature. This approach reduces the qubit requirements for data representation, since conventional quantum associative models often rely on binary representations of input data. The results were obtained by analyzing four balanced datasets (Iris, Cryotherapy, Data Bank Authentication, and Caesarian) and four imbalanced datasets (Haberman, Transfusion, Immunotherapy, and Fertility Diagnosis) showing that the efficiency of the quantum associative model is better than QkNN with the same metric in the case of a balanced dataset inclusive better than classical in the case of Caesarian. The results of the imbalanced show are inferior, with a performance difference of less than 10 % to that of the classical show for Haberman and Transfusion. Experiments to test simulation using IBM's Qiskit Library.

Keywords: Amplitude-Encoded Features · Quantum Machine Learning · Quantum Metric · Quantum Associative Model · Pattern Recognition · Quantum Similarity Measurement

1 Introduction

Quantum machine learning is an emerging area of computing that combines the principles of quantum mechanics with machine learning techniques to tackle computationally demanding problems. By exploiting phenomena such as entanglement and superposition, it offers new ways to represent and process information to efficiently solve complex mathematical problems.

Through quantum parallelism, these methods can address challenges that are prohibitively complex for classical computers, particularly in tasks involving

C. Palma-Preciado et al. (Eds.): CORE 2025, ACSAR 3, pp. 136–148, 2026.
https://doi.org/10.1007/978-3-032-08894-9_9

high-dimensional data analysis and sophisticated pattern recognition. This capability opens the door to more efficient algorithms capable of managing large-scale datasets and uncovering intricate relationships within them.

Several quantum and hybrid algorithms have been proposed; among these are quantum neural networks (QNN) [6,18,22,28], and the quantum support vector machine (QSVM) [19,24], which have demonstrated encouraging capabilities in the classification and optimization tasks. In particular, metric-based algorithms such as the quantum k nearest neighbors (QkNN) have been employing different distance metrics, including the Hamming distance [15,17,23], the Euclidean distance [27], the polar distance [7] and the amplitude encode metric [10] to analyze the performance of memory, complexity, and classification accuracy. Furthermore, different versions of quantum associative memories (QAM) [2,3,20,21,29] have been proposed as quantum analogues of classical memory that promise efficient means of associative recovery.

In this paper, we explore a novel associative model for classification tasks that utilizes a metric based on amplitude encoding [10]. This approach optimizes memory requirements compared to other models that employ the Hamming distance. Our work proposes a quantum model that computes the distance between patterns using amplitude-encoded features to recover the class label. To evaluate the performance of a new assessment model, we achieve a meticulous analysis using eight numerical datasets, with the objective of assessing the effectiveness of classification tasks.

The organization of this paper is as follows. Section 2 presents the fundamental definitions and the theory behind the associative algorithm [12], along with the different versions of the proposed quantum associative model. Section 3 details the proposed associative algorithm, highlighting the metric based on the amplitude encoding and the corresponding processes of the quantum associative algorithms. Section 4 presents the results of the computational experiments and compares them with classical algorithms. Finally, Sect. 5 concludes the paper and discusses possible directions for future work.

2 Background

The study of associative algorithms has long been a cornerstone in the development of models capable of storing and retrieving information based on pattern similarity. However, as data dimensionality and complexity grow, these classical models face inherent limitations in terms of scalability and retrieval efficiency.

Recent advances in quantum computing offer a promising avenue for addressing these challenges by leveraging quantum parallelism. The following subsections outline the foundational principles of these approaches, setting the stage for their integration into quantum architectures.

2.1 Associative Algorithm

The model associative is a supervised learning algorithm that can be utilized to perform pattern matching with the recovery pattern; this model consists of saving the associative pairs of a data (x^i, y^i) where x^i the corresponding vector of p dimension and y^i as recovery output [12] the associative model consists of two phases:

- *Learning phase*
  Transform the input vector to ensure compatibility with the memory and create the fundamental set of trains.
  Encode the input pattern into the memory to ensure that it is stored in the weight matrix $W = \sum_i y_i x_i^T$.
- *Retrieval phase*
  Given a test input x_t, the network iteratively updates the input until convergence.
  The resulting output should match or approximate one of the stored patterns.

Associative models have been widely employed in tasks such as pattern recognition and classification; however, they struggle with scalability and efficiency; therefore, principles such as superposition may be useful in overcoming this limitation.

2.2 Quantum Associative Algorithm

Quantum associative memory (QAM) models build upon the classical idea of Hopfield networks and adapt them to the quantum computing paradigm. By leveraging quantum phenomena such as superposition and entanglement, these models aim to enhance the efficiency of pattern storage and retrieval.

Some early proposals, such as those of Ventura and Martinez [25], suggest storing patterns in superposition and using amplitude amplification for the retrieval process. However, these approaches face limitations in both the retrieval phase and scalability to the input data size. This is primarily because the data is encoded directly into qubits, requiring a complex binarization process.

Subsequent research has sought to address these limitations. Zhou and Ding [29] proposed reducing complexity through phase-based encoding combined with a nonlinear search algorithm.

More recently, Sanchez et al. [21] introduced an approach that incorporates the Hamming distance in the retrieval phase, allowing identification and recovery of the stored pattern most similar to a given input.

The model proposed by Sanchez et al. [21] consists of the following steps:

- Obtain unique patterns of the fundamental set $X = \{x_1, x_2, ...x^n\}$ with n patterns and transform the training set into quantum states with the same probabilities where $x_i = \{x^1, x^2, ..., x^p\}$ with p features where x^j is a pattern with binary data $x^j \in \{0, 1\}$, where the memory with the states in superposition can be expressed as in Eq. 1

$$|m\rangle = \frac{1}{\sqrt{n}} \sum_{i=1}^{n} |x^i\rangle. \quad (1)$$

- The retrieval phase computes the Hamming distance between the input and all superposition patterns in state quantum.
- The state with the lowest value distance is chosen, and this pattern is recovered.

2.3 Quantum Random Access Memory (QRAM)

QRAM is an essential component in quantum machine learning that can then perform memory access in coherent quantum superposition. Required qubits such as the address register must contain a superposition address, as shown in Eq. 2

$$\sum_j \psi_j |j\rangle_a |D_j\rangle_d, \tag{2}$$

where $|j\rangle$ is a $j-th$ address cell and $|D_j\rangle$ is the content of the $j-th$ memory cell [9].

2.4 Metric Based on Amplitude Encoded

This metric consists of computing the similarity between features of two patterns using numerical data encoded on amplitude, employing a rotation around the y axis on a single qubit initialized in $|0\rangle$ to encode the distance as the angle of rotation. This can be expressed as

$$|d^j\rangle = \bigotimes_{i=1}^{n} \left[\cos\left(\frac{\pi\lambda_i^j}{2}\right)|0\rangle + \sin\left(\frac{\pi\lambda_i^j}{2}\right)|1\rangle \right], \tag{3}$$

with $\lambda_i^j = x_i^j - x_i^k$ and $j \in \{1, 2, ..., n\}$. Notice that the cosine term is in Eq. (3) measures the similarity between the features. When $(x_i^j - x_i^k) \to 0$ has a high degree of similarity between the corresponding features. It is also possible to express the Eq. (3) as

$$|d^j\rangle = \sum_{g=0}^{2^n-1} \gamma_g^j |g\rangle, \tag{4}$$

where

$$\gamma_g^j = \prod_{i=1}^{n} \sin\left[\frac{\pi}{2}(x_i^j - x_i^k + g_i)\right], \tag{5}$$

and g_i denotes the i-th binary digit of g [10].

3 Methodology

We employ Stratified Cross-Validation as the validation method, which is a variation of cross-validation that ensures that each fold of the data has approximately the same proportion of class labels as the original dataset; this is particularly useful when we work with an imbalanced dataset. The split is done in a way that is random, but preserves the distribution of classes in each fold. We use 90% for the training model and 10% to validate. This process is repeated 10 times, and the results are obtained by taking the average of the repetitions.

For performance comparison, we used two metrics: Accuracy and F1 score. Accuracy denotes the proportion of correctly classified patterns out of the total predictions and is widely used for evaluating classification models. However, in the context of imbalanced datasets, accuracy may not provide reliable results. In such cases, it is recommended to use the F1 score, which is defined as the harmonic mean of precision and recall.

The data analysis presented was executed using Python 3.12: specifically, the scikit-learn library to assess performance metrics and Qiskit to simulate algorithms and estimate noise. The simulations were carried out on a system with the following specifications: an Intel Core i7 10700K CPU at 3.80GHz, 48GB of RAM, and an Nvidia GeForce RTX 2060S GPU.

Table 1. Datasets information: number of patterns, features, classes and imbalance ratio (IR).

Dataset	Patterns	Features	Classes	IR
Iris	150	4	3	1.00
Cryotherapy	90	6	2	1.14
DBA	1372	4	2	1.25
Caesarian	80	5	2	1.35
Haberman	306	3	2	2.78
Transfusion	748	4	2	3.20
Immunotherapy	90	7	2	3.74
FD	100	9	2	7.33

For the training phase, it is necessary to preprocess the training dataset for categorical data, which first requires transforming it into numerical categories. Later, categorical and numerical data must be normalized to obtain a dataset when each feature is represented for $x_i \in [0, 1]$. Generate the feature sets for each class using the average data for each numerical feature and the categorical data mode.

3.1 Preprocessing

The preprocessing consists of calculating the mean of each numerical feature and the categorical mode of each class, and creating a pattern with this information that represents all the patterns of the training of each class. We use these new patterns for the train associative model. The categorical characteristics are represented with numbers and normalize the numerical and categorical features so that all features have a value $x_i \in [0,1]$. In essence, we transform the train dataset $X_T = \{x_1, x_2, ...x_n\}$ with the pattern n into $X_{T'} = \{x'_1, ...x'_c\}$ where c is the class number; this is a fundamental set of associations.

3.2 Training Phase

The training phase consists of obtaining average values for each class of each feature and initializing them as quantum states; the phase consists of the next steps.

1. Initialize a circuit with $n+m$ qubits

$$|\Psi_0\rangle = |0\rangle^{\otimes n}|0\rangle^{\otimes m}, \tag{6}$$

   where n is class number and m is feature number.
2. The circuit creates a superposition of the classes

$$\begin{aligned} |\Psi_1\rangle = U_c|\Psi_0\rangle &= \frac{1}{\sqrt{n}}\left(|10\cdots0\rangle + |010\cdots0\rangle + \cdots + |0\cdots01\rangle\right)|0\rangle^{\otimes m} \\ &= \frac{1}{\sqrt{n}}\sum_{i=1}^{n}|e_i\rangle|0\rangle^{\otimes m}, \end{aligned} \tag{7}$$

   where $|e_i\rangle$ have a $|1\rangle$ in the position i and $|0\rangle$ in the others.
3. Using the qubits of classes such as QRAM to initialize the feature, as shown in Fig. 1 set associated with the average information of the classe, as shown in Fig. 1

$$|\Psi_2\rangle = U_{inicialize}|\Psi_1\rangle = \frac{1}{\sqrt{n}}\sum_{i=1}^{n}|e_i\rangle\left(\sum_{g=0}^{2^n-1}\gamma_g^j|g\rangle\right), \tag{8}$$

   where

$$\gamma_g^j = \prod_{i=1}^{m}\sin\left[\frac{\pi}{2}(x_i^j + g_i)\right], \tag{9}$$

   and g_i denotes the i-th binary digit of g.

3.3 Classification Phase

First, we obtain the distance between the test pattern and the training data

$$|\Psi_3\rangle = U_{d_1}|\Psi_2\rangle = \frac{1}{\sqrt{n}}\sum_{i=1}^{n}|e_i\rangle|d^j\rangle, \tag{10}$$

where

$$|d^j\rangle = \sum_{i=1}^{n}\left\{\prod_{i=1}^{m}\sin\left[\frac{\pi}{2}(x_i^j - x_i^k + g_i)\right]\right\}|g\rangle, \tag{11}$$

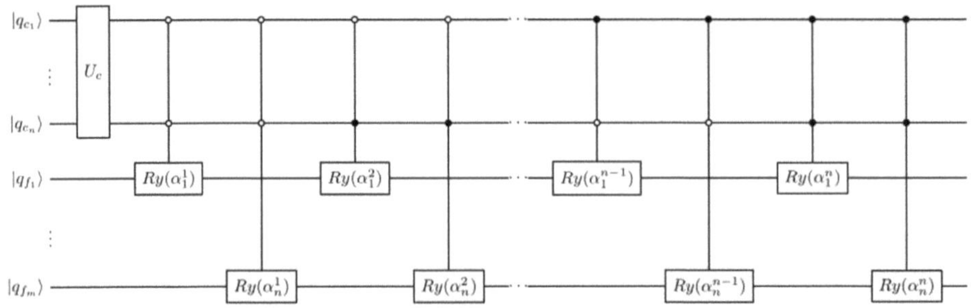

Fig. 1. Quantum circuit representing the functioning of a QRAM. The circuit prepares a superposition of classes. Classes of qubits work as address states and use controlled operations for storing information.

and g_i denotes the i-th binary digit of g. When $x_i = x_j$ we have that sine only depends on the binary digit of g; therefore, we conserve the states whose feature digit is 1, and in case $x_i \neq x_j$, we conserve terms with feature digit 0. Then we apply the X gate in the feature qubits to use the distance as in the Eq. 12

$$|\Psi_4\rangle = X|\Psi_3\rangle = \frac{1}{\sqrt{n}}\sum_{i=1}^{n}|e_i\rangle|\overline{d^j}\rangle, \tag{12}$$

where

$$\overline{d^{ij}} = \begin{cases} 0 & \text{si } x_i = x_j \\ 1 & \text{si } x_i \neq x_j. \end{cases} \tag{13}$$

Finally, we apply the control gate $CR_y(\gamma)$ for each feature and each class, if the features are different between the test and the training rote for all classes, assuming that the pattern does not belong to the class.

$$|\Psi_5\rangle = CR_y(\gamma)|\Psi_4\rangle = \frac{1}{\sqrt{n}}\sum_{i=1}^{n}|c_i\rangle|\overline{d^j}\rangle, \tag{14}$$

where $\gamma = \frac{\pi}{m}$ and c_i encode the class of patterns. Finally, we measure the class qubits and identify the majority class qubit. Figure 2 illustrates the classification phase circuit, where the distance is computed in the U_d phase and classes retrieved in the U_{as} phase.

4 Results

In this section, we present a performance comparison of the proposed QAM algorithm with the QkNN method, which employs the same metric, alongside the classical result of kNN (k = 1). The analysis utilizes a collection of eight numerical datasets: Iris [4], Cryotherapy (Cry) [5], Data Bank Authentication (DBA) [16] and Caesarian (Cae) [1], which are balanced datasets, as well as

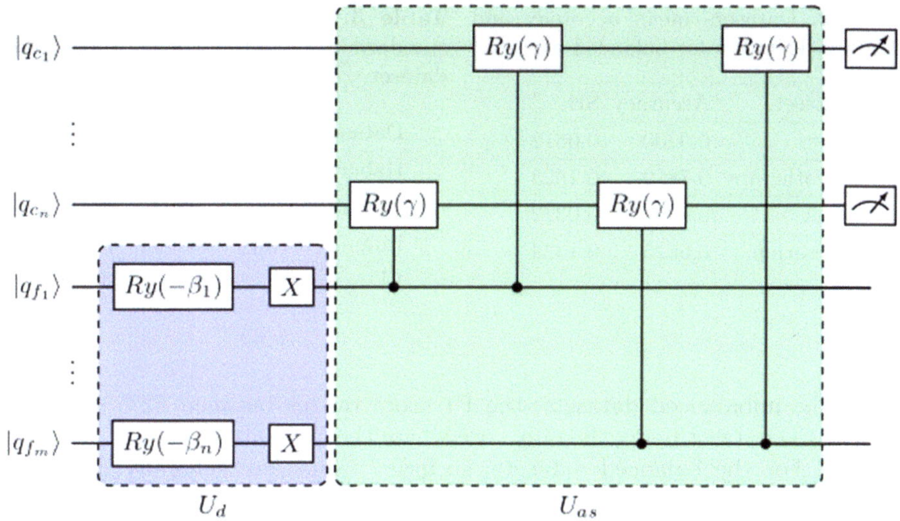

Fig. 2. Quantum circuit illustrating distance measurement and association encoding.

Haberman (Hab) [11], Transfusion (Tra) [26], Immunotherapy (Imm) [13,14] and Fertility Diagnosis (FD) [8], which represent imbalanced datasets. Detailed information on these data sets, including their imbalance ratio (IR), can be found in Table 1.

To contextualize these findings with previous work, we complement the analysis with a concise literature review of quantum nearest neighbor models that employ the same distance metric [10]. This comparison is essential to evaluate the relative performance of the proposed QAM against established quantum approaches, such as QkNN, under equivalent conditions. By analyzing both balanced and imbalanced datasets, we aim to identify the scenarios where QAM provides superior accuracy or F1 performance, highlighting the advantages of amplitude encoding and the elimination of binarization and quantum oracles. This contextualization clarifies how QAM differs from, and in certain cases surpasses, existing quantum nearest neighbor models.

The mean result and standard deviation are shown in Tables 2 and 3 obtained using the Qiskit simulator, the Fig. 3 illustrated as box-whisker plots for all datasets comparing QAM and classical kNN. The summary of the result compared to the QkNN versions and the classical kNN (k = 1) is provided in Tables 4 and 5.

4.1 Discussion

The results in Tables 2 and 3 show a standard deviation below 0.1 for iris, DBA, haberman, transfusion, and immunotherapy datasets. This indicates that these datasets produce consistent results with low variability between executions.

Table 2. Datasets mean accuracy and standard deviation for balanced dataset.

Dataset	Accuracy	SD
Iris	0.9200	0.0612
Cryotherapy	0.7889	0.1523
DBA	0.8091	0.0322
Caesarian	0.6625	0.1324

Table 3. Datasets mean F1 score and standard deviation for the imbalanced dataset.

Dataset	F1 Score	SD
Haberman	0.6202	0.0900
Transfusion	0.6302	0.0416
Immunotherapy	0.6805	0.0759
FD	0.6837	0.1238

For the imbalanced datasets, the F1 score ranges between 62% and 68%, with the FD dataset being the only case where the standard deviation is greater than 0.1. For the balanced datasets, accuracy values are generally higher. In particular, the iris dataset reaches accuracy levels of up to 92%.

Figure 3 illustrates the distribution of the F1 score and accuracy for all datasets that compare QAM and classical; it is observed that for iris and DBA, high accuracy is achieved with both models with lower variance. In the case of cryotherapy and haberman, the two models present similar accuracy; however, QAM presents greater variance. For immunotherapy, transfusion, and FD, kNN has better accuracy but greater variance. Notably, for the caesarian dataset, QAM outperforms kNN in both accuracy and variance.

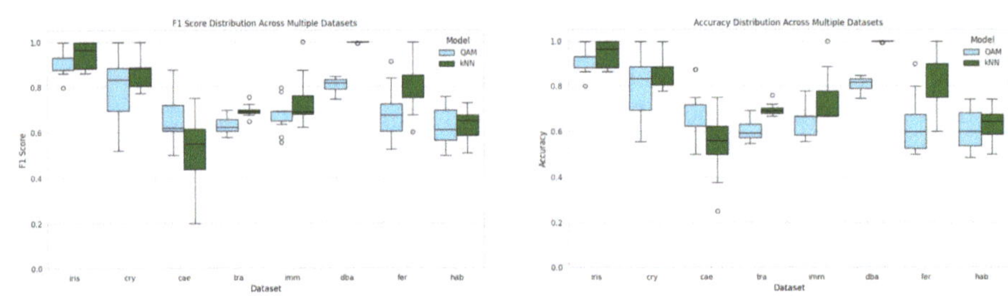

Fig. 3. Boxplot comparison of performance for the QAM model and the classical kNN model on all datasets. Left: F1 Score. Right: Accuracy.

Tables 4 and 5 compare accuracy and F1 score, respectively, between our AQM and state-of-the-art QkNN models evaluated with the same metric [10]. For balanced datasets, QAM achieves better results compared to other quantum models. Conversely, for imbalanced datasets, QkNN performs better.

One possible explanation is that, in balanced datasets, the partitioning into training and testing sets produces a feature set that is more representative for the training phase, thereby improving QAM's performance.

Table 4. Performance accuracy comparison of QkNN models, associative model, and classical kNN on the dataset.

Dataset	QkNN-Schuld	QkNN-Quezada	QAM	Classical
Iris	0.8600	0.8267	**0.9200**	0.9467
Cryotherapy	0.6889	0.7012	**0.7889**	0.8778
DBA	0.5937	0.7551	**0.8091**	0.9985
Caesarian	0.5625	0.5750	**0.6625**	0.5375
Haberman	0.1943	0.7451	0.6011	0.6369
Transfusion	0.7620	0.7673	0.6042	0.6960
Immunotherapy	0.7889	0.7889	0.6556	0.7667
FD	–	–	0.6300	0.8400

Table 5. Performance F1 Score comparison of QkNN models, associative model, and classical kNN on the dataset.

Dataset	QkNN-Schuld	QkNN-Quezada	QAM	Classical
Iris	0.8593	0.8267	0.9184	0.9454
Cryotherapy	0.6523	0.6724	0.7843	0.8758
DBA	0.5520	0.7312	0.8088	0.9985
Caesarian	0.5374	0.6889	0.6583	0.5193
Haberman	0.2864	**0.6239**	0.6202	0.6354
Transfusion	0.6619	**0.6776**	0.6302	0.6954
Immunotherapy	**0.6958**	0.6058	0.6806	0.7407
FD	-	-	0.6837	0.8258

Although QRAM can be computationally expensive to initialize the phase, in this case, one only needs to initialize as many patterns as classes. To initialize each pattern $(n + 2)$, the depth layer is required, where n is the number of features, then the training phase requires $(n + 2) * c$, where c is the number of classes.

For the associative model, the section employs two layers to compute the similitude and the $n * c$ layer to obtain the relation between the similitude for class. This proposed model does not require a large number of qubits or deep quantum circuits, making it more feasible for implementation on NISQ devices. Table 6 shows the number of qubits and the depth of each circuit for each dataset.

Table 6. Datasets information: number of patterns, features, classes, and imbalance ratio (IR).

Dataset	Qubits	QRAM depth	Depth associative model
Iris	7	18	14
Cryotherapy	8	16	14
DBA	6	12	10
Caesarian	7	14	12
Haberman	5	10	8
Transfusion	6	12	10
Immunotherapy	9	18	16
FD	11	22	20

5 Conclusions

In the same way as for classical associative models, the generation and representation of feature sets is a critical step in determining the overall performance of the quantum associative algorithm. The structure and representativeness of the input data directly influence the effectiveness of the classification.

The proposed QAM in this work operates directly with real-valued inputs, avoiding the need to convert data into binary form. This approach significantly reduces both the number of qubits required and the amount of classical preprocessing, enabling a more compact quantum representation of the input space. Such efficiency is particularly advantageous when dealing with datasets of high dimensionality, where qubit resources are limited.

In contrast to other associative models that rely on the Hamming distance and Grover's algorithm for the retrieval phase, our approach bypasses the need for binarization and the construction of complex quantum oracles. This simplifies the circuit design and improves scalability to larger datasets. As a result, the proposed model offers a practical and resource-efficient alternative for quantum pattern storage and retrieval.

The proposed model is competitive with a balanced dataset with respect to other algorithm-based metrics that use the same metric amplitude encoding, with an increase in accuracy from 5.4% to 21%, showing its potential to improve classification performance.

Future work will aim to extend the exploration of its integration with different types of data, such as images.

Acknowledgement. This work was partially supported by project No. 20231289 SIP-IPN, México. Areli-Yesareth Guerrero-Estrada acknowledges support from SECIHTI México, Grant No. 815227.

Disclosure of Interests. The authors declare no competing interests.

Availability of Data and Materials. The datasets analyzed during the current study are available in the UC Irvine machine learning repository: Iris - https://doi.org/10.24432/C56C76

Cryotherapy - https://doi.org/10.24432/C5FC7C

Blood Transfusion Service Center - https://doi.org/10.24432/C5GS39

Caesarian Section Classification - https://doi.org/10.24432/C5N59X

Fertility - https://doi.org/10.24432/C5Z01Z

Immunotherapy - https://doi.org/10.24432/C5DC72

Haberman's Survival - https://doi.org/10.24432/C5XK51

Banknote Authentication - https://doi.org/10.24432/C55P57

References

1. Amin, M., Ali, A.: Caesarian Section Classification Dataset. UCI Mach. Learn, Repository (2018)
2. Diamantini, M.C., Trugenberger, C.A.: High-capacity quantum associative memories. arXiv preprint arXiv:1506.01231 (2015)
3. Dobnikar, A., Steele, N.C., Pearson, D.W., Albrecht, R.F., Ventura, D., Martinez, T.: A quantum associative memory based on grover's algorithm. In: Artificial Neural Nets and Genetic Algorithms: Proceedings of the International Conference in Portorož, Slovenia, 1999, pp. 22–27. Springer (1999)
4. Dua, D., Graff, C.: Iris. UCI Machine Learning Repository (2019)
5. Fahime, K., Roohallah, A.M.R., Layegh, P.: Cryotherapy Dataset . UCI Machine Learning Repository (2018)
6. Farhi, E., Neven, H.: Classification with quantum neural networks on near term processors. arXiv preprint arXiv:1802.06002 (2018)
7. Feng, C., Zhao, B., Zhou, X., Ding, X., Shan, Z.: An enhanced quantum k-nearest neighbor classification algorithm based on polar distance. Entropy **25**(1), 127 (2023)
8. Gil, D., Girela, J.: Fertility. UCI Machine Learning Repository (2012). https://doi.org/10.24432/C5Z01Z
9. Giovannetti, V., Lloyd, S., Maccone, L.: Quantum random access memory. Phys. Rev. Lett. **100**(16), 160501 (2008)
10. Guerrero-Estrada, A.Y., Quezada, L., Sun, G.H.: Benchmarking quantum versions of the knn algorithm with a metric based on amplitude-encoded features. Sci. Reports **14**(1), 16697 (2024)
11. Haberman, S.: Haberman's Survival. UCI Machine Learning Repository (1999)
12. Hopfield, J.J.: Neural networks and physical systems with emergent collective computational abilities. Proc. Natl. Acad. Sci. **79**(8), 2554–2558 (1982)
13. Khozeimeh, F., Alizadehsani, R., Roshanzamir, M., Layegh, P.: Immunotherapy Dataset. UCI Machine Learning Repository (2018)
14. Khozeimeh, F., et al.: Intralesional immunotherapy compared to cryotherapy in the treatment of warts. Int. J. Dermatol. **56**(4), 474–478 (2017)
15. Li, J., Zhang, J., Zhang, J., Zhang, S.: Quantum KNN classification with k value selection and neighbor selection. IEEE Trans. Comput. Aided Design Integrated Circuits Syst. (2023)
16. Lohweg, V.: Banknote Authentication. UCI Machine Learning Repository (2013)
17. Quezada, L., Sun, G.H., Dong, S.H.: Quantum version of the k-nn classifier based on a quantum sorting algorithm. Ann. Phys. **534**(5), 2100449 (2022)

18. Rebentrost, P., Bromley, T.R., Weedbrook, C., Lloyd, S.: Quantum hopfield neural network. Phys. Rev. A **98**(4), 042308 (2018)
19. Rebentrost, P., Mohseni, M., Lloyd, S.: Quantum support vector machine for big data classification. Phys. Rev. Lett. **113**(13), 130503 (2014)
20. Salman, T., Baram, Y.: Quantum set intersection and its application to associative memory. J. Mach. Learn. Res. **13**(1), 3177–3206 (2012)
21. Sánchez-Manilla, A.A., López-Yáñez, I., Sun, G.H.: Alpha-beta hybrid quantum associative memory using hamming distance. Entropy **24**(6), 789 (2022)
22. Schuld, M., Killoran, N.: Quantum machine learning in feature hilbert spaces. Physical Rev. Lett. **122**(4), 040504 (2019)
23. Schuld, M., Sinayskiy, I., Petruccione, F.: Quantum computing for pattern classification. In: Pacific Rim International Conference on Artificial Intelligence, pp. 208–220. Springer (2014)
24. Shan, Z., et al.: Demonstration of breast cancer detection using QSVM on IBM quantum processors. Research Square (2022)
25. Ventura, D., Martinez, T.: Quantum associative memory (1998). https://arxiv.org/abs/quant-ph/9807053
26. Yeh, I.C.: Blood Transfusion Service Center. UCI Machine Learning Repository (2008)
27. Zardini, E., Blanzieri, E., Pastorello, D.: A quantum k-nearest neighbors algorithm based on the euclidean distance estimation. Quantum Mach. Intell. **6**(1), 23 (2024)
28. Zeng, Y., Wang, H., He, J., Huang, Q., Chang, S.: A multi-classification hybrid quantum neural network using an all-qubit multi-observable measurement strategy. Entropy **24**(3), 394 (2022)
29. Zhou, R., Wang, H., Wu, Q., Shi, Y.: Quantum associative neural network with nonlinear search algorithm. Int. J. Theoretical Phys. **51**(3), 705–723 (2012)

Physics-Informed Neural Networks for Approximating the Solution of the 1D Poisson Equation

Emmanuel Angel Cabrera Navarrete(✉) and Gabriela Berenice Díaz Cortès

Instituto Mexicano del Petróleo, Eje Central Lázaro Cárdenas Norte 152, Col. San Bartolo Atepehuacán, Gustavo A. Madero, 07730 Ciudad de México, Mexico
{poseangel,gbdiaz}@imp.mx

Abstract. The Poisson equation is a fundamental partial differential equation that appears in numerous physical and engineering problems, including heat conduction, electrostatics, and fluid flow.

This study presents the implementation of a Physics-Informed Neural Network (PINN) model to approximate the one-dimensional Poisson equation. Classical Neural Networks (NN) rely only on data to train a model. However, they often require a large amount of data to achieve an accurate approximation. PINNs incorporate the governing physical laws directly into the learning process, which makes them useful when there is scarce data. This work compares the approximation of the problem using three approaches: data-only, physics-only, and a hybrid approach combining both. The proposed methodology involves formulating the Poisson problem, defining the loss function according to the studied approach, and conducting a statistical analysis of experiments with different combinations of hyperparameters. Results indicate that the hybrid approach (data and physics), requires less computational work to achieve a more accurate approximation. Furthermore, it shows that the physics-based models outperform the data-based models in accuracy. The findings highlight the effectiveness of PINNs in solving differential equations, especially when data availability is limited. This work contributes to understanding the trade-offs between accuracy and computational costs, and opens the possibility for extending of their applicability to more complex real-world problems. By enabling accurate modeling with limited data, PINNs reduce the need for extensive data collection and resource-intensive simulations which can support sustainable engineering practices.

Keywords: Differential equation · Gradient descent · Physics informed neural network · Poisson equation

1 Introduction

The description of physical phenomena has been made throughout the development of Partial Differential Equations (PDEs). Only a few PDEs have an

C. Palma-Preciado et al. (Eds.): CORE 2025, ACSAR 3, pp. 149–167, 2026.
https://doi.org/10.1007/978-3-032-08894-9_10

analytical solution; the rest are treated with numerical methodologies. However, for large and complex systems, the solution of these equations is computationally expensive and advanced techniques are required to reduce costs [1,2]. Therefore, new approaches are studied and the Physics-Informed Neural Network (PINNs) have emerged as a possible way to reduce computational costs [3,4].

Traditional numerical methods such as the Finite Difference Method (FDM) [5], Finite Volume Method (FVM) [6], and Finite Element Method (FEM) [7] have long been used to solve PDEs by discretizing the domain and obtaining numerical approximations. While effective, these methods can be computationally demanding, especially for complex geometries or high-dimensional problems. PINNs offer a mesh-free alternative, enabling efficient and scalable solutions in data-scarce or nonlinear scenarios.

PINNs are a class of neural networks that incorporate the governing principles of physical phenomena into their architecture, typically represented as mathematical models expressed through PDEs. They can be combined with data obtained from the observation of the phenomena. This hybrid approach gives us a more general model that help us understand the physical phenomena and to improve the approximations of the model.

1.1 Literature Review

Several studies have integrated knowledge of physical systems into the training of machine learning models, laying the foundation for what is now known as physics-informed machine learning [8,9]. One of the earliest efforts to apply neural networks to the solution of differential equations was by Meade and Fernandez [10], who demonstrated how feed-forward neural networks could be used to numerically solve linear ordinary differential equations.

The earliest studies that formally defined these methodologies were introduced by Raissi et al. [11,12], aimed at estimating missing data in complex systems by incorporating information from the physical system into the training of a learning model.

In recent years, research on the applications and development of PINN has increased, as shown in Fig. 1. A self-conducted study has identified the most common research topics. In computational physics, they have been used to simulate complex systems and solve PDEs with high fidelity [13,14]. In geosciences, PINNs have facilitated seismic inversion and subsurface modeling by integrating physical constraints into data-driven workflows [15,16]. Fluid dynamics has emerged as a particularly active area, with studies addressing turbulence, multiphase flows, and lubrication problems using PINNs[17–21]. Moreover, PINNs have proven effective in solving inverse problems, where the goal is to infer unknown parameters or governing equations from observed data [13,22]. Recent applications into quantum mechanics have also shown promise, with quantum-enhanced PINNs offering new methods for modeling multi-variable systems governed by quantum laws [23].

Multiple review articles have synthesized the state of the art in PINNs, highlighting their strengths, limitations, and future directions [24]. These studies underscore the versatility of PINNs and their potential to unify data-driven and physics-based modeling approaches.

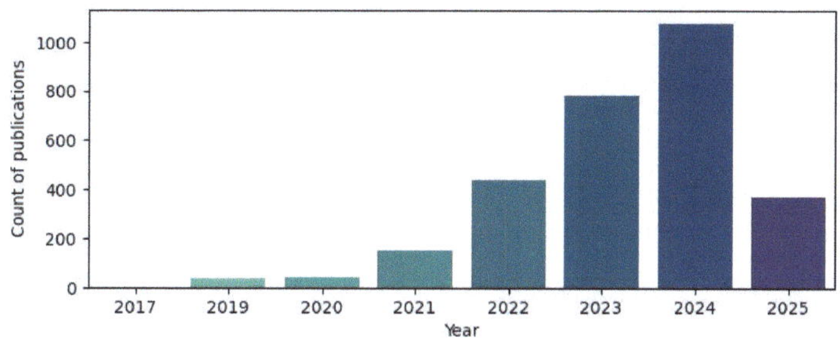

Fig. 1. Number of publications related to the implementation of PINNs per year.

To contextualize the development and growing relevance of PINNs, Table 1 presents a selection of key studies and review articles. These papers were selected based on their foundational contributions to the PINN framework, their coverage of diverse application areas, and their methodological innovations. The inclusion of works such as those by Raissi et al. [11,12] and Karniadakis et al. [3] ensures representation of the theoretical underpinnings and evolution of PINNs. More recent studies, such as those by Zhao et al. [25] and Sánchez-López and Díaz-Cortés [20], explore specialized applications in fluid dynamics and optimization strategies. Additionally, the work by Diab and Al Kobaisi [21] demonstrates the adaptability of PINNs in porous media flow problems, such as the hyperbolic Buckley-Leverett equation, highlighting the versatility of the framework.

1.2 Structure of This Work

Building upon the expanding research on PINNs, this work presents an implementation of various PINNs models for approximating solutions of the one-dimensional Poisson equation. The document is structured as follows:

The first section introduces the problem description, followed by the formulation of the loss function, which incorporates both physical laws and data, and the proposed neuronal network architecture.

The second section presents numerical experiments, that illustrate the proposed PINN configurations. The analytical solution is used to evaluate the accuracy of the results, using the Root Mean Squared Error (RMSE) as a comparative metric. To evaluate computational efficiency, the number of floating-point operations (Flops) is also considered. Additionally, a statistical analysis was conducted on a series of experiments to assess the impact of hyperparameters on the quality of the obtained solutions.

The results have been carefully analyzed to highlight the role and influence of the hyperparameter set in shaping the model's behavior. By examining these

Table 1. Summary of Selected Review Papers on PINNs

Reference	Focus Area	Key Contributions
Raissi et al. (2017) [11]	General PINN methodology	Introduces the original Physics-Informed Neural Network (PINN) framework for solving nonlinear PDEs using deep learning; demonstrates data-driven solution of differential equations by embedding physical laws into the loss function
Raissi et al. (2017) [12]	General PINN methodology	Extends the PINN framework to identify unknown nonlinear PDEs from data by learning both the solution and the governing equations; demonstrates data-driven discovery of physics laws through neural networks
Karniadakis et al. (2021) [3]	General PINN framework	Introduces and formalizes the concept of physics-informed machine learning; reviews core methodologies, architectures, and applications of PINNs across scientific domains; highlights strengths in data-scarce regimes and discusses challenges like stiffness, generalization, and scalability
Almqvist (2021) [18]	PINNs/Reynolds equation	Constructs a meshless PINN to solve the Reynolds boundary value problem; matches analytical solutions and highlights PINNs' potential for generalization to more complex problems
Diab and Al Kobaisi (2021) [21]	Porous media/Buckley-Leverett problem	Proposes a PINN-based solution for the hyperbolic Buckley-Leverett problem with a non-convex flux function
Zhao et al. (2024) [25]	Complex fluid dynamics	Reviews PINN applications in turbulence, multiphase flows, and multiscale modeling; discusses architectural design, optimization strategies, and future challenges
Sánchez-López and Díaz-Cortés (2025) [20]	Fluid Dynamics/Reynolds equation	Develops and optimizes a PINN to solve the 1D stationary Reynolds equation, systematically studies hyperparameters, and highlights the potential of PINN for complex fluid applications

hyperparameters, the study provides deeper insight into their impact on model accuracy. A key contribution of this work is the comparative analysis of three modeling approaches: data-only, physics-only, and a hybrid approach that combines both data and physical laws.

2 Methodology

The behavior of physical models is typically described by differential equations, whose solutions are often approximated using numerical methods. Physics-Informed Neural Networks (PINNs) are a state-of-the-art approach for approximating these solutions u, by the use of a neural network model $\hat{u}(\theta, x)$ as a function of the set of parameters θ. The goal is to approximate $\hat{u} \approx u$, achieved by optimizing the neural network parameters θ. The residual form of the differential equation is given by Eq. (1),

$$\mathcal{N}\left[u(x); x\right] = 0, \qquad x \in \Omega, \tag{1}$$

$$\mathcal{B}\left[u(x); x\right] = 0, \qquad x \in \partial\Omega. \tag{2}$$

In Eq. (1), $\mathcal{N}$ is a differential operator (linear or nonlinear), subject to the initial/boundary condition $\mathcal{B}$, Eq. (2), where x represents points in the domain Ω and on the boundary $\partial\Omega$.

The objective is to minimize the following loss function:

$$\begin{aligned}\mathcal{L}(\theta) = \frac{w_c}{N_c}\sum_{i}^{Nc}\left|\left|\mathcal{N}\left[\hat{u}(\theta, x_c^i); x_c^i\right]\right|\right|^2 + \frac{w_b}{N_b}\sum_{i}^{Nb}\left|\left|\mathcal{B}\left[\hat{u}(\theta, x_b^i); x_b^i\right]\right|\right|^2 \\ + \frac{w_d}{N_d}\sum_{i}^{Nd}\left|\left|\hat{u}_D(\theta, x_d^i) - u_D\right|\right|^2,\end{aligned} \tag{3}$$

where w_c, w_b, and w_d are weights associated with terms that integrate the loss function; in this work, they are set to 1. The first two terms enforce the differential equation and boundary condition constraints, while the last term represents the data loss, which is optional when data is available [26]. The optimization process minimizes the loss function Eq. (3), which integrates both data constraints and physics-based restrictions, ensuring that the learned solution remains consistent with the underlying physical laws.

2.1 Case Study

In this section, the problem is defined as a particular case of the 1D Poisson equation with Dirichlet boundary conditions:

$$\frac{d^2u(x)}{dx^2} = 1, \qquad x \in [0, 1], \tag{4}$$

where u is the solution to Eq. (4), subject to the boundary conditions

$$u(0) = 1, \quad u(1) = 2, \tag{5}$$

with an analytical solution

$$u(x) = \frac{1}{2}(x^2 + x) + 1. \tag{6}$$

The goal is to approximate Eq. (6) using a PINN model $\hat{u}(\theta, x)$, where θ is the set of parameters. This approach involves formulating the loss function $\mathcal{L}$, which incorporates the components of the differential Eq. (4) in $\mathcal{L}_{physics}$, the boundary conditions Eq. (5) in $\mathcal{L}_{BC}$, and the phenomenon observations in $\mathcal{L}_{data}$.

$$\mathcal{L}(\theta) = \underbrace{\langle(\hat{u}'' - 1)^2\rangle}_{\mathcal{L}_{physics}} + \underbrace{(\hat{u}(0) - 1)^2 + (\hat{u}(1) - 2)^2}_{\mathcal{L}_{BC}} + \underbrace{(\hat{u}_D - u_D)^2}_{\mathcal{L}_{data}}, \tag{7}$$

the terms $u''(x)$ and $\hat{u}''(x)$ represent the second derivatives of u and $\hat{u}$ with respect to x, respectively. In the case of data loss component $\mathcal{L}_{data}$, u_D denotes the known data $u(x_D)$, while $\hat{u}_D$ corresponds to the approximation $\hat{u}(x_D)$.

In our case, the proposed PINN model is defined by the expression,

$$\hat{u}(x) = W_i^1 \varphi(W_i^0 x + b_i^0) + b^1. \tag{8}$$

A diagram that describes the architecture of the model is shown in Fig. 2. The set of parameters θ is composed by $\{W_i^0, W_i^1, b_i^0, b^1\}$, also it is defined φ as the activation function. For this case, φ is a sigmoid function, defined as:

$$\varphi(\epsilon) = \frac{1}{1 + e^{-\epsilon}}, \quad \mathbb{R} \to [0, 1]. \tag{9}$$

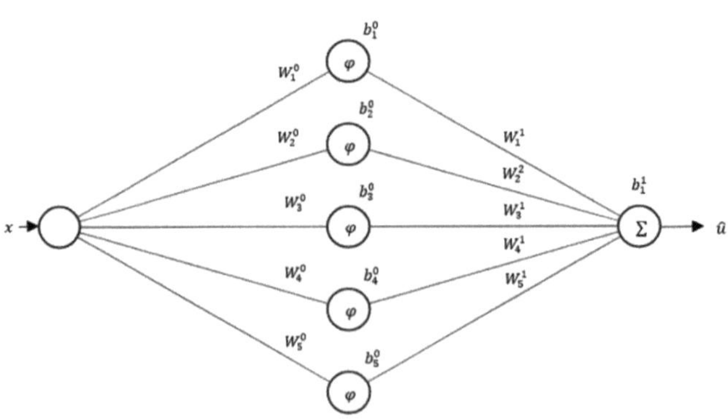

Fig. 2. Proposed neural network model for solving the PINN.

To adjust the model parameters during the training phase, a gradient descent algorithm is implemented, represented by Eq. (10).

$$\theta^{k+1} = \theta^k - \eta \frac{\partial \mathcal{L}(\theta)}{\partial \theta}. \tag{10}$$

The function $\mathcal{L}$ is differentiated with respect to each parameter and multiplied by a factor η, known as the learning rate. Lower η values result in precise but slow convergence, whereas higher η values lead to faster but less accurate convergence. Therefore, the appropriate η value must be determined based on the studied function.

The parameter updates at each iteration k are represented as follows:

$$\begin{aligned} W_i^{1,k+1} &= W_i^{1,k} + \eta \frac{\partial \mathcal{L}(\theta)}{\partial W_i^1}, \qquad & W_i^{0,k+1} &= W_i^{0,k} + \eta \frac{\partial \mathcal{L}(\theta)}{\partial W_i^0}, \\ b^{1,k+1} &= b^{1,k} + \eta \frac{\partial \mathcal{L}(\theta)}{\partial b^1}, \qquad & b_i^{0,k+1} &= b_i^{0,k} + \eta \frac{\partial \mathcal{L}(\theta)}{\partial b_i^0}. \end{aligned} \tag{11}$$

Furthermore, the terms that constitute the loss function Eq. (7), as formulated in Eq. (8), are defined as follows,

$$\begin{aligned} \hat{u}(x) &= \sum_{n=1}^{N} W_i^1 \varphi(W_i^0 x + b_i^0) + b^1, \\ \hat{u}(0) &= \sum_{n=1}^{N} W_i^1 \varphi(b_i^0) + b^1, \\ \hat{u}(1) &= \sum_{n=1}^{N} W_i^1 \varphi(W_i^0 + b_i^0) + b^1, \\ \hat{u}''(x) &= \sum_{n=1}^{N} W_i^1 (W_i^0)^2 \varphi''(W_i^0 x + b_i^0). \end{aligned} \tag{12}$$

In Eq. (12) the terms φ' and φ'' are the first and second derivatives of the activation function, Eq. (9).

2.2 Numerical Experimentation

To compare data-driven and physics-informed models, three configurations: Case 1, Case 2 and Case are proposed. These configurations incorporate different terms in the loss function: Case 1 incorporates only the data term ($\mathcal{L}_{data}$), Case 2 includes physics ($\mathcal{L}_{physics}$) and boundary conditions ($\mathcal{L}_{BC}$) terms, and Case 3 integrates all loss terms: data ($\mathcal{L}_{data}$), physics ($\mathcal{L}_{physics}$) and boundary conditions ($\mathcal{L}_{BC}$).

The domain discretization is determined by the number of collocation points N_i, where u and $\hat{u}$ are computed. The hyperparameters, detailed in Table 2, include the number of neurons (Nn), training epochs (N_e), and data points used during training (Tb).

Table 2. Hyperparameters for the proposed models.

Hyperparameter	PINN 1	PINN 2
N_i	20	20
η	0.002	0.002
Nn	2	5
N_e	1000	1000
Tb	20	20

3 Results

3.1 Case 1: Data Informed Model

In the first experiment (Case 1), the loss function relied exclusively on the $\mathcal{L}_{data}$ component. By focusing only on minimizing the discrepancy between the predicted values $\hat{u}$ and u. The data-only model serves as a baseline for understanding the neural network's approximation without incorporating the governing laws of the system. The comparison between the models and the analytical solution is illustrated in Figs. 3 and 4, while the corresponding loss function curves are displayed in Figs. 5 and 6.

The models approximation struggle to accurately represent the 1D Poisson analytical solution, Eq. (6), exhibiting difficulties in correctly approximating certain features, such as the boundary conditions (see Figs. 3 and 4).

As the number of neurons Nn increases, the model's accuracy improves. For $Nn = 2$ and $Nn = 5$ we obtain RMSE=0.059666 and RMSE=0.030518 respectively (see Table 4). Additionally, both loss curves display a slight linear convergence trend (see Figs. 5 and 6), approaching values near 10^{-3}, yet neither curve stabilizes at a definitive value.

To enhance the approximation using a data-informed model a more complex configuration was proposed, increasing the number of collocation points to $Ni = 40$, the number of neurons to $Nn = 50$, and the learning rate to $\eta = 0.01$ (see Fig. 7). This adjustment reduced the error to RMSE=0.002429, requiring fewer epochs (approximately 400, Fig. 8) to reach a stable solution, compared to the models with $Nn = 2$ and $Nn = 5$ (Figs. 5 and 6). Although, a higher value of η, helps to reach a faster convergence, increasing the number of Ne and Nn implies a higher computational cost. This approach opens the possibility of enhancing the model's results by integrating the mathematical expression that describes the system's behavior into the loss function.

3.2 Case 2: Physics Informed Model

The second experiment (Case 2) was conducted using a loss function exclusively relied on $\mathcal{L}_{physics}$ and $\mathcal{L}_{BC}$, without incorporating data-driven term $\mathcal{L}_{data}$. By focusing solely on the physical constraints represented by the differential equation and boundary conditions, this approach aimed to approximate the solution

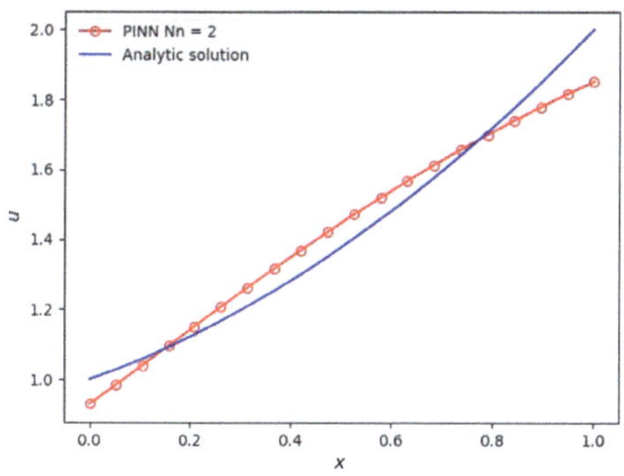

Fig. 3. Approximation of the Poisson equation using a data-informed model with $Nn = 2, Tb = 20$ and $\eta = 0.002$.

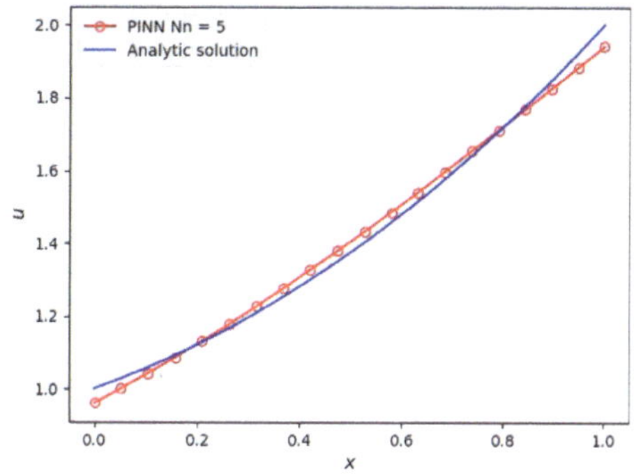

Fig. 4. Approximation of the Poisson equation using a data-informed model with $Nn = 5, Tb = 20$ and $\eta = 0.002$.

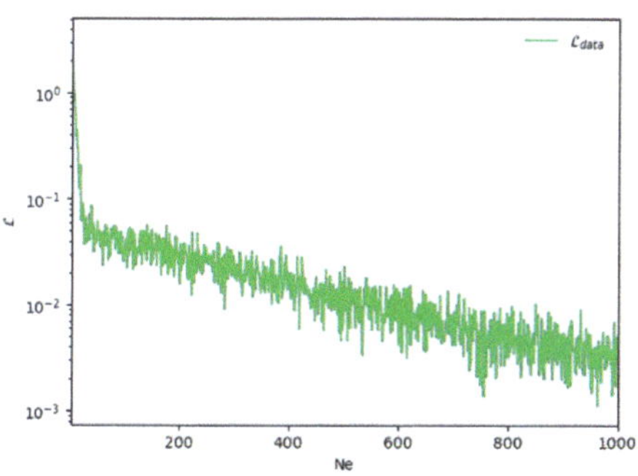

Fig. 5. Loss function curve of the data informed model with $Nn = 2, Tb = 20$ and $\eta = 0.002$.

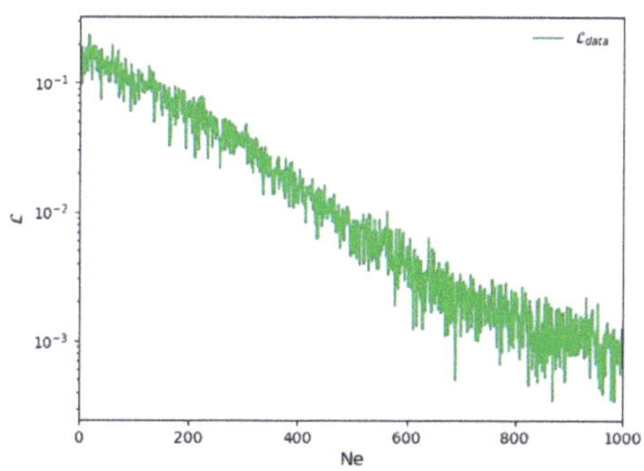

Fig. 6. Loss function curve of the data informed model with $Nn = 5, Tb = 20$ and $\eta = 0.002$.

$\hat{u}$ purely through adherence to the governing laws of the system. Model comparisons for $Nn = 2$ and $Nn = 5$ are illustrated in Figs. 9 and 10. The loss function curves are displayed in Figs. 11 and 12.

Both models exhibit a close approximation to the analytical solution with errors $RMSE = 0.007414$ and $RMSE = 0.004371$ for $Nn = 2$ and $Nn = 5$ respectively (see Table 4), which magnitude is lower than the data-informed models. Physics-informed models show an improved performance of the loss function curve, reaching a stable convergence closer to the 300 epochs, to a value around 10^{-2} (see Figs. 11 and 12). However, the loss curves for the boundary conditions exhibit some instability toward convergence, unlike the $\mathcal{L}_{physics}$ term, the values of $\mathcal{L}_{BC}$ oscillate around a value closer to 10^{-3}. The data term $\mathcal{L}_{data}$ may be necessary to constrain variations in the boundary condition approximation, providing additional regulation and improving overall stability.

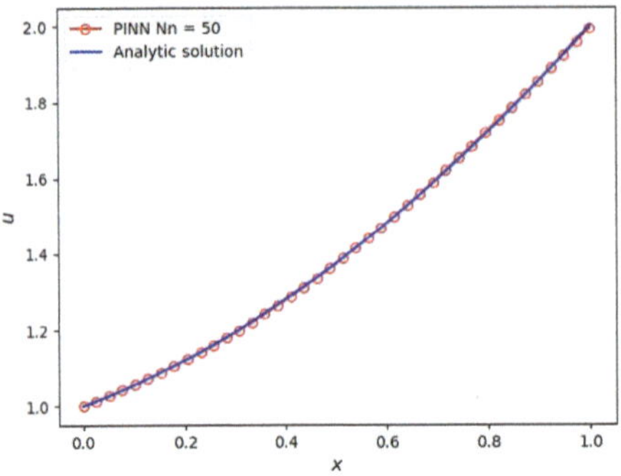

Fig. 7. Approximation of the Poisson equation using a data-informed model with $Nn = 50, Tb = 200$ and $\eta = 0.01$.

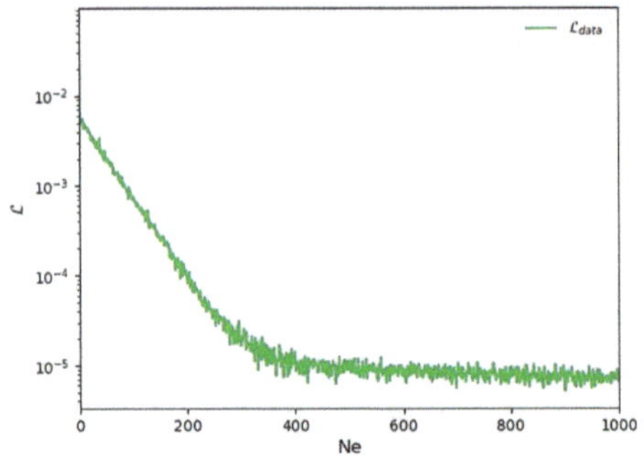

Fig. 8. Loss function curve of the data-informed model with $Nn = 50, Tb = 200$. and $\eta = 0.01$.

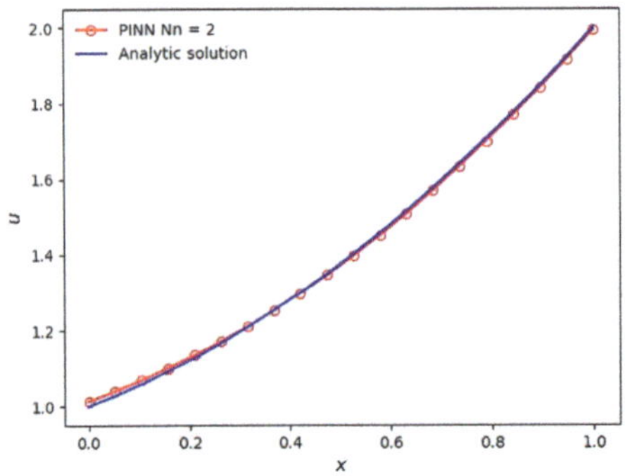

Fig. 9. Approximation of the Poisson equation using a physics informed model with $Nn = 2, Tb = 20$ and $\eta = 0.002$.

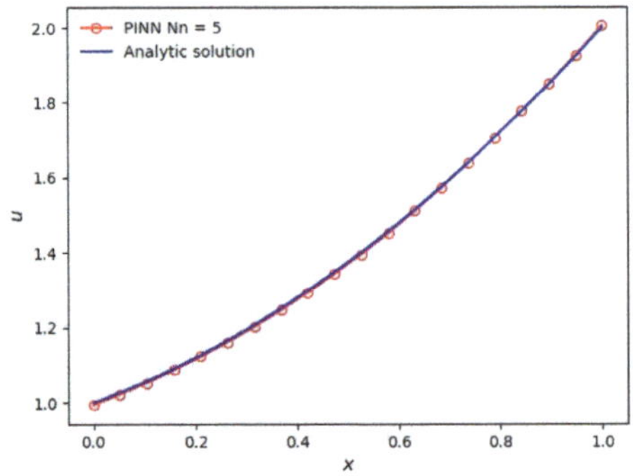

Fig. 10. Approximation of the Poisson equation using a physics informed model with $Nn = 5, Tb = 20$ and $\eta = 0.002$.

The results demonstrate that relying just on physics-based components highlights the model's capacity to produce accurate approximations in data-scarce scenarios, by leveraging the physical principles inherent to the system.

3.3 Case 3: Physics and Data Informed Model

The third experiment (Case 3) was conducted using the loss function integrated by the physics-informed $\mathcal{L}_{physics}$, boundary conditions $\mathcal{L}_{BC}$ and data-informed $\mathcal{L}_{data}$ components. This hybrid approach aimed to leverage the strengths of both methodologies by incorporating observational data, while ensuring adherence to the physical constraints governing the system. The data points u_D, in loss term $\mathcal{L}_{data}$, were calculated using Eq. 6. The proposed approximations are shown alongside the analytical solution in Fig. 13 and 14. Likewise, Fig. 15 and 16 display the loss function curves of the aforementioned models.

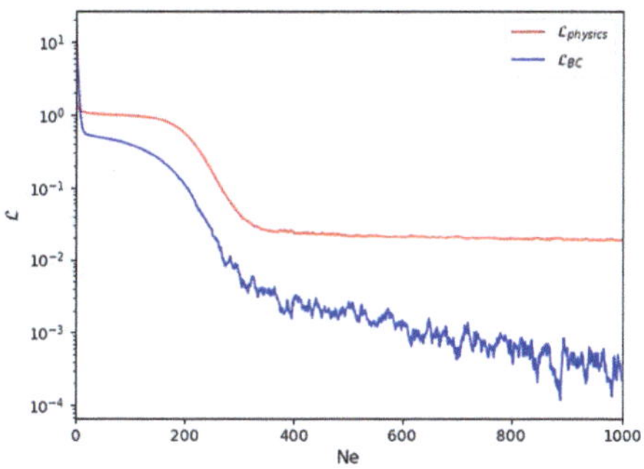

Fig. 11. Loss function curve of the physics informed model with $Nn = 2, Tb = 20$ and $\eta = 0.002$.

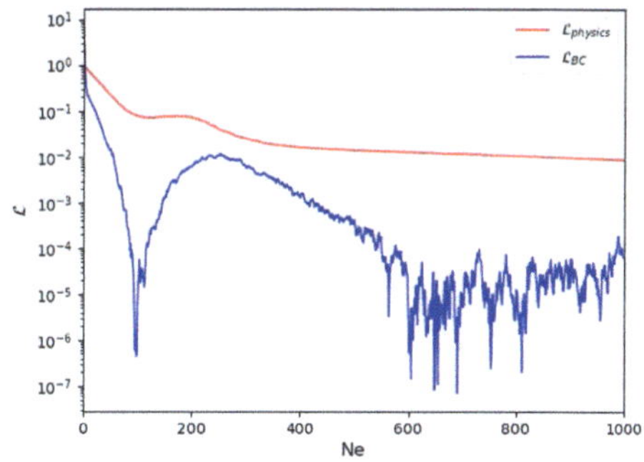

Fig. 12. Loss function curve of the physics informed model with $Nn = 5, Tb = 20$ and $\eta = 0.002$.

The results showed that combining data and physics-informed components improves the approximations (see Figs. 13 and 14), with errors $RMSE = 0.005831$ and $RMSE = 0.002421$ for $Nn = 2$ and $Nn = 5$ respectively (see Table 4), having the lowest errors given the studied hyperparameters in the Table 2. The loss curves exhibit stable convergence in the early epochs (200–300), (see Figs. 15 and 16). Instability is observed in the boundary condition loss function ($\mathcal{L}_{BC}$) and the data loss function ($\mathcal{L}_{data}$). Moreover, the data term plays a crucial role in regulating variations in the boundary conditions, reinforcing the model's ability to align with observed data.

By balancing the contributions of $\mathcal{L}_{data}$, $\mathcal{L}_{physics}$ and $\mathcal{L}_{BC}$, the models achieved a more accurate approximation of $\hat{u}$, enhancing its predictive capabilities within the domain of the provided data.

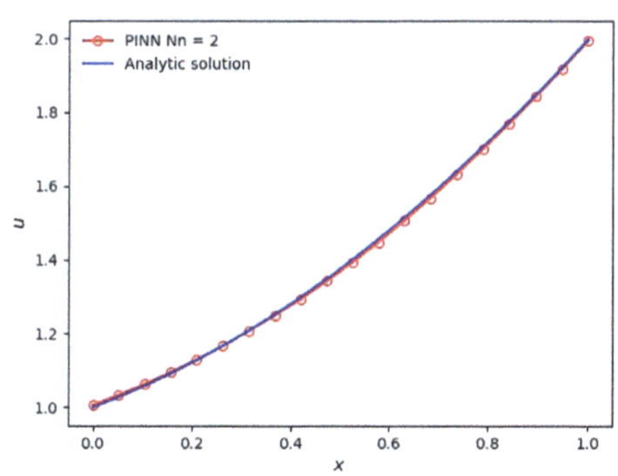

Fig. 13. Approximation of the Poisson equation using a physics and data informed model with $Nn = 2, Tb = 20$ and $\eta = 0.002$.

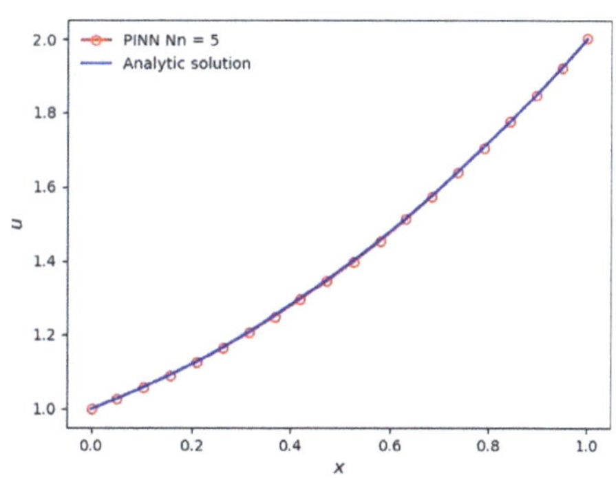

Fig. 14. Approximation of the Poisson equation using a physics and data informed model with $Nn = 5, Tb = 20$ and $\eta = 0.002$.

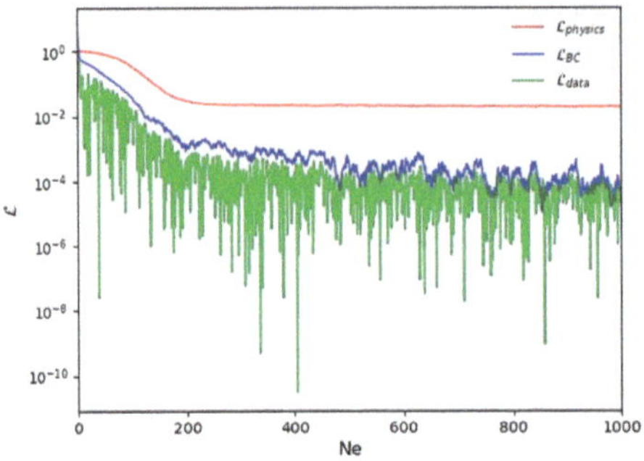

Fig. 15. Loss function curve of the physics and data informed model with $Nn = 2, Tb = 20$ and $\eta = 0.002$.

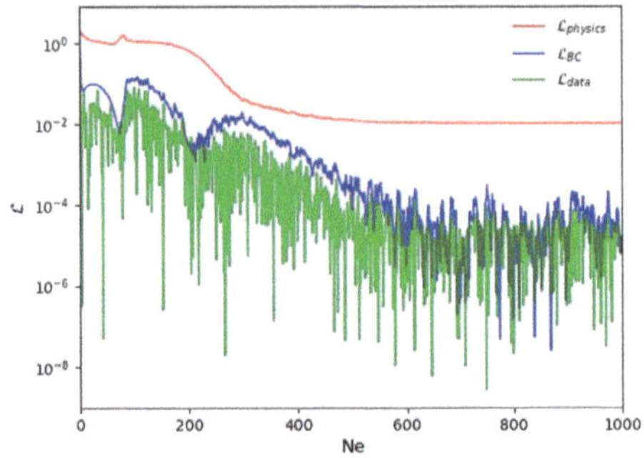

Fig. 16. Loss function curve of the physics and data informed model with $Nn = 5, Tb = 20$ and $\eta = 0.002$.

3.4 Analysis of Results

In this section, the results obtained from previous experiments (Sects. 3.1, 3.2 and 3.3) are analyzed. Measuring the discrepancy between the approximations and the analytical solution is crucial for assessing model accuracy. The RMSE serves as a robust indicator of how closely each model aligns with expected outcomes, defined as:

$$RMSE = \sqrt{\sum_{i}^{n} \frac{(u_i - \hat{u}_i)^2}{n}}, \tag{13}$$

it calculates the average magnitude of the discrepancies between the analytical solution and the predictions made by the specific model.

Additionally, an analysis of the computational cost associated with key operations was conducted in terms of floating-point operations (Flops). This analysis offers valuable insights into the efficiency of the proposed models. Table 3 presents the estimated Flops required for essential computations, including: the forward approximation, derivative evaluations, sigmoid activations, and the components of the loss function.

Table 4 presents a comparison of the studied models, comparing their performance in terms of the RMSE and the computational cost, measured by number of Flops per epoch. These results are directly informed by the operation-level analysis summarized in Table 3, which details the estimated Flops required for the components of the model. All computational costs are reported per epoch for clarity, though training spans 1000 epochs in total.

For $Nn = 2$, the data-informed error was relatively high at 0.059666, but incorporating physics and boundary loss components, it was reduced to 0.007414. The physics and data loss approach lowers the RMSE to 0.005831, demonstrating the benefits of integrating both physical and data loss components. The

Table 3. Summary of Flops per operation for a single value x.

$W_i^1, W_i^0, b_i^0 \in \mathbb{R}^n, \quad x, \epsilon \in \mathbb{R}, \quad n \in \mathbb{Z}, n > 0$		
Notation	Operation	Flops
z_i	$W_i^0 x + b_i^0$	$2n$
$\hat{u}$	$\sum W_i^1 \varphi(z_i) + b^1$	$10n$
$\hat{u}'$	$\sum W_i^1 W_i^0 \varphi'(z_i)$	$21n - 1$
$\hat{u}''$	$\sum W_i^1 (W_i^0)^2 \varphi''(z_i)$	$26n - 1$
$\varphi(\epsilon)$	$\frac{1}{1+e^{-\epsilon}}$	4
$\varphi'(\epsilon)$	$\varphi(\epsilon)(1 - \varphi(\epsilon))$	9
$\varphi''(\epsilon)$	$\varphi(\epsilon)(1 - \varphi(\epsilon))(1 - 2\varphi(\epsilon))$	11
$\mathcal{L}_{\text{data}}$	$(u_D - \hat{u}_D)^2$	$10n + 2$
$\mathcal{L}_{\text{physics}}$	$(\hat{u}'' - 1)^2$	$26n + 1$
$\mathcal{L}_{\text{BC}}$	$(\hat{u}(0) - 1)^2 + (\hat{u}(1) - 2)^2$	$20n + 4$
$\mathcal{L}_{\text{physics}} + \mathcal{L}_{\text{BC}}$	$(\hat{u}'' - 1)^2 + (\hat{u}(0) - 1)^2 + (\hat{u}(1) - 2)^2$	$46n + 5$
$\mathcal{L}_{\text{data}} + \mathcal{L}_{\text{physics}} + \mathcal{L}_{\text{BC}}$	$(u_D - \hat{u}_D)^2 + (\hat{u}'' - 1)^2 + (\hat{u}(0) - 1)^2 + (\hat{u}(1) - 2)^2$	$56n + 7$

Table 4. Summary of PINN models parameters, RMSE and Flops.

PINN hyperparameters, $\mathcal{L}$, RMSE and Flops								
Ne	Tb	η	Nn	$\mathcal{L}$	RMSE	Flops per		
						$\hat{u}$	$\mathcal{L}$	Tb
1000	20	0.002	2	$\mathcal{L}_{data}$	0.059666	20	22	840
				$\mathcal{L}_{physics} + \mathcal{L}_{BC}$	0.007414	20	97	2340
				$\mathcal{L}_{data} + \mathcal{L}_{physics} + \mathcal{L}_{BC}$	0.005831	20	119	2780
			5	$\mathcal{L}_{data}$	0.030518	50	22	1440
				$\mathcal{L}_{physics} + \mathcal{L}_{BC}$	0.004371	50	97	2940
				$\mathcal{L}_{data} + \mathcal{L}_{physics} + \mathcal{L}_{BC}$	0.002421	50	119	3380
	200	0.01	50	$\mathcal{L}_{data}$	0.002429	500	502	200400

computational cost remains low across these configurations, with 20 Flops per approximation $\hat{u}$ and up to 119 Flops for the loss $\mathcal{L}$ evaluation.

Similarly, for $Nn = 5$, a comparable pattern emerges: the data-informed error starts at 0.030518, while the physics-informed approach reduces it to 0.004371, and the combined approach minimizes it to 0.002421. While the accuracy improves, the computational cost also increases, with 50 Flops per approximation $\hat{u}$ and up to 119 Flops for the loss $\mathcal{L}$ highlighting the trade-off between model complexity and performance.

For models with a number of neurons of $Nn = 2$ and $Nn = 5$, incorporating the data loss ($\mathcal{L}_{data}$), physics loss ($\mathcal{L}_{physics}$), and boundary condition loss ($\mathcal{L}_{BC}$) results in the lowest RMSE ($\lesssim 0.006$), (see Table 4), achieving the best overall performance. This aligns with the Flops analysis, where the full loss function requires 56n+7 operations, indicating a higher computational cost but improved accuracy.

The data-informed model with $Nn = 50$ achieves a low error value of 0.002429, suggesting that increasing hyperparameter values, such as: the number of neurons $Nn = 50$, collocation points $N_i = 40$, training batch size $Tb = 200$, and learning rate $\eta = 0.01$ (as seen in Sect. 3.1) enhances accuracy and generalization. However, this improvement comes at a higher computational cost, with 500 Flops per approximation $\hat{u}$ and 502 Flops for the loss $\mathcal{L}$.

The results indicate that physics-and data-informed models outperform data only-informed models with similar hyperparameter configurations(see Table 4). Moreover, achieving an error comparable to the best performing physics-and data-informed model requires greater computational effort, with Flops per approximation $\hat{u}$ ranging from 50 to 500, and for the Tb Flops per epoch increase from 3380 to 200400.

3.5 Statistics of Physics-Informed and Physics and Data-Informed Models

This section outlines the statistical metrics derived from numerical experiments conducted with various values of η and Tb (Table 5), while keeping $N_i = 20$ and $N_e = 1000$ constant. To gain a comprehensive understanding of the physics-informed and data-informed models, 100 experiments were performed for each unique combination of parameters. These experiments evaluated the statistical properties of the models, resulting in the calculation of the mean and standard deviation for each case.

The analysis aims to highlight how parameter variations influence the performance and reliability of the models, providing insights into the robustness and consistency under different experimental conditions. The outcomes of the numerical experiments for physics-informed and physics and data-informed models are shown in Fig. 17 and Fig. 18, which illustrate the mean and standard deviation of the experiments as a function of the hyperparameter combinations, offering a detailed representation of statistical metrics. The corresponding data values are presented in Table 6 and Table 7.

Table 5. Hyperparameter set used in the experiments.

Hyperparameter	Values
Learning rate (η)	{0.001, 0.002, 0.005, 0.01}
Neurons per layer (Nn)	{2, 5, 10}
Batch size (Tb)	{20, 50, 100, 200}

The results indicate that increasing the number of neurons Nn generally leads to lower mean and standard deviation values. For $Nn = 2$, the mean is

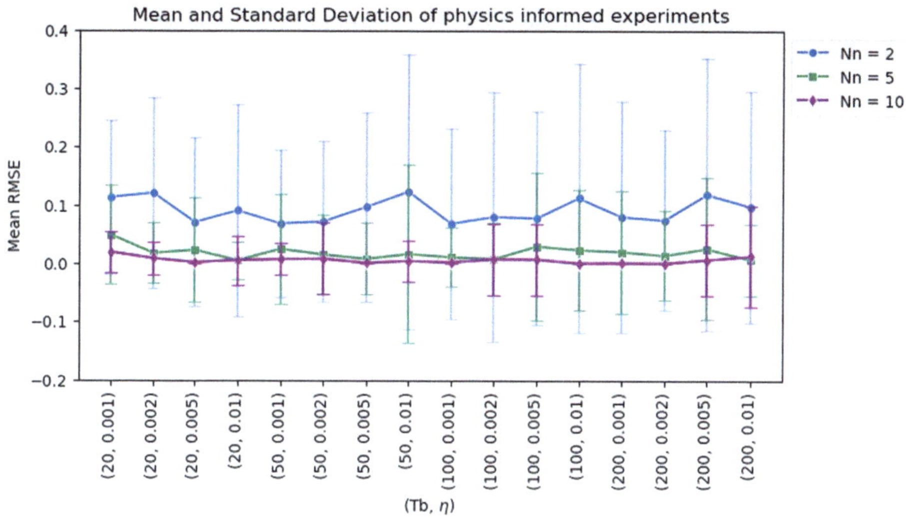

Fig. 17. Mean (dots) and standard deviation (vertical lines) obtained from the physics-informed experiments $\mathcal{L} = \mathcal{L}_{physics} + \mathcal{L}_{BC}$.

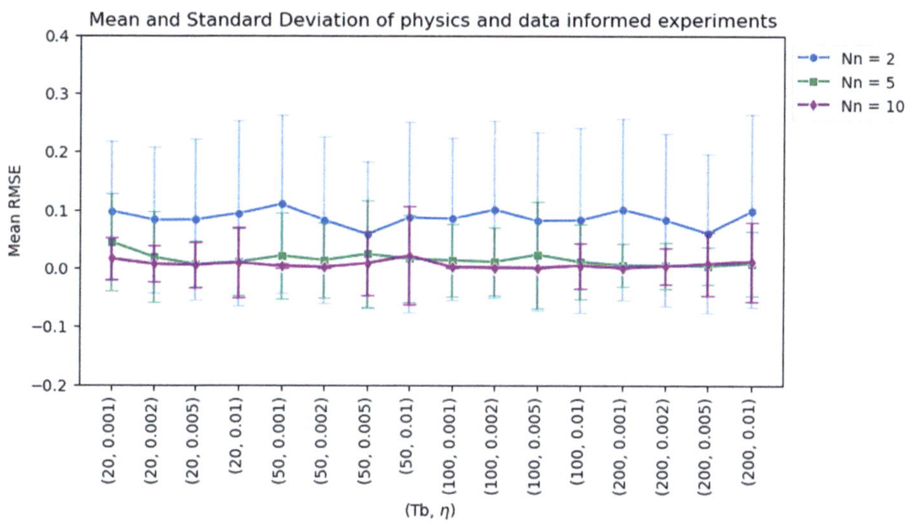

Fig. 18. Mean (dots) and standard deviation (vertical lines) obtained from the physics- and data-informed experiments $\mathcal{L} = \mathcal{L}_{data} + \mathcal{L}_{physics} + \mathcal{L}_{BC}$.

approximately 0.1, whereas for $Nn = 5$ and $Nn = 10$, the mean drops below 0.05, suggesting enhanced accuracy in the models' predictive performance. For the physics and data-informed experiments, smaller learning rates $(0.001, 0.002)$ demonstrate greater stability, exhibiting lower standard deviations and contributing to improved approximation results.

Table 6. Table with the mean and the standard deviation (Std) of the physics-informed experiments. Best results are highlighted for both mean and Std values.

Tb	lr	Mean			Std		
		Nn = 2	Nn = 5	Nn = 10	Nn = 2	Nn = 5	Nn = 10
20	0.001	0.097	0.044	0.016	0.120	0.084	0.036
	0.002	0.083	0.019	0.007	0.126	0.079	0.032
	0.005	0.083	0.007	**0.005**	0.138	0.039	**0.030**
	0.01	0.094	0.011	0.010	0.159	0.057	0.060
50	0.001	0.110	0.021	0.003	0.153	0.074	0.004
	0.002	0.082	0.014	**0.002**	0.143	0.064	**0.001**
	0.005	0.058	0.025	0.009	0.125	0.092	0.054
	0.01	0.087	0.017	0.022	0.164	0.074	0.085
100	0.001	0.085	0.014	0.002	0.139	0.063	0.001
	0.002	0.101	0.011	0.001	0.153	0.058	0.001
	0.005	0.081	0.024	**0.000**	0.153	0.092	**0.000**
	0.01	0.083	0.012	0.004	0.159	0.064	0.039
	0.001	0.101	0.006	**0.001**	0.156	0.037	**0.001**
	0.002	0.083	0.005	0.003	0.148	0.040	0.031
	0.005	0.060	0.004	0.008	0.136	0.032	0.054
	0.01	0.099	0.008	0.012	0.166	0.056	0.068

Larger Tb values (approaching 200) tend to produce more stable standard deviations (around 0.05). RMSE mean values demonstrate greater stability as the number of neurons Nn increases (Table 7). For $Nn = 10$, mean values tend to be closer to 0.01, indicating that adjusting the learning rate η is necessary to maintain consistent performance. Smaller Tb values (approximately 20) show greater variability in both mean values and standard deviations. In some cases, the mean fluctuates around 0.1, while standard deviations exceed 0.05, indicating instability in learning.

Mean RMSE for both physics-informed and physics- and data-informed models remain within a comparable magnitude range (below 0.2 for all values of Nn and η, (see Tables 6 and 7). However, the physics-informed experiments demonstrate greater variability in standard deviation, indicating potential convergence instability. This is consistent with findings from previous studies, which have reported similar instability in physics-informed models [20], particularly when compared to their physics-and-data-informed counterparts.

Table 7. Table with the mean and the standard deviation (Std) of the physics and data-informed experiments. Best results are highlighted for both mean and Std values.

Tb	lr	Mean			Std		
		Nn = 2	Nn = 5	Nn = 10	Nn = 2	Nn = 5	Nn = 10
20	0.001	0.113	0.049	0.020	0.132	0.085	0.035
	0.002	0.121	0.018	0.009	0.164	0.052	0.028
	0.005	0.071	0.023	**0.002**	0.146	0.090	**0.002**
	0.01	0.090	0.005	0.006	0.182	0.032	0.042
50	0.001	0.068	0.025	0.007	0.126	0.094	0.028
	0.002	0.072	0.015	0.008	0.139	0.069	0.061
	0.005	0.097	0.008	**0.001**	0.162	0.061	**0.001**
	0.01	0.123	0.016	0.004	0.236	0.153	0.035
100	0.001	0.068	0.011	0.002	0.163	0.050	**0.001**
	0.002	0.080	0.008	0.007	0.215	0.062	0.061
	0.005	0.078	0.030	0.007	0.184	0.127	0.062
	0.01	0.112	0.023	**0.000**	0.231	0.104	0.001
200	0.001	0.080	0.020	0.001	0.198	0.105	0.001
	0.002	0.074	0.014	**0.000**	0.155	0.077	**0.000**
	0.005	0.118	0.026	0.006	0.234	0.122	0.062
	0.01	0.098	0.007	0.013	0.199	0.062	0.087

4 Conclusions

In this study, a particular solution of the one-dimensional Poisson equation was approximated using various PINN models, including data-informed, physics-informed, and hybrid approaches (physics-and data-informed). A statistical analysis was conducted through experiments involving different hyperparameter configurations for the physics-informed and physics-and data-informed models.

Results shows that physics and data-informed models outperformed data-only models, with RMSE dropping from 0.059666 to 0.005831 for $Nn = 2$, and from 0.030518 to 0.002421 for $Nn = 5$, while a data-only model with higher hyperparameters achieved a similar RMSE of 0.002429 but at a significantly higher computational cost. The mean RMSE value improves as Nn increases, with average values from approximately 0.089 for $Nn = 2$ to 0.006 for $Nn = 10$. This trend highlights the advantage of larger network architectures in both physics-informed and physics-and-data-informed models. Higher learning rates η (0.005 and 0.01) result in lower mean values but greater standard deviations, reaching up to 0.236 in some cases. However, lower learning rates ($\eta = 0.001$) stabilize the standard deviation (values below 0.2), though at the expense of higher mean RMSE values (some exceeding 0.1).

These findings highlight the potential of physics- and data-informed neural networks that achieve a better approximations than a data only model. Furthermore, they present the importance of balancing hyperparameters, such as the number of neurons per layer (Nn), learning rate (η), and training batch size (Tb) to optimize the performance and reliability of PINNs. By improving efficiency and accuracy, such models can contribute to more sustainable computational practices.

4.1 Future Work

Future research can explore deeper architectures and extend PINNs to more complex domains, such as high-dimensional PDEs and nonlinear systems. Emphasis should be placed on balancing accuracy, stability, and computational efficiency through informed hyperparameter tuning.

Acknowledgement. The authors thankfully acknowledge the computer resources, technical expertise and support provided by the Laboratorio Nacional de Supercómputo del Sureste de México, CONACYT member of the network of national laboratories, Proyect: 202203073N.

Disclosure of Interests. The authors have no competing interests to declare that are relevant to the content of this article.

References

1. Díaz-Cortés, G.B., Vuik, C., Jansen, J.D.: On POD-based deflation vectors for DPCG applied to porous media problems. J. Comput. Appl. Math. **330**(Suppl. C), 193–213 (2018)
2. Díaz-Cortés, G.B., Vuik, C., Jansen, J.D.: Accelerating the solution of linear systems appearing in two-phase reservoir simulation by the use of pod-based deflation methods. Comput. Geosci. **25**(5), 1621–1645 (2021)
3. Karniadakis, G.E., Kevrekidis, I.G., Lu, L., Perdikaris, P., Wang, S., Yang, L.: Physics-informed machine learning. Nat. Rev. Phys. **3**(6), 422–440 (2021)
4. Huang, B., Wang, J.: Applications of physics-informed neural networks in power systems - a review. IEEE Trans. Power Syst. **38**(1), 572–588 (2023)
5. Smith, G.D.: Numerical Solution of Partial Differential Equations: Finite Difference Methods, 3 edn. Oxford University Press (1985)
6. Moukalled, F., Mangani, L., Darwish, M.: The Finite Volume Method in Computational Fluid Dynamics: An Advanced Introduction with OpenFOAM and Matlab. Springer (2016)
7. Zienkiewicz, O.C., Taylor, R.L., Zhu, J.Z.: The Finite Element Method: Its Basis and Fundamentals, 6 edn. Elsevier (2005)
8. Raissi, M., Perdikaris, P., Karniadakis, G.E.: Inferring solutions of differential equations using noisy multi-fidelity data. CoRR, abs/1607.04805 (2016)
9. Raissi, M.: Deep hidden physics models: deep learning of nonlinear partial differential equations (2018)
10. Meade Jr, A.J., Fernandez, A.A.: The numerical solution of linear ordinary differential equations by feed-forward neural networks. Math. Comput. Model. **19**(12), 1–25 (1994)

11. Raissi, M., Perdikaris, P., Karniadakis, G.E.: Physics informed deep learning (part I): data-driven solutions of nonlinear partial differential equations. CoRR, abs/1711.10561 (2017)
12. Raissi, M., Perdikaris, P., Karniadakis, G.E.: Physics informed deep learning (part II): data-driven discovery of nonlinear partial differential equations. CoRR, abs/1711.10566 (2017)
13. Raissi, M., Perdikaris, P., Karniadakis, G.E.: Physics-informed neural networks: a deep learning framework for solving forward and inverse problems involving nonlinear partial differential equations. J. Comput. Phys. **378**, 686–707 (2019)
14. Farea, A., Yli-Harja, O., Emmert-Streib, F.: Understanding physics-informed neural networks: techniques, applications, trends, and challenges. In: Proceedings of the Conference Name (2024)
15. Zheng, Y., Wang, Y.: Ground-penetrating radar wavefield simulation via physics-informed neural network solver. Geophysics **88**(2), KS47–KS57 (2023)
16. Li, P., Grana, D., Liu, M.: Bayesian neural network and Bayesian physics-informed neural network via variational inference for seismic petrophysical inversion. Geophysics **89**(6), M185–M196 (2024)
17. Cai, S., Mao, Z., Wang, Z., Yin, M., Karniadakis, G.E.: Physics-informed neural networks (PINNs) for fluid mechanics: a review (2021)
18. Almqvist, A.: Fundamentals of physics-informed neural networks applied to solve the reynolds boundary value problem. In: Proceedings of the Conference Name (2021)
19. Jin, X., Cai, S., Li, H., Karniadakis, G.E.: NSFnets (Navier-Stokes flow nets): physics-informed neural networks for the incompressible Navier-stokes equations. J. Comput. Phys. **426**, 109951 (2021)
20. Sánchez-López, Z., Díaz-Cortés, G.B.: Optimizing a physics-informed neural network to solve the reynolds equation. Revista Mexicana de Física **71**(020601), 1–18 (2025)
21. Diab, W., Kobaisi, M.A.: PINNs for the solution of the hyperbolic Buckley-Leverett problem with a non-convex flux function (2021)
22. Zhang, Yijie, Zhu, Xueyu, Gao, Jinghuai: Seismic inversion based on acoustic wave equations using physics-informed neural network. IEEE Trans. Geosci. Remote Sens. **61**, 1–1 (2023)
23. Panichi, G., Corli, S., Prati, E.: Quantum physics informed neural networks for multi-variable partial differential equations (2025)
24. Li, Z.: A review of physics-informed neural networks. Appl. Comput. Eng. **133**, 165–173 (2025)
25. Zhao, C., Zhang, F., Lou, W., Wang, X., Yang, J.: A comprehensive review of advances in physics-informed neural networks and their applications in complex fluid dynamics. Phys. Fluids **36**(10), 101301 (2024)
26. Hao, Z., et al.: PINNacle: a comprehensive benchmark of physics-informed neural networks for solving PDEs (2024)

Modeling the Diffusion Equation with Physics-Informed Neural Networks (PINNs) and Artificial Neural Networks (ANNs)

Zoila Sánchez López(✉), Gabriela Berenice Díaz Cortés, Galileo Domínguez Zacarías, and Gorgonio Fuentes Cruz

Instituto Mexicano del Petróleo, Eje Central Lázaro Cárdenas Norte 152, Col. San Bartolo Atepehuacán, Gustavo A. Madero, C.P. 07730 Ciudad de México, Mexico
soydzoi@gmail.com, {gbdiaz,gdzacari,gfuentes}@imp.mx

Abstract. Physics-Informed Neural Networks (PINNs) offer a powerful approach for solving differential equations by integrating physical laws directly into the training process, specifically into the loss function. This study explores the application of both PINNs and traditional artificial neural networks (ANNs) to simulate pressure behavior, modeled by the diffusion equation, which is key to reservoir characterization through well pressure tests. Two scenarios are analyzed: in the first, a PINN solves the one-dimensional diffusion equation in Cartesian coordinates, representing linear flow. Its predictions are compared with results obtained using the finite difference method and with the analytical solution. In the second scenario, an ANN is trained with semi-analytical data generated from the Laplace-domain solution of the radial diffusion equation, which is numerically inverted using the Stehfest method. This network accurately reproduces the pressure response during a drawdown test. The results show that both PINNs and ANNs are capable of approximating complex solutions with high fidelity, supporting their potential for pressure test analysis and real-time decision-making in petroleum engineering.

Keywords: Diffusion Equation · Radial Flow · Linear Flow · Well Pressure Tests · Petroleum Engineering

1 Introduction

In 2017, Raissi and collaborators [1,2] introduced an innovative strategy for solving differential equations by combining machine learning with physical knowledge. This approach was later consolidated in a 2019 publication [3], giving rise to the concept known as Physics-Informed Neural Networks (PINNs). The core idea behind this methodology is the direct incorporation of the governing physical laws into the loss function of the neural network, enabling the training process to rely not only on observational data but also on fundamental physical principles. By integrating mathematical models with measurable data, PINNs can

C. Palma-Preciado et al. (Eds.): CORE 2025, ACSAR 3, pp. 168–186, 2026.
https://doi.org/10.1007/978-3-032-08894-9_11

be applied to both forward problems—where the goal is to predict the behavior of a system from known equations—and inverse problems—where unknown model parameters are inferred from observed data. The authors demonstrated the effectiveness of this method by applying it to representative nonlinear partial differential equations, such as the Schrödinger, Burgers, and Allen-Cahn equations [3].

Unlike traditional numerical methods—such as finite differences, finite volumes, and finite elements—which are generally not designed to directly incorporate observational data during the solution process, PINNs propose an integrative approach. This approach enables the fusion of physical knowledge and available data within a unified computational framework [4,5]. Thanks to this dual capability, PINNs can address both forward and inverse problems involving partial differential equations (PDEs), whether linear or nonlinear.

PINNs have proven effective in solving complex problems across various fields, such as hemodynamics, elastic models, geosciences, and industrial processes [6]. In all these disciplines, their versatility—including the ability to adapt to situations where the underlying physical model is not fully known—is widely supported in the literature. Cuomo et al. (2022) [6] provide a comprehensive review that compiles specific references and detailed examples of these applications, along with an in-depth analysis of the development and use of PINNs, highlighting their hybrid nature that combines physical models with data. Complementarily, Ganga and Uddin (2024) [7] examine the evolution of PINNs, the potential of their variants to overcome existing limitations, and their application to fluid flow problems.

Beyond these general developments, several studies have specifically focused on fluid dynamics, where innovative approaches have further showcased the strengths of PINNs [8]. Reported applications include scenarios with limited training data [9], incomplete or noisy boundary conditions, and inverse problems [10]. Additional works have addressed cases with partial knowledge of the physical system and scarce data [11], irregular geometries without requiring datasets [12], and ill-posed problems such as those with unknown boundary conditions [13]. In some instances, PINNs have even been successfully applied without relying on experimental data or prior simulations [14].

In particular, within petroleum engineering, PINNs have been employed to solve the Buckley–Leverett problem, characterized by a non-convex flux function and extensively studied in the analysis of two-phase flows in porous media [15,16]. Traditional numerical approaches in petroleum engineering can be computationally intensive or inadequate for certain scenarios. PINNs provide a compelling alternative by incorporating physical constraints such as Darcy's law or the Navier–Stokes equations directly into the learning process. Their application spans several areas, including reservoir simulation and pressure distribution prediction, which are critical for optimizing hydrocarbon recovery strategies [17].

Latrach et al. (2024) [18] present a review of PINNs and their applications in the oil and gas industry, as well as in carbon and hydrogen storage and geothermal systems. This review highlights a wide range of applications, including drilling engineering, reservoir engineering and fluid flow, production forecasting and optimization, and CO_2 storage.

Other important applications include history matching, a process of adjusting reservoir models to fit historical production data and thus improving their reliability [8]. Enhanced oil recovery (EOR) techniques also benefit from PINNs by simulating methods such as water flooding and gas injection, enabling scenario evaluation and process optimization [19]. Furthermore, PINNs facilitate real-time monitoring and management of reservoirs by providing faster and more efficient solutions compared to conventional methods [20].

It has been shown that Physics-Informed Neural Networks (PINNs) can achieve a significant reduction in computational time compared to conventional time-domain simulation methods [21]. These capabilities suggest that the application of PINNs in petroleum engineering—such as in reservoir simulations, multiphase flow modeling, or injection processes—could help reduce computational costs and energy consumption, promoting more sustainable modeling and operational practices in the field.

Specifically, for well pressure testing, Badawy and Gildin (2023) [22] applied PINNs to solve both forward and inverse problems related to the one-dimensional diffusivity equation in Cartesian coordinates, using production data to estimate key reservoir properties such as horizontal permeability and boundary distance. They also analyzed radial flow in a circular reservoir under various well operating conditions, identifying limitations in using a single PINN; consequently, they adopted a domain decomposition method to improve accuracy [23].

Another recent proposal is the La-PPINN method introduced by Fan et al. (2025) [24], which integrates pressure test observations with Laplace-space models to estimate both reservoir and well parameters. Their results demonstrated accurate recovery of pressure profiles and effective parameter inversion, even in noisy environments, for complex systems such as dual-porosity, triple-porosity, and composite reservoirs.

In this work, we focus on exploring the application of both PINNs and ANNs to model pressure behavior governed by the diffusion equation, a fundamental aspect of reservoir characterization through well pressure tests. We analyze different scenarios to assess the capabilities and limitations of these approaches in simulating pressure responses relevant to petroleum engineering.

It is important to highlight the fundamental differences between our approach and the methodologies presented in the previously cited works [22,24]. Both studies incorporate experimental or field data for training; however, our proposal does not yet integrate such data, although its inclusion is planned for future work.

Reference [22] addresses the one-dimensional diffusion equation in Cartesian coordinates under conditions of constant well pressure and no-flow at the boundaries, simulating a buildup test. In contrast, our work considers a non-homogeneous Neumann boundary condition representing constant flow at the well, corresponding to a drawdown test. Additionally, we compare our results with those obtained using the finite difference method and analytical solutions to validate the model. In the radial case, we employ the Stehfest numerical inversion method to obtain a semi-analytical solution that serves as a reference for training a traditional artificial neural network in the time-space domain—an approach not considered in [22]. This highlights the diversity of possible strategies to address modeling problems in reservoir engineering.

Unlike [24], where the neural network is trained directly in the Laplace domain and the results are subsequently inverted to the time-space domain, our approach conducts the entire training process within the time-space domain. The Laplace transform is employed solely to generate a semi-analytical reference solution. Furthermore, the code developed in this study is publicly available on GitHub at https://github.com/gbdiazc/PINN_Difussion_Equation, fostering reproducibility and scientific transparency.

2 Theory

2.1 Physics-Informed Neural Networks for Solving PDEs

The PINN framework extends conventional neural networks by embedding the physics of the problem into the loss function. The goal is to find a neural approximation $\boldsymbol{u}_\theta(\boldsymbol{x}, t)$ that satisfies a given partial differential equation (PDE), along with its initial and boundary conditions [3]. The residual of a general PDE is expressed as:

$$\mathcal{R}(t, \boldsymbol{x}) = \frac{\partial \boldsymbol{u}(\boldsymbol{x}, t)}{\partial t} + \mathcal{N}[\boldsymbol{u}(\boldsymbol{x}, t)] = 0, \quad \boldsymbol{x} \in \boldsymbol{\Omega}, \quad t \in [0, T], \tag{1}$$

subject to:

$$\boldsymbol{u}(t = 0, \boldsymbol{x}) = g(\boldsymbol{x}), \quad \boldsymbol{x} \in \boldsymbol{\Omega}, \tag{2}$$

$$\mathcal{B}[\boldsymbol{u}(\boldsymbol{x}, t)] = 0, \quad \boldsymbol{x} \in \partial\boldsymbol{\Omega}, \quad t \in [0, T]. \tag{3}$$

Here, $\mathcal{N}[\cdot]$ denotes a (linear or nonlinear) differential operator, and $\mathcal{B}[\cdot]$ is an operator representing the boundary conditions (Dirichlet, Neumann, Robin, or periodic). The vector $\boldsymbol{x} = (\boldsymbol{x_1}, \ldots, \boldsymbol{x_d}) \in \boldsymbol{\Omega}$ is the spatial coordinate, that in general could be in $\mathbb{R}^d$, and $t \in [0, T]$ is the temporal coordinate. The spatial domain and the boundary of the domain where the PDE is defined are represented by $\boldsymbol{\Omega}, \boldsymbol{\partial\Omega} \in \mathbb{R}^d$, respectively.

The neural network employed is a fully connected feedforward architecture composed of an input layer, multiple hidden layers, and a final output layer. If $\boldsymbol{z}^0 = (\boldsymbol{x}, t)$ is the input layer, $\boldsymbol{z}^l = (\boldsymbol{x}, t)$ represents the intermediate layers, where $1 \leq l \leq L - 1$, and $\boldsymbol{z}^L = (\boldsymbol{x}, t)$ is the output layer, then the final output of the network, $u_\theta(\boldsymbol{z})$, can be expressed as a linear combination $\left(\boldsymbol{w}^l \boldsymbol{z}^l + \boldsymbol{b}^l\right)$ using the weight matrices $\boldsymbol{w}^L$ and bias vectors $\boldsymbol{b}^L$ of the l-th layer, together with activation functions $\varphi(\cdot)$, which may be linear or nonlinear [25,26]. That is, the forward pass of the network is given by:

$$u_\theta(z) := \boldsymbol{w}^L \boldsymbol{\varphi}^L \left(\boldsymbol{w}^{L-1} \boldsymbol{\varphi}^{L-1} \left(\cdots \boldsymbol{\varphi}^1 \left(\boldsymbol{w}^0 z + \boldsymbol{b}^0\right) \cdots\right) + \boldsymbol{b}^{L-1}\right) + \boldsymbol{b}^L. \tag{4}$$

If the PDE depends on the variables $\boldsymbol{x}, t$, a set of points $\boldsymbol{x}_i, t_i$ in the domain $\boldsymbol{\Omega}$ are selected to train the network. This set of points $\boldsymbol{z}^0$ will be the input to the network. In the output layer $\boldsymbol{z}^L$, the expected approximation $u_\theta(\boldsymbol{x}, t)$ is obtained. The solution $\boldsymbol{u}(t, \boldsymbol{x})$ of the PDE is approximated with the output of a Neural Network $\boldsymbol{u}_\theta(t, \boldsymbol{x})$. The total loss is a weighted sum of several components:

$$\mathcal{L}(\boldsymbol{\theta}) = \boldsymbol{\omega}_f \mathcal{L}_{PDE}(\boldsymbol{\theta}) + \boldsymbol{\omega}_{BC} \mathcal{L}_{BC}(\boldsymbol{\theta}) + \boldsymbol{\omega}_{IC} \mathcal{L}_{IC}(\boldsymbol{\theta}) + \boldsymbol{\omega}_D \mathcal{L}_{Data}(\boldsymbol{\theta}), \tag{5}$$

where the first term corresponds to the residual of the PDE ($\mathcal{L}_{PDE}$). The second term accounts for the boundary conditions ($\mathcal{L}_{BC}$), and the third incorporates the initial conditions ($\mathcal{L}_{IC}$), and the last term is related to the observation data ($\mathcal{L}_{Data}$) if they are available [27]. Where $\boldsymbol{\omega}_f$, $\boldsymbol{\omega}_{BC}$, $\boldsymbol{\omega}_{IC}$, and $\boldsymbol{\omega}_D$ are the weights associated with each of the loss terms in Eq. (5).

In this work, all weights are set to one, i.e., $\boldsymbol{\omega}_f = \boldsymbol{\omega}_{\mathrm{BC}} = \boldsymbol{\omega}_{\mathrm{IC}} = \boldsymbol{\omega}_D = 1$, and each component of the loss function is computed using the mean squared error (MSE), as follows [6,8,27]:

$$\begin{aligned}
\mathcal{L}_{PDE}(\boldsymbol{\theta}) &= \frac{1}{N_r} \sum_{i=1}^{N_r} \left\| \mathcal{R}_\theta(t_r^i, \boldsymbol{x}_r^i) \right\|^2, \\
\mathcal{L}_{IC}(\boldsymbol{\theta}) &= \frac{1}{N_{IC}} \sum_{i=1}^{N_{IC}} \left\| \boldsymbol{u}_\theta(0, \boldsymbol{x}_{IC}^i) - g(\boldsymbol{x}_{IC}^i) \right\|^2, \\
\mathcal{L}_{BC}(\boldsymbol{\theta}) &= \frac{1}{N_{BC}} \sum_{i=1}^{N_{BC}} \left\| \mathcal{B}[\boldsymbol{u}_\theta](t_{BC}^i, \boldsymbol{x}_{BC}^i) \right\|^2, \\
\mathcal{L}_{Data}(\boldsymbol{\theta}) &= \frac{1}{N_D} \sum_{i=1}^{N_D} \left\| \boldsymbol{u}_\theta(t_D^i, \boldsymbol{x}_D^i) - u_D^{*i} \right\|^2.
\end{aligned} \tag{6}$$

The sets of points $\{(t_r^i, \boldsymbol{x}_r^i)\}_{i=1}^{N_r}$, $\{\boldsymbol{x}_{IC}^i\}$, and $\{(t_{BC}^i, \boldsymbol{x}_{BC}^i)\}$ are used to enforce the residual, initial, and boundary conditions, respectively. When training is performed using only data, the loss function consists solely of the term $\mathcal{L}_{\mathrm{Data}}(\boldsymbol{\theta})$, effectively reducing the model to a traditional artificial neural network (ANN). In other words, a traditional ANN can be regarded as a particular case of the PINN framework in which no physical constraints are imposed. This situation corresponds to setting the weights associated with the physical terms to zero, that is, $\boldsymbol{\omega}_f = \boldsymbol{\omega}_{IC} = \boldsymbol{\omega}_{BC} = 0$ in Eq. (5), thereby reducing the PINN model to a standard ANN trained solely on labeled data (see Fig. 1).

We denote the set of trainable parameters $\boldsymbol{w}^l$ and $\boldsymbol{b}^l$ for each layer l as a single vector $\boldsymbol{\theta}$, defined as:

$$\boldsymbol{\theta} = \{\boldsymbol{w}^1, \boldsymbol{w}^2, \ldots, \boldsymbol{w}^L, \boldsymbol{b}^1, \boldsymbol{b}^2, \ldots, \boldsymbol{b}^L\}. \tag{7}$$

These parameters are randomly initialized and updated through gradient-based optimization, aiming to minimize the loss function $\mathcal{L}(\boldsymbol{\theta})$. A typical gradient descent step is given by:

$$\boldsymbol{\theta}_{n+1} = \boldsymbol{\theta}_n - \eta \nabla_{\boldsymbol{\theta}} \mathcal{L}(\boldsymbol{\theta}_n), \tag{8}$$

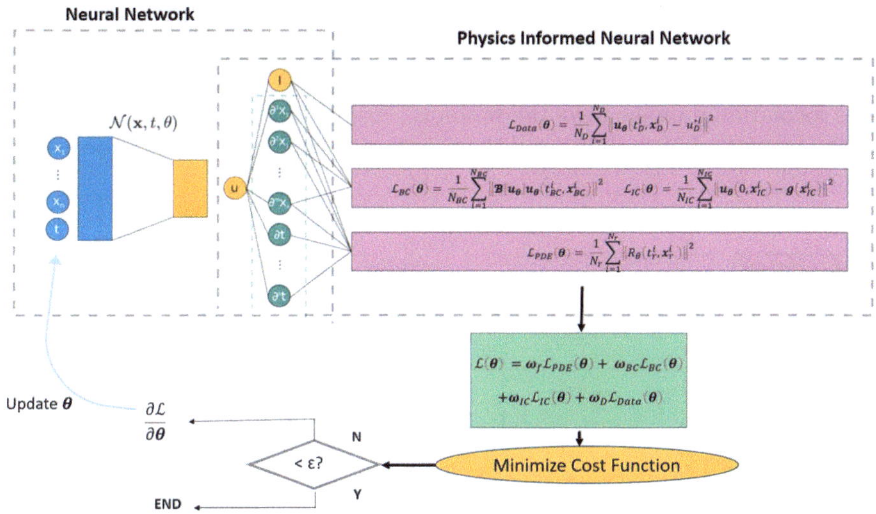

Fig. 1. Building blocks of a Physics-Informed Neural Network (PINN). Adapted from [6].

where η denotes the learning rate, and $\nabla_{\boldsymbol{\theta}}\mathcal{L}(\boldsymbol{\theta}_n)$ is the gradient of the loss with respect to the parameters. More explicitly, each parameter is updated as:

$$\boldsymbol{w}_{n+1}^{l} = \boldsymbol{w}_{n}^{l} - \eta \frac{\partial \mathcal{L}(\boldsymbol{\theta})}{\partial \boldsymbol{w}_{n}^{l}},$$
$$\boldsymbol{b}_{n+1}^{l} = \boldsymbol{b}_{n}^{l} - \eta \frac{\partial \mathcal{L}(\boldsymbol{\theta})}{\partial \boldsymbol{b}_{n}^{l}}. \tag{9}$$

2.2 Pressure Test

The diffusion equation serves as the fundamental model for analyzing well pressure tests, which aim to quantitatively evaluate reservoir characteristics. In this study, we consider two classical cases governed by this equation. A brief overview of the physical context of these tests is provided below.

A pressure test involves perturbing the reservoir pressure and observing the resulting bottom-hole pressure (p_{wf}) over time. In single-well tests, the response is recorded at the same well where the disturbance is applied. The analysis of this pressure behavior allows the estimation of average reservoir parameters within the drainage area of the well. The most frequently applied pressure tests in petroleum engineering are the pressure drawdown and the pressure buildup tests. In this work, we focus exclusively on the Drawdown test.

Drawdown Test. This test consists of producing the well at a constant flow rate and measuring the bottom-hole pressure as it evolves with time. Typically, the test is preceded by a shut-in period, allowing the reservoir to reach a uniform pressure distribution (see Fig. 2).

The drawdown test is mainly used to estimate the reservoir permeability and assess formation damage near the wellbore. Additionally, it can provide insights into the reservoir pore volume and the presence of heterogeneities in the drainage region [28].

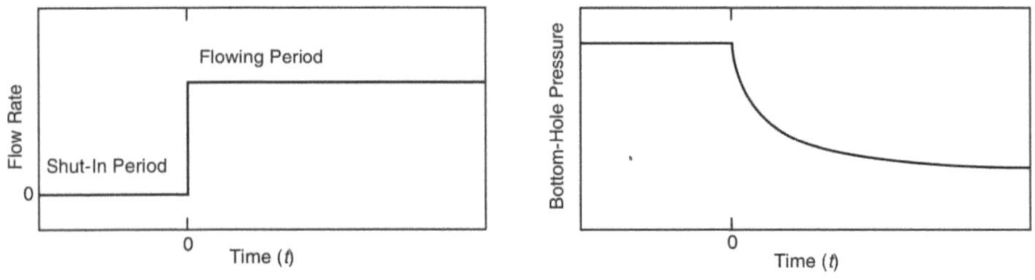

(a) (b)

Fig. 2. Schematic representation of (a) flow rate and (b) bottom-hole pressure during a pressure drawdown test. Adapted from [29].

Buildup Test. In contrast, a pressure buildup test begins by shutting in a well that has been flowing at a constant rate. After shut-in, the bottom-hole pressure is recorded over time to capture the recovery behavior of the reservoir. For accurate analysis, the well should be produced long enough prior to shut-in to reach a pseudo-steady state.

The recorded pressure increase provides valuable information about reservoir properties such as average pressure in the drainage area, effective permeability, and the skin factor near the wellbore [30]. Figure 3 illustrates the typical constant-rate production period and the expected pressure recovery trend during shut-in.

One of the challenges of drawdown testing lies in maintaining a truly constant flow rate, which is often difficult in practice. This limitation makes interpretation more complex. In contrast, buildup tests offer the advantage of imposing a constant surface rate (zero), simplifying the mathematical treatment. For this reason, pressure buildup tests are commonly preferred for evaluating permeability and wellbore damage [30].

2.3 Problem Statement

In this section, particular cases of the diffusion equation are presented, specifically linear and radial flow. The linear flow case will be modeled using Physics-Informed Neural Networks (PINNs), while the radial flow case will be addressed using Artificial Neural Networks (ANNs).

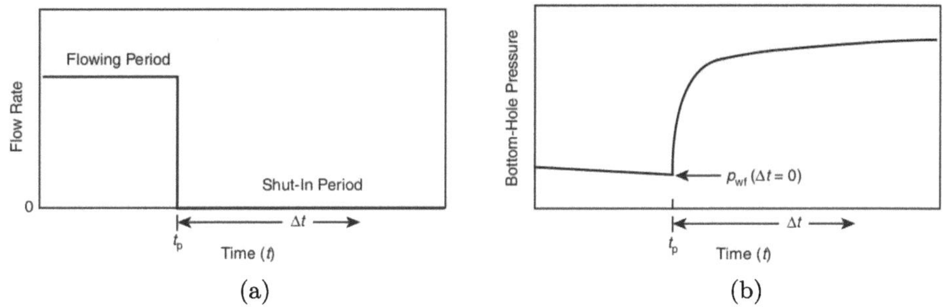

Fig. 3. Schematic representation of (a) flow rate and (b) bottom-hole pressure for a pressure buildup test. Adapted from [29].

Diffusion Equation for Single-Phase Fluid Flow. For a slightly compressible fluid flowing through a porous medium, the general form of the diffusivity equation is:

$$\nabla^2 p = \frac{\phi \mu c_t}{k} \frac{\partial p}{\partial t}, \tag{10}$$

where p is the pressure, ϕ is the porosity, μ is the fluid viscosity, $c_t = c_f + c_\phi$ is the total compressibility (the sum of fluid and formation compressibility), k is the permeability, and t is time. The left-hand side of the equation, $\nabla^2 p$, represents the spatial distribution of pressure and depends on the geometry of the flow domain.

In this study, we consider two one-dimensional geometries: linear and radial flow, whose Laplacian terms are defined as:

- **Linear flow:**

$$\nabla^2 p = \frac{\partial^2 p}{\partial x^2}. \tag{11}$$

- **Radial flow:**

$$\nabla^2 p = \frac{1}{r} \frac{\partial}{\partial r} \left(r \frac{\partial p}{\partial r} \right). \tag{12}$$

This diffusivity model originates from the combination of three physical laws: (1) the mass conservation principle via the continuity equation, (2) the momentum balance through Darcy's law, and (3) a constitutive relationship or equation of state.

The linear formulation is especially relevant when analyzing pressure behavior in hydraulically fractured horizontal wells, typically found in unconventional, low-permeability formations. On the other hand, the radial case is commonly applied to vertical wells operating in conventional reservoirs.

For the derivation of the Diffusivity Equation for Radial Flow of a Single-Phase Liquid with Small and Constant Compressibility, several assumptions are made: radial flow, laminar flow (also known as Darcy flow), constant permeability and compressibility of the porous medium, negligible gravitational effects, isothermal conditions, and small, constant fluid compressibility. Additionally, it is assumed that the product of compressibility and the square of the pressure gradient, $c \cdot (\nabla p)^2$, is negligible [30].

Diffusivity Equation in 1D Cartesian Coordinates (Linear Flow). The propagation of pressure in a porous medium under linear flow conditions is described by the diffusivity equation in one-dimensional Cartesian coordinates. Substituting Eq. 11 into the general form of Eq. 10 yields the governing expression:

$$\frac{\partial^2 p}{\partial x^2} = \frac{\phi \mu c_t}{k} \frac{\partial p}{\partial t}, \tag{13}$$

where p denotes pressure, ϕ is the porosity of the formation, μ is the viscosity of the fluid, $c_t = c_f + c_\phi$ represents the total compressibility, and k is the permeability of the porous medium.

To generalize the problem and facilitate its numerical treatment, we introduce a dimensionless formulation. This transformation not only simplifies the analysis but also allows for a better comparison between different systems. The dimensionless form of the diffusion equation becomes:

$$\frac{\partial^2 p_D}{\partial x_D^2} = \frac{\partial p_D}{\partial t_D}, \quad 0 < x_D < 1, \quad 0 < t_D \leq T, \tag{14}$$

where p_D, x_D, and t_D are the dimensionless pressure, distance, and time, respectively.

The dimensionless initial and boundary conditions correspond to a reservoir with an initially uniform pressure distribution, a constant production rate at the inner boundary ($x_D = 0$), and a no-flow condition at the outer boundary ($x_D = 1$). These are expressed as:

$$p_D(x_D, 0) = 0, \tag{15}$$

$$\left.\frac{\partial p_D}{\partial x_D}\right|_{x_D=0} = -1, \tag{16}$$

$$\left.\frac{\partial p_D}{\partial x_D}\right|_{x_D=1} = 0. \tag{17}$$

The dimensionless variables are defined by the following relations:

$$x_D = \frac{x}{x_e}, \tag{18}$$

$$p_D = p_{DC} \cdot \frac{kA}{qB\mu x_e}(p_i - p), \tag{19}$$

$$t_D = t_{DC} \cdot \frac{k}{\phi \mu c_t x_e^2} t, \tag{20}$$

where x_e is the external boundary of the reservoir, A is the cross-sectional area of flow, q is the production rate, B is the formation volume factor, and p_i is the initial reservoir pressure [31].

The conversion factors t_{DC} and p_{DC}, used to transform between physical units and the dimensionless formulation, are provided in Table 1:

Table 1. Conversion Factors for Parameters with Different Units in Linear Flow.

Parameter	Darcy Units	Field Units	SI Units
t_{DC}	1	2.637×10^{-3}	3.557×10^{-6} (in hours)
p_{DC}	1	1.127×10^{-3}	8.527×10^{-5}

Diffusivity Equation in 1D Cylindrical Coordinates (Radial Flow). Pressure diffusion in a porous medium under radial flow conditions is governed by the radial form of the diffusion equation. Substituting Eq. 12 into the general diffusion equation (Eq. 10) yields the diffusivity equation for horizontal radial flow, neglecting angular and vertical components:

$$\frac{1}{r}\frac{\partial}{\partial r}\left(r\frac{\partial p}{\partial r}\right) = \frac{\phi \mu c_t}{k}\frac{\partial p}{\partial t}, \tag{21}$$

which can be equivalently expressed as:

$$\frac{\partial^2 p}{\partial r^2} + \frac{1}{r}\frac{\partial p}{\partial r} = \frac{\phi \mu c_t}{k}\frac{\partial p}{\partial t}, \tag{22}$$

where p represents pressure, r is the radial coordinate, ϕ is the formation porosity, μ is the fluid viscosity, $c_t = c_f + c_\phi$ denotes the total compressibility, and k is the permeability of the porous medium.

To facilitate both analytical and numerical treatment, we introduce dimensionless variables that transform the problem as follows:

$$\frac{\partial^2 p_D}{\partial r_D^2} + \frac{1}{r_D}\frac{\partial p_D}{\partial r_D} = \frac{\partial p_D}{\partial t_D}, \quad 1 \le r_D \le r_{De}, \quad t_D > 0, \tag{23}$$

where p_D, r_D, and t_D are dimensionless pressure, radius, and time, respectively.

The problem is defined by the following initial and boundary conditions, corresponding to a reservoir initially at uniform pressure, a constant flow rate at the wellbore ($r_D = 1$, inner boundary condition), and no flow at the external radius ($r_D = r_{De}$, outer boundary condition):

$$\begin{aligned} p_D(r_D, 0) &= 0, \\ r_D \left.\frac{\partial p_D}{\partial r_D}\right|_{r_D=1} &= -1, \\ r_D \left.\frac{\partial p_D}{\partial r_D}\right|_{r_D=r_{De}} &= 0. \end{aligned} \tag{24}$$

The dimensionless variables are defined by:

$$r_D = \frac{r}{r_w}, \tag{25}$$

$$r_{De} = \frac{r_e}{r_w}, \tag{26}$$

$$p_D = p_{DC} \cdot \frac{2\pi kh}{q\mu B}(p_i - p), \tag{27}$$

$$t_D = t_{DC} \cdot \frac{k}{\phi\mu c_t r_w^2} t, \tag{28}$$

where r_w is the well radius, r_e is the external boundary radius of the reservoir, h is the reservoir thickness, q is the production rate, B is the formation volume factor, and p_i is the initial reservoir pressure [31].

The conversion factors t_{DC} and p_{DC}, used to translate between dimensional and dimensionless variables in different unit systems, are listed in Table 2.

Table 2. Conversion Factors for Parameters with Different Units in Radial Flow.

Parameter	Darcy Units	Field Units	SI Units
t_{DC}	1	2.637×10^{-4}	3.557×10^{-6}
p_{DC}	2π	7.081×10^{-3}	5.356×10^{-4}

3 Experiments

This section presents two numerical experiments designed to evaluate the performance of different neural network-based approaches for solving diffusion problems.

The first experiment (Case 1) addresses the solution of the one-dimensional diffusion equation in Cartesian coordinates, which is representative of linear flow in porous media. In this case, a Physics-Informed Neural Network (PINN) is implemented, and its performance is compared with the classical finite difference method Backward Time Centered Space (BTCS), using the analytical solution as a reference to compute the Mean Squared Error (MSE) and the Root Mean Squared Error (RMSE). This case serves as a starting point to evaluate the accuracy and robustness of the PINN in comparison with conventional approaches and the analytical solution.

The second experiment (Case 2) focuses on modeling radial flow in porous media, described by the one-dimensional diffusion equation in cylindrical coordinates. Unlike the first case, here an Artificial Neural Network (ANN) is trained exclusively with data generated from the analytical solution in the Laplace domain, numerically inverted using the Stehfest algorithm. This data-driven approach evaluates the generalization capability of the neural network when trained with semi-analytical solutions, in the context of a drawdown test without considering skin or storage effects.

3.1 Case 1: Modeling the 1D Cartesian Diffusion Equation Using PINNs

In this case, the Physics-Informed Neural Network (PINN) and the Backward Time Centered Space (BTCS) finite difference method are evaluated against the analytical solution of the Diffusivity Equation in 1D Cartesian Coordinates (Linear Flow), defined in Problem Statement.

To assess the accuracy of the methods, the Mean Squared Error (MSE) and the Root Mean Squared Error (RMSE) are calculated. Specifically, the PINN results are compared with the analytical solution, and the BTCS finite difference results are also compared with the same analytical solution.

In the context of the Physics-Informed Neural Network (PINN) methodology, the mathematical model is defined through a residual function that must be satisfied throughout the spatiotemporal domain. The corresponding residual equation is:

$$\mathcal{R}(t, \boldsymbol{x}_D) = \frac{\partial \boldsymbol{P}_D(\boldsymbol{x}_D, t_D)}{\partial t_D} - \frac{\partial^2 \boldsymbol{P}_D(\boldsymbol{x}_D, t_D)}{\partial x_D^2} = 0, \quad \boldsymbol{x}_D \in [0,1], \quad t_D \in [0,1], \tag{29}$$

subject to the following initial and boundary conditions:

$$\begin{aligned} \boldsymbol{P}_D(\boldsymbol{x}_D, t_D = 0) &= 0, \quad 0 \leq x_D \leq 1, \\ \left.\frac{\partial \boldsymbol{P}_D}{\partial x_D}\right|_{\boldsymbol{x}_D = 0} &= -1, \\ \left.\frac{\partial \boldsymbol{P}_D}{\partial x_D}\right|_{\boldsymbol{x}_D = 1} &= 0. \end{aligned} \tag{30}$$

The network architecture and training parameters used for the Physics-Informed Neural Network (PINN) are summarized in Table 3. The number of collocation points N_r used to evaluate the PDE residual $\mathcal{R}_\theta$, as well as the number of points for the initial condition N_{IC} and boundary conditions N_{BC}, is set to 150 each. The network consists of 4 hidden layers with 80 neurons per layer and uses the hyperbolic tangent activation function. All loss weights (residual, initial, and boundary) are set to 1.0. The model is trained for 1000 epochs using a learning rate of 0.002.

Table 3. PINN Training Parameters

Parameter	Value	Parameter	Value
N_r, N_{IC}, N_{BC}	150	Learning Rate	0.002
Weight Residual	1.0	Activation Function	Hyperbolic Tangent
Weight Initial	1.0	Layers	4
Weight Boundary	1.0	Neurons per Layer	80
Epochs	1000		

As shown in Fig. 4, the convergence of the cost function with respect to the epochs in a Log-Log scale is presented for each of the components: the residual loss $\mathcal{L}_{PDE}(\boldsymbol{\theta})$ in red, the initial loss $\mathcal{L}_{IC}(\boldsymbol{\theta})$ in green, the boundary loss $\mathcal{L}_{BC}(\boldsymbol{\theta})$ in yellow, and the total loss $\mathcal{L}(\boldsymbol{\theta})$ in blue.

It is observed that the loss associated with the differential equation, $\mathcal{L}_{PDE}(\boldsymbol{\theta})$ (in red), converges faster compared to the other components. However, some oscillations appear toward the final stages of training, which require further analysis to understand their origin and potential impact on the final solution.

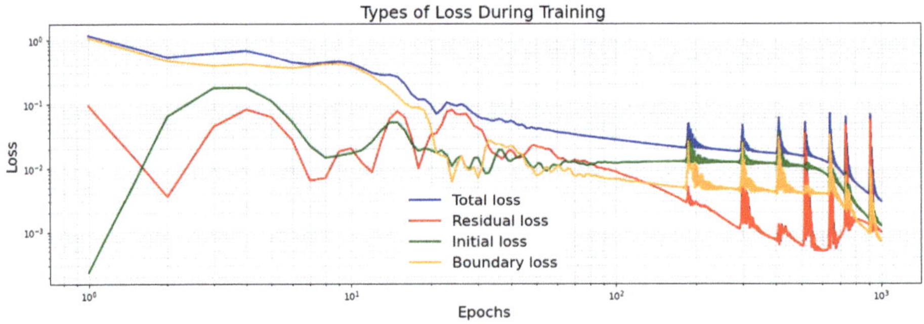

Fig. 4. Convergence of the cost function as a function of epochs in a log-log scale.

The results of Case 1 are presented in Fig. 5, showing the three solutions (PINN, finite differences, and analytical) in 3D: position on the x-axis, time on the t-axis, and pressure on the z-axis. Figure 6 illustrates the comparison between the PINN and analytical solutions in color maps, where the x-axis represents position, the y-axis represents time, and the color scale represents pressure values. The first two plots (from left to right) display both solutions, while the third plot shows the mean squared error (MSE) between them. The color scale in the third plot indicates the MSE values.

Table 4 provides a comparison between the PINN and Finite Differences methods with respect to the analytical solution, evaluating the Root Mean Squared Error (RMSE). These values provide an indication of the accuracy of each method in relation to the exact solution.

It can be observed that the obtained solutions are very similar, with a very small error. In the case of the finite differences method with the analytical solution, the RMSE is 8.85×10^{-4}, while for the PINN method, the RMSE is 4.38×10^{-3}. Although the finite differences method exhibits a smaller error, the PINN method, while slightly less accurate, still provides results that are quite close to the exact solution.

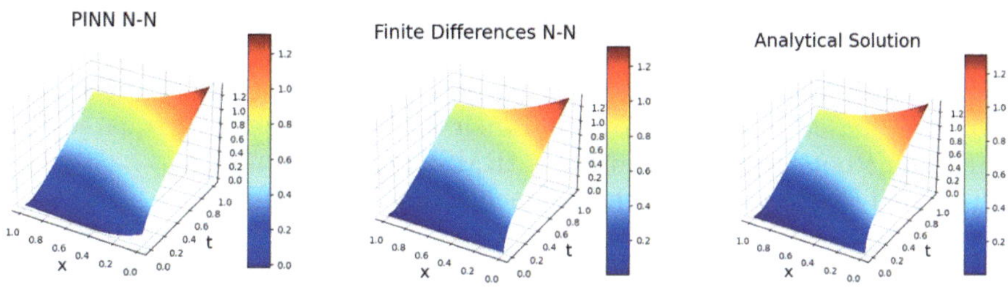

(a) (b) (c)

Fig. 5. Comparison of three solutions: (a) Physics-Informed Neural Network (PINN), (b) finite differences, and (c) analytical solution. The x-axis represents position, the t-axis represents time, and the z-axis represents pressure.

Table 4. RMSE and MSE Comparison Between Methods

Comparison	RMSE	MSE
PINN vs Analytical	4.38×10^{-3}	1.92×10^{-5}
Finite Differences vs Analytical	8.85×10^{-4}	7.83×10^{-7}

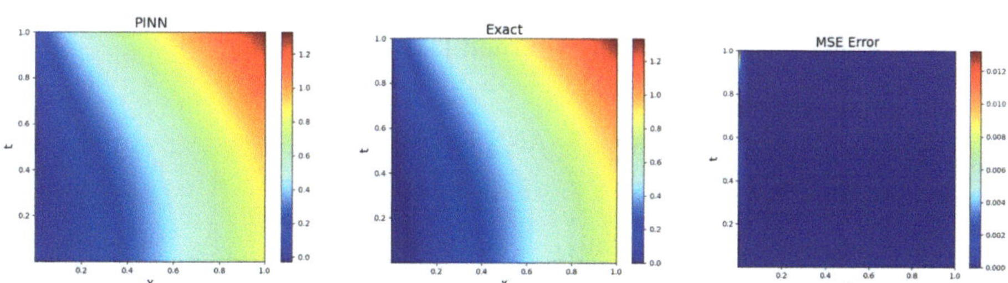

(a) (b) (c)

Fig. 6. Comparison of three color maps of the solutions: (a) Physics-Informed Neural Network (PINN), (b) analytical, and (c) MSE error between them. The x-axis represents position, and the t-axis represents time.

3.2 Case 2: Modeling the 1D Diffusion Equation in Cylindrical Coordinates Using Data-Driven ANNs

In this work, an Artificial Neural Network (ANN) is trained using data generated by the Stehfest algorithm, a numerical method for inverting Laplace transforms when the solution is known in the Laplace domain and needs to be recovered in the time domain. Specifically, the algorithm is applied to invert the Laplace-domain solution of the radial diffusion equation for the flow scenario described in Problem Statement. The resulting time-domain approximation is referred to as the semi-analytical solution. Subsequently, a drawdown test is simulated without considering skin or storage effects, using both the semi-analytical and the neural network-based solutions. To assess their accuracy, the Mean Squared Error (MSE) and Root Mean Squared Error (RMSE) are computed.

The analytical solution in the Laplace domain is given by:

$$\bar{p}_D(u, r_D) = -\frac{1}{u^{3/2}}\left[\frac{K_1(\sqrt{u}r_{eD})I_0(\sqrt{u}r_D) + I_1(\sqrt{u}r_{eD})K_0(\sqrt{u}r_D)}{K_1(\sqrt{u}r_{eD})I_1(\sqrt{u}) - I_1(\sqrt{u}r_{eD})K_1(\sqrt{u})}\right], \tag{31}$$

where I_n and K_n denote the modified Bessel functions of the first and second kind, respectively.

The Artificial Neural Network (ANN) was trained over 1000 epochs using a learning rate of 0.002. It employed four hidden layers with 80 neurons each and the hyperbolic tangent as the activation function. The corresponding configuration details are summarized in Table 5.

Figure 7 displays the solutions obtained using the Artificial Neural Network (ANN) in blue and the semi-analytical solution derived via the Stehfest method in black. The neural network was trained with normalized and dimensionless data. The left panel shows the normalized and dimensionless solution, while the right panel presents the dimensionless pressure response. Additionally, the derivative of the pressure with respect to time, computed from the semi-analytical solution using Bourdet's method [32], is shown in red.

Table 5. ANN Parameters

Parameter	Value
Learning Rate	0.002
Activation Function	Hyperbolic Tangent
Layers	4
Neurons per Layer	80
Epochs	1000

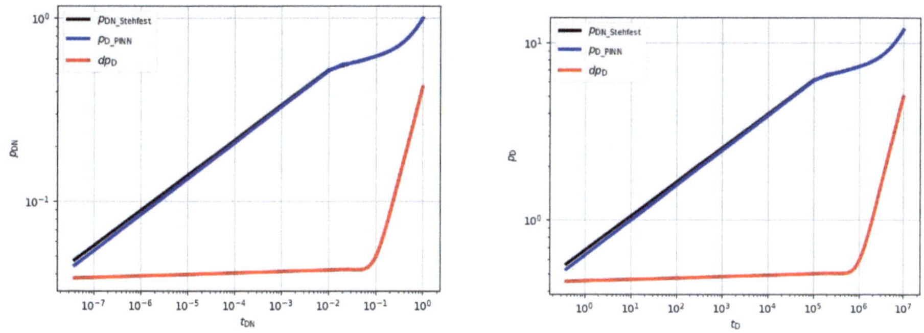

(a) (b)

Fig. 7. Comparison of solutions obtained with PINN (blue) and the Stehfest method (black): (a) normalized and dimensionless form, and (b) dimensionless form.

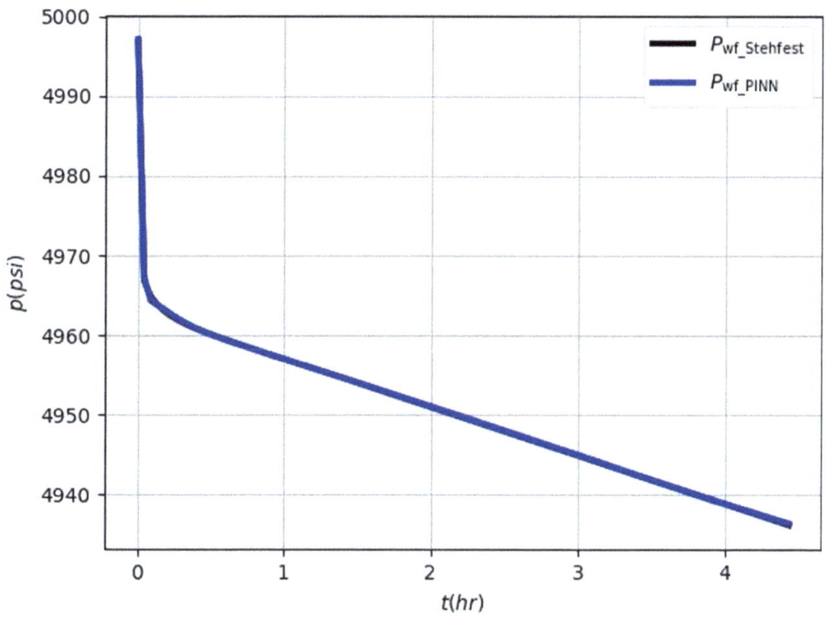

Fig. 8. Comparison of bottom-hole pressure (BHP) as a function of time during the drawdown test, obtained using the ANN (blue) and the Stehfest algorithm (black).

A drawdown test is subsequently simulated without considering skin or storage effects, using both the semi-analytical and neural network-based solutions. Figure 8 presents the bottom-hole pressure (BHP), expressed in psi as a function of time in hours, for both approaches. To evaluate their performance, the Mean Squared Error (MSE) and Root Mean Squared Error (RMSE) are calculated. Table 6 summarizes the RMSE values for the dimensionless pressure p_D, quantifying the discrepancy between the PINN and the Stehfest-based solutions.

The RMSE $= 1.98 \times 10^{-3}$ and MSE $= 3.92 \times 10^{-6}$ indicate a high level of agreement between the two methods.

Table 6. Comparison of RMSE and MSE Between ANN and Stehfest

Comparison	RMSE	MSE
ANN vs Stehfest	1.98×10^{-3}	3.92×10^{-6}

4 Conclusions

In this work, the diffusion equation was modeled using two types of neural networks: Physics-Informed Neural Networks (PINNs) and Artificial Neural Networks (ANNs). Two different cases were studied to evaluate the performance of these methods in solving flow problems in porous media.

In Case 1, the one-dimensional diffusion equation in Cartesian coordinates – representing linear flow in porous media – was solved. A Physics-Informed Neural Network (PINN) was implemented and its performance compared against the classical Backward Time Centered Space (BTCS) finite difference method, using the analytical solution as a reference. The comparison was made by evaluating the Root Mean Squared Error (RMSE). The Finite Differences method showed a smaller deviation, with an RMSE of 8.85×10^{-4}, while the PINN method resulted in an RMSE of 4.38×10^{-3}. These results indicate that both methods yield solutions very close to the analytical reference, with the Finite Differences method being slightly more accurate.

In Case 2, radial flow in porous media—described by the diffusion equation in cylindrical coordinates—was modeled. An Artificial Neural Network (ANN) was trained using data generated from the analytical solution in the Laplace domain, which was numerically inverted using the Stehfest algorithm. The RMSE obtained was 1.98×10^{-3}, demonstrating a strong agreement between the ANN and the Stehfest algorithm. This confirms that the NN-based solution provides a reliable approximation to the semi-analytical method, supporting its applicability in well pressure testing within porous media.

5 Future Work

For future work, it is proposed to train the neural network by incorporating into the loss function the contributions from the radial diffusion equation, as well as the losses associated with the initial and boundary conditions. This approach effectively transforms the ANN into a PINN.

Additionally, the integration of experimental or field data during training is considered, with the goal of obtaining a more accurate and physically consistent solution that better reflects the real behavior of the system.

Acknowledgments. The authors thankfully acknowledge the computer resources, technical expertise and support provided by the Laboratorio Nacional de Supercómputo del Sureste de México, CONACYT member of the network of national laboratories, Proyect: 202203073N.

Disclosure of Interests. The authors declare that there are no conflicts of interest related to this work.

References

1. Raissi, M., Perdikaris, P., Karniadakis, G.E.: Physics informed deep learning (part i): data-driven solutions of nonlinear partial differential equations. arXiv preprint arXiv:1711.10561 (2017)
2. Raissi, M., Perdikaris, P., Karniadakis, G.E.: Physics informed deep learning (part ii): data-driven discovery of nonlinear partial differential equations. arXiv preprint arXiv:1711.10566 (2017)
3. Raissi, M., Perdikaris, P., Karniadakis, G.E.: Physics-informed neural networks: a deep learning framework for solving forward and inverse problems involving nonlinear partial differential equations. J. Comput. Phys. (2019)
4. Díaz-Cortés, G.B., Vuik, C., Jansen, J.D.: On POD-based Deflation Vectors for DPCG applied to porous media problems. J. Comput. Appl. Math. **330**(Suppl. C), 193–213 (2018)
5. Díaz-Cortés, G.B., Vuik, C., Jansen, J.D.: Accelerating the solution of linear systems appearing in two-phase reservoir simulation by the use of pod-based deflation methods. Comput. Geosci. **25**(5), 1621–1645 (2021)
6. Cuomo, S., Cola, V.S.D., Giampaolo, F., Rozza, G., Raissi, M., Piccialli, F.: Scientific machine learning through physics-informed neural networks: where we are and what's next. J. Sci. Comput. **92**(3), 88 (2022)
7. Ganga, S., Uddin, Z.: Exploring physics-informed neural networks: from fundamentals to applications in complex systems. arXiv preprint arXiv:2410.00422 (2024)
8. Cai, S., Wang, Z., Wang, S., Karniadakis, G.E.: Physics-informed neural networks for heat transfer problems. J. Heat Transfer **143**(6), 060801 (2021)
9. Rao, C., Sun, H., Liu, Y.: Physics-informed deep learning for incompressible laminar flows. Theor. Appl. Mech. Lett. **10**(3), 207–212 (2020)
10. Jin, X., Cai, S., Li, H., Karniadakis, G.E.: Nsfnets (navier-stokes flow nets): physics-informed neural networks for the incompressible navier-stokes equations. J. Comput. Phys. **426**, 109951 (2021)
11. He, Q., Barajas-Solano, D., Tartakovsky, G., Tartakovsky, A.M.: Physics-informed neural networks for multiphysics data assimilation with application to subsurface transport. Adv. Water Resour. **141**, 103610 (2020)
12. Sun, L., Gao, H., Pan, S., Wang, J.-X.: Surrogate modeling for fluid flows based on physics-constrained deep learning without simulation data. Comput. Methods Appl. Mech. Eng. **361**, 112732 (2020)
13. Cai, S., Wang, Z., Wang, S., Perdikaris, P., Karniadakis, G.E.: Physics-informed neural networks for heat transfer problems. J. Heat Transf. **143**(6), 060801 (2021)

14. Raghu, S., Nayek, R., Chalamalla, V.: Physics informed neural networks for free shear flows. arXiv preprint arXiv:2404.03542 (2024)
15. Abreu, E., Florindo, J.B.: A study on a feedforward neural network to solve partial differential equations in hyperbolic-transport problems. In: Paszynski, M., Kranzlmüller, D., Krzhizhanovskaya, V.V., Dongarra, J.J., Sloot, P.M.A. (eds.) ICCS 2021. LNCS, vol. 12743, pp. 398–411. Springer, Cham (2021). https://doi.org/10.1007/978-3-030-77964-1_31
16. Almajid, M.M., Abu-Al-Saud, M.O.: Prediction of porous media fluid flow using physics informed neural networks. J. Pet. Sci. Eng. **208**, 109205 (2022)
17. Yang, L., Perdikaris, P.: Physics-informed neural networks for solving multiscale stochastic PDEs. arXiv (2021)
18. Latrach, A., Malki, M.L., Morales, M., Mehana, M., Rabiei, M.: A critical review of physics-informed machine learning applications in subsurface energy systems. Geoenergy Sci. Eng. **239**, 212938 (2024)
19. He, J., Li, L., Xu, J., Karniadakis, G.E.: Physics-informed neural networks for nonlinear system identification. SIAM J. Sci. Comput. **43**(1), A313–A337 (2021)
20. Zhang, J., Zhao, J., Wang, S., Wang, H.: Physics-informed neural networks for power system dynamic security assessment and control. arXiv (2020)
21. Stiasny, J., Chatzivasileiadis, S.: Physics-informed neural networks for time-domain simulations: accuracy, computational cost, and flexibility. Electric Power Syst. Res. **224**, 109748 (2023)
22. Badawi, D., Gildin, E.: Physics-informed neural network for the transient diffusivity equation in reservoir engineering. arXiv preprint arXiv:2309.17345 (2023)
23. Jagtap, A.D., Kharazmi, E., Karniadakis, G.E.: Conservative physics-informed neural networks on discrete domains for conservation laws: applications to forward and inverse problems. Comput. Methods Appl. Mech. Eng. **365**, 113028 (2020)
24. Fan, D., et al.: A framework of parallel physics-informed neural network with laplace transform for well testing interpretation. Phys. Fluids **37**(1) (2025)
25. López, Z.S., Cortés, G.B.D., Zacarías, G.D.: Cuando la física y la inteligencia artificial se unen para modelar fluidos. Materiales Avanzados **41**(5), 63–70 (2024)
26. Sánchez-López, Z., Díaz-Cortés, G.B.: Optimizing a physics-informed neural network to solve the reynolds equation. Revista Mexicana de Física **71**, 020601 (2025)
27. Wang, S., Sankaran, S., Wang, H., Perdikaris, P.: An expert's guide to training physics-informed neural networks. arXiv preprint arXiv:2308.08468 (2023)
28. Ahmed, T., Meehan, D.N.: Introduction to enhanced oil recovery. Adv. Reservoir Manag. Eng. **2**, 541–85 (2012)
29. Ahmed, T., Meehan, N.: Advanced reservoir management and engineering (2012). ISBN: 978-0-1238-5548-0
30. Lee, J., Rollins, J.B., Spivey, J.P.: Pressure Transient Testing (2003)
31. Blasingame, T.A.: Pete 620 class notes: Lecture 20. module 4 - reservoir flow - dimensionless variables. Class notes (PDF), course PETE 620 – Fluid Flow in Petroleum Reservoirs, Texas A&M University (2009). https://blasingame.engr.tamu.edu/?start=pete%2Fblasingame.engr.tamu.edu%2Fz_zCourse_Archive%2FP620_09C%2FP620_09C_Lectures%2F
32. Bourdet, D., Whittle, T.M., Douglas, A.A., Pirard, Y.M.: A new set of type curves simplifies well test analysis. World Oil **196**(6), 95–106 (1983)

Fuzzy Inference Systems with Evolutionary Optimization for Timely Harvest Prediction: A Case Study

Jesús Emmanuel Brizuela Ramírez(✉), Omar Sánchez Alaniz, Miguel Ángel Vejar Cortes, Salvador Ávila Ramírez, and Abel Romero Ruíz

División de Estudios de Posgrado e Investigación, Tecnológico Nacional de México Campus Colima, Av. Tecnológico No. 1 Villa de Álvarez, 28976 Villa de Álvarez, Colonia Liberación, Mexico

{g2346011,ngarcia,g2346016,g2346017,g2346010, g2346015}@colima.tecnm.mx

Abstract. This paper presents a fuzzy inference system (FIS) enhanced through genetic algorithms (GAs) to predict the optimal harvest time for *Stevia rebaudiana* based on climatological data. The proposed Mamdani-type FIS integrates five key meteorological variables—solar radiation, humidity, dew point, total precipitation, and average precipitation—to estimate the °Brix value, which indicates the crop's sweetness and readiness for harvest. Three types of membership functions (triangular, trapezoidal, and Gaussian) were optimized using evolutionary encoding strategies, where each chromosome encodes the type and parameters of the membership functions. A total of 90 parameters were evolved across 20 generations using selection, crossover, and mutation operators. The system's rules were derived from expert knowledge and refined with data-driven insights. Validation was conducted using an 80-20 hold-out strategy and evaluated through metrics such as mean squared error (MSE) and accuracy. Results demonstrate that the trapezoidal configuration achieved the highest accuracy (96.43%) and the lowest MSE (0.0357), outperforming both triangular and Gaussian configurations. These findings validate the effectiveness of integrating fuzzy logic and evolutionary algorithms in precision agriculture, offering a non-destructive, interpretable, and robust method for harvest prediction.

Keywords: Fuzzy Inference System · Genetic Algorithm · Stevia Harvest Prediction · °Brix · Precision Agriculture

1 Introduction

Modern agriculture must optimize its practices amid increasing climate variability and resource constraints. To address this, computer science offers advanced tools for modeling and prediction in uncertain environments [1]. Techniques such as artificial intelligence (AI), machine learning (ML), and fuzzy inference systems (FIS) have proven

C. Palma-Preciado et al. (Eds.): CORE 2025, ACSAR 3, pp. 187–201, 2026.
https://doi.org/10.1007/978-3-032-08894-9_12

particularly valuable in precision agriculture [2]. One major challenge is accurately predicting optimal harvest time, as it directly influences the crop's quality and market value [3]. Key environmental factors—temperature, humidity, solar radiation, and precipitation—play a crucial role in crop development and ripening [4]. In *Stevia rebaudiana*, °Brix values serve as a primary indicator of maturity, yet traditional methods to measure them are often destructive and inefficient [5].

Fuzzy logic (FL), introduced by Zadeh in 1965, enables the modeling of uncertainty by assigning degrees of membership rather than binary classifications [6, 7]. This makes it ideal for expressing imprecise agronomic concepts such as "optimal temperature" or "suitable maturity". Unlike opaque ML or DL models, FIS are interpretable through linguistic rules derived from expert knowledge, making them suitable for transparent decision-making [8].

Genetic algorithms (GAs), inspired by natural evolution, are widely used for optimization tasks. They evolve populations of candidate solutions through selection, crossover, and mutation to reach near-optimal configurations [9, 10]. Their effectiveness in tuning fuzzy models and exploring complex solution spaces has been validated in recent studies [11, 12].

This study proposes a Mamdani-type FIS for predicting stevia harvest time using climatological variables. The system is trained on data from the NASA POWER platform and refined through a genetic algorithm. The central hypothesis is that this hybrid FL-GA approach can non-destructively and accurately estimate optimal harvest timing, thereby enhancing agronomic decision-making.

2 Literature Review

A literature review was conducted to explore the application of fuzzy logic (FL) in agriculture, with a focus on crop optimization and climate-based decision-making. Several studies demonstrate FL's potential in diverse contexts. In [13], FL was applied to develop an automated irrigation model for cotton that adjusted water supply based on soil and climate conditions. Similarly, [14] implemented FL to regulate greenhouse environments, while [15] integrated FL with IoT and LoRa for smart irrigation, improving water efficiency.

Other contributions include the combination of FL with multi-criteria analysis and GIS for soil fertility assessment [16], and a systematic review confirming FL's utility in irrigation, yield forecasting, and environmental monitoring [17]. Additional studies applied FL with IoT sensors for adaptive irrigation control [18], and used Arduino-Simulink platforms to manage irrigation pumps based on environmental data [19].

Furthermore, [20] proposed a fuzzy decision support system for estimating crop water needs, and [21] utilized FL for interpreting complex weather data to support agricultural decisions under uncertainty.

Collectively, these studies highlight FL's capacity to manage uncertainty in agroclimatic systems and improve decision-making in irrigation and environmental control. However, a clear research gap exists regarding its application to harvest prediction based on meteorological variables in *Stevia rebaudiana*. The use of genetic algorithms is also suggested to reduce subjectivity in fuzzy set design, enabling automated parameter tuning from historical data.

3 Theoretical Background

Fuzzy logic [22] is a reasoning system designed to handle propositions with truth values between absolute false (0) and absolute true (1). Unlike binary logic, FL expresses degrees of truth, making it well-suited for modeling uncertainty and imprecision in dynamic agricultural contexts [23]. Grounded in linguistic concepts such as "high temperature" or "moderate rainfall," FL enables the translation of expert knowledge into interpretable, rule-based systems [24].

Fuzzy inference systems (FIS) [25] apply this framework through four stages:

- Fuzzification: Conversion of crisp input values into fuzzy values by assigning degrees of membership to different linguistic sets using membership functions.
- Rule evaluation: Application of fuzzy logical operators (such as minimum or product) to activate the relevant rules based on observed conditions.
- Aggregation: Combination of the fuzzy outputs of all activated rules into a single fuzzy output set.
- Defuzzification: Conversion of the aggregated fuzzy set into a specific numerical value, useful for decision-making or prediction.

Two main FIS models exist: Mamdani, which produces fuzzy outputs requiring defuzzification [26], and Sugeno, which uses weighted averages or linear functions for more efficient computation [27].

Mamdani models, in particular, have shown strong applicability in agriculture due to their interpretability and robustness in adapting to environmental variability. Their success in harvest prediction and crop management has been demonstrated in multiple studies [28, 29].

4 Methodology

The proposed system integrates FL with genetic algorithms to develop an intelligent model for harvest prediction. The system is composed of three main modules: (1) a preprocessing unit that normalizes and structures meteorological data, (2) a fuzzy inference system (FIS) that transforms climatic inputs into linguistic variables and predicts the Brix degree using expert-defined rules, and (3) an optimization engine based on genetic algorithms that tunes the membership functions of the FIS for enhanced performance. This hybrid architecture ensures both interpretability and adaptability, making it suitable for decision-making in agricultural environments with high uncertainty.

4.1 Input Variables

The proposed model integrates key climatic variables that influence the growth and quality of *Stevia rebaudiana*. To capture these relationships, historical data from the period 2016–2024 were collected through the NASA POWER platform (Power Data Access Viewer), which provides daily meteorological measurements. These data were complemented by agricultural records provided by producers from Rancho Tajeli, including harvest dates, quarterly yields, and achieved Brix degrees.

With the support of agronomy experts, five meteorological variables were selected as input factors based on their influence on photosynthesis, glycoside accumulation, and water stress:

- ALLSKY_KT (Clear Sky Index): Represents the fraction of solar radiation that reaches the Earth's surface. High values favor photosynthesis and the synthesis of sweetening compounds. In the dataset, values ranged from 0.48 to 0.71, with a mean of 0.61.
- QV2M (Specific Humidity at 2 meters): Indicates the amount of water vapor in the air. Extreme values can affect plant transpiration and nutrient uptake. Observed values ranged from 7.80 to 16.78 g/kg, with an average of 11.91.
- T2MDEW (Dew Point Temperature at 2 meters): Reflects the saturation point of air moisture. Higher values may promote fungal diseases, while lower values suggest drier air conditions.Recorded values ranged from 7.94°C to 20.03°C, with an average of 13.58°C.
- PRECTOTCORR_SUM (Total Accumulated Precipitation): Represents the total quarterly rainfall received by the crop. Moderate water stress can enhance glycoside concentration. Values ranged from 1.99 mm to 182.89 mm, with a mean of 53.12 mm.
- PRECTOTCORR (Average Precipitation): Indicates the average daily precipitation rate, affecting root development and water availability. Values ranged from 0.07 mm/day to 5.97 mm/day, averaging 1.77 mm/day.

The selection of these variables is supported by scientific literature [30–32], which demonstrates their impact on stevia productivity and sweet compound content. Prior to their incorporation into the FIS, each time series was normalized and adjusted to its historical range to ensure a robust and appropriate fuzzification process.

4.2 Output Variables

The output variable of the FIS corresponds to the predicted Brix degree (°Brix) in stevia leaves. This parameter is used as a key indicator for determining the optimal harvest time [33]. Three linguistic categories were defined—low, medium, and high—based on thresholds established by experts from Rancho Tajeli:

- Low (<22 °Brix): The plant has not yet reached the appropriate concentration of sweetening compounds.
- Medium (22–27 °Brix): Intermediate maturation stage. Harvest may be acceptable depending on external conditions.
- High (>27 °Brix): Represents the optimal state of sweetness and quality for harvest.

This fuzzy classification allows the system to issue comprehensible and practical recommendations, facilitating accurate and timely agronomic decision-making.

4.3 Membership Functions

Membership functions (MFs) are an essential component of Fuzzy Inference Systems (FIS) as they enable the mapping of crisp values to degrees of membership within linguistic sets [34]. Among the most commonly used functions (Figure 1) are triangular (a), defined by three parameters that establish a simple linear transition; trapezoidal (b), which extend this concept by including a central zone of maximum membership; and Gaussian (c), which provide a smooth and continuous representation based on the mean and standard deviation [35, 36].

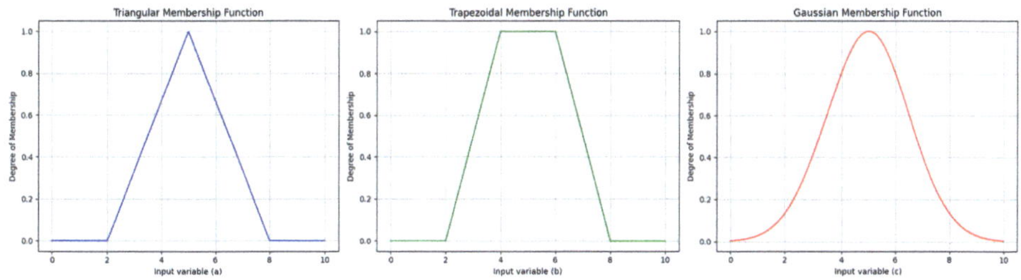

Fig. 1. Types of membership functions: (a) triangular, (b) trapezoidal, and (c) Gaussian

Recent advances in the literature have promoted the use of adaptive membership functions, whose parameters are not manually defined but instead optimized through computational methods such as evolutionary heuristics, fuzzy clustering, neural networks, or machine learning [37–39]. These approaches allow the generation of more accurate MFs tailored to the nature of the data, enhancing the robustness of the FIS and its generalization capacity in uncertain contexts.

4.4 Genetic Algorithms and Parameter Optimization

In order to reduce dependence on manual design of membership functions and improve the accuracy of the FIS, a strategy based on Genetic Algorithms (GAs) was adopted for adaptive parameter optimization. GAs are an evolutionary search technique inspired by the theory of natural selection [9, 40]. They rely on the representation of potential solutions through encoded chromosomes, which evolve through operators such as selection, crossover, and mutation [10].

In this study, GAs were employed as an optimization mechanism to adaptively tune the membership functions (MFs) of the Mamdani-type FIS, aimed at predicting Brix degrees in *Stevia rebaudiana* leaves. Each individual in the evolutionary population represents a complete encoding of the FIS, including the defining parameters of the membership functions and the type of function used (triangular, trapezoidal, or Gaussian). This approach enables efficient exploration of the solution space, taking into account both the parametric and topological configurations of the fuzzy logic system.

4.5 Chromosome Encoding

Each chromosome in the evolutionary process was structured as a vector comprising 90 real-valued parameters, corresponding to the complete configuration of the fuzzy inference system. This dimensionality results from the encoding of six variables: five meteorological inputs—ALLSKY_KT, QV2M, T2MDEW, PRECTOTCORR_SUM, and PRECTOTCORR—and one output variable representing the predicted °Brix value. For each variable, three fuzzy linguistic sets were defined: "low," "medium," and "high." Each linguistic set was encoded using five genes: four genes specifying the defining parameters of the membership function—interpreted as inflection points in the case of triangular (trimf) and trapezoidal (trapmf) functions, or as the mean and standard deviation for Gaussian (gaussmf) functions—and one additional gene indicating the type of membership function used.

This gene adopts an integer value: 0 for triangular, 1 for trapezoidal, and 2 for Gaussian. As a result, each variable contributes 15 genes to the chromosome (3 linguistic sets × 5 genes), and the entire system, comprising six variables, yields a total of 90 genes per chromosome. This encoding framework allows for the simultaneous optimization of both the shape and type of membership functions, facilitating the adaptive design of the fuzzy model through evolutionary search.

4.6 Evaluation and Fitness Function

The fitness function was defined as the inverse of the mean squared error (MSE) between the predictions generated by the FIS and the actual Brix degree values. The evaluation of each individual consisted of the following steps:

1. Construction of the FIS using the encoded MFs.
2. Application of six Mamdani-type fuzzy rules defined by domain experts.
3. Simulation of the model on the training dataset.
4. Calculation of the MSE and assignment of the corresponding fitness value.

This procedure allowed for the identification of individuals with higher predictive capability, promoting their reproduction in successive generations.

4.7 Evolutionary Process

The evolutionary process was developed over 20 generations with an initial population of 50 individuals. The genetic algorithm parameters were configured as follows:

- Selection: Tournament of size 3.
- Crossover: Blend operator (cxBlend) with $\alpha = 0.5$.
- Mutation: Gaussian mutation (mutGaussian) with mean $\mu = 0$, standard deviation $\sigma = 1$, and an individual mutation probability of 0.2.
- Replacement: Selection of the best individuals for the next generation.

This configuration maintained a balance between exploration and exploitation, ensuring convergence towards optimal FIS configurations.

4.8 Structural Representation of the Chromosome

Figure 2 presents the structural representation of a chromosome used in the evolutionary optimization process. This architecture establishes a direct link between fuzzy logic and

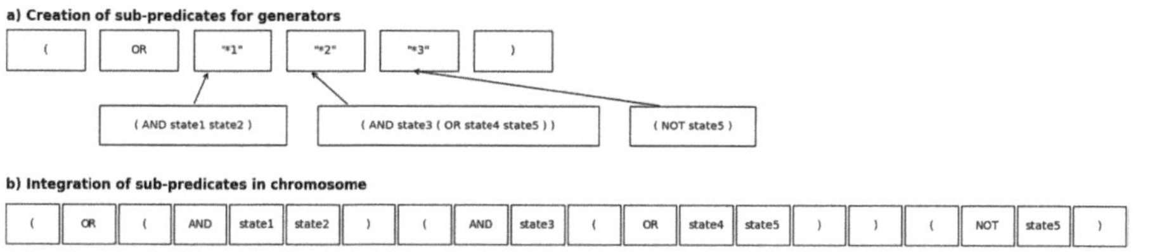

Fig. 2. Structural Representation of the Chromosome and Subpredicates

evolutionary learning techniques, enabling the automated generation of both membership functions and logical rule structures within the fuzzy inference system.

Each chromosome is composed of a series of genes, where every set of five genes defines a fuzzy subpredicate. These genes encode both the type and the parameters of the membership functions—triangular, trapezoidal, or Gaussian—depending on the gene configuration. The subpredicates generated in this manner are logically grouped to reflect compound relationships among variables. For instance, constructs such as (AND state1 state2), (AND state3 (OR state4 state5)), or (NOT state5) represent basic logical expressions encoded within the chromosome.

These logical substructures are then assembled into a hierarchical framework that defines the overall fuzzy rule base. A representative example of this assembly is:

(OR (AND state1 state2) (AND state3 (OR state4 state5)) (NOT state5)).

This composition guarantees that the resulting rule set is syntactically valid, hierarchically consistent, and capable of expressing complex nonlinear interactions among meteorological inputs.

In implementation, this integration is handled by the evaluate(...) function, which decodes the chromosome, constructs the ctrl.Antecedent and ctrl.Consequent objects for each variable, and defines the fuzzy rules using ctrl.Rule. Logical connectors (AND, OR, NOT) and the corresponding linguistic labels are systematically applied. This process ensures that each chromosome yields not only an optimized set of membership function parameters but also a semantically coherent and interpretable rule base, resulting in a robust and adaptive fuzzy inference system.

4.9 Input Membership Functions

In this research, an adaptive fuzzy modeling approach was adopted, in which the membership functions (MF) associated with the input variables were generated through evolutionary algorithm (EA) optimization. This strategy allowed for the elimination of manual parameter design, reducing the subjectivity inherent in the classical configuration of fuzzy sets and promoting precise tuning adapted to real meteorological data.

Each individual in the genetic population encoded a complete set of parameters that defined both the type of MF (triangular, trapezoidal, or Gaussian) and their characteristic values. For each of the five input meteorological variables, three linguistic sets ("low", "medium", "high") were generated, and their parameterization was evaluated using a fitness function based on the mean squared error (MSE) between the predicted values and the Brix degrees observed in historical data.

Three functional configurations were considered to represent the input functions:

- Triangular (trimf): Defined by three points (a, b, c), these provided good accuracy in contexts with well-defined transitions between classes.
- Trapezoidal (trapmf): Parameterized by four points (a, b, c, d), these captured stable regions in the data and showed greater tolerance to noise or local inaccuracies.
- Gaussian (gaussmf): Characterized by a mean and standard deviation, these exhibited smooth and continuous behavior, especially useful in environments with gradual variability.

The optimization was performed independently for each function type, thus constructing three complete fuzzy models with functions of the trimf, trapmf, or gaussmf type exclusively. The best individual from each run determined the final configuration used in the performance comparison of the FIS.

4.10 Output Membership Functions

The output variable of the FIS, the predicted Brix degrees in *Stevia rebaudiana* leaves, was modeled using three linguistic categories: "low", "medium", and "high". These labels were based on empirical thresholds defined by agronomy experts from the Rancho Tajeli and were subsequently refined through EA to achieve better alignment with historical data.

Each of the three output functions was represented using the same three functional configurations applied to the inputs:

- Triangular (trimf): These favored clear discrimination between discrete maturity states, with a representative central vertex.
- Trapezoidal (trapmf): These allowed for capturing stable maturity ranges with high membership, useful for representing acceptable agronomic conditions.
- Gaussian (gaussmf): These provided smooth transitions between classes, being especially suitable in scenarios with ambiguity in the measurement of maturity.

As with the input variables, the output MFs were optimized separately for each type. These parameterizations were combined with their respective input functions to construct three complete versions of the FIS, each based on an exclusive type of function (trimf model, trapmf model, gaussmf model).

This comparative design allowed for determining which functional configuration offered the best fit to the observed data, contributing to the generation of a more robust, interpretable, and generalizable fuzzy model.

4.11 Fuzzy Rule Base

The core operation of the FIS is constituted by its rule base [41], formulated under a linguistic structure of the type IF [condition] THEN [output]. These rules were initially defined by agronomy experts based on empirical knowledge of the climatic behavior of the stevia crop and were later refined through exploratory analysis of meteorological and production data.

The following are the six fundamental rules implemented in the system:

- IF Radiation = High AND Humidity = Low AND Dew = Low AND Accumulated Precipitation = Low, THEN °Brix = Low.
- IF Radiation = Medium AND Humidity = Medium AND Dew = Medium AND Accumulated Precipitation = Medium, THEN °Brix = Medium.
- IF Radiation = Low AND Humidity = High AND Dew = High AND Accumulated Precipitation = High, THEN °Brix = High.
- IF Accumulated Precipitation = High OR Average Precipitation = High, THEN °Brix = High.
- IF Accumulated Precipitation = Medium OR Average Precipitation = Medium, THEN °Brix = Medium.
- IF Accumulated Precipitation = Low OR Average Precipitation = Low, THEN °Brix = Low.

These rules allow for the representation of typical climatic combinations and their effects on the sweetening quality of the crop, promoting linguistic interpretations consistent with agronomic experience. Their integration into the system contributes to the transparency and interpretability of the model, facilitating its adoption in agricultural decision-making environments.

4.12 Model Validation

The validation of the proposed FIS was performed using the hold-out cross-validation strategy [42] with an 80-20 split. For this, the historical dataset corresponding to the period 2015–2024 was used, with 80% allocated for model training and the remaining 20% for validation. This methodology allowed for the assessment of the system's stability within the same time frame [43, 44].

To quantify the model's performance, the following metrics were used:

Mean Squared Error (MSE): Evaluates the average squared errors between the values predicted by the model and the actual observed values. A lower MSE indicates higher prediction accuracy [45].

$$\frac{1}{N}\sum_{i=1}^{n}(yi - \hat{y}i)^2 \tag{1}$$

where:

- n = total number of samples.
- yi = actual value.
- $\hat{y}i$ = predicted value by the model.
- $(yi - \hat{y}i)^2$ = the square of the error (difference between actual and predicted).

Accuracy: The total percentage of correct predictions (harvest or no harvest) compared to the total number of cases [46].

$$Accuracy = \frac{TP + TN}{TP + TN + FP + FN} \tag{2}$$

where:

- TP (True Positives): Cases correctly predicted as "Harvest".
- TN (True Negatives): Cases correctly predicted as "No Harvest".
- FP (False Positives): Cases incorrectly classified as "Harvest".
- FN (False Negatives): Cases incorrectly classified as "No Harvest".

Confusion Matrix: A table that shows the distribution of true and false predictions [47]. It is interpreted as shown in Table 1.

Table 1. Confusion Matrix

	Prediction: No Harvest	Prediction: Harvest
Actual: No Harvest	TN (True Negatives)	FP (False Positives)
Actual: Harvest	FN (False Negatives)	TP (True Positives)

These metrics allowed verification that the optimized FIS is not only interpretable and based on expert knowledge but also effective at predicting the sweetening content of *Stevia rebaudiana* leaves under real production conditions. The validation showed a good fit of the model to external climatic conditions, confirming its usefulness as a decision-support tool in agronomic decision-making.

5 Results

The performance of the proposed FIS was evaluated using three different MF configurations: triangular, trapezoidal, and Gaussian. The evaluation was conducted exclusively on the validation set, following the 80-20 hold-out cross-validation strategy outlined in Section 4.12. For each configuration, the best-performing individual obtained through GA optimization was selected to assess the model.

The triangular MF configuration yielded an accuracy of 92.86% and a mean squared error (MSE) of 0.0714. This setup demonstrated solid predictive performance, characterized by clear transitions between linguistic terms and a favorable balance between accuracy and sensitivity.

The trapezoidal MF configuration achieved the highest overall performance, with an accuracy of 96.43% and the lowest MSE of 0.0357. Its robustness to data noise and ability to represent stable membership regions contributed to its superior results, including perfect sensitivity during validation.

In contrast, the Gaussian MF configuration resulted in an accuracy of 78.57% and a considerably higher MSE of 0.2143. While Gaussian functions are well-suited for modeling smooth and continuous transitions, their application in this case was less effective, likely due to their sensitivity to local data variability and difficulty capturing abrupt class boundaries.

The results (Table 2) indicate that this configuration faced significant difficulties in detecting positive cases (harvests), suggesting that Gaussian functions were not suitable for the nature of the validation data or the characteristics of the problem addressed.

Table 2. Results by Membership Function

FM	Accuracy	MSE	TN	FP	FN	TP
TRIMF	92.86%	0.0714	21	1	1	5
TRAPMF	**96.43%**	**0.0357**	**21**	**1**	**0**	**6**
GAUSSMF	78.57%	0.2143	22	0	6	0

The FIS models using triangular, trapezoidal, and Gaussian functions were evaluated. The trapezoidal function provided the best performance with the highest accuracy (96.43%) and the lowest MSE (0.0357). The triangular model was also effective, with a good balance between accuracy and sensitivity, while the Gaussian model showed weaker performance, particularly in detecting positive harvest cases.

In order to further assess the effectiveness of the proposed fuzzy logic approach, two additional models were implemented and evaluated using the same validation dataset: a multilayer perceptron (MLP) neural network and a baseline fuzzy inference system without genetic optimization.

The MLP model achieved an accuracy of 83.33% and a perfect recall of 100%, although it produced false positives, resulting in a precision of only 50%. The non-optimized FIS obtained an accuracy of 66.67%, a recall of 100%, and a precision of 33.33%, indicating a tendency to overpredict harvests. In contrast, the GA-optimized FIS with trapezoidal membership functions outperformed both alternatives, achieving the highest accuracy (96.43%) and maintaining perfect sensitivity without sacrificing precision. These results (Table 3) confirm that evolutionary optimization significantly enhances the performance and reliability of fuzzy inference models for harvest prediction tasks.

Table 3. Comparative Metrics of Selected Models

FM	Accuracy (%)	Precision (%)	Recall (%)	F1-Score (%)
MLP	83.33	50	100	66.67
FIS +GA (Trapezoidal MF)	**96.43**	**100**	**100**	**100**
Non-optimized FIS	66.67	33.33	100	50

6 Discussion

This study confirms the potential of combining FL with GA for predicting the optimal harvest time in *Stevia rebaudiana* crops. The use of a Mamdani-type FIS enabled the encoding of expert agronomic knowledge into interpretable linguistic rules, making the model particularly suitable for real-world agricultural applications.

The GA successfully optimized MF parameters for three configurations: triangular, trapezoidal, and Gaussian. Among these, the trapmf achieved the best performance, with an accuracy of 96.43% and the lowest MSE of 0.0357. Its robustness against climatic variability and ability to capture stable membership regions contributed to its superior detection of positive harvest cases.

The trimf also performed well (92.86% accuracy), offering a simpler alternative with slightly lower precision but good generalization. In contrast, the gaussmf reached only 78.57% accuracy and failed to detect positive cases. This underperformance is likely due to the sensitivity of Gaussian curves to noise and dispersion in the input data.

A notable contribution is the use of a chromosome encoding scheme that simultaneously represents MF parameters and function types. This enabled a comprehensive search of the solution space and allowed the automatic construction of complete fuzzy rule sets. The approach balances model interpretability with adaptability, making it particularly attractive for decision-making in precision agriculture.

7 Conclusion

The integration of FIS with evolutionary optimization presents a promising solution for predicting the optimal harvest time in *Stevia rebaudiana* cultivation. The GA-optimized FIS proved to be an accurate and robust tool, particularly when using trapezoidal membership functions. This configuration showed the highest precision and sensitivity to the complex environmental conditions influencing harvest timing.

The model's interpretability and adaptability make it especially suitable for deployment in small and medium-sized agricultural operations. Future work may extend this system through real-time sensor integration, mobile platforms, or expanded datasets to improve its precision and scalability in diverse cultivation environments.

Data Availability and Acknowledgments. A subset of the dataset used in this study is available for reproducibility purposes at [https://github.com/Brizram23/Fuzzy-Inference-Systems-with-Evolutionary-Optimization-for-Timely-Harvest-Prediction-A-Case-Study.git]. It includes normalized input variables and corresponding Brix degree values, and is provided for non-commercial and educational use only.

The authors thank the agronomic staff of Rancho Tajeli for their valuable collaboration in providing harvest records, field data, and domain expertise. This work was supported by the Secretaría de Ciencia, Humanidades, Tecnología e Innovación (SECIHTI) and the Tecnológico Nacional de México, Campus Colima, whose institutional support made this research possible.

Declaration of Conflict of Interest. The authors declare that there are no competing financial or non-financial interests that could have influenced the results or interpretations presented in this manuscript.

References

1. Russell, S., Norvig, P.: Artificial Intelligence: A Modern Approach, 4th edn. Pearson Education (2021)
2. Liakos, K.G., Busato, P., Moshou, D., Pearson, S., Bochtis, D.: Machine learning in agriculture: a review. Sensors **18**(8), 2674 (2018). https://doi.org/10.3390/s18082674

3. Brandle, J.E., Rosa, N.: Heritability and effect of harvest management on stevioside content in Stevia rebaudiana. Can. J. Plant Sci. **72**(4), 1263–1270 (1992). https://doi.org/10.4141/cjps92-155
4. Hatfield, J.L., Boote, K.J., Kimball, B.A., et al.: Climate impacts on agriculture: implications for crop production. Agron. J. **103**(2), 351–370 (2011). https://doi.org/10.2134/agronj2010.0303
5. Arif, K.M., Jaywant, S.A., Singh, H.: Sensors and instruments for brix measurement: a review. Sensors **22**(7), 2695 (2022). https://doi.org/10.3390/s22072695
6. Zadeh, L.A.: Fuzzy sets. Inf. Control. **8**(3), 338–353 (1965). https://doi.org/10.1016/S0019-9958(65)90241-X
7. Klir, G.J., Folger, T.A.: Fuzzy Sets, Uncertainty, and Information. Prentice Hall (1988)
8. Padrón-Tristán, J.F., Cruz-Reyes, L., Espín-Andrade, R.A., Llorente-Peralta, C.E.: Desempeño vs interpretabilidad en sistemas difusos: una breve revisión. Computación y Sistemas **25**(3), 489–499 (2021). https://doi.org/10.13053/CyS-25-3-4023
9. Holland, J.H.: Adaptation in Natural and Artificial Systems. University of Michigan Press (1975)
10. Goldberg, D.E.: Genetic Algorithms in Search, Optimization and Machine Learning. Addison-Wesley (1989)
11. Arellano-Verdejo, J., Guzmán-Arenas, A., Godoy-Calderón, S., Barrón-Fernández, R.: Efficiently finding the optimum number of clusters in a dataset with a new hybrid differential evolution algorithm: DELA. Comput. Sist. **18**(2), 313–327 (2014). https://doi.org/10.13053/cys-18-2-1995
12. Melin, P., Castillo, O., Ramírez, E., Soria, J., Valdez, F.: Optimización genética de sistemas difusos tipo-2 intervalares para control inteligente. Comput. Sist. **17**(2), 179–188 (2013). https://doi.org/10.13053/cys-17-2-1360
13. Bin, L., Shahzad, M., Khan, H., Bashir, M.M., Ullah, A., Siddique, M.: Sustainable smart agriculture farming for cotton crop: a fuzzy logic rule based methodology. Sustainability **15**(18), 13874 (2023). https://doi.org/10.3390/su151813874
14. Riahi, J., Nasri, H., Mami, A., Vergura, S.: Effectiveness of the fuzzy logic control to manage the microclimate inside a smart insulated greenhouse. Smart Cities **7**(3), 1304–1329 (2024). https://doi.org/10.3390/smartcities7030065
15. Artetxe, E., Barambones, O., Martín Toral, I., Uralde, J., Calvo, I., del Rio, A.: Smart IoT irrigation system based on fuzzy logic, LoRa, and cloud integration. Electronics **13**(10), 1949 (2024). https://doi.org/10.3390/electronics13101949
16. Saraswat, A., Ram, S., AbdelRahman, M.A.E., et al.: Combining fuzzy, multicriteria and mapping techniques to assess soil fertility for agricultural development. Land **12**(4), 860 (2023). https://doi.org/10.3390/land12040860
17. Widayat, I.W., Arsyad, A.A., Mantau, A.J., Adhitya, Y., Köppen, M.: Fuzzy methods in smart farming: a systematic review. Informatica **48**, 1–37 (2024). https://doi.org/10.15388/23-INFOR511
18. Abdullah, N., Durani, N.A.B., Shari, M.F.B., et al.: Towards smart agriculture monitoring using fuzzy systems. IEEE Access **9**, 4097–4111 (2021). https://doi.org/10.1109/ACCESS.2021.3054444
19. Singh, A.K., Tariq, T., Ahmer, M.F., Sharma, G., Bokoro, P.N., Shongwe, T.: Intelligent control of irrigation systems using fuzzy logic controller. Energies **15**(19), 7199 (2022). https://doi.org/10.3390/en15197199
20. Hasan, I., Srivastava, A., Khan, Z.R., Rizvi, S.A.M.: A novel fuzzy inference-based decision support system for crop water optimization. SN Oper. Res. Forum **4**(2), 38 (2023). https://doi.org/10.1007/s44196-023-00123-z
21. Małolepsza, O., Mikołajewski, D., Prokopowicz, P.: Using fuzzy logic to analyse weather conditions. Electronics **14**(1), 85 (2025). https://doi.org/10.3390/electronics14010085

22. Zadeh, L.A.: Outline of a new approach to the analysis of complex systems and decision processes. IEEE Trans. Syst. Man Cybern. **SMC-3**(1), 28–44 (1973). https://doi.org/10.1109/TSMC.1973.5408575
23. Padrón-Tristán, J.F., Cruz-Reyes, L., Espín-Andrade, R.A., Llorente-Peralta, C.E.: Compensatory fuzzy logic genetic algorithm for classification problems: a case study. Comput. Sist. **28**(3), 1257–1274 (2024). https://doi.org/10.13053/cys-28-3-4789
24. Guillaume, S.: Designing fuzzy inference systems from data: an interpretability-oriented review. IEEE Trans. Fuzzy Syst. **9**(3), 426–443 (2001). https://doi.org/10.1109/91.928739
25. Lee, C.C.: Fuzzy logic in control systems: Fuzzy logic controller—Part II. IEEE Trans. Syst. Man Cybern. **20**(2), 419–435 (1990). https://doi.org/10.1109/21.52552
26. Mamdani, E.H., Assilian, S.: An experiment in linguistic synthesis with a fuzzy logic controller. Int. J. Man Mach. Stud. **7**(1), 1–13 (1975). https://doi.org/10.1016/S0020-7373(75)80002-2
27. Takagi, T., Sugeno, M.: Fuzzy identification of systems and its applications to modeling and control. IEEE Trans. Syst. Man Cybern. **15**(1), 116–132 (1985). https://doi.org/10.1109/TSMC.1985.6313399
28. Vejar-Cortés, A.-P., García-Díaz, N., Soriano-Equigua, L., Ruiz-Tadeo, A.-C., Álvarez-Flores, J.-L.: Determination of crop soil quality for stevia rebaudiana bertoni morita II using a fuzzy logic model and a wireless sensor network. Appl. Sci. **13**(17), 9507 (2023). https://doi.org/10.3390/app13179507
29. Papadopoulos, A., Kalivas, D., Hatzichristos, T.: Decision support system for nitrogen fertilization using fuzzy theory. Comput. Electron. Agric. **78**(2), 130–139 (2011). https://doi.org/10.1016/j.compag.2011.06.002
30. Yadav, A.K., Singh, B., Dhyani, D., Ahuja, P.S.: A review on the improvement of Stevia rebaudiana (Bertoni). Can. J. Plant Sci. **91**(1), 1–27 (2011). https://doi.org/10.4141/CJPS10036
31. Celaya, L., Ferreyra, D., Kolb, E., Koslobsky, N.K.: Extraction of stevioside and rebaudioside a from stevia rebaudiana by percolation with ethanol-water solvents. Rev. Ciencia Tecnol. (38), 61–70 (2022). https://doi.org/10.36995/j.recyt.2022.38.007
32. Pal, P.K., Yadav, A.K., Singh, S., Roy, S.: Effect of water stress on growth and steviol glycoside content in Stevia rebaudiana. Ind. Crops Prod. **66**, 170–176 (2015). https://doi.org/10.1016/j.indcrop.2014.12.031
33. Kader, A.A.: Flavor quality of fruits and vegetables. J. Sci. Food Agric. **88**(11), 1863–1868 (2008). https://doi.org/10.1002/jsfa.3293
34. Ross, T.J.: Fuzzy Logic with Engineering Applications, 3rd edn. Wiley (2010)
35. Zimmermann, H.J.: Fuzzy Set Theory—and Its Applications, 2nd edn. Kluwer Academic Publishers (1991)
36. Cox, E.: Fuzzy fundamentals. IEEE Spectr. **29**(10), 58–61 (1992). https://doi.org/10.1109/6.163347
37. Jang, J.-S.R.: ANFIS: adaptive-network-based fuzzy inference system. IEEE Trans. Syst. Man Cybern. **23**(3), 665–685 (1993). https://doi.org/10.1109/21.256541
38. Bezdek, J.C., Ehrlich, R., Full, W.: FCM: the fuzzy c-means clustering algorithm. Comput. Geosci. **10**(2–3), 191–203 (1984). https://doi.org/10.1016/0098-3004(84)90020-7
39. Saatchi, R.: Fuzzy logic concepts, developments and implementation. Information **15**(10), 656 (2024). https://doi.org/10.3390/info15100656
40. Mitchell, M.: An Introduction to Genetic Algorithms. MIT Press (1998)
41. Lee, C.C.: Fuzzy logic in control systems: fuzzy logic controller—part I. IEEE Trans. Syst. Man Cybern. **20**(2), 404–418 (1990). https://doi.org/10.1109/21.52551
42. Kohavi, R.: A study of cross-validation and bootstrap for accuracy estimation and model selection. In: Proceedings of the 14th International Joint Conference on Artificial Intelligence, pp. 1137–1145 (1995)

43. Bergmeir, C., Benítez, J.M.: On the use of cross-validation for time series predictor evaluation. Inf. Sci. **191**, 192–213 (2012). https://doi.org/10.1016/j.ins.2011.12.028
44. Roberts, D.R., Bahn, V., Ciuti, S., et al.: Cross-validation strategies for data with temporal, spatial, hierarchical, or phylogenetic structure. Ecography **40**(8), 913–929 (2017). https://doi.org/10.1111/ecog.02881
45. Chai, T., Draxler, R.R.: Root mean square error (RMSE) or mean absolute error (MAE)? – arguments for avoiding RMSE in favor of MAE. Geosci. Model Dev. **7**(3), 1247–1250 (2014). https://doi.org/10.5194/gmd-7-1247-2014
46. Tharwat, A.: Classification assessment methods. Appl. Comput. Inform. **17**(1), 168–192 (2018). https://doi.org/10.1016/j.aci.2018.08.003
47. Sokolova, M., Lapalme, G.: A systematic analysis of performance measures for classification tasks. Inf. Process. Manage. **45**(4), 427–437 (2009). https://doi.org/10.1016/j.ipm.2009.03.002

Impact of Binarization on the Performance of Associative Memories in Machine Learning

Jorge Emmanuel Zamora Zamora[1(✉)], Rodolfo Salgado Rivera[1], Cornelio Yañez Marquez[1], Elias Jesús Ventura Molina[2], and Antonio Alarcón-Paredes[1]

[1] Centro de Investigación en Computación del Instituto Politcénico Nacional, CIC IPN, Mexico City, Mexico
{jzamoraz2024,rsalgador2024,cyanez,aalarcon}@cic.ipn.mx
[2] Centro de Innovación y Desarrollo Tecnológico en Cómputo del Instituto Politcénico Nacional, CIC IPN, Mexico City, Mexico

Abstract. Associative memories (AM) deliver instant recall and tolerate noisy inputs, yet their effectiveness hinges on how numeric data are translated into bits. This study benchmarks five integer-to-binary schemes with different approaches, code—within the classic Lernmatrix associative memory. Fourteen public datasets with varied sizes, feature counts, and class balances were converted to non-negative integers, harmonized to a common bit-width, binarized, and validated by Leave-One-Out cross-validation. Balanced-accuracy results show that Parity + RNS (mean BA = 0.6826) and Gray code (0.6788) provide the most informative representations, leading eight of the fourteen datasets. Straight Binary and BCD excel only in niche cases, whereas IEEE-754 mantissa remains the least effective (0.6457). The distributed residues of Parity + RNS and the one-bit transitions of Gray code make class boundaries easier to separate, boosting accuracy by more than five percentage points over less suitable encodings. These results demonstrate that careful bit-level design can markedly improve one-shot associative classifiers, underscoring the importance of representation as an independent lever for optimizing lightweight, interpretable learning systems.

Keywords: Associative memory · Lernmatrix · Binarization · Gray code · Residue number system · Balanced accuracy

1 Introduction

Artificial-intelligence algorithms now equal or surpass human performance in tasks such as image and text recognition [15]. Their success, however, comes at the cost of growing model size, energy demand, and long training times. Most state-of-the-art systems rely on many iterations of gradient descent to refine

C. Palma-Preciado et al. (Eds.): CORE 2025, ACSAR 3, pp. 202–214, 2026.
https://doi.org/10.1007/978-3-032-08894-9_13

millions of parameters [20]. This workflow may be impractical on edge devices or in time-critical settings.

Associative memories (AM) address this limitation. These pattern-storage and retrieval systems, inspired by the psychological concept of association, can learn a new example in a single pass, and recover it in microseconds [24]. The Lernmatrix, a feed-forward associative memory introduced by Karl Steinbuch [25] exemplifies this simplicity: it reinforces co-occurring bits with a direct correlation rule, and produces a class decision without any iterative optimization. The price is lower accuracy than that of modern ensembles, raising the question of how far one can push performance without sacrificing the one-shot property.

A key but understudied lever is the *bit-level representation* of the input data. Real-world features are usually floating-point numbers that must be converted to binary vectors before they can drive the Lernmatrix. Straight binary is the default, yet alternatives exist. Gray code flips only one bit between successive integers, Binary-Coded Decimal (BCD) preserves decimal structure, the IEEE-754 mantissa compresses magnitudes logarithmically, and a Residue Number System (RNS) spreads information across several residues. So far, there hasn't been a study that compares these encoding methods in the same way. Because of that, it's tough to figure out which coding scheme is the best choice.

In the last decade, research on AM has gained new momentum, driven by the need for transparent, low-latency classifiers. Operate where deep models are impractical [30]. Three complementary lines of work were reviewed: representation-level enhancements, novel associative classifiers, and Theoretical advances in bidirectional memories.

The classification power of an AM is strongly affected by the way input patterns are encoded before they are stored. In [26] was introduced a Möbius-based numerical transform that removes subtractive noise and raises Lernmatrix balanced accuracy by up to six percentage points on twenty imbalanced datasets. That approach changes the *numerical* scale before any bit conversion. In contrast, the raw integers were kept and study how five alternative integer-to-binary encodings alter performance when every other experimental factor is held constant.

Several authors have proposed new AM architectures that rival mainstream learners. The Naïve Associative Classifier (NAC) couples a mixed-type dissimilarity measure with a transparent weighting scheme and surpasses support-vector machines and decision trees on four financial datasets [27]. While NAC tackles heterogeneous attributes, our study preserves the original Lernmatrix correlation-learning rule and focuses exclusively on the influence of the binary *representation.*

Bidirectional AM extend the original Lernmatrix by allowing recall in both directions (pattern $\leftrightarrow$ class). The α-β BAM family guarantees perfect recall capacity $2 \cdot \min(n, m)$ under bounded noise, with formal proofs and practical demonstrations [3]. A later monograph consolidates fifteen years of α-β theory and variants [32]. These works underscore that capacity and stability depend on how information is distributed across synapses, reinforcing our motivation to examine bit-level encodings.

Earlier studies either introduced numerical transforms [26], redesigned the similarity operator [27], or modified the learning dynamics [32]. The intention was to take an orthogonal perspective: without altering the classic correlation update of the Lernmatrix, A systematic evaluation was presented, across fourteen heterogeneous datasets, of how five integer encodings (straight binary, Gray, BCD, IEEE-754 mantissa, Parity + RNS) influence its classification accuracy. Our results complement existing architectural and theoretical advances, filling a gap in the literature on representation-driven performance in AM.

2 Materials and Methods

This section presents the methodological framework used to examine how different integer-to-binary encodings shape the behavior of a Lernmatrix associative memory. It introduces the datasets and the preprocessing required to obtain a uniform numerical representation, then outlines the encoding alternatives and the construction of binary inputs and targets. The following subsections expand each component in turn.

2.1 Binarization Methods

Five classical coding schemes were tested: *Straight Binary* ($\log_2$), *Gray Code*, *Binary-Coded Decimal (BCD)*, *IEEE-754 Mantissa Only* and the *combined Parity & Residue Number System (RNS)* encoding. Each integer vector row is mapped to a binary sequence of length $d \times b$ under scheme $s \in \mathcal{S}$.

Successive Divisions (Decimal to Binary Conversion). This classic method converts a decimal number to its binary representation by repeatedly dividing it by 2, saving the residue at each step, and reading these residues in reverse order [4].

For example, to convert the number 25, it does at following:

$$\begin{aligned} 25 \div 2 &= 12, \ \text{residue } \mathbf{1} \\ 12 \div 2 &= 6, \ \text{residue } \mathbf{0} \\ 6 \div 2 &= 3, \ \text{residue } \mathbf{0} \\ 3 \div 2 &= 1, \ \text{residue } \mathbf{1} \\ 1 \div 2 &= 0, \ \text{residue } \mathbf{1} \end{aligned}$$

$\therefore$ The result is: **11001**.

Gray Code. Gray code is a binary representation in which two consecutive numbers differ by only one bit, reducing errors during transitions. To obtain the Gray code, the most significant bit is preserved, and an XOR operation is applied between each pair of consecutive bits [13]. For example, for the number 25 (binary 11001).

$$\begin{aligned}\text{First bit: } &\mathbf{1}\\ \text{Second bit: } &1 \oplus 1 = \mathbf{0}\\ \text{Third bit: } &1 \oplus 0 = \mathbf{1}\\ \text{Fourth bit: } &0 \oplus 0 = \mathbf{0}\\ \text{Fifth bit: } &0 \oplus 1 = \mathbf{0}\end{aligned}$$

$\therefore$ The number 25 is represented in Gray code as **10101**.

BCD (Binary-Coded Decimal). BCD encoding represents each decimal digit with 4 bits, maintaining the decimal structure of the number [31]. For example, the number 25 is divided into two digits:

$$2 \rightarrow 0010$$
$$5 \rightarrow 0101$$

$\therefore$ The number 25 is represented in BCD as: **0010 0101**.

IEEE 754 (Floating-Point Representation). The IEEE 754 standard defines the representation of real numbers in floating-point format in digital systems. In the single-precision format (32 bits), a number is divided into one sign bit, 8 bits for the exponent (with a bias of 127), and 23 bits for the mantissa [10].

For example, the number 10.75 is normalized to 1.01011×2^3; the exponent 3 is adjusted to 130 (binary 10000010), and the mantissa is derived from the fractional part, resulting in **01000001001011000000000000000000**.

Parity + Residue Number System (RNS) Encoding. This hybrid code turns a non-negative integer into a single-bit string in three plain steps:

1. Residues. Pick a small set of pairwise-coprime moduli—here $\{3, 5, 7\}$—and compute the remainders of the number with each modulus.
2. Fixed-width binary. Encode every residue with just enough bits to cover its range (01 for mod 3, 000 for mod 5, 100 for mod 7, etc.) and concatenate the blocks [17].
3. Even-parity bit. Count the 1's in the concatenated residue string. If the count is odd, append `1`; if it is already even, append `0`. This single bit lets any receiver detect a one-bit error [22].

Example (25).

$$25 \bmod 3 = 1 \rightarrow 01, \quad 25 \bmod 5 = 0 \rightarrow 000, \quad 25 \bmod 7 = 4 \rightarrow 100$$

Concatenate the residue blocks: 01000100 (two 1's, already even). Parity bit = 0.

010001000

Thus, the final Parity + RNS representation of 25 is the 9-bit string 010001000, combining the space efficiency of RNS with a built-in single-bit error check.

2.2 Associative Memories

An associative memory is a system capable of learning and recognizing pairs of patterns, even when the input data are altered. Its primary goal is to reconstruct complete patterns from modified versions. In the case of binary patterns, alterations may be additive, subtractive, or mixed [14].

AM remains relevant due to their robustness against data alterations, fast learning capability (one-shot learning), ease of implementation, and, in some cases, their ability to recover 100% of the original information. Furthermore, their relationship to autoencoders maintains their significance within the field of deep learning. However, they also present certain limitations, such as the requirement to use numerical patterns, restrictions on the types of numbers they can recognize, and the risk of saturation when storing too many associations within a finite space.

2.3 Lernmatrix

The *Lernmatrix* proposed by Karl Steinbuch in 1961 was the first modern associative memory model. It uses a synaptic matrix $\mathbf{M}$ that connects n input features (*characteristic lines*) to m output classes (*meaning lines*) [25]. This matrix has:

- m rows (one for each output class);
- n columns (one for each input feature);

Each element m_{ij} indicates how strongly feature j supports class i: positive values mean supporting evidence, while negative values indicate contradiction.

Training Phase: For each pattern-class pair $(\mathbf{x}^\mu, \mathbf{y}^\mu)$, weights are adjusted through

$$m_{ij}^{\text{new}} = m_{ij}^{\text{current}} + \begin{cases} +\varepsilon & \text{si } y_i^\mu = 1 \wedge x_j^\mu = 1, \\ -\varepsilon & \text{si } y_i^\mu = 1 \wedge x_j^\mu = 0, \\ 0 & \text{en otro caso.} \end{cases} \tag{1}$$

That is:

1. Take the current value m_{ij},
2. Add the corresponding adjustment ($+\varepsilon$, $-\varepsilon$ or 0),
3. Store the result as the new weight value.

This reinforces features that consistently accompany their class and weakens those that are absent when the class is activated.

Recovery phase: pattern classification For a test pattern x, the network decides the class in three quick steps:

1. *Score vector:* compute $\mathbf{s} = \mathbf{M}\mathbf{x}$, where each entry s_i is the total "vote" accumulated for class i.
2. *Pick the best class:* find $k = \arg\max_i s_i$, the index with the largest score.
3. *Build the one-hot output* $\mathbf{y}$: set $y_k = 1$ and all other $y_i = 0$. Example: for the classes [Cat, Dog, Fox] and $k = 3$ (Fox), $\mathbf{y} = [0, 0, 1]$.

The Lernmatrix associative memory introduced foundational ideas that modern associative memories, such as Willshaw's correlograph. Its main drawback is synaptic saturation: when many similar patterns are stored, overlapping connections blur class boundaries and generate ambiguous outputs. This ambiguity remains a central obstacle that limits the practical scalability of these memories.

2.4 Datasets

Machine learning algorithms, ideally, must be evaluated for their robustness across different scenarios and problem domains. In this context, several datasets were obtained from the KEEL platform [5], a free repository designed to provide reference benchmarks for analyzing the behavior of learning algorithms.

Primarily two-class datasets with exclusively numerical attributes were selected; categorical variables and missing values were excluded, and no class balancing was applied. The selected datasets are presented in Table 1.

3 Methodology

The intention was to assess the effect of five integer-to-binary encoding—straight binary ($\log_2$), Gray code, BCD, IEEE-754 mantissa, and a combined Parity + RNS—on the accuracy of Lernmatrix associative memory.

Fourteen KEEL datasets were chosen to span 28–5,300 instances, 2–1,070 features, and imbalance ratios from 0.24 to 2.77. Every dataset is imputed, label-encoded, shifted to remove negatives, and scaled to integers. A uniform bit-width is then applied before being binarized with each scheme.

Performance is estimated via Leave-One-Out cross-validation; Balanced Accuracy is recorded for every fold and averaged per dataset $\times$ encoding pair. Figure 1 summarizes the seven-phase pipeline—from raw data to metric aggregation—that underpins all experiments.

This section describes in detail the seven phases of our methodology process for evaluating the impact of different binarization schemes on a Lernmatrix associative memory. Figure 1 illustrates the overall flow.

Table 1. Summary of selected datasets

Dataset	Instances	Features	IR
Iris [9]	150	4	1.00
Appendicitis [28]	106	7	0.24
Banana [18]	5300	2	0.81
Contraceptive [16]	1473	9	1.88
Electricity [12]	2400	9	1.47
Haberman [11]	306	3	2.77
Heart [2]	270	13	1.25
Nutt [19]	28	1070	1.00
Pima [7]	768	8	1.86
Titanic [8]	2201	3	2.09
Australian [21]	690	14	1.24
Bupa [1]	345	6	1.37
Ionosphere [23]	351	33	1.78
Monk [29]	432	6	1.11

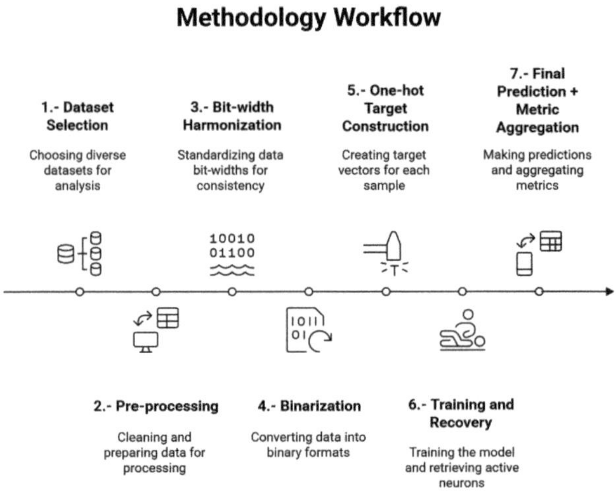

Fig. 1. End-to-end workflow implemented in this study.

3.1 Phase 1: Dataset Selection

Fourteen publicly available datasets that have a variety of sizes (from a few to hundreds, even thousands of patterns), dimensionalities (4–50 features) and imbalance ratios were used. Table 1 summarizes their characteristics. Treating each dataset independently ensures our conclusions generalize across domains.

3.2 Phase 2: Pre-processing

Preprocessing was required before transforming the selected datasets, as the binarization schemes considered act on integer values. Hence, each dataset followed four steps.

1. *Imputation.* If any dataset had missing values, these missing data were filled with the class column mean.
2. *Categorical encoding.* Nominal attributes (if any) are converted via label encoding into integer data.
3. *Remove negatives.* To get rid of the negative values, it was necessary to search for the minimum. For each attribute a_j, compute $\delta_j = -\min(a_j)$ and add it to all values so that the minimum becomes 0. This preserves relative distances and guarantees non-negative integers.
4. *Decimal removal.* Let $d_{\max}$ be the maximum number of decimal places across the dataset. Multiply every value by $10^{d_{\max}}$ and round to the nearest integer.

These steps produces an integer matrix $\mathbf{X} \in \mathbb{Z}_{\geq 0}^{N \times d}$.

3.3 Phase 3: Bit-Width Harmonization

Compute for each attribute column:

$$\begin{aligned} b_j &= \lceil \log_2(\max(a_j) + 1) \rceil , \\ b &= \max_i b_i . \end{aligned} \tag{2}$$

Using the global bit-width b, to represent every integer entry with exactly b bits, ensuring fixed-length binary vectors of dimension $d \times b$.

3.4 Phase 4: Binarization

Five classical coding schemes were tested: *Two's Complement*, *Gray Code*, *Binary-Coded Decimal (BCD)*, *IEEE-754 Mantissa Only*, and *Residue Number System (RNS)*. Each integer vector row is mapped to a binary sequence of length $d \times b$ under scheme $s \in \mathcal{S}$.

3.5 Phase 5: One-Hot Target Construction

For each of the N samples, build a 1-of-N target vector $\mathbf{y}^{(k)} \in \{0, 1\}^N$ with a single 1 at position k. These serve as the desired outputs for the associative recall in the Lernmatrix.

3.6 Phase 6: Training and Recovery (LOO-CV)

Perform Leave-One-Out cross-validation: for each probe sample $(\mathbf{x}, y)$,

$$D_{\text{train}} = D \setminus \{(x, y)\}. \tag{3}$$

Then

1. Store all binarized training patterns and their one-hot targets in a new version of the Lernmatrix.
2. Present the probe's binary vector, obtaining a retrieved vector $\mathbf{r} \in \{0, 1\}^N$. Entries $r_k = 1$ mark "fired" memory neurons corresponding to candidate patterns.

3.7 Phase 7 Recovery Add on & Metric Aggregation

After retrieval, the Lernmatrix often activates more than one memory cell, producing a candidate set $\mathcal{K} = \{k \mid r_k = 1\}$. To choose the single candidate that best matches the probe, the **Euclidean distance** was used [6].

Intuition. For two points in a 2-D plane, $A(x_1, y_1)$ and $B(x_2, y_2)$, the Euclidean distance is

$$d(A, B) = \sqrt{(x_2 - x_1)^2 + (y_2 - y_1)^2}. \tag{4}$$

This idea was applied to our d-dimensional feature space.

Formal Definition. For every activated index $k \in \mathcal{K}$ compute

$$d_k = \sqrt{\sum_{j=1}^{d} \left(a_j(x) - a_j\left(x^{(k)}\right)\right)^2}. \tag{5}$$

where $a_j(\mathbf{x})$ is the (pre-processed) value of feature j for the probe and $a_j(\mathbf{x}^{(k)})$ is the same feature for the candidate pattern stored at index k. The candidate with the smallest distance wins:

$$k^{\star} = \arg\min_{k \in \mathcal{K}} d_k, \qquad \hat{y} = \text{IndexToClass}(k^{\star}). \tag{6}$$

Balanced Accuracy (BA). After obtaining the predicted class $\hat{y}$, update the Balanced Accuracy counters

$$\text{BA} = \frac{1}{2}\left(\frac{\text{TP}}{\text{TP} + \text{FN}} + \frac{\text{TN}}{\text{TN} + \text{FP}}\right). \tag{7}$$

Averaging BA over all N Leave-One-Out folds returns one final score for each binarization scheme s.

4 Results

Balanced Accuracy (BA) for the five binarization schemes was computed on fourteen public, binary-class datasets under a Leave-One-Out protocol. Table 2 summarizes the per-dataset outcomes and the cross-dataset mean. On average, **Parity+RNS** and **Gray** rank highest (mean BA = 0.6826 and 0.6788), followed by straight binary ($\log_2$) and BCD, whereas **IEEE-754 mantissa** attains the lowest mean (0.6457).

At the dataset level, Parity+RNS or Gray is the sole top performer in **8 of 14** datasets (excluding ties). Ties occur in a few cases (e.g., *Titanic*, *Iris (1)*). For context, the non-binarized baselines at the right of Table 2—Random Forest and Naïve Bayes—reach mean BA of 0.8014 and 0.7440, respectively.

Table 2. Balanced Accuracy (BA) obtained with each binarization scheme on the 14 benchmark datasets.

Dataset	$\log_2$	Gray	BCD	IEEE754	Parity+RNS	RF	NB
Iris (1)	0.8200	**0.8600**	**0.8600**	0.6500	0.7800	0.91	0.93
Iris (2)	**0.9266**	0.8666	0.8733	0.6660	0.8800	0.94	0.95
Appendicitis	0.7641	0.7641	0.7924	**0.7925**	0.7830	0.75	0.78
Banana	0.6321	0.6326	**0.6958**	0.6054	0.6232	0.89	0.58
Contraceptive	0.4297	**0.4514**	0.4223	0.4379	0.4257	0.52	0.49
Electricity	0.7708	0.8070	0.7459	**0.8329**	0.8175	0.97	0.75
Haberman	0.6275	**0.6699**	0.6666	0.6111	0.6405	0.55	0.58
Heart	0.6370	0.6444	0.5518	0.6444	**0.6518**	0.81	0.83
Nutt	0.5000	0.5000	0.4761	0.4761	**0.6082**	0.78	0.75
Pima	0.6107	0.6209	0.5951	**0.6406**	0.6192	0.73	0.72
Titanic	0.6902	**0.6905**	**0.6905**	**0.6905**	0.6901	0.68	0.70
Australian	0.6608	0.6666	0.6463	0.6811	**0.6971**	0.86	0.75
Bupa	0.5884	**0.5942**	0.5478	0.5710	0.5621	0.71	0.59
Ionosphere	0.8290	0.8148	0.7635	0.7492	**0.8575**	0.92	0.83
Monk	0.5555	0.6666	0.5550	0.6342	**0.7222**	1.00	0.93
Mean	0.6695	0.6788	0.6580	0.6457	**0.6826**	**0.8014**	0.7440

5 Discussions

Two patterns emerge from Table 2. First, **Parity+RNS** and **Gray** consistently yield the most separable bit patterns, explaining their lead in eight datasets and their highest means. Second, **IEEE-754 mantissa** underperforms on several corpora, suggesting that its logarithmic scaling can blur small numerical differences after binarization.

A representational rationale is plausible. Gray code changes only one bit between successive integers, preserving local neighborhoods in Hamming space. Parity+RNS distributes information across independent residue blocks and appends a parity bit, which tends to increase inter-class separability. Finally, results vary across datasets—an empirical echo of the No-Free-Lunch principle—so no encoding dominates universally; the best choice depends on data distribution and task difficulty.

6 Conclusions

The goal of this paper was to study how the choice of binary encoding influences the performance of a Lernmatrix associative memory. The results reveal a clear trade-off between speed and precision. A Random Forest model that iterates over the data achieves approximately 0.80 balanced accuracy, while the fastest single-pass option—the Lernmatrix—tops out about a dozen points lower. This gap reflects the cost of one-shot learning and the model's ability to fit comfortably within a kilobyte range.

Within these constraints, the method of representation significantly impacts performance. The combined *Parity + RNS* code, along with *Gray code*, produces the most interpretable bit patterns for the matrix, winning eight out of fourteen datasets and averaging 0.68 balanced accuracy. In contrast, standard straight binary or BCD methods perform well on only a few datasets, and IEEE-754 performs poorest when the data cover only a narrow numeric range and the task is already straightforward, most clearly in the two-class Iris subset. In other words, our results echo the No-Free-Lunch principle [33]: even the most sophisticated encoding shines on some datasets and stumbles on others; There's no one-size-fits-all algorithm.

For practitioners, the key takeaway is clear: choose Parity + RNS for the highest balanced accuracy, with Gray Code as a strong alternative. When iterative training is permissible and achieving absolute accuracy is the priority, conventional ensembles like Random Forest remain the most effective choice.

Future work will explore two main directions. First, the idea is to develop a data-driven selection of RNS moduli. This automatic procedure analyzes the numerical range and distribution of a dataset to select a set of pairwise coprime moduli that provide the most informative residue representation. Second, the plan is to investigate techniques that allow the learning matrix to enhance classification, aiming to achieve balanced accuracy values that can compete with state-of-the-art classifiers while preventing weight saturation.

Acknowledgments. The authors gratefully acknowledge the support of the *Secretaría de Ciencia, Humanidades, Tecnología e Innovación* (SECTIHI) and the *Laboratorio de Computo Inteligente del Centro de Investigación en Computación, Instituto Politécnico Nacional (CIC-IPN)*, whose resources and guidance were essential for completing This study.

Disclosure of Interests. The authors declare that they have no competing interests.

References

1. Liver disorders, published: UCI Machine Learning Repository
2. Statlog (heart), published: UCI Machine Learning Repository
3. Acevedo-Mosqueda, M.E., Yáñez-Márquez, C., López-Yáñez, I.: Alpha–beta bidirectional associative memories: theory and applications
4. Al-Khaleel, O., Al-Qudah, Z., Al-Khaleel, M., Papachristou, C.: High performance FPGA-based decimal-to-binary conversion schemes for decimal arithmetic. Microprocess. Microsyst. **37**(3), 287–298 (2013). https://doi.org/10.1016/j.micpro.2013.01.002, https://www.sciencedirect.com/science/article/pii/S0141933113000136
5. Alcalá-Fdez, J., Fernández, A., Luengo, J., Derrac, J., García, S.: KEEL data-mining software tool: data set repository, integration of algorithms and experimental analysis framework. **17**(2), 255–287. http://dblp.uni-trier.de/db/journals/mvl/mvl17.html#Alcala-FdezFLDG11
6. Blanco-Mallo, E., Morán-Fernández, L., Remeseiro, B., Bolón-Canedo, V.: Do all roads lead to rome? studying distance measures in the context of machine learning. Patt. Recogn. **141**, 109646 (2023). https://doi.org/10.1016/j.patcog.2023.109646, https://www.sciencedirect.com/science/article/pii/S0031320323003473
7. Chang, V., Bailey, J., Xu, Q.A., Sun, Z.: Pima indians diabetes mellitus classification based on machine learning (ML) algorithms **35**(22), 16157–16173. https://doi.org/10.1007/s00521-022-07049-z, https://link.springer.com/10.1007/s00521-022-07049-z
8. Cukierski, W.: Titanic - machine learning from disaster. https://kaggle.com/competitions/titanic
9. Fisher, R.A.: Iris, published: UCI Machine Learning Repository
10. George, A.M., Sharma, R., Rao, S.: IEEE 754 floating-point addition for neuromorphic architecture. Neurocomputing **366**, 74–85 (2019), https://doi.org/10.1016/j.neucom.2019.05.093, https://www.sciencedirect.com/science/article/pii/S0925231219308884
11. Haberman, S.: Haberman's survival, published: UCI Machine Learning Repository
12. Hebrail, G., Berard, A.: Individual household electric power consumption, published: UCI Machine Learning Repository
13. Hori, S., Mikawa, K.: Gray code generation of binary trees encoded in left-child sequences. Theoret. Comput. Sci. **1048**, 115366 (2025). https://doi.org/10.1016/j.tcs.2025.115366, https://www.sciencedirect.com/science/article/pii/S0304397525003044
14. Kage, H.: Implementing associative memories by echo state network for the applications of natural language processing. Mach. Learn. Appl. **11**, 100449 (2023). https://doi.org/10.1016/j.mlwa.2023.100449, https://www.sciencedirect.com/science/article/pii/S2666827023000026
15. Li, Z., Zhu, Z., Gui, X., Luo, Y.: this is human intelligence debugging artificial intelligence: examining how people prompt gpt in seeking mental health support. Int. J. Hum. Comput Stud. **203**, 103555 (2025). https://doi.org/10.1016/j.ijhcs.2025.103555, https://www.sciencedirect.com/science/article/pii/S1071581925001120
16. Lim, T.S.: Contraceptive method choice, published: UCI Machine Learning Repository
17. Lyakhov, P., et al.: A novel sign detection method in residue number system based on Chinese remainder theorem with fractional values. Microprocess. Microsyst. **102**, 104940 (2023). https://doi.org/10.1016/j.micpro.2023.104940, https://www.sciencedirect.com/science/article/pii/S0141933123001849

18. Md. Ataur Rahman: Banana dataset, https://doi.org/10.21227/dn9b-9y70
19. Nutt, C.L., et al.: Gene expression-based classification of malignant gliomas correlates better with survival than histological classification **63**(7), 1602–1607, publisher: American Association for Cancer Research Inc
20. Puangpontip, S., Hewett, R.: On using deep learning for business analytics: At what cost? Procedia Comput. Sci. **207**, 3738–3747 (2022). https://doi.org/10.1016/j.procs.2022.09.434, https://www.sciencedirect.com/science/article/pii/S1877050922013278, knowledge-Based and Intelligent Information Engineering Systems: Proceedings of the 26th International Conference KES2022
21. Quinlan, R.: Statlog (australian credit approval), published: UCI Machine Learning Repository
22. Ranjan, R., Swain, D., Paikaray, B.: Efficient key management and cipher text generation using BCD coded parity bits. Procedia Comput. Sci. **57**, 703–709 (2015). https://doi.org/10.1016/j.procs.2015.07.455, https://www.sciencedirect.com/science/article/pii/S1877050915019845, 3rd International Conference on Recent Trends in Computing 2015 (ICRTC-2015)
23. Sigillito, V., W.S.H.L., Baker, K.: Ionosphere, published: UCI Machine Learning Repository
24. Simas, R., Sa-Couto, L., Wichert, A.: Classification and generation of real-world data with an associative memory model. Neurocomputing **551**, 126514 (2023). https://doi.org/10.1016/j.neucom.2023.126514, https://www.sciencedirect.com/science/article/pii/S0925231223006379
25. Steinbuch, K.: Die lernmatrix - the beginning of associative memories. In: Eckmiller, R. (ed.) Advanced Neural Computers, pp. 21–29. North-Holland, Amsterdam (1990). https://doi.org/10.1016/B978-0-444-88400-8.50007-8, https://www.sciencedirect.com/science/article/pii/B9780444884008500078
26. Velázquez-Rodríguez, J.L., Villuendas-Rey, Y., Camacho-Nieto, O.,Yáñez-Márquez, C.: A novel and simple mathematical transform improves the perfomance of lernmatrix in pattern classification **8**(5), 732. https://doi.org/10.3390/math8050732, https://www.mdpi.com/2227-7390/8/5/732
27. Villuendas-Rey, Y., Rey-Benguría, C.F., Ferreira-Santiago, , Camacho-Nieto, O., Yanez-Marquez, C.: The naïve associative classifier (NAC): a novel, simple, transparent, and accurate classification model evaluated on financial data **265**, 105–115. https://doi.org/10.1016/j.neucom.2017.03.085, https://linkinghub.elsevier.com/retrieve/pii/S0925231217310123
28. Weiss, S.M., Kulikowski, C.A.: Computer systems that learn: classification and prediction methods from statistics, neural nets, machine learning, and expert systems. Morgan Kaufmann Publishers Inc
29. Wnek, J.: MONK's problems, published: UCI Machine Learning Repository
30. Ya, C.: Toward the bleaching of the black boxes: Minimalist machine learning
31. Yazdanian-Amiri, Z., Valinataj, M.: High-speed binary coded decimal digit multipliers with multiple error detection. Integration **93**, 102073 (2023). https://doi.org/10.1016/j.vlsi.2023.102073, https://www.sciencedirect.com/science/article/pii/S0167926023001153
32. Yáñez-Márquez, C., López-Yáñez, I., Aldape-Pérez, M., Camacho-Nieto, O., Argüelles-Cruz, A.J., Villuendas-Rey, Y.: Theoretical foundations for the alpha-beta associative memories: 10 years of derived extensions, models, and applications **48**(2), 811–847. https://doi.org/10.1007/s11063-017-9768-2, http://link.springer.com/10.1007/s11063-017-9768-2
33. Zhang, X., et al.: No free lunch theorem for privacy-preserving LLM inference. Artif. Intell. **341**, 104293 (2025). https://doi.org/10.1016/j.artint.2025.104293, https://www.sciencedirect.com/science/article/pii/S0004370225000128

An Integer Quadratically Constrained Program for the Firefighter Problem: an Empirical Evaluation

Lourdes Beatriz Cajica-Maceda[1], Zaida Adriana Gárate-Cahuantzi[1], and Jesús García-Díaz[1,2](✉)

[1] Coordinación de Ciencias Computacionales, Instituto Nacional de Astrofísica, Óptica y Electrónica, Luis Enrique Erro, 72840 Puebla, Mexico
{bcajica,zaicahuantzi}@inaoep.mx

[2] Secretaría de Ciencia, Humanidades, Tecnología e Innovación, Av. Insurgentes Sur, 03940 Mexico City, Mexico
jesus.garcia@secihti.mx

Abstract. The Firefighter Problem (FP) is a graph-theoretical problem that represents the containment of diffusive processes such as fires or epidemics. This paper proposes a novel integer quadratically constrained program (IQCP) for the FP that substantially reduces the number of decision variables relative to Hartnell's classical integer linear program (ILP). While Hartnell's ILP has $2nT$ binary variables, the proposed IQCP has $nT + n$ binary variables, where n is the order of the graph and T is an upper bound on the number of steps until the fire spreads no more. To assess the practical effectiveness of the proposed IQCP, we conduct a series of experiments using Erdős–Rényi instances spanning a range of densities, and state-of-the-art optimization solvers with default settings and a common stopping criterion (proving optimality). We also examine sensitivity to instance properties, finding conditions under which models with quadratic constraints yield shorter execution times. From these experiments, we observe that the IQCP can serve as an efficient alternative under specific conditions; specifically, when the number of fire sources and firefighters is small.

Keywords: Firefighter problem · Integer quadratically constrained program · Integer linear program · NP-hard · Combinatorial optimization

1 Introduction

The Firefighter Problem (FP) is a classical graph-theoretical problem introduced by Bert Hartnell in 1995 [9,14]. It models the containment of a diffusive process (such as a fire, flood, or epidemic) that spreads over the vertices of a graph G in discrete time steps. The objective is to defend a subset of vertices such that the total number of *burned* vertices is minimized once the process terminates. The input consists of a graph G, a subset $F \subseteq V(G)$ of initially burning vertices, and

C. Palma-Preciado et al. (Eds.): CORE 2025, ACSAR 3, pp. 215–225, 2026.
https://doi.org/10.1007/978-3-032-08894-9_14

a positive integer k representing the number of available *firefighters* per time step [9,20].

Initially, all vertices in $V(G) - F$ are unburned. At each step, up to k new vertices can be defended. After the defense, the fire spreads from each burning vertex to its undefended neighbors. The process continues until no further spread is possible. By the end, each vertex is either burned, defended, or protected (unburned and never defended) [9,14,20].

Figure 1 illustrates optimal solutions for two instances: (a) $F = \{v_7\}$ and (b) $F = \{v_5\}$, both with $k = 1$. In (a), vertices v_1, v_4, and v_7 are burned; vertices v_2, v_5, and v_8 are defended; and v_3, v_6, and v_9 are protected.

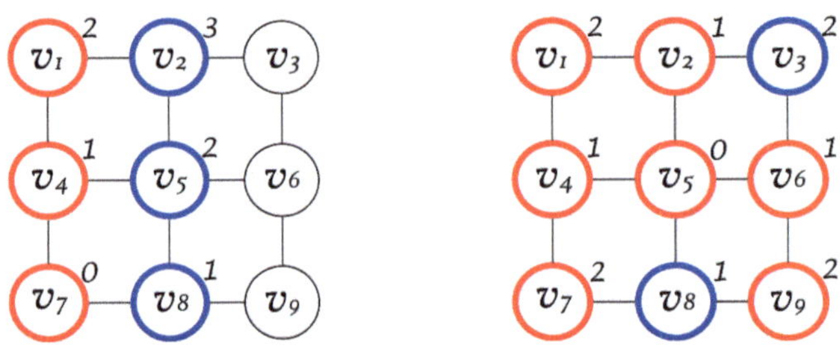

Fig. 1. Optimal solution of two instances for the FP. In both, $k = 1$. Beside each vertex is the step at which it gets burned (red) or defended (blue). The first graph has $F = \{v_7\}$ and $OPT = 3$, and the second graph has $F = \{v_5\}$ and $OPT = 7$.

As a basic model of contention, the FP has gained growing relevance over the years. Many of its theoretical properties have been studied, and many generalizations have been proposed [13,18,23]. Section 2 lists the related work for the FP, including the integer linear program (ILP) introduced by Hartnell. To our knowledge, Hartnell's program is the only one available in the literature for arbitrary graphs. This paper presents an alternative IP for the FP with fewer decision variables than Hartnell's, but at the expense of having some quadratic constraints. Nevertheless, as shown in Sect. 3, it can be almost as convenient as Hartnell's under specific circumstances. Namely, when the input instance is a random graph [4], Branch-and-Bound-based optimization solvers are used [1,12], and the number of fire sources and firefighters is small.

2 Literature Review

The FP is recognized as NP-hard when considering bipartite graphs [20], cubic graphs [16], trees with a maximum degree of three [20] and a pathwidth of three [6], co-bipartite graphs [6], and unit disk graphs [11]. However, it is solvable in polynomial time for caterpillars and P-trees [20], interval graphs, split graphs, permutation graphs, P_k-free graphs for any fixed k [11], and also for graphs with a maximum degree of three [10], where the fire starts at a vertex with a degree of at most two.

The principal extensions of the FP include variations where the number of firefighters available at any given step varies [21], versions focusing on shielding specific vertex subsets [5,16], and those where protection spreads from each defended vertex to its adjacent non-burning vertices [2,3]. Additional FP variants incorporate more realistic vertex defense constraints. For example, the geometric firefighter problem [17,18,23] assesses the speed of building barriers to contain a fire; here, the fire ignites at a point within a polygon and uniformly spreads outward at a constant speed. In this scenario, a firefighter erects a sequence of one-dimensional barriers at a steady pace, potentially different from the fire's spread speed. The moving firefighter [13] variant accounts for the travel time needed for a firefighter to reach new vertices and the time required to defend a vertex upon arrival.

Program 1 shows Hartnell's ILP for the FP. The input is a graph $G = (V, E)$, a set $F \subseteq V$, and two positive integers T and k. For simplicity, let us assume that $V = \{v_1, v_2, ..., v_n\}$. The number of steps until the fire spreads no more is T; naturally, such a value is upper bounded by $n = |V|$, but also by the distance between the fire sources and their most distant vertex. In the beginning, all vertices are undefended (See line 2 of Program 1), and only vertices in F are burned (See line 3). Notice that $b_{i,t} = 1$ ($d_{i,t} = 1$) indicates that the vertex v_i is burned (defended) at step t; otherwise, $b_{i,t} = 0$ ($d_{i,t} = 0$).

Constraints from lines 12 and 13 ensure that once a vertex is burned or defended, it remains in that state, respectively. The restriction from line 21 requires a vertex with a burned neighbor to get burned or defended, but not both, as specified by the bound in line 14. The requirement in line 26 guarantees that no more than k new vertices are defended at each step. Finally, line 15 prevents a vertex from burning if it does not have burned neighbors in its closed neighborhood. This ILP has $2nT$ binary variables and $4nT+2mT+T$ constraints, where $n = |V|$ and $m = |E|$. Notice that the $2mT$ constraints come from lines 18 to 24, where $\sum_{v_i \in V} d(v_i) = 2m$ by the so-called handshaking lemma [7].

Notice that the restriction from line 15 can be removed because the Objective function (See line 9) is enough to prevent a vertex from being burned if it does not have burned neighbors. Besides, notice that Constraints (1) (See line 26) and Constraints (2) are equivalent in the sense that the size of an optimal solution is the same regardless of the inequality being used (See Proposition 1 and Fig. 2).

$$\forall t \in [1, T] \quad , \sum_{v_i \in V} (d_{i,t} - d_{i,t-1}) \leq k \tag{1}$$

$$\forall t \in [1, T] \quad , \sum_{v_i \in V} d_{i,t} \leq tk \tag{2}$$

Proposition 1. *The size of an optimal solution of Hartnell's ILP is the same if Constraints (2) are used instead of Constraints (1).*

Program 1. Hartnell's ILP

Require: A graph G, a set $F \subseteq V(G)$, and two positive integers T and k
Ensure: An optimal defense sequence $[d_{i,t}]_{|V(G)|\times T}$

`/* Initialization */`
1: **for** $v_i \in V(G)$ **do**
2: $\quad d_{i,0} = 0$ ▷ Initially, all vertices are not defended
3: $\quad b_{i,0} = \begin{cases} 1 & \text{if } v_i \in F \\ 0 & \text{otherwise} \end{cases}$ ▷ Initially, only vertices in F are burned
4: $\quad$ **for** $t = 1$ **to** T **do**
5: $\qquad b_{i,t} \in \{0,1\}$ ▷ All variables are binary
6: $\qquad d_{i,t} \in \{0,1\}$
7: $\quad$ **end for**
8: **end for**

`/* Objective function */`
9: **minimize** $\sum_{v_i \in V(G)} b_{i,T}$

`/* Constraints */`
10: **for** $v_i \in V(G)$ **do**
11: $\quad$ **for** $t = 1$ **to** T **do**
12: $\qquad b_{i,t} \geq b_{i,t-1}$ ▷ Burned vertices remain burned
13: $\qquad d_{i,t} \geq d_{i,t-1}$ ▷ Defended vertices remain defended
14: $\qquad b_{i,t} + d_{i,t} \leq 1$ ▷ Vertices can't be burned and defended simultaneously
15: $\qquad \sum_{v_j \in N[v_i]} b_{j,t-1} \geq b_{i,t}$ ▷ Vertices require a burned neighbor to be burned
16: $\quad$ **end for**
17: **end for**
18: **for** $v_i \in V(G)$ **do**
19: $\quad$ **for** $v_j \in N(v_i)$ **do**
20: $\qquad$ **for** $t = 1$ **to** T **do**
21: $\qquad\quad b_{i,t} + d_{i,t} \geq b_{j,t-1}$ ▷ Vertices with burned neighbors must be burned or defended
22: $\qquad$ **end for**
23: $\quad$ **end for**
24: **end for**
25: **for** $t = 1$ **to** T **do**
26: $\quad \sum_{v_i \in V(G)} (d_{i,t} - d_{i,t-1}) \leq k$ ▷ At most k new vertices are burned at each time step
27: **end for**

`/* Solution */`
28: **return** $[d_{i,t}]_{|V(G)|\times T}$ ▷ An optimal defense sequence is codified into variables $d_{i,t}$

Proof. While Constraints (1) guarantee that at most k new vertices are defended at each step of the diffusion process, Constraints (2) ensure that the accumulated number of defended vertices at step t is at most tk. Both cases work thanks to the restriction on line 13 in Program 1, which keeps track of all previously defended vertices. Since Constraints (2) count the number of accumulated defended vertices, it is possible that at some step i only $k'_i < k$ vertices are defended, and at some future step $j > i$ some extra $k - k'_i$ vertices are defended. In such a scenario, the contention capacity of the vertices defended at step j cannot exceed the capacity they would have had if defended earlier, at iteration i. Thus, the size of the optimal solution of Hartnell's ILP is the same regardless of using Constraints (1) or Constraints (2).

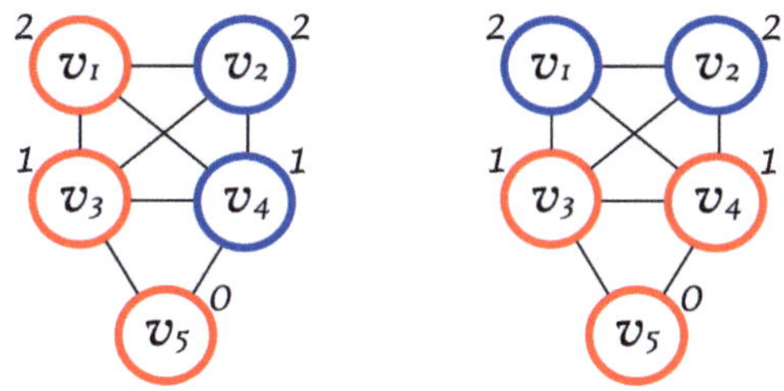

Fig. 2. Hartnell's ILP optimal solutions using Constraints (1) and (2), respectively. In both cases, $k = 1$ and the fire starts from vertex v_5. Notice that both solutions have a size of three. The first graph has one defended vertex per round, and the second graph has two defended vertices at the last round.

3 An Integer Quadratically Constrained Program

Program 2 defines the proposed IQCP. Its variables are defined and initialized at lines 1–9. Since this program codifies both burned and defended vertices in the same set of variables $x_{i,t}$, n extra decision variables, $x_{1,T+1}$ to $x_{n,T+1}$, are added to discern between burned and defended vertices. In more detail, if a vertex v_i is burned or defended at step t, $x_{i,t} = 1$; otherwise, $x_{i,t} = 0$. If vertex v_i is burned, $x_{i,T+1} = 0$; if it is defended, $x_{i,T+1} = 1$. The constraints on line 14 guarantee that vertices with burned (closed) neighbors get burned or defended, which also guarantees that burned vertices remain burned up to the final step. The restriction from line 22 ensures that all protected vertices are not marked as defended. Besides, this same restriction guarantees that all defended vertices remain defended. The bound in line 19 guarantees that the accumulated number of firefighters at each step is not greater than tk. Since line 22 guarantees that all defended vertices remain defended, keeping track of accumulated defended vertices does not alter the size of the optimal solution (See Proposition 1). The Objective function (See line 10) seeks to minimize the number of pairs $(x_{i,T}, x_{i,T+1}) = (1, 0)$, which correspond to burned vertices.

Program 2. Proposed IQCP

Require: A graph G, a set $F \subseteq V(G)$, and two positive integers T and k
Ensure: An optimal defense sequence $[x_{i,t}]_{|V(G)| \times T}$

`/* Initialization */`
for $v_i \in F$ **do**
  $x_{i,T+1} = 0$ ▷ Initially, all vertices are not defended
end for
for $v_i \in V(G)$ **do**
  $x_{i,0} = \begin{cases} 1 & \text{if } v_i \in F \\ 0 & \text{otherwise} \end{cases}$ ▷ Initially, only vertices in F are burned
  for $t = 1$ **to** $T + 1$ **do**
    $x_{i,t} \in \{0, 1\}$ ▷ All variables are binary
  end for
end for

`/* Objective function */`
minimize $\sum_{v_i \in V(G)} (x_{i,T} - x_{i,T+1})$

`/* Constraints */`
for $v_i \in V(G)$ **do**
  for $v_j \in N[v_i]$ **do**
    for $t = 1$ **to** T **do**
      $x_{i,t} \geq x_{j,t-1} - x_{j,T+1}$ ▷ Vertices with burned neighbors get burned or defended
    end for
  end for
end for
for $t = 1$ **to** T **do**
  $\sum_{v_i \in V(G)} x_{i,t} x_{i,T+1} \leq tk$ ▷ No more than tk vertices can be defended at each round
end for
for $v_i \in V(G)$ **do**
  $x_{i,T} \geq x_{i,T+1}$ ▷ Defended vertices remain defended
end for

`/* Solution */`
return $[x_{i,t}]_{|V(G)| \times T+1}$ ▷ An optimal defense sequence is codified into variables $x_{i,t}$

The proposed IQCP has $nT + n$ binary variables and $2mT + T + n$ constraints. Although it has fewer variables and constraints than Hartnell's ILP, it has quadratic constraints, which might be a disadvantage when using Branch-and-Bound-based solvers. Although non-exact algorithmic techniques, such as metaheuristics, might be better suited for programs with quadratic constraints [8, 15, 19, 22], we only tested the proposed IQCP using exact solvers.

4 Experimental Results

To test the practicality of Hartnell's ILP and the proposed IQCP, we ran a series of experiments using Erdős-Rényi graphs and two of the most advanced optimization solvers: Gurobi and SCIP [1,12]. Table 1 presents the hardware and software setup for all experiments. The implemented code is publicly available at https://github.com/NodesOnFire/firefighter_programs.

Table 1. Hardware and software setup

Hardware	
CPU	Intel Core i5-10300H
CPU frequency	2.5 GHz
RAM	32 GB
OS	Windows 11
Software	
Gurobi	12.0.0
SCIP	9.2.2
Interface	Python pyomo

Figures 3, 4, 5 and 6 show the average execution time and standard deviation reported by Gurobi and SCIP over the giant component of 30 Erdős-Rényi graphs with $n = 100$ and different values of p. In more detail, 30 $G(n, p)$ random graphs of order n were generated for each parameter p from the critical point $1/n$ to $3/n$ [4]. From them, the giant component was extracted. Then, Gurobi and SCIP were executed over each giant component using their default parameters; the average time required to find the optimal solution is reported along with its standard deviation. In Figs. 3 and 4, one fire source is randomly selected and $k = 1$. In Figs. 5 and 6, two fire sources are randomly selected and $k = 1$.

For both SCIP and Gurobi, the stop condition is to find an optimal solution. The general approach of both solvers is to reduce the original problem into many smaller subproblems that are easier to solve; this is the Branch-and-Bound approach. If the original problem is an ILP, the subproblems are usually linear programs (LP) that can be tackled through the simplex algorithm or interior point methods. If the input program has quadratic constraints, the solver explores an outer approximation of the feasible region using relaxations; as the exploration advances, the outer approximation gets refined. Therefore, this approach tends to converge more slowly to the optimal solution. The experimental results below indicate that, in certain instances, a formulation with fewer variables may yield advantages, even in the presence of quadratic constraints and when using Branch-and-Bound-based solvers.

Figures 3 and 4 show how Hartnell's ILP (Program 1) and the proposed IQCP (Program 2) compare to each other when using Gurobi as a comparison point.

From Fig. 3 we can see that, on average, Gurobi was faster for solving the FP using the IQCP in 13 out of 21 values of p. This indicates that, under certain circumstances, a quadratic program may be as useful or even better than a linear program when the number of variables of the former is considerably smaller. From Fig. 4 we can see that, on average, SCIP was faster for solving the FP using the ILP in 14 out of 21 values of p. Nevertheless, the performance of SCIP using the IQCP is, in most cases, very similar to that of using the ILP. Figures 3 and 4 also show that, in general, Gurobi is more efficient than SCIP for solving the FP.

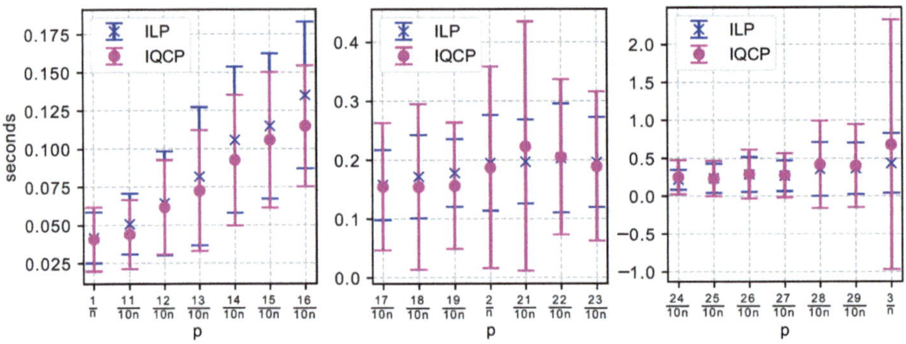

Fig. 3. Average running time and standard deviation reported by Gurobi over the giant component of 30 Erdős-Rényi graphs with $n = 100$ for each $p \in [1/n, 3/n]$. The number of fire sources and firefighters is one.

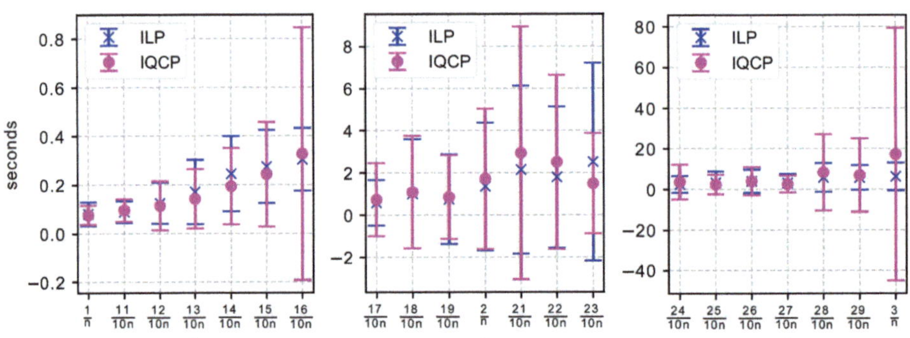

Fig. 4. Average running time and standard deviation reported by SCIP over the giant component of 30 Erdős-Rényi graphs with $n = 100$ for each $p \in [1/n, 3/n]$. The number of fire sources and firefighters is one.

Figures 5 and 6 compare Hartnell's ILP and the proposed IQCP using Gurobi and SCIP, respectively, but with two fire sources instead of one. This seems to make the problem a little harder to solve. Namely, both solvers required more time to get the optimal solution, and both solvers performed better using the ILP than the IQCP. However, as before, the difference in performance between the two programs is not so disproportionate.

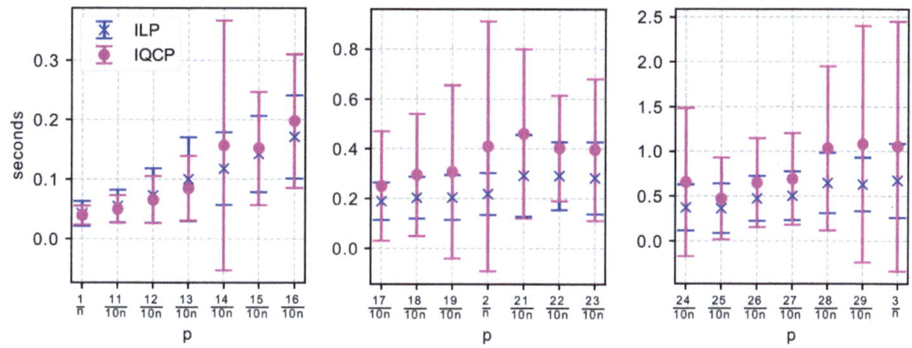

Fig. 5. Average running time and standard deviation reported by Gurobi over the giant component of 30 Erdős-Rényi graphs with $n = 100$ for each $p \in [1/n, 3/n]$. The number of fire sources is two, and the number of firefighters is one.

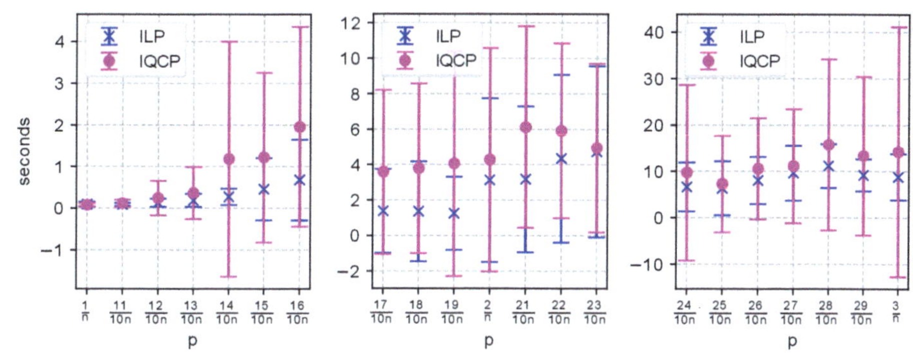

Fig. 6. Average running time and standard deviation reported by SCIP over the giant component of 30 Erdős-Rényi graphs with $n = 100$ for each $p \in [1/n, 3/n]$. The number of fire sources is two, and the number of firefighters is one.

5 Discussion

As the Firefighter Problem (FP) is NP-hard, all of its mathematical formulations—including Hartnell's ILP and the proposed IQCP—are inherently NP-hard as well. In theory, both models are equally complex. However, in practice, the ILP tends to be more tractable, particularly when employing exact methods such as Branch-and-Bound. Solvers like Gurobi and SCIP exploit this strategy by decomposing the original problem into smaller subproblems, which are typically solved using linear programming techniques such as the simplex or interior-point methods.

By contrast, the IQCP's quadratic constraints require the solver to approximate the feasible region using successive relaxations. Although this approach refines the search space progressively, it often results in a slower convergence to the optimal solution. Despite this, empirical evidence suggests that the IQCP can outperform the ILP under certain conditions—specifically, when the number of fire sources and firefighters is small. These results highlight the potential of IQCP as a competitive alternative in specialized scenarios. Future work will explore its performance using heuristic and metaheuristic methods, which might better exploit the structure of its feasible region.

6 Conclusion

Since its introduction in 1995, the FP has garnered increasing interest due to its practical relevance and rich theoretical foundations. Hartnell's ILP remains the standard formulation for arbitrary graphs. In this study, we proposed an alternative model—an integer quadratically constrained program (IQCP)—that reduces the number of variables at the expense of introducing quadratic constraints. Although this might seem disadvantageous at first glance, our empirical results demonstrate that the IQCP performs competitively under certain conditions, particularly when using Branch-and-Bound solvers like Gurobi and SCIP on Erdős-Rényi graphs.

We have made our implementation and experimental setup publicly available to facilitate reproducibility and comparison with other methods. Future work includes a more rigorous statistical evaluation and an exploration of heuristic and metaheuristic techniques, as well as experiments on more complex and challenging instances.

Acknowledgments. We acknowledge Secretaría de Ciencia, Humanidades, Tecnología e Innovación (SECIHTI) and Instituto Nacional de Astrofísica, Óptica y Electrónica (INAOE) for providing the necessary resources for the development of this research.

Disclosure of Interests. The authors have no competing interests to declare that are relevant to the content of this article.

References

1. Achterberg, T.: Scip: solving constraint integer programs. Math. Program. Comput. **1**(1), 1–41 (2009)
2. Anshelevich, E., Chakrabarty, D., Hate, A., Swamy, C.: Approximation algorithms for the firefighter problem: cuts over time and submodularity. In: Dong, Y., Du, D.-Z., Ibarra, O. (eds.) ISAAC 2009. LNCS, vol. 5878, pp. 974–983. Springer, Heidelberg (2009). https://doi.org/10.1007/978-3-642-10631-6_98

3. Anshelevich, E., Chakrabarty, D., Hate, A., Swamy, C.: Approximability of the firefighter problem. Algorithmica **62**, 520–536 (2012)
4. Barabási, A.L.: Network Science. Cambridge University Press, Cambridge (2016)
5. Bazgan, C., Chopin, M., Ries, B.: The firefighter problem with more than one firefighter on trees. Discret. Appl. Math. **161**, 899–908 (2013)
6. Chlebíková, J., Chopin, M.: The firefighter problem: further steps in understanding its complexity. Theoret. Comput. Sci. **676**, 42–51 (2017)
7. Diestel, R.: Graph Theory, vol. 173. Springer, Cham (2025)
8. Díaz-Ayón, J.A., Carrillo-Ruiz, M.: Optimización de despacho económico con algoritmo de luciérnagas. In: Santiago-Díaz, M.C. (ed.) Aplicaciones de las ciencias computacionales en sistemas inteligentes y ciberseguridad, pp. 23–34 (2022)
9. Finbow, S., Hartnell, B., Li, Q., Schmeisser, K.: On minimizing the effects of fire or a virus on a network. J. Comb. Math. Comb. Comput. **33**, 311–322 (2000)
10. Finbow, S., King, A., MacGillivray, G., Rizzi, R.: The firefighter problem for graphs of maximum degree three. Discret. Math. **307**, 2094–2105 (2007)
11. Fomin, F.V., Heggernes, P., van Leeuwen, E.J.: The firefighter problem on graph classes. Theoret. Comput. Sci. **613**, 38–50 (2016)
12. Gurobi Optimization, LLC: Gurobi optimizer reference manual (2025). https://www.gurobi.com. Accessed 02 June 2025
13. Gutiérrez-De-La-Paz, B.R., García-Díaz, J., Menchaca-Méndez, R., Montenegro-Meza, M.A., Menchaca-Méndez, R., Gutiérrez-De-La-Paz, O.A.: The moving firefighter problem. Mathematics **11**(1), 179 (2023). https://doi.org/10.3390/math11010179
14. Hartnell, B.: Firefighter! an application of domination. In: Proceedings of the 24th Manitoba Conference on Combinatorial Mathematics and Computing. University of Manitoba, Winnipeg, ON, Canada
15. Houssein, E.H., Saeed, M.K., Hu, G., Al-Sayed, M.M.: Metaheuristics for solving global and engineering optimization problems: review, applications, open issues and challenges. Arch. Comput. Methods Eng. **31**(8), 4485–4519 (2024)
16. King, A., MacGillivray, G.: The firefighter problem for cubic graphs. Discret. Math. **310**, 614–621 (2010)
17. Klein, R., Levcopoulos, C., Lingas, A.: Approximation algorithms for the geometric firefighter and budget fence problems. In: Pardo, A., Viola, A. (eds.) LATIN 2014. LNCS, vol. 8392, pp. 261–272. Springer, Heidelberg (2014). https://doi.org/10.1007/978-3-642-54423-1_23
18. Klein, R., Levcopoulos, C., Lingas, A.: Approximation algorithms for the geometric firefighter and budget fence problems. Algorithms **11**(45) (2018)
19. Kumar, M., Aryabartta, S., Mitra, P.: A comparison of different metaheuristics for the quadratic assignment problem in accelerated systems. Appl. Soft Comput. **100**, 106927 (2021)
20. MacGillivray, G., Wang, P.: On the firefighter problem. JCMCC J. Comb. Math. Comb. Comput. **47**, 57–78 (2003)
21. Ng, K.L., Raff, P.: A generalization of the firefighter problem on $\mathbb{Z} \times \mathbb{Z}$. Discret. Appl. Math. **156**, 730–745 (2008)
22. Tasgetiren, M.F., Pan, Q.K., Suganthan, P.N., Dizbay, I.E.: Metaheuristic algorithms for the quadratic assignment problem. In: 2013 IEEE Symposium on Computational Intelligence in Production and Logistics Systems (CIPLS), pp. 131–137 (2013)
23. Zambon, M.J., de Rezende, P.J., de Souza, C.C.: Solving the geometric firefighter routing problem via integer programming. Eur. J. Oper. Res. **274**, 1090–1101 (2019)

BREX: *Blend of Ranked-Sequential Algorithms Executed* for Boosting-Based Classification Applied to Wine Dataset

Acevedo-Sánchez Gerardo[1], Alarcón-Paredes Antonio[1], Yáñez-Márquez Cornelio[1](✉), and Camacho-Nieto Óscar[2]

[1] Centro de Investigación en Computación, Ciudad de México, México
{gacevedos2024,aalarcon,cyanez}@cic.ipn.mx
[2] Centro de Innovación y Desarrollo Tecnológico en Cómputo, Instituto Politécnico Nacional, Ciudad de México, México
oscarc@cic.ipn.mx

Abstract. Class imbalance and large number of classes severely degrade the classifiers' performance while increasing computational costs. Some approaches are either computationally expensive or oversimplify the problem into a binary problem. To tackle these issues, the objective was to develop a *Blend of Ranked-sequential Algorithms Executed* for boosting-based classification (BREX), a hybrid hierarchical model combining Machine Learning techniques with a deterministic validation Leave-One-Out. BREX was applied in the white wine dataset with extreme imbalance class ($n = 4898$, $m = 12$, 7-classes, $IR = 439.6$). Fifteen classifiers were chosen, ranked and executed by computational simplicity strategy. Weighted-average measures (Recall, Specificity, Balanced Accuracy (BA), Precision, F1-score, MCC) were computed for performance evaluation. In the first stage (Euclidean) 3018 instances (61.6%) were classified reaching Recall = 0.62, Specificity = 0.81, BA = 0.71, Precision = 0.62, F1-score = 0.61, and MCC = 0.43; meanwhile, at the final stage (XGBoost) 4777 instances (97.5%) were classified reaching near-optimal performance with 0.98, 0.99, 0.98, 0.97, 0.98, and 0.96, respectively. BREX outperformed top standalone algorithms: Random Forest (best independent performer with 3521 predicted and BA = 0.77), IB1 (3299 predicted), and XGBoost (3276 predicted), showing a 27.2% improvement in BA. Computationally, BREX completed classification in 2.85 min (27.9 patterns/second), significantly faster than Random Forest (38.7 min; 13.6 × slower). This demonstrates BREX's dual advantage in predictive accuracy and efficiency. Our proposal introduces a novel sequential algorithmic complexity structure that optimizes resource usage, representing a breakthrough for robust classification in extreme imbalance scenarios with optimal speed-performance trade-offs.

Keywords: Sequential classification · Boosting · LOOCV · Extreme imbalance

C. Palma-Preciado et al. (Eds.): CORE 2025, ACSAR 3, pp. 226–244, 2026.
https://doi.org/10.1007/978-3-032-08894-9_15

1 Introduction

The rise of Machine Learning (ML) and Deep Learning (DP) models faces two fundamental paradoxes: firstly, the No Free Lunch theorem, which warns that no algorithm is optimal for all problems, and secondly, the curse of dimensionality and cardinality, which directly impact performance and computational costs [1–3]. These paradoxes become critical constraints for academic and research environments with restricted infrastructure. In this context, a need arises to develop frameworks prioritizing efficiency without relying on complementary technologies such as specialized GPUs.

Development research has been documented to overcome these limitations in the field of machine learning with the aim of maximizing the prediction through the performance of learning models. In this respect, some alternative techniques to implementing machine learning algorithms individually have emerged. Boosting, cascades, and others are frameworks that attempt to optimize resources by processing only critical subsets of data, reducing the dimensional overhead of datasets [4, 5]. Other systematic alternatives, such as stacking, minimizing the overfitting through meta-learning, mitigating costly processing [6, 7], or bagging, which requires parallelization that sometimes in the face of specific scenarios, becomes inaccessible on standard hardware [8]. This suggests that the future of ML and intelligent computing lies in the generation of environments or architectures that smartly manage algorithms, mitigating hardware limitations by transforming them into opportunities for methodological innovation.

In Pattern Classification, among others, approaches that integrate multiple algorithms as a development strategy to solve problems are booming [6, 9]. For example, methods such as boosting and stacking process instances iteratively, where each classifier correcting errors of previous one [9, 10]. This philosophy, called *progressive refinement*, is applied in the prediction of various knowledge areas, where transferring misclassified instances between stages improves performance on imbalanced data [4–6]. However, among these processing alternatives, key differences emerge, marked by those that prioritize adaptivity or dynamic weighting [7, 8]. Some applications suggest that sequential approaches outperform single models run alone, as contextualized within a wider scope of techniques integrating boosting, stacking, cascading, and bagging techniques partially or fully [6, 11, 12]. Therefore, this work aimed to develop an innovative model that combines ML techniques with hybrid and hierarchical architecture. The proposed model is designed to address extreme class imbalance by selecting and executing algorithms in a progressive sequence, from simple to complex, reducing the dataset cardinality stage-by-stage using Leave-One-Out validation. This approach attempts to improve predictive performance while ensuring feasible runtimes on standard hardware.

2 Literature Review

In the domain of boosting, contemporary ensembles integrate adaptive resampling techniques to mitigate extreme class imbalances. Noteworthy approaches include CSBBoost, which incorporates cluster-based SMOTE oversampling and undersampling strategies, reporting 12–15% improvements in recall and F1-score for minority classes compared to traditional methods [13]. Parallel architectures such as DUEN (Dynamic Undersampling Ensemble) dynamically adjust sampling distributions during training, iteratively feeding critical instances back to the model to reduce biases in successive iterations [14]. Complementarily, Gradient Boosted Decision Trees (GBDT) with cost-sensitive loss functions optimize error weighting, achieving gains of up to 18% in balanced accuracy for medical diagnosis [15]. Edge computing applications, such as SMOTE-XGBoost hybrids, demonstrate that embedded resampling schemes maintain classification efficacy (F1-score > 0.92) under sub-50ms latency constraints [16, 17].

For balanced cascades, the HEM-BCWF (Hybrid Ensemble Model with Balanced Cascade, Windowing, and Filters) introduces an adaptive window-based filtering mechanism where each stage selectively processes complex patterns, reducing overfitting by 30% in data with imbalance ratios (*IR*) > 200 [18]. Edge-deployed systems like EdgeCascade tier specialized models (Random Forest, SVM) and route only 15–20% of ambiguous instances to computationally expensive stages (e.g., CNNs), optimizing the accuracy-latency tradeoff (AUC: 0.97; inference: < 100 ms) in IoT streams [19].

In stacking, advanced meta-learners employ error feedback mechanisms to reweigh misclassified instances. For cybersecurity, variants like ProbStack integrate base-layer predictors with Bayesian networks, elevating AUC by 8.5% through uncertainty calibration [20]. In financial fraud detection, hierarchical ensembles with 15 base models outperform standalone XGBoost and LightGBM in F1-score (0.96 vs. 0.89) by prioritizing corrections in high-ambiguity regions [21]. Nevertheless, these approaches face challenges in bias propagation when inter-class boundaries are diffused [7].

Although these approaches share techniques like SMOTE/ADASYN and cost-sensitive weighting to handle imbalances, their core innovation lies in dynamically coordinating complementary algorithms: cascade systems progressively divide the feature space (e.g., HEM-BCWF), stacking architectures combine errors from lower layers using meta-classifiers (XGBoost, neural networks), and boosting schemes iteratively refine training distributions (e.g., DUEN, CSBBoost). However, the hold-out/*k*-fold validation showing bias in samples with high variability, or the predominant use of independent models (i.e., SVM, Random Forest, or XGBoost), are issues for improvement. This highlights the need for novel models with robust validation strategies and adaptive architectures that adjust complexity per instance in the classification task.

3 Materials and Methods

This section details the experimental setup for evaluating the BREX model, covering dataset characteristics, validation strategy, classifier selection/ranking, performance measures, computational resources, and implementation specifics.

3.1 Data Collection

The BREX model's efficacy in scenarios involving extreme imbalance and many classes was tested by analyzing the white wine dataset from public repositories UCI Urvine (https://archive.ics.uci.edu/). The dataset corresponds to physicochemical characteristics for determining the quality of wine [22]. The dataset ($m \times n$) exhibited cardinality (n) of 4898 patterns or instances, dimensionality (m) of 12 attributes, seven classes, and an extremely high Imbalance Ratio (*IR*) with 439.6.

3.2 Validation Method

The Leave-One-Out (LOOCV) method was selected for training (E) and testing (P), which is a special variant of the k-fold-cross-validation where $k = n$ (cardinality of dataset). This method involves partitioning of dataset into E and P, for each iteration leave one pattern for test, and the remaining patterns ($n - 1$) for training. This process is repeated n-times until all the patterns have been tested. Contrary to others, LOOCV is computationally intensive for large datasets with many patterns [23, 24]. However, since it is deterministic it does not require a random seed for reproducibility.

3.3 Model Description

The *Blend of Ranked-sequential Algorithms Executed* (BREX) for classification is a novel model proposed for pattern classification, designed with the strengths of boosting-based learning and deterministic validation. The model's ranked and sequential execution of multiple classification algorithms is performed (Fig. 1A). The BREX model works by processing n-instances by stages, for each one, the classification is performed by a blend of classifiers strategically ranked according to the increasing algorithmic complexity (Fig. 1A and 1B). The boosting-based sequential structure allows each classifier to handle the subset of data that remains misclassified by the preceding one. In other words, BREX carries forward the classification errors from one stage to the next. The process continues iteratively: at each stage, a classifier is trained and tested with the LOOCV method on the misclassified instances from the previous stage. The sequential refinement proceeds until all dataset instances are correctly classified, or until the full sequence of classifiers has been exhausted (Fig. 1B). Overall, the BREX model efficiently combines three features that make it a model of computational intelligence:

- A hierarchical algorithmic sequence that starts with computationally simple models (i.e., Euclidean, kNN, and IBk).
- Progressive forwarding of misclassified instances (complex) to later stages with powerful models (e.g., Random Forest or XGBoost).
- LOOCV validation that avoids bias and randomness of other methods.

Regarding the structure of BREX regarding state-of-the-art developments, it contrasts with available approaches. The *stacking* shows parallels in the combination of multiple classifiers, but the structure is a meta-learning: a final model synthesizing base predictions, as opposed to the linear sequence of BREX, where each algorithm operates exclusively on errors of the previous one (Fig. 1) [7, 11]. In many applications, stacking prioritizes algorithmic diversity over complexity progression, as does BREX [9].

The *cascade* systems are most analogous to BREX due to both filtering instances from early stages (simple classifiers) and delegating complex cases to later stages. However, typical cascades use confidence thresholds to forward instances [5], while BREX delegates all misclassified instances without intermediate evaluation. Finally, the *bagging* contrasts strongly: due to the parallel processing of independent models (e.g. Random Forest) ignores sequential synergy [8]. Meanwhile, the bagging reduces variance through averaging, BREX minimizes bias through cumulative refinement. Finally, the comparison of our model against others shows that the model employs an innovative

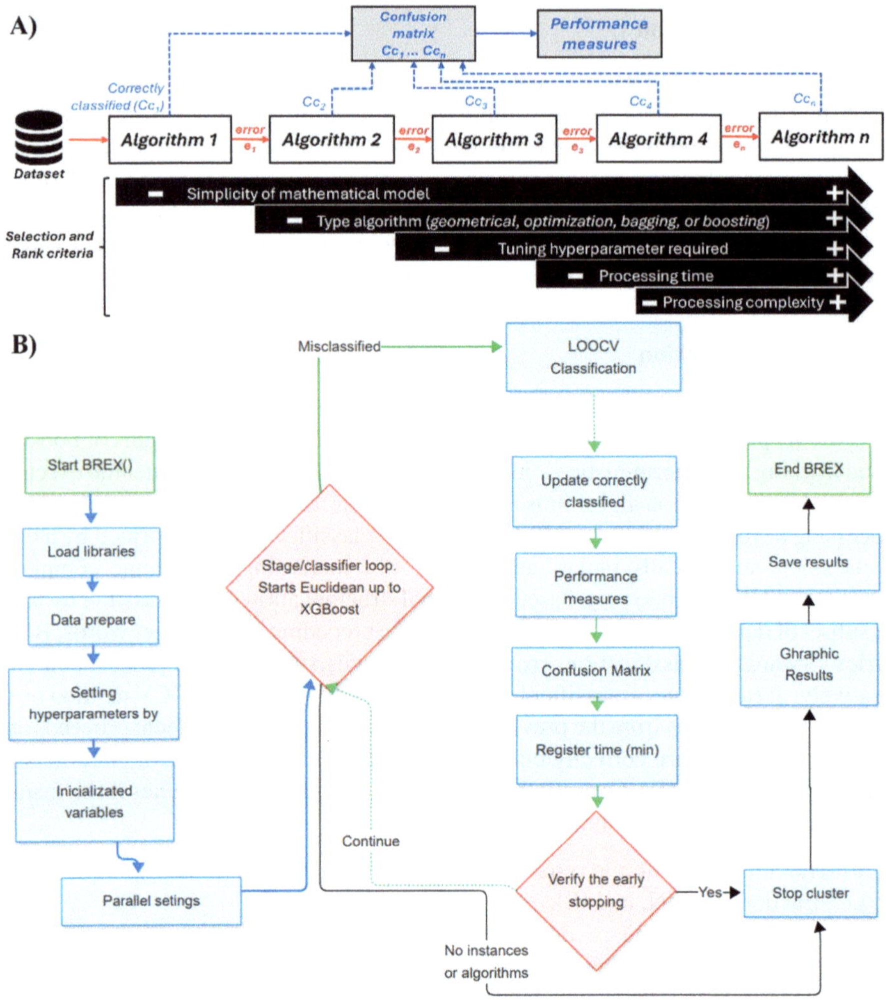

Fig. 1. **A)** Process of the BREX model showing the sequential classification, which carries errors from before subsequent classifiers until all patterns are correctly classified, or all classifiers have been trained and tested. The classifiers are chosen, ranked, and executed by complexity level, starting with the simplest and increasing complexity with more powerful classifiers. **B)** Flowchart of the BREX model showing the sequential process of the algorithm. An important subprocess is the diamond decision which shows that unclassified instances are forwarded to the next stage.

approach as it integrates cascade efficiency with boosting adaptability, but imposes structural rigor absent in other methods through a blend of selection and ranked algorithms based on their mathematical complexity. The BREX model innovation lies in linking algorithmic complexity with sequential progression, optimizing both performance and computational cost in highly complex domains (Fig. 1A and Fig. 1B).

3.4 Classifiers Selected and Ranked

A distinctive feature of the BREX model is the smart *ranking and selection strategy* of algorithms. The classifiers were chosen based on their relevance, suitability, and ability to solve problems in the classification task effectively. Meanwhile, the ranking of the classifiers was determined by three main criteria: 1) computational complexity (training time and memory usage); 2) interpretability (model transparency); and 3) the ability to capture complex decision boundaries (nonlinearity capability). The algorithms with a lower computational cost and a higher level of interpretability were placed earlier in the sequence (e.g., Euclidean or 1NN classifiers), which are expected to handle easy-to-classify instances. As the process advances, more powerful and complex algorithms (e.g., RF, GBM, or XGBoost) are employed to tackle the increasingly difficult patterns that simpler classifiers could not resolve (Fig. 1A, 1B, and Table 1). Essentially, BREX's strategy offers three key advantages:

1. *Efficiency.* By allowing simple classifiers to handle the bulk of easily separable instances, the computational load on more complex classifiers is reduced.
2. *Performance.* By concentrating the effort of sophisticated algorithms on the most challenging patterns, the overall classification performance is improved, especially in scenarios with imbalanced datasets or overlapping classes.
3. *Deterministic approach.* By reducing the dataset cardinality starting with simple to powerful algorithms, it allows a LOOCV to be implemented effectively.

Table 1. Selection and ranking of Machine Learning algorithms through model type, nonlinear capability, training, interpretability, and computational complexity criteria.

Algorithm	Model type	Nonlinear capability	Training	Interpretability	Computational complexity	Rank
Euclidean	Distance-based	✕	Light	☑ High	○ Very low	1
1NN	Distance-based	✕	✕	☑ High	○ Low	2
kNN (k = 3 and 5)	Distance-based	Light	✕	☑ High	○ Low-Middle	3-4
IBk (k = 1, 3 and 5)	Instance-based	Light	Light	☑ High	○ Low-Middle	5-7
Naive Bayes	Probabilistic	✕	Fast	☑ High	○ Very low	8
LDA	Linear	✕	☑ Very fast	☑ High	○ Low	9
CART	Simple decision tree	☑	☑	☑ Middle-High	○ Middle	10
C5.0	Optimized with boosting	☑	☑	☑ Middle	○ Middle	11
SVM	Optimization	☑ (kernel)	☑ Fitting required	◆ Middle	● High	12
Random Forest	Ensemble (bagging)	☑	☑ Slow	◆ Middle	● High	13
GBM	Ensemble (sequential boosting)	☑☑	☑ Slow	✕ Low	● High	14
XGBoost	GBM optimized	☑☑☑	☑ Slow	✕ Low	●● Very high	15

3.5 Description of Classifiers Used

A total of 15 algorithms were chosen and ranked for training and testing encompassing distance-based, trees, linear combinations, probabilistic, optimal hyperplanes, and ensemble (Table 1). The following section provides a brief description:

- Euclidean Classifier. A pattern classifier based on the Euclidean distance between each pattern and the overall class average.
- k-Nearest Neighbors (1NN and kNN). Simple algorithms are widely used in Pattern Recognition and Machine Learning. 1NN classifies a test pattern by assigning the nearest neighbor's class from the training set (E). kNN ($k > 1$) assigns the class via majority vote among k nearest neighbors in E [25–27].
- Instance-Based k (IB1 and IBk). An enhanced kNN version that handles mixed data (numeric, categorical, or missing). Use the Heterogeneous Euclidean-Overlap Metric (HEOM) dissimilarity measure. The kNN algorithm classifies based on the k-nearest training patterns [28].
- Decision Tree (C4.5 and C5.0). Divides datasets into homogeneous subsets through nodes. Recursively selects optimal attributes and splitting thresholds using criteria like Information Gain (IG), Gini Index (Gi), or Information Gain Ratio (IGR), until stop conditions are met [29].
- Linear Discriminant Analysis (LDA). A supervised algorithm that finds linear feature combinations maximizing inter-class separation while minimizing intra-class variance [30].
- Support Vector Machine (SVM). Identifies an optimal hyperplane in d-dimensional space to separate classes, maximizing the margin to the closest patterns of each class [31].
- Bayesian Algorithms (Naive Bayes). Classifiers based on probability (Bayes' theorem). Naive Bayes assumes independence among all attributes [32].
- Random Forest. An ensemble method combining multiple decision trees. Each tree trains on a random data subset (bagging) with random feature selection. It classifies via majority vote across all trees [33].
- Gradient Boosting Machine (GBM). An ensemble algorithm that sequentially trains weak learners (e.g., trees), correcting previous errors by minimizing a loss function [34].
- Extreme Gradient Boosting (XGBoost). An optimized, scalable GBM version that accelerates training and improves performance using parallel/distributed computing and advanced tree methods [2].

3.6 Performance Measures

The imbalanced datasets (i.e., $IR > 1.5$) require performance measures that address the class imbalance effects, where standard Accuracy is limited [24]. The confusion matrix (CM) is essential for evaluating the performance of classifiers. The CM breaks predictions into four values: True Positives (TP), True Negatives (TN), False Positives (FP), and False Negatives (FN). From these values, key measures for imbalanced data are derived, including Recall, Specificity, Balanced Accuracy, Precision, F1-score, and Matthews Correlation Coefficient (MCC) [35, 36]. Due to the nature of the study's multiclass dataset, which comprises seven classes, performance measures were determined through the one-versus-all approach [36]. Furthermore, a correction for class imbalance was implemented, and the weighted average per measure were computed.

3.7 Computer Resources

The analyses were performed using an 8-core, 16-thread AMD Ryzen™ 7 7730U processor with integrated AMD Radeon™ GPUs and 40 GB of RAM (8 GB soldered DDR4-3200 and 32 GB SO-DIMM DDR4-3200). For all selected classifiers in the BREX process and single calculation, the available cores were used for computational parallelization to accelerate the analysis process using the *doParallel* package [37].

3.8 Analyses and Software

The *Blend of Ranked-sequential algorithms Executed* (BREX) model was implemented using packages and functions of RStudio for preprocessing and management data (*dplyr*, *tidyverse*, *tidyr*, and *magrittr*), parallel computing (*doParallel* and *foreach*), models and classification fitting (*caret*, *e1071*, *class*, *C50*, *randomForest*, *xgboost*, *gbm*, *naivebayes*, *rpart*, *RWeka*, and *MASS*), and visualization (*ggplot2*) [37]. All functions used were articulated in six phases that make up the BREX model's algorithmic process: 1) *Input parameters* including a data frame, a class or target variable, and k-folds (default $k = n$, i.e., LOOCV); 2) *Core Workflow* which includes the initialization loading of more than 20 libraries, pre-processing, conversion of the target to factor and management of row names, and the implementation of classifier blend using 15 algorithms without tunning hyperparameters; 3) *Sequential Processing*, which iterates sequential classifiers; 4) *Performance tracking*, which computes measures and generates confusion matrices by stage; 5) *Visualization*, which generates and saves as *png* the plots of confusion matrices per classifier, measures progress, and execution time profiling; and 6) *Output* which returns a list with the final results (Fig. 1B).

4 Results

This section presents the results obtained from executing the BREX model on the white wine dataset. It includes a comparison of predictions at each stage, from the Euclidean classifier to XGBoost, as well as the performance when the same algorithms are executed independently.

4.1 BREX Execution Flow on the White Wine Dataset

The implementation of BREX on white wine dataset (n = 4898, IR = 439.6) started with the Euclidean algorithm (stage 1), correctly classifying 3018 instances (61.6% of the total), showing moderate initial measures: BA = 0.71, Recall = 0.62, Specificity = 0.81, Precision = 0.62, F1-score = 0.61, and MCC = 0.43. At this stage, 1880 instances remained misclassified (Fig. 2A, 2D, and Table 2). The kNN family (stages 2–4) contributed 679 new classified instances (1NN = 205, 3NN = 265, and 5NN = 209), accounting for the cumulative to 3697 (75.5% of the dataset). This progress significantly increased performance measures: BA = 0.81 (+0.10), Recall = 0.75 (+0.14), Specificity = 0.87 (+0.06), Precision = 0.76 (+0.14), F1-score = 0.75 (+0.14) and MCC = 0.63 (+0.20). In this dataset, efficiency exhibited a proportional increase in accordance with the k-value. At the end of the 5NN stage, a total of 1201 unclassified instances remained for subsequent stages (Fig. 2 and 2D). The IBk family (stages 5–7) classified an additional 635 instances (IB1 = 386, IB3 = 142, IB5 = 107), totaling 4332 instances (88.4%). Notably, performance improvements were observed: BA = 0.91 (+0.10), Recall = 0.88 (+0.13), Specificity = 0.94 (+0.07), Precision = 0.88 (+0.12), F1 = 0.88 (+0.13), and MCC = 0.83 (+0.20). In contrast to the performance of kNN, efficiency decreased after IB1. At the end of IB5, using seven simple distance-based algorithms, only 566 instances (11.6%) advanced to the next powerful algorithms (Fig. 2B, 2D and Table 2).

Table 2. Performance results of the BREX sequential classification model, including per-stage and accumulated measures.

Stage	Predicted		Errors	Measure performance						Time (min)	
	By stage	Accumulated	Accumulated	BA	Recall	Specificity	Precision	F1	MCC	By stage	Accumulated
Euclidian	3018	3018	1880	0.714	0.616	0.811	0.614	0.615	0.430	0.64	0.64
1NN	205	3223	1675	0.749	0.658	0.840	0.659	0.659	0.495	0.19	0.83
3NN	271	3494	1404	0.787	0.713	0.861	0.710	0.711	0.573	0.08	0.91
5NN	210	3704	1194	0.815	0.756	0.873	0.751	0.751	0.633	0.07	0.99
IBk1	381	4085	813	0.882	0.834	0.929	0.833	0.833	0.754	0.50	1.49
IBk3	140	4225	673	0.902	0.863	0.941	0.866	0.863	0.797	0.29	1.78
IBk5	111	4336	562	0.915	0.885	0.944	0.882	0.883	0.829	0.24	2.01
Naive Bayes	145	4481	417	0.943	0.915	0.971	0.921	0.916	0.875	0.06	2.08
LDA	123	4604	294	0.954	0.940	0.968	0.939	0.938	0.910	0.06	2.14
CART	87	4691	207	0.972	0.958	0.986	0.957	0.956	0.937	0.07	2.21
C5.0	40	4731	167	0.977	0.966	0.988	0.965	0.965	0.949	0.05	2.26
SVM	34	4765	133	0.981	0.973	0.989	0.972	0.972	0.960	0.05	2.31
RF	14	4779	119	0.984	0.976	0.993	0.975	0.975	0.964	0.08	2.39
GBM	10	4789	109	0.986	0.978	0.993	0.977	0.977	0.967	0.06	2.45
XGBoost	8	4797	101	0.987	0.979	0.994	0.979	0.979	0.969	0.74	3.19

The Naive Bayes (stage 8) and LDA (stage 9) models classified 136 and 125 instances respectively, accumulating 4593 instances out of 4898 total (93.8%). In these two stages of probability and linear function, the measures reached: BA = 0.95 (+0.04), Recall = 0.94 (+0.05), Specificity = 0.96 (+0.02), Precision = 0.91 (+0.03), F1-score = 0.94 (+0.06) and MCC = 0.91 (+0.08). The remaining 305 misclassified instances (6.2%) were passed to the tree-based algorithm processes (Fig. 2, 2D, and Table 2). The decision trees (stages 10–11: CART and C5.0) added 105 classified instances (CART = 63, C5.0 = 42), totaling 4698 (95.9%). At this stage, the measures have shown an improvement of 0.02–0.03 compared to previous stages: BA = 0.97 (+0.02), Recall = 0.96 (+0.02), Specificity = 0.99 (+0.02), Precision = 0.96 (+0.05), F1-score = 0.96 (+0.02) and MCC = 0.94 (+0.03). At the end of C5.0 (stage 11), a total of 200 instances (4.1%) moved to classifiers of higher mathematical complexity (Fig. 2 and 2D, Table 2). The SVM (stage 12) classified only 43 of the 200 residual instances possibly due to complex nonlinear patterns, accumulating 4741 classified instances (96.8%). The measures exhibited a modest increase from the previous stage: BA = 0.98 (+0.01), Recall = 0.97 (+0.01),

Specificity = 0.99 (+0.00), Precision = 0.97 (+0.01), F1-score = 0.97 (+0.01) and MCC = 0.95 (+0.01), leaving 157 instances (3.2%) for ensembles (Fig. 2, 2D, and Table 2).

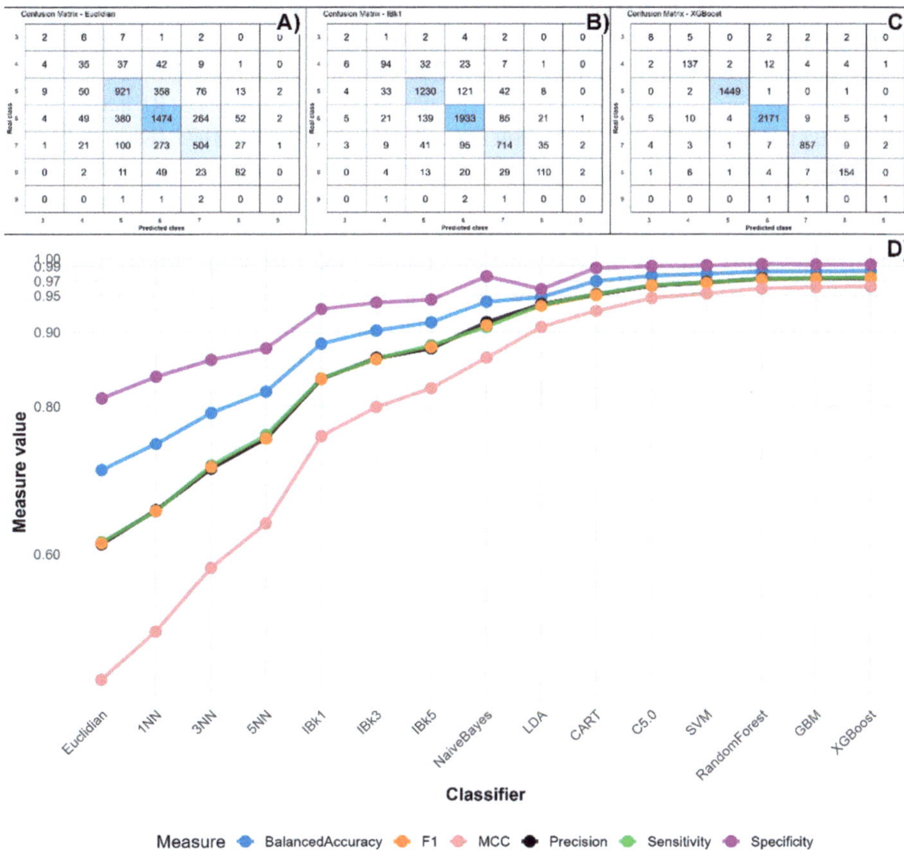

Fig. 2. Results of BREX model in the white wine dataset. **A)** Confusion matrix of Euclidean algorithm placed in first stage, **B)** Confusion matrix of IB1 algorithm placed in fifth stage, **C)** Confusion matrix of XGBoost algorithm placed in last stage, and **D)** Accumulated progress of performance measures as weighted-average.

The ensembles (stages 13–15: Random Forest, GBM, XGBoost) together classified only 36 additional instances (RF = 18, GBM = 14, XGBoost = 4), totaling 4777 of the 4898 in the full dataset (97.5%). The final measures were near-optimal: BA = 0.98, Recall = 0.98, Specificity = 0.99, Precision = 0.97, F1-score = 0.98 and MCC = 0.96. The remaining 121 instances (2.5%) were misclassified, confirming a high complexity in the pattern structure (Fig. 2C, 2D and Table 2). In summary, the BREX model was able to classify 97.5% of the patterns with incremental improvements in performance across the sequence of algorithms executed. The initial stages (kNN and IBk) provided the greatest reduction in instances, while the final stages (SVM and ensemble) classified complex patterns with marginal but critical improvements to overall performance.

Comparing the BREX model with independently executed algorithms confirmed significant superiority. While our model achieved measures ranging from 0.96 to 0.99, the three most effective algorithms executed independently in the white wine dataset were Random Forest (3521 predicted), IB1 (3299 predicted) and XGBoost (3276 predicted). The best independent algorithms only achieved: Recall = 0.72 (RF), Specificity = 0.84 (IB1), BA = 0.77 (RF), Precision = 0.72 (RF), F1-score = 0.71 (RF), and MCC = 0.57 (RF) (Fig. 3, Table 3). The maximum performance reached measures of BA = 0.77 (0.73–0.77) and F1-score = 0.71 (0.66–0.71). The remaining algorithms showed lower performance, with predicted between 2170–3018 and BA = 0.60–0.71 (Fig. 3, Table 3). This gap confirms the strategic advantage of the BREX model when combining algorithms sequentially. It is noteworthy that the best independent models include instance-based methods (IBk1) and ensembles (RF and XGBoost). However, the moderate performance reached (e.g., BA $\leq$ 0.77 or F1-score $\leq$ 0.71) evidence limitations in handling complex class imbalance (Fig. 3, Table 3).

Table 3. Performance measures of classifiers independently executed.

Classifier	Predicted	Errors	BA	Recall	Specificity	Precision	F1	MCC	Time (min)
Euclidian	3018	1880	0.714	0.616	0.811	0.614	0.61	0.43	0.58
1NN	3018	1880	0.714	0.616	0.811	0.614	0.61	0.43	0.13
3NN	2437	2461	0.618	0.498	0.739	0.489	0.49	0.24	0.11
5NN	2378	2520	0.603	0.486	0.721	0.471	0.48	0.22	0.14
IBk1	3299	1599	0.755	0.674	0.836	0.670	0.67	0.51	17.97
IBk3	2771	2127	0.670	0.566	0.775	0.560	0.56	0.35	25.81
IBk5	2752	2146	0.660	0.562	0.758	0.554	0.55	0.33	27.88
Naive Bayes	2170	2728	0.606	0.443	0.770	0.462	0.43	0.23	0.30
LDA	2615	2283	0.619	0.534	0.705	0.512	0.51	0.27	0.39
CART	2651	2247	0.619	0.541	0.697	0.499	0.5	0.27	2.15
C5.0	2938	1960	0.698	0.600	0.795	0.594	0.6	0.4	4.16
SVM	2619	2279	0.599	0.535	0.664	0.547	0.48	0.26	32.38
RF	3505	1393	0.768	0.716	0.820	0.723	0.71	0.56	39.48
GBM	2717	2181	0.636	0.555	0.716	0.513	0.52	0.3	21.96
XGBoost	3276	1622	0.735	0.669	0.801	0.670	0.66	0.49	50.01

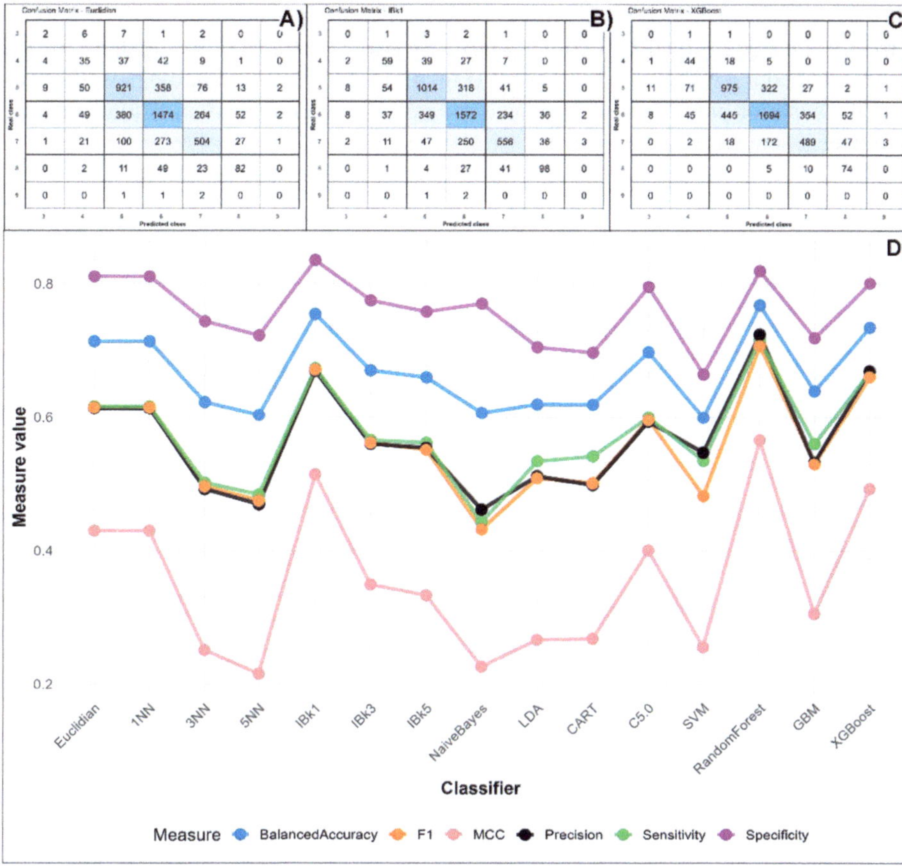

Fig. 3. Results of 15 machine learning algorithms executed independently in the white wine dataset. **A)** Confusion matrix of Euclidean algorithm, **B)** Confusion matrix of IB1 algorithm, **C)** Confusion matrix of XGBoost algorithm, **D)**. Progress of performance measures as the weighted-average of each algorithm.

The BREX model overcame the extreme imbalance condition ($IR = 439.6$) through staged architecture, optimizing the progressive reduction of complexity. Therefore, validation in this dataset leads to the conclusion that BREX consistently outperformed all independent algorithms, even the most robust ensembles. Improvements in key measures (MCC: + 0.40 over the best independent) and the efficient handling of complex instances support the innovative design (Fig. 3 and 4, Table 3).

A comparison of the independent running algorithms over time shows that BREX's final run time on the dataset was significantly faster than that of any standalone model. BREX's classification duration was 2.85 min across the entire model sequence and was associated with 4777 predicted and BA = 0.98 (Fig. 4A, Table 2). This represents a predictive ability and computational efficiency of 27.9 patterns per second that were correctly classified on a dataset with extreme imbalance ($IR = 439.6$). In contrast, Random Forest achieved the best performance in the independent process with 3,521 predicted and a BA of 0.77, but it took 38.7 min to complete, equivalent to 1.5 patterns per second correctly classified (Fig. 4B). In other words, RF was 13.6 times slower than the BREX model and had a BA that was 0.21 lower (Fig. 4B, Table 3). These findings further validate the superior predictive performance and resource-efficient computations obtained with BREX sequential classification.

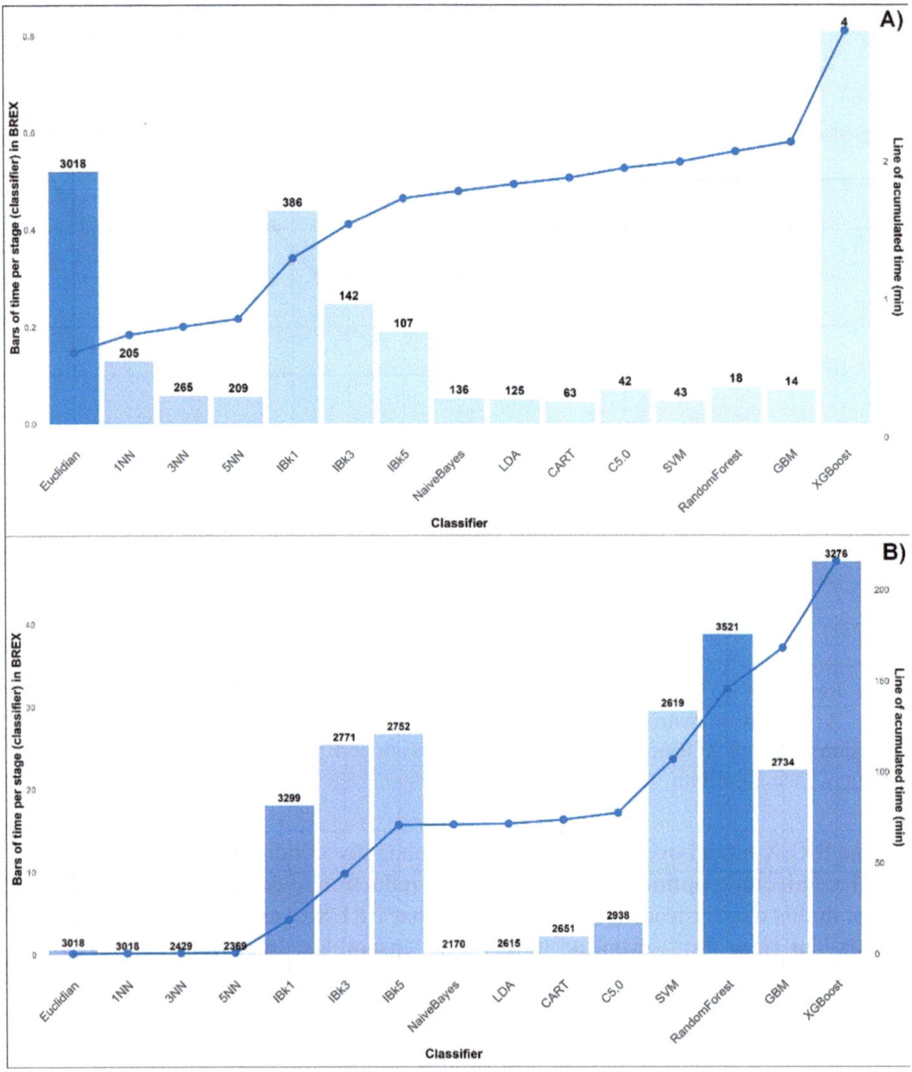

Fig. 4. Comparative of execution time between the BREX model (**A**) and independently executed algorithms (**B**). Bars show the time in minutes (min) per classifier, with the number of correctly classified instances at the top. The line shows the cumulative process.

5 Discussion

The BREX model's results on the white wine dataset ($n = 4898$, $IR = 439.6$) are contrasted with recent studies using the same data domain published in the UCI Wine Quality public repository and others, such as Kaggle. The *first contrasting difference* found was that BREX is the first and only sequential model addressing extremely complex problems in the artificial intelligence domain of this type of dataset. The *second contrasting difference* was that these datasets are not used with the original structure but mostly converted to a two-class problem explaining the wine color i.e., white or red, or merging quality classes into two types i.e., low or high wine quality, obtaining near-optimal performance measures greater than 0.98 [39, 40]. In the context of platforms such as Kaggle (https://www.kaggle.com/), proposals to address this issue are predominantly aligned with a two-class approach, accompanied by a range of methodologies that yield divergent outcomes. However, an attempt to predict wine quality with seven classes and extreme imbalance ($IR = 439.6$) as proposed by BREX has only been attempted by Niyogisubizo *et al.* [41], although with poor to moderate results on at least five powerful classifiers such as SVM, RF, and ensembles. Thus, these results reveal significant improvements in the BREX model's performance measures, validation method, and handling of extreme class imbalance.

The *third contrasting difference* was that only the BREX model employed a deterministic validation, such as LOOCV, from end-to-end. This contrasts with most papers, which resort to k-fold cross-validation experiments using the classical $k = 5$ or 10, and the hold-out with partitioning 70–30%. These methods are computationally faster but statistically less rigorous than LOOCV [7, 38–40]. The observed discrepancy in performance can be partially attributed to methodological differences. For instance, BREX achieves an MCC of 0.97, whereas other proposals achieve an MCC ranging from 0.68 to 0.82 [38–40]. The optimal performance of LOOCV in the BREX model is attributable to its selective sequential nature. For instance, the model processes 4,898 patterns in 2.85 min, whereas a standalone Random Forest requires 38.7 min. The efficiency of the process is achieved by the preliminary refinement of "easy" patterns, thereby reserving resources for the truly challenging and complex patterns. Notably, LOOCV implementation achieves unique efficiency through three principles:

1. *Staged implementation*: Strategically, the LOOCV is not executed on the entire dataset (computationally prohibitive), but only on the subset of misclassified instances in the previous stage.
2. *Progressive reduction*: In initial stages (e.g., Euclidean, $n = 4898$), the LOOCV operates on the entire dataset, but the cost is mitigated by simple mathematical algorithms. Moving forward, later stages (e.g., SVM, $n = 200$) handle reduced sets where LOOCV is feasible even on commodity hardware.
3. *Cumulative validation*: Each algorithm is validated only with the instances that reach its stage, avoiding redundant evaluations.

The *fourth contrasting difference* was the performance and robustness in our model reaching e.g., BA = 0.98, F1-score = 0.98 at the final stage, exceeding the maximum reported in the literature with F1-score = 0.89 employing SVM with hierarchical Bayesian optimization [38]. Other independent models such as Random Forest and

XGBoost, powerful high-precision algorithms, showed F1-score lower than 0.86 due to unmitigated class imbalance [40]. Regarding class imbalance handling, BREX raises Recall measure from 0.62 at the initial stage with the Euclidean algorithm to 0.98 in the final stage with XGBoost, without applying specific balancing techniques, while other approaches employed SMOTE-ENN only achieving Recall = 0.83 [42]. Conversely, the Specificity value of 0.99 in the BREX model stands in contrast to the ensemble stacking model, which has values lower than 0.91 [39].

Notably, in addition to the sequential and hierarchical ranking of the algorithms, a determining factor in the BREX model strategy is LOOCV as a validation method. This is a deterministic method, unlike k-fold or hold-out models. Unlike the existing state-of-the-art, our model applies LOOCV at each stage (sequential algorithms), providing reproducibility and low bias compared to global k-fold that exhibited sensitivity and underestimation of variance in imbalanced data [23]. The BREX model's efficiency is demonstrated by a processing time of 2.85 min on a dataset of 15 x 4898 using standard hardware, while similar implementations of algorithms, such as SVM, can take over 4 h and produce moderate results [38]. Furthermore, BREX ensures reproducibility and consistency due to its deterministic LOOCV approach.

The BREX model architecture leverages sequential versus the parallelism employed in models such as stacking or voting [6]. The process reduced the dataset by 78.5% with simple distance or tree-based algorithms before running powerful algorithms such as SVM and ensembles, thereby optimizing resources. Approaches such as Random Forest, GBM, or XGBoost process the entire dataset, increasing computational cost without proportional gain in performance as was evidenced in our study by independently running these algorithms, the time increased by up to 5–13 times [40–42]. In the case of the BREX model, less than 7% of the dataset patterns, considered as complex instances, reached the ensemble stages, and only less than 10% were classified, while standard methods such as deep stacking and other approaches require full processing of the dataset in computationally expensive algorithms [39]. A *final contrasting difference* was the practical application of BREX that was executed on standard hardware with reasonable processing time (2.85 min), while other solutions with metaheuristics e.g., grid search + SVM require availability of specific GPUs (e.g., more than 15 min) [40].

6 Conclusions

In summary, the BREX model is a new benchmark for modeling classification tasks applied to extreme imbalanced datasets. Our model outperforms state-of-the-art results in all studied performance measures while reducing computational time by five to thirteen times, despite the use of deterministic validation. The BREX model's hierarchical sequential approach with deterministic validation mitigates the limitations of conventional methods (k-fold or hold-out) in environments with technical, technological, and infrastructure constraints. These results emphasize the need for methodological innovations to address real-world problems and the integration of an algorithmic-mathematical complexity model.

The BREX model is a significant breakthrough in machine learning and intelligent computing. The model achieves a balance between speed, performance, reproducibility, accessibility, and robustness in complex processes. Furthermore, our proposal introduces a distinctive innovation: an ascending algorithmic complexity structure that optimizes computational efficiency. In contrast, algorithms such as ensembles and systems such as cascades generally manage complexity through randomization or weight adjustment. These features are incorporated into the BREX model within the ecosystem of boosting-based sequential methods, highlighting the trade-off between algorithmic hierarchy and cumulative error handling. Integrating Leave-One-Out Cross-Validation (LOOCV) as a deterministic method in BREX is an innovative solution that addresses the tension between statistical rigor and computational efficiency. Unlike traditional stochastic methods that depend on random partitions, LOOCV provides deterministic and reproducible results through an intelligent and exhaustive approach: each input serves as a validation set once, eliminating sampling biases. This rigor is essential in academic research, where reproducibility is essential.

7 Limitations and Future Work

Although our BREX model exhibited optimal results, the validation was limited to the white wine dataset for proof-of-concept. Therefore, addressing performance in other domains with high imbalance or other complexity indicators is essential for future work. For instance, LOOCV's feasibility depends on data reduction between stages or classifiers. Therefore, an empirical comparison of the BREX model with other hybrid models, such as stacking, voting, or cascade classifiers, across multiple datasets could also be performed. This would allow for a broader validation of BREX's scalability and generalization capabilities beyond the wine dataset. Nevertheless, for datasets where early classifiers resolve few instances, computational gains should be demonstrated. Conversely, the 121 misclassified instances (2.5%) are due to features indicating unresolved bias, class overlap or noise, which can be addressed using alternative methods outside classical machine learning algorithms. These methods can include *ad hoc* algorithms, metaheuristics, and deep learning approaches, among others.

Acknowledgments. This work was supported by a scholarship from Mexico's Secretariat of Science, Humanities, Technology and Innovation (SECIHTI). The authors additionally acknowledge the Centro de Investigación en Computación of the Instituto Politécnico Nacional (CIC-IPN) for the institutional support throughout this research.

Declaration of Interest. The authors declare no conflict of interest.

References

1. Wolpert, D.H., Macready, W.G.: No free lunch theorems for optimization. IEEE Trans. Evol. Comput. **1**(1), 67–82 (1997). https://doi.org/10.1109/4235.585893
2. Chen, T., Guestrin, C.: XGBoost: a scalable tree boosting system. In: Proceedings of the 22nd ACM SIGKDD International Conference on Knowledge Discovery and Data Mining (2016). https://doi.org/10.1145/2939672.2939785
3. He, H., Garcia, E.A.: Learning from Imbalanced Data. IEEE Trans. Knowl. Data Eng. **21**(9), 1263–1284 (2009). https://doi.org/10.1109/TKDE.2008.239

4. Zhang, Y., Li, Q., Wang, T.: Boosting-based iterative error transfer for short-term energy load forecasting. Energy **291**, 130451 (2024). https://doi.org/10.1016/j.energy.2024.130451
5. Wang, H., Liu, X., Chen, G.: Sequential deep learning for imbalanced environmental data: a case study on PM2.5 prediction. Front. Environ. Sci. **11**, 1295526 (2023). https://doi.org/10.3389/fenvs.2023.1295526
6. Khan, A.A., Chaudhari, O., Chandra, R.: A review of ensemble learning and data augmentation models for class imbalanced problems: combination, implementation and evaluation. Expert Syst. Appl. **244**, 122778 (2024). https://doi.org/10.1016/j.eswa.2023.122778
7. Ahmad, S., Khan, M.A., Al-Jumeily, D.: Dynamic weighted stacking for medical diagnostic systems under high-dimensional imbalance. Expert Syst. Appl. **207**, 117947 (2022). https://doi.org/10.1016/j.eswa.2022.117947
8. Al-Sai, Z., Abdullah, R., Husin, M.H.: Optimizing industrial process efficiency through ensemble learning: a comparative study of bagging and random forest approaches. J. Ind. Inf. Integr. **35**, 100542 (2023). https://doi.org/10.1016/j.jii.2023.100542
9. Liu, R., Zhang, J., Zhou, Y.: Ensemble learning with feature selection for industrial fault diagnosis in IoT-enabled manufacturing systems. J. Manuf. Syst. **68**, 15–28 (2023). https://doi.org/10.1016/j.jmsy.2023.03.005
10. Chen, X., Wang, Z., Li, J.: Comparative analysis of boosting algorithms for high-dimensional imbalanced data: accuracy optimization strategies. Knowl.-Based Syst. **228**, 107279 (2021). https://doi.org/10.1016/j.knosys.2021.107279
11. Zhou, L., Xu, B., Tang, W.: Sequential classification model for software defect prediction using hybrid feature spaces. Electronics **12**(15), 3354 (2023). https://doi.org/10.3390/electronics12153354
12. Sami, N.M., Naeini, M.: Machine learning applications in cascading failure analysis in power systems: a review. Electr. Power Syst. Res. **232**, 110415 (2024). https://doi.org/10.1016/j.epsr.2024.110415
13. Salehi, A.R., Khedmati, M.: A cluster-based SMOTE both-sampling (CSBBoost) ensemble algorithm for classifying imbalanced data. Sci. Rep. **14**, 5152 (2024). https://doi.org/10.1038/s41598-024-55598-1
14. Ren, H., Tang, Y., Dong, W., Ren, S., Jiang, L.: DUEN: dynamic ensemble handling class imbalance in network intrusion detection. Expert Syst. Appl. (advance online publication) (2023). https://doi.org/10.1016/j.eswa.2023.120420
15. Zhang, X., Yu, L.: Consumer credit risk assessment: a review from the state-of-the-art classification algorithms, data traits, and learning methods. Expert Syst. Appl. **237**, 121484 (2024). https://doi.org/10.1016/j.eswa.2023.121484
16. Han, Y., Wei, Z., Huang, G.: An imbalance data quality monitoring based on SMOTE-XGBOOST supported by edge computing. Sci. Rep. **14**, 10151 (2024). https://doi.org/10.1038/s41598-024-60600-x
17. Mangina, V.S.: Adaptive boosting with dynamic weight adjustment. ArXiv. (2024). https://arxiv.org/abs/2406.00524
18. Zhao, H., et al.: An ensemble learning approach with gradient resampling for class-imbalance problems. INFORMS J. Comput. **35**(4), 747–763 (2023). https://doi.org/10.1287/ijoc.2023.1274
19. Izonin, I., Tkachenko, R., Krak, I., Berezsky, O., Shevchuk, I., Shandilya, S.K.: A cascade ensemble-learning model for deployment at the edge. Front. Environ. Sci. **11**, 1295526 (2023). https://doi.org/10.3389/fenvs.2023.1295526
20. Bakasa, W., Viriri, S.: Stacked ensemble deep learning for pancreas cancer classification using extreme gradient boosting. Front. Artif. Intell. **6**, 1232640 (2023). https://doi.org/10.3389/frai.2023.1232640
21. Zhu, S., et al.: A financial fraud prediction framework based on stacking ensemble learning. Systems **12**(12), 588 (2024). https://doi.org/10.3390/systems12120588

22. Cortez, P., Cerdeira, A., Almeida, F., Matos, T., Reis, J.: Wine Quality. UCI Mach. Learn. Repos. (2009). https://doi.org/10.24432/C56S3T
23. Adin, A., Teixeira, E.K., Lenzi, A., Liu, Z., Martínez-Minaya, J., Rue, H.: Automatic cross-validation in structured models: is it time to leave out leave-one-out? Spat. Stat. **62**, 100843 (2024). https://doi.org/10.1016/j.spasta.2024.100843
24. Velázquez-Rodríguez, J.L., Villuendas-Rey, Y., Camacho-Nieto, O., Yáñez-Márquez, C.: A novel and simple mathematical transform improves the performance of Lernmatrix in pattern classification. Mathematics **8**(5), 732 (2020). https://doi.org/10.3390/math8050732
25. Miranda-Vega, J.E., Rivas-López, M., Fuentes, W.F.: K-nearest neighbor classification for pattern recognition of a reference source light for machine vision system. IEEE Sens. J. **21**(10), 11514–11521 (2020). https://doi.org/10.1109/JSEN.2020.3024094
26. Taunk, K., De, S., Verma, S., Swetapadma, A.: A brief review of nearest neighbor algorithm for learning and classification. In: 2019 International Conference on Intelligent Computing and Control Systems (ICCS), pp. 1255–1260 (2019). https://doi.org/10.1109/ICCS45141.2019.9065747
27. Cover, T.M., Hart, P.E.: Nearest neighbor pattern classification. IEEE Trans. Inf. Theory **13**(1), 21–27 (1967)
28. Venkatesh, B., Singh, D.A.A.G., Leavline, E.J.: Pragmatic investigation on performance of instance-based learning algorithms. Artif. Intell. Evol. Comput. Eng. Syst. 633–642 (2017). https://doi.org/10.1007/978-981-10-3174-8_53
29. Mienye, I.D., Jere, N.: A survey of decision trees: concepts, algorithms, and applications. IEEE Access **12**, 86716–86727 (2024). https://doi.org/10.1109/ACCESS.2024.3416838
30. Zhao, S., Zhang, B., Yang, J., Zhou, J., Xu, Y.: Linear discriminant analysis. Nat. Rev. Methods Primers **4**(1), 70 (2024). https://doi.org/10.1038/s43586-024-00346-y
31. Vapnik, V.N., Golowich, S.E., Smola, A.J.: Support vector method for function approximation, regression estimation and signal processing. Adv. Neural Inf. Process. Syst. **9**, 281–287 (1996). https://www.scirp.org/reference/referencespapers?referenceid=2869180
32. Sun, S.: A review of deterministic approximate inference techniques for Bayesian machine learning. Neural Comput. Appl. **23**, 2039–2050 (2013). https://doi.org/10.1007/s00521-013-1445-4
33. Breiman, L.: Random forests. Mach. Learn. **45**, 5–32 (2001). https://doi.org/10.1023/A:1010933404324
34. Natekin, A., Knoll, A.: Gradient boosting machines, a tutorial. Front. Neurorobot. **7**, 21 (2013). https://doi.org/10.3389/fnbot.2013.00021
35. Amin, F., Mahmoud, M.: Confusion matrix in binary classification problems: a step-by-step tutorial. J. Eng. Res. **6**(5), 1–12 (2022). https://digitalcommons.aaru.edu.jo/erjeng/vol6/iss5/1
36. Cheng, Z., Zhang, X.Y., Liu, C.L.: Unified classification and rejection: a one-versus-all framework. Mach. Intell. Res. **21**, 870–887 (2024). https://doi.org/10.1007/s11633-024-1514-4
37. RStudio Team: RStudio: Integrated Development Environment for R (2024.09.1+394). Posit Software (2024). https://posit.co/download/rstudio/
38. Jain, K., Kaushik, K., Gupta, S.K., et al.: Machine learning-based predictive modelling for the enhancement of wine quality. Sci. Rep. **13**, 17042 (2023). https://doi.org/10.1038/s41598-023-44111-9
39. Kumari, S., Misra, A., Wahi, A., Rathore, P.S.: Quality of red wine: analysis and comparative study of machine learning models. In: 2023 5th International Conference on Inventive Research in Computing Applications (ICIRCA), pp. 769–772 (2023). https://doi.org/10.1109/ICIRCA57980.2023.10220857
40. Er, Y., Atasoy, A.: The classification of white wine and red wine according to their physicochemical qualities. Int. J. Intell. Syst. Appl. Eng. **4**(Special Issue-1), 23–26 (2016). https://doi.org/10.18201/ijisae.265954

41. Niyogisubizo, J., Ninteretse, J.D.D., Nziyumva, E., Nshimiyimana, M., Murwanashyaka, E., Habiyakare, E.: Towards predicting the quality of red wine using novel machine learning methods for classification, data visualization, and analysis. Artif. Intell. Appl. **3**(1), 31–42 (2024). https://doi.org/10.47852/bonviewAIA42021999
42. Koranga, M., Pandey, R., Joshi, M., Kumar, M.: Analysis of white wine using machine learning algorithms. Mater. Today: Proc. **46**, 11087–11093 (2021). https://doi.org/10.1016/j.matpr.2021.02.229

Impact of Data Augmentation Applied to Fundus Images Used in a Swin Transformer V2-Based Model for the Detection of Age-Related Macular Degeneration

Roberto Marquez Castro[1], Jorge Ernesto González Díaz[1], José Luis Sánchez Cervantes[1(✉)], Yara Anahí Jiménez Nieto[2], and Adolfo Rodríguez Parada[2]

[1] Tecnológico Nacional de México/I. T. Orizaba, Av. Oriente 9 No. 852. Col Emiliano Zapata, CP. 94320 Orizaba, México
{m16011135,d04010291,jose.sc}@orizaba.tecnm.mx

[2] School of Business and Technologies Ixtaczoquitlan Campus, Universidad Veracruzana, Sumidero - Dos Rios State Highway, Km 1, Ixtaczoquitlán, México
{yjimenez,adrodriguez}@uv.mx

Abstract. The use of data augmentation in medical images has become an effective technique to improve the performance of deep learning models, especially when dealing with a limited dataset. This technique involves applying transformations such as rotations, scaling, and brightness adjustments to the original images, which allows for the generation of artificial variations and thus increases the diversity of the dataset. This study investigates the impact of data augmentation on retinal images affected by Age-Related Macular Degeneration (AMD), one of the leading causes of vision loss in older adults. To achieve this, the Swin Transformer V2 model was used, a deep learning model based on the transformer architecture, known for its ability to capture spatial patterns in high-resolution images. Various data augmentation techniques were applied, evaluating their effect on the accuracy and generalization ability of the models trained with Swin Transformer V2 for AMD detection. The results show that the use of these techniques not only improves the accuracy of the models but also optimizes their ability to generalize, achieving an accuracy of 88.64%, which is crucial for the early detection of this disease. In this way, the study emphasizes the value of data augmentation in computer-assisted diagnosis in the field of visual health, contributing to better clinical management of AMD and the improvement of diagnostic methods in modern medicine.

Keywords: Age-related macular degeneration · Data augmentation · Deep learning · Swin transformer V2

C. Palma-Preciado et al. (Eds.): CORE 2025, ACSAR 3, pp. 245–257, 2026.
https://doi.org/10.1007/978-3-032-08894-9_16

1 Introduction

Age-Related Macular Degeneration (AMD) is one of the leading causes of vision loss in older adults, affecting a large percentage of the global population [1]. This condition impacts the macula, the central part of the retina, and can lead to the gradual loss of central vision, making it difficult to perform everyday activities such as reading or driving [2]. Early detection of AMD is crucial for effective treatment, as it can slow its progression and preserve vision. However, early identification of this disease is often hindered by the variability of retinal images and the complexity of their clinical interpretation [3].

From a computer vision perspective, this challenge translates into the need to automatically extract relevant visual features from retinal images that may appear subtly different across patients and stages of the disease. Traditional diagnostic methods are often subjective and require expert interpretation, making them time-consuming and prone to variability. Therefore, developing automated, accurate, and efficient classification systems becomes a critical goal for supporting clinical decision-making and improving access to early diagnosis.

Deep learning models have shown great effectiveness in detecting ocular pathologies, especially when advanced image processing techniques are used. A prominent approach to improving the performance of these models, particularly when available data is limited, is data augmentation. This technique involves applying transformations to the original images, such as rotations, scaling, and brightness adjustments, to generate additional variations and thus increase the diversity of the training dataset [4]. This methodology is especially useful in the field of medical imaging, where datasets can be small or imbalanced [5].

In this regard, the Swin Transformer V2 model has emerged as an effective tool for medical image analysis. Based on transformer architecture, this model has shown good results in capturing large-scale spatial patterns and improving accuracy in image classification tasks [6]. Its ability to process high-resolution images and learn hierarchical representations makes it an excellent option for detecting AMD. This study analyzes the impact of data augmentation on the accuracy and generalization ability of a Swin Transformer V2-based model for identifying AMD in retinal images.

This article is structured as follows: Sect. 2 reviews prior research on AMD and ocular disease detection using CNNs and Transformers, emphasizing the role of data augmentation in enhancing deep learning performance. Section 3 outlines the dataset, preprocessing steps, and applied augmentation strategies. Section 4 presents results, including accuracy, recall, F1-score, and visualizations like confusion matrices and ROC curves, comparing the three models. Section 5 discusses how augmentation affects performance. Section 6 concludes with key findings and future directions, such as using larger datasets and real-world clinical validation.

2 State of the Art

Below is a brief description of several related studies on data augmentation.

The use of CNNs to detect AMD in retinal fundus images was addressed in [7]. The authors propose using data augmentation to artificially increase the number of training images and improve the model's generalization ability. Their research employed classic techniques such as rotation, horizontal/vertical flipping, and scaling, achieving a model accuracy of up to 99.45% by applying 16 times data augmentation to the dataset. This approach allowed the model to handle greater variability and become more robust against distortions in clinical images.

In a parallel study, a different approach by integrating Swin Transformer with data augmentation techniques such as MixUp and CutMix for classifying various ocular pathologies, including diabetic retinopathy and AMD was adopted in [8]. The results demonstrated that the Swin Transformer, combined with these augmentation techniques, not only improved the model's ability to classify the images correctly but also significantly increased the model's robustness to unseen variations in the images. This approach achieved an average accuracy of 97%, highlighting the ability of Transformers to learn long-term dependencies between pixels, which is crucial in complex medical tasks such as detecting ocular diseases.

On the other hand, a pretrained CNN with data augmentation on retinal fundus images to detect diabetic retinopathy was used in [9]. In their study, they applied transformations such as random cropping, rotation, and brightness/contrast adjustments. By comparing the CNN's results with and without augmentation, they found that using data augmentation allowed the model to achieve 97.4% accuracy, significantly improving its classification ability under varying lighting conditions and image quality, which are common in clinical images.

In recent research, a Swin Transformer-based model for classifying diabetic retinopathy using retinal fundus images was proposed in [10]. The study highlights the model's ability to extract hierarchical spatial features with high accuracy and robustness, even under limited data conditions. The authors employed data augmentation strategies such as flipping, rotation, and color jittering to enhance generalization and prevent overfitting. Their results demonstrated that vision transformer architectures are well-suited for retinal disease classification tasks and can outperform conventional CNNs in specific settings.

A classification model for multi-fundus diseases using retinal OCT images and the Swin Transformer V2 architecture was proposed in [11]. Their approach leverages the model's hierarchical self-attention to extract detailed features across multiple scales, achieving high performance in disease classification tasks. The study also incorporates preprocessing techniques and cross-validation to ensure generalization, reporting an accuracy of 99.52% on a diverse dataset. This work highlights the effectiveness of Swin Transformer V2 in ophthalmic imaging and supports its application in automated diagnostic systems for retinal diseases.

According to the demonstration presented in [12], the use of CNNs to detect diabetic retinopathy with data augmentation can substantially increase accuracy, reaching 97.5% by incorporating techniques such as rotation, transposition, and brightness variations in the training of a deep neural network model. The model was also validated using a real clinical image dataset, demonstrating its applicability in medical settings. In [13], data augmentation techniques were adopted to improve a CNN's performance on retinal fundus images for detecting AMD. The combination of vertical flip, rotation, and zoom allowed the model to achieve 96.8% accuracy, compared to 94.5% without augmentation. This study highlights how data augmentation improves the model's ability to generalize.

On the other hand, a hybrid architecture combining Swin Transformer V2 with augmentation techniques such as MixUp and CutMix was proposed in [14]. In their application to AMD detection in retinal fundus images, the model achieved 98.1% accuracy, showing how using Swin Transformer combined with data augmentation can improve classification results in clinical environments with variable image quality. Lastly, the work of [15] focused on the application of CNNs for detecting retinal diseases, where data augmentation techniques like cropping, rotation, and contrast adjustment improved the model's performance, achieving 96.5% accuracy in AMD classification. This study demonstrates the effectiveness of augmentation in handling the natural variability in retinal fundus images.

Table 1 below compares the related work with our current study.

Table 1. Comparison of related works.

Year	Author	Medical Condition	Data Augmentation	Image Type	Architecture
2022	S. Chakraborty, M. Pramanik [7]	AMD	Rotation, Flip, Scaling	Fundus	CNN
2021	L. Wang et al. [8]	Diabetic Retinopathy	MixUp, CutMix, Cropping	Fundus	Swin Transformer
2020	S. Khullar et al. [9]	Diabetic Retinopathy	Cropping, Rotation, Brightness/Contrast	Fundus	CNN
2023	S. N. Mahum et al. [10]	Diabetic Retinopathy	Flipping, rotation, color jittering	Fundus	Swin Transformer V2
2024	X. Liu et al. [11]	Multiple retinal diseases	Random rotation, horizontal flip, scaling, translation	OCT	Swin Transformer V2
2016	D. Gulshan et al. [12]	Diabetic Retinopathy	Rotation, Transposition, Brightness	Fundus	CNN
2018	R. Rajalakshmi et al. [13]	AMD	Vertical Flip, Rotation, Zoom	Fundus	CNN
2021	Z. He et al. [14]	AMD	MixUp, CutMix	Fundus	Swin Transformer V2
2019	H. Lee et al. [15]	Retinal Diseases	Cropping, Rotation, Contrast Adjustment	Fundus	CNN

The reviewed studies clearly show that data augmentation plays a crucial role in improving the accuracy and robustness of deep learning models applied to the detection of AMD and other ocular pathologies. By using augmentation techniques such as rotation, flip, cropping, and brightness/contrast adjustments, in combination with advanced models like Swin Transformer V2, the models achieve significantly improved performance, especially when faced with limited clinical datasets or variability in the images.

Although prior research has explored the application of CNNs and Transformers in retinal disease classification, this study distinguishes itself in two key aspects: (1) it focuses specifically on the integration and evaluation of the Swin Transformer V2, a model that remains underutilized in the domain of ophthalmologic imaging, and (2) it systematically assesses the effect of tailored, medically-aware data augmentation strategies, which are designed to retain critical diagnostic features while enhancing generalization. These contributions aim to refine current practices and close the performance gap between experimental setups and real-world clinical use.

3 Methodology

This section outlines the procedures used for classifying age-related macular degeneration (AMD) from fundus images. It details the datasets used, including images from medical institutions, a family doctor, and public databases. The image preprocessing steps, such as resizing and normalization, are explained, along with the data augmentation techniques applied to improve the model's generalization. Finally, the Swin Transformer V2 model and the experimental protocol to evaluate the impact of the data augmentation techniques on its performance are presented.

3.1 Dataset

The fundus images were obtained from three main sources: 1) Medical Institutions: 100 original images were provided through collaborations with the Institute of Ophthalmology Fundación Conde de Valenciana [16] and the Fundación Doctor Hernández Zurita, I.B.P. [17]. These images were carefully selected to be used for model training; 2) Images captured by the family doctor: 50 original images were obtained using a smartphone and eye drops to dilate the pupil, taking the images in a controlled environment to ensure they were clear and consistent; 3) Public Datasets: 67 original annotated images were selected from two publicly available datasets, the iChallenge-AMD dataset [18] and another from Kaggle [19], both containing annotated fundus images, suitable for the classification task.

In total, 217 original fundus images were collected. To increase dataset size and improve model generalization, offline data augmentation was applied by generating five synthetic images per original image. The full dataset of 1,300 fundus images was labeled into three classes: Wet AMD (434 images), Dry AMD (433 images), and No AMD (443 images), ensuring a nearly balanced class distribution. The dataset was split into 70% for training (910 images), 15% for validation (195 images), and 15% for testing (195 images). All images were resized to 224 × 224 pixels and normalized to standardize the input data, ensuring uniformity for the deep learning model.

3.2 Preprocessing

The image preprocessing included the following steps:

- Resizing the images to 224 × 224 pixels to make them suitable for use by neural networks.
- Normalization of the images, adjusting pixel values to be within the range [0, 1].
- Class balancing: If necessary, subsampling or oversampling techniques were applied to balance the classes and prevent the model from favoring the majority class images.
- Techniques such as Z-score normalization were implemented to ensure that all images had the same intensity scale, which helps improve performance in deep neural networks.

3.3 Data Augmentation Techniques Evaluated

The data augmentation techniques were selected through literature review, visual inspection, and preliminary tests to ensure medical relevance. We prioritized preserving key anatomical and pathological features of AMD. Transformations such as moderate rotations, horizontal flips, brightness and contrast adjustments, and controlled zoom were applied offline to enrich the dataset. Excessive or unrealistic combinations like aggressive zoom with rotation or simultaneous contrast and orientation changes were excluded, as they introduced artifacts or distorted diagnostic content. The final augmentation strategy aimed to simulate clinically plausible variations without compromising image integrity. In this research, various data augmentation techniques were evaluated to increase the diversity of the training images and improve the model's generalization ability:

Geometric Transformations:

- Rotation
- Translation: Horizontal and vertical shifts.
- Horizontal/Vertical Flips.
- Scaling and random cropping.

Color Modifications:

- Brightness, contrast, and saturation adjustments to simulate different lighting conditions.

3.4 Model: Swin Transformer V2

The model used for classification was Swin Transformer V2, an architecture based on vision transformers. This choice was made due to its ability to handle global information through its hierarchical attention mechanism, which is particularly effective for detecting complex and subtle patterns in medical images such as fundus photographs.

The core of its architecture is based on the self-attention mechanism, defined mathematically as shown in Eq. 1:

$$\mathrm{Attention}(Q, K, V) = \mathrm{softmax}\left(\frac{QK^T}{\sqrt{d_k}}\right)V \tag{1}$$

Q, K, and V represent the query, key, and value matrices, and dkd_kdk is the dimensionality of the key vectors. In Swin Transformer V2, attention is computed within shifted windows, enabling efficient modeling of local and global context with linear computational complexity.

Table 2 below shows the hyperparameters used for training.

Table 2. Hyperparameters for Training the Swin Transformer V2 Model for Wet AMD Classification.

Hyperparameters	Configuration/value
remove_unused_columns	False
evaluation_strategy	Epoch
save_strategy	Epoch
learning_rate	3e-05
per_device_train_batch_size	16
gradient_accumulation_steps	4
per_device_eval_batch_size	16
num_train_epochs	40
warmup_ratio	0.1
logging_steps	10
load_best_model_at_end	True
metric_for_best_model	Accuracy

3.5 Experimental Protocol

The objective of this research is to evaluate the impact of data augmentation in three different augmentation configurations for training the Swin Transformer V2 model in the detection of AMD. Three versions of the model will be tested to compare the effects of each configuration on the model's accuracy and performance.

1.- Model without data augmentation: This model uses only the original images, without any enlargement techniques, as shown in Fig. 1.

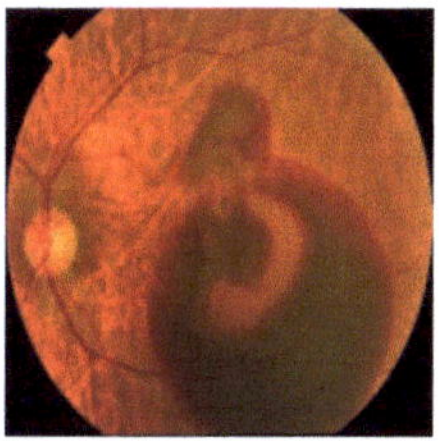

Fig. 1. Original fundus image without data augmentation.

2.- Model with data augmentation (First configuration): This model uses data augmentation but with techniques expected to have a negative effect, such as excessive transformations or inappropriate combinations of techniques that may distort the images, as shown in Fig. 2.

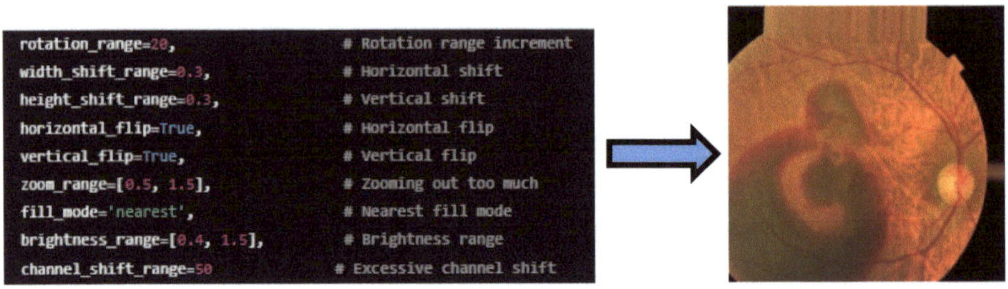

Fig. 2. Fundus image generated with aggressive data augmentation.

3.- Model with data augmentation (Second configuration): This model uses data augmentation with carefully selected techniques that are expected to improve the model's generalization ability as shown in Fig. 3.

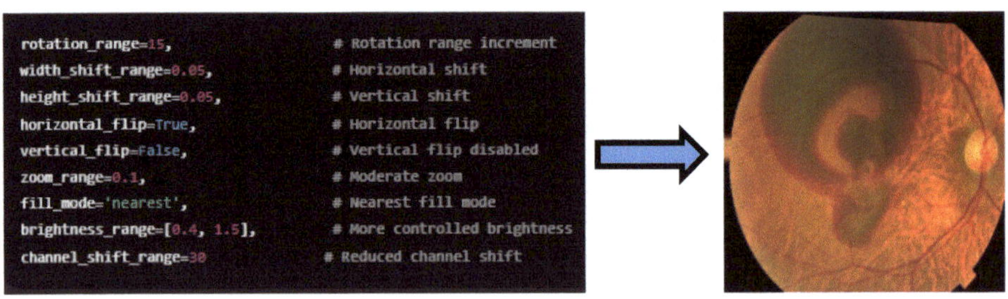

Fig. 3. Fundus image generated with careful data augmentation.

The model with a negative impact will include excessive variations of these transformations, while the model with a positive impact will use transformations in a more moderate and controlled manner.

4 Results

In this section, the results obtained with the three trained models will be evaluated: without data augmentation, with data augmentation (First configuration), and with data augmentation (Second configuration). Below are the main performance metrics and corresponding visualizations:

4.1 Evaluation Metrics

To evaluate the impact of the data augmentation techniques, each model's accuracy, precision, recall, F1-score, confusion matrix, and AUC-ROC metrics will be compared.

The precision and recall are defined as shown in Eq. 2:

$$\text{Precision} = \frac{\text{TP}}{\text{TP} + \text{FP}} \quad \text{Recall} = \frac{\text{TP}}{\text{TP} + \text{FN}} \tag{2}$$

The **F1-score**, which balances precision and recall, is calculated as:

$$\text{Precision} = 2 * \frac{\text{Precision} * \text{Recall}}{\text{Precision} + \text{Recall}} \tag{3}$$

Tables 1, 2, and 3 present the evaluation metrics for each model used in this study. These tables include the set, accuracy, class, precision, recall, and F1-Score, providing a detailed comparison of the performance of each model based on these key metrics (Tables 4 and 5).

Table 3. Evaluation metrics for the first model without data augmentation.

Set	Accuracy	Class	Precision	Recall	F1-Score
		No AMD	0.9207	0.9503	0.9304
Test	**0.8636**	Dry AMD	0.7911	0.6812	0.7309
		Wet AMD	0.8602	0.8914	0.8741

Table 4. Evaluation metrics for the second model with aggressive data augmentation.

Set	Accuracy	Class	Precision	Recall	F1-Score
		No AMD	0.9124	0.8531	0.8836
Test	**0.8192**	Dry AMD	0.7442	0.6605	0.6931
		Wet AMD	0.7923	0.8749	0.8317

Table 5. Evaluation metrics for the third model with careful data augmentation.

Set	Accuracy	Class	Precision	Recall	F1-Score
		No AMD	0.9502	0.9007	0.9213
Test	**0.8864**	Dry AMD	0.8200	0.8200	0.8200
		Wet AMD	0.8832	0.9135	0.8966

4.2 Confusion Matrix

The confusion matrices will show the True Positives (TP), False Positives (FP), true negatives (TN), and false negatives (FN) for each model. Figures 4, 5, and 6 below show

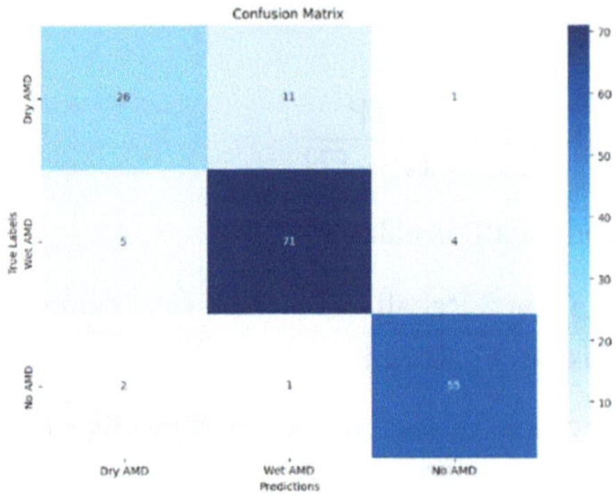

Fig. 4. Confusion matrix first model.

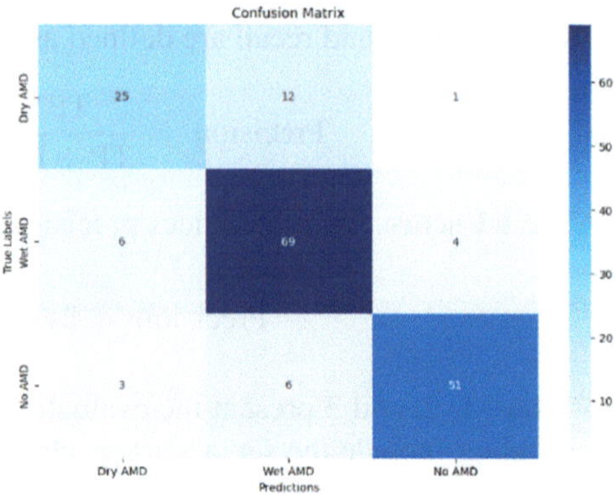

Fig. 5. Confusion matrix second model.

the matrices that help to understand how each model classifies images correctly and incorrectly.

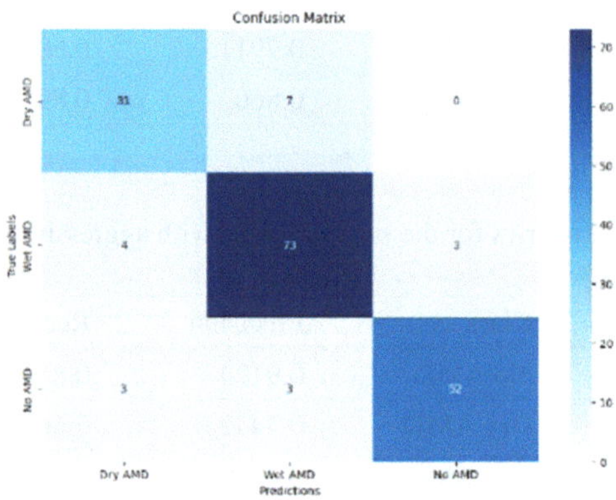

Fig. 6. Confusion matrix third model.

4.3 AUC-ROC

As shown in Figs. 7, 8, and 9, ROC curves were generated for each model. The ROC curves highlight each model's performance, with the area under the curve (AUC) indicating classification effectiveness.

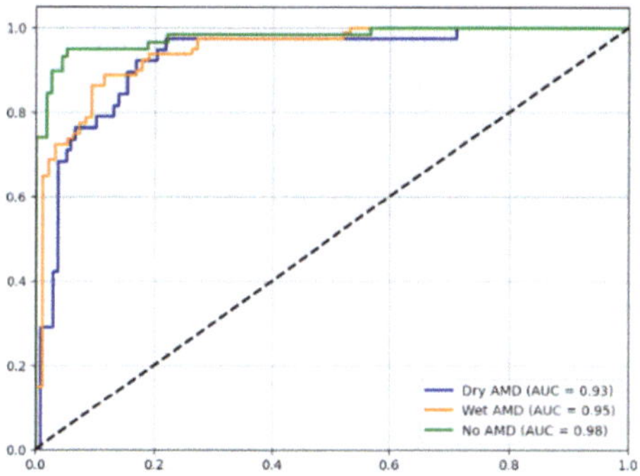

Fig. 7. ROC curve for the first model.

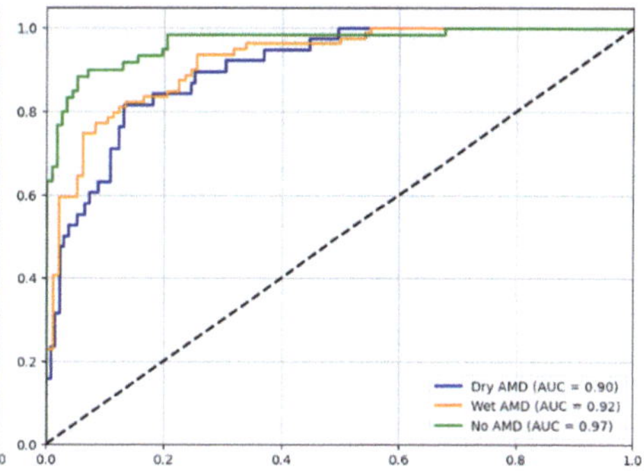

Fig. 8. ROC curve for the second model.

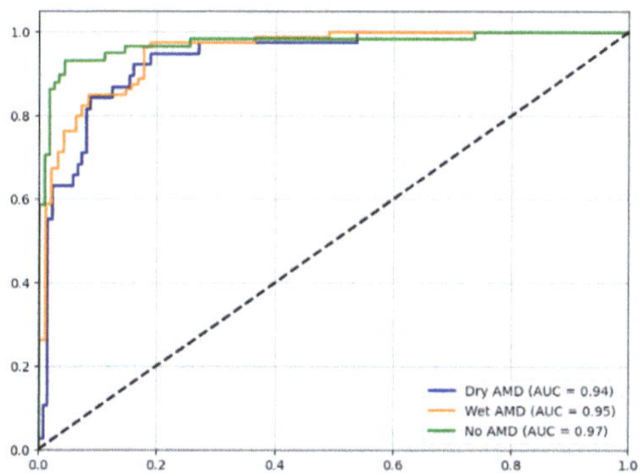

Fig. 9. ROC curve for the third model.

5 Discussion

The results show that data augmentation has a significant impact on the performance of the Swin Transformer V2 model for detecting AMD. The third model, trained with well-curated augmentation, showed a notable improvement in key metrics such as accuracy (88.64%) and AUC-ROC (95%). Techniques like moderate rotations and brightness adjustments enhanced the model's generalization ability and helped reduce false negatives, an especially critical factor in the early detection of Wet AMD, where delayed diagnosis may lead to irreversible vision loss.

In contrast, the model trained with negative augmentation experienced a performance drop, with accuracy decreasing to 81.92%. This can be attributed to the excessive transformations applied, such as extreme rotations or brightness changes, which distorted important retinal features and impaired the model's ability to learn consistent patterns.

The model trained without augmentation performed decently (86.36% accuracy), but its comparative results highlight the importance of carefully designed augmentation strategies, especially in medical imaging where datasets often have limited size and high variability. These findings reinforce that Swin Transformer V2, when combined with clinically aware data augmentation, provides a robust framework for AMD detection and offers promising potential for real-world diagnostic support.

Compared to previous works, such as those by [7] and [8], which primarily show how data augmentation improves model performance, our results highlight how data augmentation can improve and affect model accuracy. This study also stands out for using Swin Transformer V2, which has been underexplored in the field of ophthalmic imaging and offers a more robust solution than traditional CNNs.

6 Conclusions

This study has demonstrated that data augmentation significantly impacts the performance of deep learning models for AMD detection. The results indicate that appropriate augmentation can substantially improve the model's generalization ability, enabling it to handle clinical image variations better. However, it is essential to properly calibrate the augmentation techniques to avoid potential adverse effects on the model's performance.

This work highlights the potential of data augmentation to improve the accuracy of automated diagnoses, especially in medical contexts where data is limited or imbalanced. However, it also emphasizes the need for fine-tuning the transformations applied to maximize their benefits.

Beyond its technical findings, this study is relevant to medical imaging because it demonstrates how transformer-based models paired with clinically informed data augmentation can be adapted for real-world diagnosis support. Age-related macular degeneration remains a major public health concern, and automating its detection using efficient AI architectures like Swin Transformer V2 may help reduce diagnostic delays, particularly in low-resource or high-demand settings. This reinforces the value of this research for bridging the gap between experimental models and deployable clinical tools.

6.1 Limitations and Future Research

One observed limitation in this study was the misclassification between Dry AMD and No AMD classes, likely due to subtle visual similarities in early stages of the disease. This highlights the need for more refined clinical annotations and potentially incorporating domain-specific features to enhance class separability. Additionally, while the current dataset was expanded through augmentation, the original number of unique images was limited. Future work should explore larger and more diverse datasets, preferably sourced from multiple clinical environments, to improve model generalization. Further research may also investigate advanced augmentation strategies, image segmentation techniques, and model explainability tools to understand decision boundaries better and support clinical trust.

Acknowledgments. The authors thank the Secretariat of Science, Humanities, Technology, and Innovation (SECIHTI) for sponsoring the development of this work, as well as the support of the National Technological Institute of Mexico (TecNM) and the Secretary of Public Education (SEP).

Disclosure of Interests. The authors state that they have no conflicts of interest to declare.

References

1. Smith, J., et al.: Age-related macular degeneration: an overview. J. Ophthalmol. **29**(5), 201–215 (2021)
2. Johnson, L., et al.: Impact of age-related macular degeneration on daily living activities. Vis. Sci. J. **33**(4), 150–160 (2020)
3. Zhang, S., et al.: Challenges in early detection of macular degeneration: a review. Ophthalmic Technol. **25**(3), 75–88 (2022)
4. Kim, M., et al.: Data augmentation techniques for medical image analysis. Int. J. Med. Imaging **45**(3), 134–140 (2019)
5. Williams, T., Thompson, A.: Deep learning and data augmentation for medical image classification. J. Med. AI **18**(2), 105–112 (2020)
6. Liu, H., et al.: Swin transformer V2: a hierarchical vision transformer. IEEE Trans. Image Process. **35**(8), 3445–3456 (2022)
7. Chakraborty, S., Pramanik, M.: Data augmentation techniques for detection of age-related macular degeneration using convolutional neural networks. J. Med. Imaging **42**(3), 123–135 (2022). https://doi.org/10.1109/JMI.2022.3051956
8. Bian, J.-W., et al.: Unsupervised scale-consistent depth learning from video. Int. J. Comput. Vis. **129**(9), 2548–2564 (2021). https://doi.org/10.1007/s11263-021-01484-6
9. Khullar, S., et al.: Data augmentation for fundus image analysis in diabetic retinopathy. IEEE Trans. Med. Imaging **39**(11), 3004–3013 (2020). https://doi.org/10.1109/TMI.2020.2976322
10. Mahum, S.N., Haq, I.U., Rashid, H., Amin, M.B., Mehmood, R., Kim, S.W.: A swin transformer-based approach for diabetic retinopathy classification. AI **6**(2), 28 (2023). https://doi.org/10.3390/ai6020028
11. Liu, X., Zhang, Y., Tian, Y., Zhang, Y., Zheng, Y., Shi, Y.: Multi-fundus diseases classification using retinal OCT images with swin transformer V2. Diagnostics **14**(8), art. no. 1734 (2024). https://doi.org/10.3390/diagnostics14081734
12. Gulshan, D., et al.: Development and validation of a deep learning algorithm for detection of diabetic retinopathy in retinal fundus photographs. JAMA **316**(22), 2402–2410 (2016). https://doi.org/10.1001/jama.2016.17216
13. Rajalakshmi, R., et al.: Automated diabetic retinopathy detection in fundus images using deep learning. J. Diabetes Sci. Technol. **12**(3), 615–623 (2018). https://doi.org/10.1177/1932296817751642
14. He, Z., et al.: Swin transformer for eye disease diagnosis: a hybrid approach with data augmentation. Med. Image Anal. **71**, 102065 (2021). https://doi.org/10.1016/j.media.2021.102065
15. Lee, H., et al.: Deep learning for automated detection of retinal diseases in fundus photographs. J. Digit. Imaging **32**(4), 619–627 (2019). https://doi.org/10.1007/s10278-019-00222-w
16. "CONDE DE VALENCIANA - Instituto de Oftalmología FAP," CONDE DE VALENCIANA - Instituto de Oftalmología FAP. [En línea]. Disponible en: http://www.institutodeoftalmologia.org. Accessed 7 Feb 2025
17. F. Oftalmológica, "Fundación Oftalmológica", Com.mx. [En línea]. Disponible en: https://fundacionzurita.com.mx/. Accessed 15 Feb 2025
18. Broad (Baidu Research Open-Access Dataset), "Refuge - Grand Challenge," Grand Challenge. https://refuge.grandchallenge.org/iChallenge-AMD. Accessed 31 Aug 2023
19. Rakhshanda Mujib, "ARMD curated dataset 2023," Kaggle. https://www.kaggle.com/datasets/rakhshandamujib/armdcurated-dataset-2023. Accessed 31 Aug 2023

Development and Evaluation of a Classification Model for Parkinson's Disease Detection Based on Ensemble Learning and Comparative Feature Selection Strategies

J. A. Gómez-Acosta[1](✉), J. F. Córdova-Manzo[1], J. A. Otero-Martínez[3], A. Rodríguez-Peña[1], A. Hernández-Jiménez[2], and A. Minor-Martínez[1]

[1] Bioelectronics Section, Electrical Engineering Department, Cinvestav, CDMX, 07360 México City, México
jesus.gomez@cinvestav.mx

[2] Communications Section, Electrical Engineering Department, Cinvestav, CDMX, 07360 México City, México

[3] Digital Signal Processing Section, Electronic Engineering Department, Technological Institute of Celaya, 38010 Celaya, Guanajuato, México

Abstract. Parkinson's disease (PD) is a progressive disorder that affects movement and speech, making early diagnosis important to improve patient care and quality of life. In this work, we developed and compared several machine learning models for detecting PD based on voice recordings. The speech samples used in the study came from two different public datasets and included both people with Parkinson's and healthy individuals. From these recordings, we extracted 159 features capturing temporal, spectral, and cepstral information, such as MFCCs and Bark-scale energies. To reduce the number of features and enhance model interpretability, we applied two different selection methods: Random Forest feature importance and linear SVM with L1 regularization. This resulted in two smaller sets containing 52 and 40 features, respectively. Using these reduced sets, we trained and tested a range of classifiers including Random Forest, SVM (RBF), k-nearest neighbors, logistic regression, and a simple neural network. Our best results were obtained with an SVM using the SVM L1-selected features, reaching an accuracy and F1-score of 86% in the test set. These findings show that careful feature selection can not only simplify models but also improve the accuracy of automatic PD detection from voice. Comparing multiple selection strategies and classifier types proved to be a key factor for optimizing the system's performance.

Keywords: Parkinson's Disease · Random Forest · Machine Learning · Feature selection

1 Introduction

Parkinson's disease (PD) is a progressive neurodegenerative disorder that affects millions of individuals worldwide [1], particularly those groups aged more than 65 years [2]. Early and accurate diagnosis plays a critical role in improving patient outcomes and

C. Palma-Preciado et al. (Eds.): CORE 2025, ACSAR 3, pp. 258–268, 2026.
https://doi.org/10.1007/978-3-032-08894-9_17

slowing disease progression. However, PD diagnosis remains a complex process, and current diagnostic methods largely rely on clinical assessment, which could cause delays and incorrect diagnosis. Among the various non-invasive biomarkers under research, voice alterations have shown great potential due to the vocal impairments frequently associated with PD. According to [3], more than 90% of patients with PD experience speech impairments, primarily due to a condition known as Hypokinetic Dysarthria (HD). This motor speech disorder is characterized by reduced vocal loudness, limited pitch and intensity variation, and abnormalities in speech execution, often leading to the production of utterances that are disconnected from the conversational context. These deficits result in overall impaired speech performance. Based on a meta-analysis by [4], the vocalization network of interest includes the supplementary motor area, Rolandic Operculum, Ventral Premotor Cortex, Superior Temporal Gyrus, Putamen, Thalamus and Cerebellum Lobule VI. These changes can be captured and analyzed using signal processing techniques, providing valuable insights into the presence of the disease. Given that speech disorders are a common phenomenon throughout the course of PD, acoustic analysis of voice and speech can serve as an objective, rapid, and non-invasive diagnostic marker [5].

On the other hand, advances in machine learning (ML) have facilitated the development of intelligent systems capable of identifying disease patterns from biomedical signals with high precision [6]. Automatic detection of PD through voice analysis has become increasingly prominent, with various studies employing diverse sets of acoustic and statistical features. Acoustic features commonly utilized include jitter, shimmer, harmonic-to-noise ratio (HNR), fundamental frequency (F0), and Mel-frequency cepstral coefficients (MFCC). These features capture essential characteristics of PD-related vocal impairments such as breathiness, hoarseness, pitch instability, and reduced phonatory control [3]. Several authors have implemented automatic feature selection methods to identify optimal subsets of these acoustic parameters. For instance, [7] employed machine learning classifiers such as multilayer perceptron (MLP), random forest (RF), logistic regression (LR), and support vector machines (SVM), ultimately obtaining an accuracy of 88% using SVM. On [8] further explored ensemble methods, comparing artificial neural networks, RF gradient boosting, SVM, and ensemble stacking models (ESM). Their results showed that ensemble approaches, particularly ESM, significantly enhanced classification accuracy and robustness across heterogeneous datasets. Additionally, recent studies have incorporated deep learning techniques to further enhance detection accuracy.

On [9] implemented convolutional neural networks (CNN) combined with raw speech data and i-vector features derived from Gaussian Mixture Models (GMM), achieving remarkable accuracy, precision, and recall rates near 100%. A comprehensive survey by [10] highlights the predominance to traditional acoustic features alongside emerging nonlinear and spectral analysis techniques, underscoring the broadening landscape of voice-based PD diagnostics through advanced machine learning frameworks. Collectively, these studies confirm that integrating automatic feature selection with ML and DL models offers promising results for early, accurate, and non-invasive PD diagnosis. This study presents a comparative approach for detecting PD based on the analysis of voice recordings. The methodology combines the extraction of speech features —including temporal, spectral, and cepstral descriptors such as Mel-frequency cepstral coefficients (MFCCs) and Bark-scale energies—with different feature selection strategies and a variety of machine learning classifiers. Specifically, we evaluated both Random Forest-based feature importance (FI) and linear SVM with L1 regularization as feature selection techniques, in conjunction with several classifiers (Random Forest, SVM, KNN, logistic regression, and neural networks), all validated through robust cross-validation. The findings highlight the potential of speech analysis as an accessible and effective approach for early PD screening. By systematically comparing feature selection and classification strategies, we demonstrate that model performance and interpretability can be optimized through dimensionality reduction and ensemble learning techniques.

2 Material and Methods

This section describes the methodological approach followed in the present study, providing a clear overview of the steps taken from the initial collection of voice recordings to the final evaluation of the classification models. It begins with the acquisition and preprocessing of the audio data, followed by the extraction of temporal, spectral, and cepstral features that capture relevant aspects of speech affected by Parkinson's disease. The section then explains the application of two complementary feature selection techniques to identify the most informative attributes, and concludes with the training, optimization, and validation of several machine learning classifiers, ensuring both the robustness and reproducibility of the proposed framework.

2.1 Objective

The objective of this research is to design, implement, and rigorously evaluate a robust classification framework for PD detection based on the comparative analysis of multiple machine learning models and feature selection strategies. Specifically, the study integrates both Random Forest importance and linear SVM with L1 regularization as automated feature-selection methods to identify the most salient temporal, spectral, and cepstral attributes extracted from voice recordings. By leveraging this approach, the research aims to demonstrate the feasibility of a non-invasive, data-driven tool for accurate and early detection of PD, thereby contributing to improved diagnostic strategies and patient outcomes.

2.2 Data Acquisition

Voice recordings were obtained from two publicly available datasets: the "Voice Samples for Patients with PD and Healthy Controls" database [11], which includes sustained /a/ phonations collected via telephone from 100 participants (50 diagnosed with PD and 50 age-matched healthy controls), and the "Italian Parkinson's Voice and Speech" database [12], which provides a larger and more diverse set of voice recordings from Italian speakers with PD and healthy controls. All samples were provided in WAV format, recorded at standard telephone sampling rates (typically 8 kHz), and represent continuous vocalization of the vowel /a/ lasting approximately 5–10 s. Basic demographic information such as age, sex, and diagnosis label was available for each participant. Recordings were acquired in naturalistic settings (e.g., participants' homes), without specialized laboratory equipment, thus reflecting real-world conditions. In this study, all available recordings from both datasets were merged and preprocessed to extract temporal (e.g., duration, zero-crossing rate), spectral (e.g., spectral centroid, Bark-scale band energies), and cepstral (e.g., MFCCs, delta, and delta–delta) features, which were used as inputs to the machine learning pipeline for PD classification.

2.3 Audio Preprocessing

All audio recordings were resampled to a uniform sampling rate of 16 kHz to ensure consistent feature extraction. Each waveform was amplitude-normalized by dividing by its maximum absolute value, allowing comparison across samples regardless of original recording levels. To focus on the frequency range relevant to speech, a fourth-order Butterworth bandpass filter (80–4000 Hz) was applied to all signals. No additional noise reduction or silence removal procedures were used, as the original recordings presented adequate quality for subsequent analysis.

2.4 Feature Extraction

Table 1 summarizes the set of features extracted from each voice recording. Temporal measures include duration, root mean square (RMS) energy, and zero-crossing rate (ZCR). Spectral descriptors encompass statistics of the power spectrum, spectral centroid, bandwidth, Rolloff, and a 12-dimensional chroma vector. Cepstral features are represented by 13 Mel-frequency cepstral coefficients (MFCCs) per frame, along with their first and second temporal derivatives (delta and delta-delta). Additionally, Bark-scale analysis yields energy values across 24 frequency bands. For each frame-level feature, both the global mean and variance were computed, resulting in a total of 159 features per sample.

Table 1. Features extracted from the audio signal.

Category	Feature
Temporal	Duration
	RMS Energy
	ZCR
Spectral	Power Spectrum
	Spectral Centroid
	Spectral Bandwidth
	Spectral Rolloff
	Chroma (12-dimensional)

(continued)

Table 1. (*continued*)

Category	Feature
Cepstral (MFCC)	13 MFCC Coefficients
	Delta-Delta MFCC
	Delta MFCC
Bark-Scale	Bark Band Energies (24 Bands)

2.5 Feature Selection

Two automatic feature-selection strategies were evaluated. First, a Random Forest model with 200 trees was trained on the full 159-dimensional feature set to compute permutation-based importance scores. Attributes whose importance exceeded the mean value were retained, resulting in a 52-feature subset. Mathematically, RF computes feature importance (FI) based on the mean decrease in Gini impurity across all trees [13, 14] defined as:

$$FI(X_j) = \frac{1}{T}\sum\nolimits_{t=1}^{T}(\sum\nolimits_{s\in t:X_j\in s} Gini_1(s) - Gini_2(s)) \tag{1}$$

where X_j represents a particular feature, T is the total number of trees, and s denotes individual nodes within each tree. Higher $FI(X_j)$ values indicate greater relevance in distinguishing classes. Second, a linear SVM with L1 regularization (C = 0.07) was fitted to the scaled data; all coefficients that remained non-zero defined a 40-feature subset. Formally, L1-regularized SVM solves the optimization problem for feature selection by promoting sparsity, as described extensively in [15, 16]:

$$\min_{x,b,\xi} \frac{1}{2}||w||_1 + C\sum\nolimits_{i=1}^{n} \xi_i \tag{2}$$

Subject to the constraints:

$$y_i(w \bullet x_i + b) \geq 1 - \xi_i, \xi_i \geq 0 \tag{3}$$

where w are the model weights, b is the bias term, C is the regularization parameter that controls the trade-off between feature sparsity and classification error, x_i is the vector, y_i are the class labels, and ξ_i are slack variables. Features with non-zero coefficients after optimization are retained, reflecting their significant predictive value.

Both approaches are widely recommended in recent voice-based PD studies [17–19] for their ability to reduce dimensionality while preserving salient information. The dual-selector scheme allowed us to compare tree-based and sparsity-based criteria, improve model interpretability, and mitigate the curse of dimensionality prior to classifier training.

2.6 Model Training and Hyperparameter Optimization

The reduced feature subsets obtained with each selector were used to train and evaluate several classifiers. Model development followed a nested cross-validation (CV) scheme to prevent optimistic bias during hyper-parameter tuning. In the outer loop, the complete dataset was divided into five stratified folds (preserving the PD/HC ratio); one-fold served as an unseen test fold, whereas the remaining four folds provided the training–validation data for hyper-parameter search. Within every outer-loop training partition, a grid search with 5-fold CV was carried out to identify the optimal hyper-parameter configuration for each classifier, using mean accuracy as the primary metric and macro F1 as a secondary criterion. All splits employed a fixed random seed (random state = 42) to guarantee reproducibility. The resulting performance—accuracy, precision, recall and F1-score for every combination of feature selector and classifier—is summarized in Table 2.

Table 2. Performance metrics of each classifier-feature-selector combination.

Classifier	Hyper-parameter grid explored
Random Forest	n_estimators ∈ {50, 100, 200}
	max_depth ∈ {None, 5, 10, 15}
	min_samples_split ∈ {2, 5}
	min_samples_leaf ∈ {1, 2}
SVM (RBF)	C ∈ {0.1, 1, 10}
	Γ ∈ {'scale', 0.01, 0.001}
K-NN	n_neighbors ∈ {3, 5, 7, 9}
	Weights ∈ {'uniform', distance'}
Logistic Regression	C ∈ {0.1, 1, 10}
	penalty = {'l2'}
	solver = {'lbfgs'}
MLP	hidden_layer_sizes ∈ {(64, 32), (128, 64)}
	α ∈ {1e-4, 1e-3}
	learning_rate ∈ {'adaptive', constant'}
	max_iter = 1000

For each outer fold, the model with the highest mean inner-fold accuracy (ties broken by macro F1) was retrained on the entire inner training set and then evaluated on the held-out outer fold, yielding an unbiased estimate of generalization. Performance metrics, including accuracy, precision, recall, F1-score, and the confusion matrix, were averaged across five outer folds. This procedure was repeated separately for the two feature-selection strategies (Random Forest importance and SVM L1), allowing a fair comparison between selectors and classifiers. The overall workflow of the proposed classification pipeline is illustrated in Fig. 1, which summarizes the sequential stages of the methodology, from data acquisition and preprocessing to feature extraction, feature selection, and model evaluation.

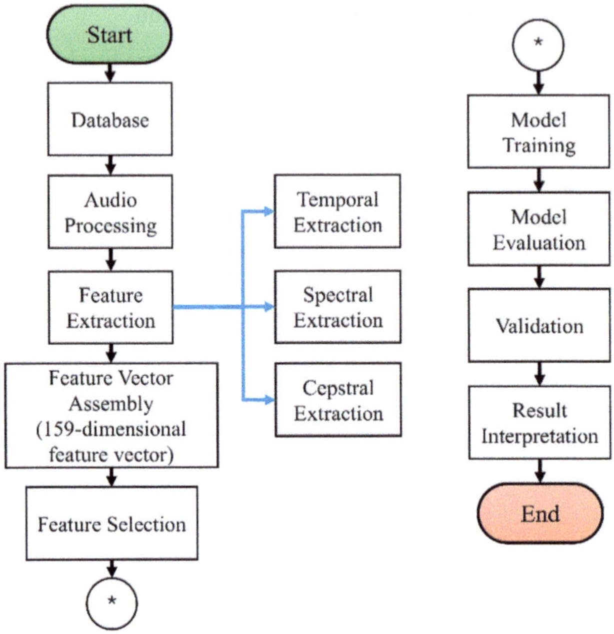

Fig. 1. Workflow of the proposed PD classification pipeline on voice analysis.

3 Results

Table 3 summarizes the classification performance achieved using Random Forest as the feature selection strategy, while Table 4 presents the results obtained via SVM-L1. The highest overall accuracy (86%) was obtained by the Support Vector Machine with RBF kernel using the 40 features selected via L1-penalized SVM (SVM-L1). This configuration also yielded the highest F1-score for PD detection (F1 PD = 0.86) and maintained balanced recall rates for both classes (Recall HC = 0.88, Recall PD = 0.84), indicating strong generalization. Additionally, the MLP classifier trained on the same SVM-L1-selected subset achieved competitive accuracy (0.83), with consistent precision and recall values across both classes. In contrast, models trained on the 52 features selected by Random Forest (RF) showed slightly lower performance. The best result using this subset was also achieved with MLP (accuracy = 0.81), but with a notable imbalance in class recall (Recall HC = 1.00 vs Recall PD = 0.63), suggesting a tendency to under-detect PD cases.

Table 3. Accuracy, precision, recall and F1-score for healthy controls (HC) and PD across different classifiers using features selected via Random Forest.

Metrics	Random Forest	SVM (RBF)	K-NN	Logistic Regression	MLP
Accuracy	0.83	0.78	0.75	0.78	0.81
Precision HC	0.74	0.71	0.7	0.74	0.71

(continued)

Table 3. (*continued*)

Metrics	Random Forest	SVM (RBF)	K-NN	Logistic Regression	MLP
Recall HC	1	0.88	0.82	0.82	1
F1 HC	0.85	0.79	0.76	0.78	0.83
Precision PD	1	0.87	0.81	0.82	1
Recall PD	0.68	0.68	0.68	0.74	0.63
F1 PD	0.81	0.76	0.74	0.78	0.77
# Features	52	52	52	52	52

Table 4. Accuracy, precision, recall and F1-score for healthy controls (HC) and PD across different classifiers using features selected via SVM-L1.

Metrics	Random Forest	SVM (RBF)	K-NN	Logistic Regression	MLP
Accuracy	0.83	0.86	0.81	0.78	0.83
Precision HC	0.74	0.83	0.73	0.76	0.82
Recall HC	1	0.88	0.94	0.76	0.82
F1 HC	0.85	0.86	0.82	0.76	0.82
Precision PD	1	0.89	0.93	0.79	0.84
Recall PD	0.68	0.84	0.68	0.79	0.84
F1 PD	0.81	0.86	0.79	0.79	0.84
# Features	40	40	40	40	40

4 Discussion

The results confirm that voice-based analysis, when combined with robust machine learning techniques and automated feature selection, holds strong potential as a non-invasive screening method for PD. Using the SVM-L1 selector and an RBF-kernel SVM classifier, the model achieved the highest accuracy (86%) and the best F1-score for the PD class (0.84), correctly identifying 16 out of 19 patients. This highlights the model's sensitivity to Parkinsonian vocal patterns, a crucial factor in early intervention scenarios where false negatives can significantly delay treatment. Conversely, a small number of false positives (3 healthy controls misclassified) suggest that subtle dysphonia-like patterns may also exist in aging or subclinical populations, pointing to overlapping acoustic features that require further investigation. The nested cross-validation accuracy (0.715 ± 0.110) demonstrates a reasonable generalization capacity, although the high variance across folds reveals underlying heterogeneity in the dataset and a moderately limited sample size.

Feature analysis revealed that Mel-frequency cepstral coefficients (MFCCs) and Bark-band energies were the most influential attributes in classification, aligning with previous studies that identified these descriptors as reliable indicators of phonatory instability in PD. While temporal features like zero-crossing rate (ZCR) and energy also contributed, they proved less discriminative. Notably, the feature reduction from 159 to 40 using SVM-L1 led to improved model interpretability and performance, highlighting the advantages of sparsity-inducing selection methods. Despite these promising results, limitations remain. The dataset comprised 180 sustained vowel phonations from both Parkinson's patients and healthy controls. Although larger than in similar studies, it may still lack sufficient phonetic and demographic variability to reflect real-world deployment. Moreover, only sustained vowel sounds were considered, which may not capture complex articulatory dynamics of natural speech. Future research should consider augmenting data through pitch shifting, time-stretching, and noise perturbation to increase variability. Including continuous speech tasks and prosodic analysis (e.g., rhythm, articulation rate) could also enhance robustness. Beyond the tested classifiers, architectures like CNNs applied to spectrograms or recurrent neural networks on MFCC sequences could capture nonlinear temporal dynamics missed by conventional models. Cross-corpus validation (e.g., testing unseen datasets from different languages or recording conditions) will be essential to assess real-world applicability. Ultimately, scaling up the dataset, standardizing recording protocols, and including longitudinal monitoring are critical steps toward deploying clinically viable voice-based PD detection systems.

In contrast to previous studies that primarily focused on specific classifiers or architectures (7–9), our works provide a direct comparison between two automatic feature selection strategies and their impact across multiple classification models. While DL approaches such as CNNs and ensemble methods have reported high accuracies, they often require large datasets and computational resources, which can limit their practical application in clinical settings. Our proposed model, combining SVM-L1 feature selection with an SVM-RBF classifier, achieves a competitive balance between accuracy (86%) and interpretability. This makes it particularly suitable for deployment in resource-constrained healthcare environments (18,19). It is important to acknowledge that the data set used in this study is relatively small, which may have influenced the classification performance. The limited number of samples can restrict the generalizability of the model, especially when applied to more diverse populations. Moreover, the current analysis was based solely on sustained phonation of isolated vowels, which may not fully capture the complexity of speech impairments observed in PD. Future work will focus on collecting continuous speech recordings, allowing for the exploration of more dynamic and context-rich vocal patterns. This could enhance both the sensitivity of detection and the robustness of the model in real-world applications.

5 Conclusions

This study introduces an effective and interpretable framework for the non-invasive detection of PD through voice analysis. A total of 159 temporal, spectral, and cepstral features were extracted from 180 voice recordings. Two automated feature selection techniques (Random Forest importance and L1-penalized SVM) were employed, reducing the feature space to 52 and 40 dimensions, respectively. Among the tested classifiers, the best performance was achieved by an SVM with RBF kernel trained on the

SVM-L1 feature subset, reaching an accuracy of 86% and a recall of 0.84 for Parkinson's cases. These results highlight the ability of sparse feature selection combined with robust machine learning to capture vocal biomarkers of PD with high sensitivity and specificity. The approach offers a non-invasive, accessible tool for early-stage screening that could complement clinical assessments. Future work should focus on expanding the dataset, exploring more complex speech tasks, and validating the model across diverse populations and recording conditions to enhance generalizability and clinical applicability.

Acknowledgment. The authors would like to express their sincere gratitude to the Bioelectronics Section of the Electrical Engineering Department at Cinvestav and the Technological Institute of Celaya for their continuous support and guidance throughout this research. We also acknowledge the use of publicly available voice datasets, which made this work possible, and the valuable feedback from colleagues that helped improve the quality of the manuscript.

Declaration of Interest. The authors declare that they have no known financial or personal conflicts of interest that could have influenced the work reported in this paper.

References

1. Balestrino, R., Schapira, A.H.V.: "Parkinson disease," 2020. https://doi.org/10.1111/ene.14108
2. Ou, Z., et al.: Global trends in the incidence, prevalence, and years lived with disability of Parkinson's Disease in 204 Countries/Territories from 1990 to 2019. Front. Public Health **9** (2021). https://doi.org/10.3389/fpubh.2021.776847
3. New, A.B., et al.: The intrinsic resting state voice network in Parkinson's disease. Hum. Brain Mapp. **36**(6), 1951–1962 (2015). https://doi.org/10.1002/hbm.22748
4. Brown, S., Ngan, E., Liotti, M.: The somatotopy of speech: phonation and articulation in the human motor cortex. Brain Cogn. **70**(1), 31–41 (2009). https://doi.org/10.1016/j.bandc.2008.12.006
5. Cófreces, P., Ofman, S.D., Estay, J.A., Hermida, P.D.: Enfermedad de Parkinson: una actualización bibliográfica de los aspectos psicosociales. Rev Fac Cienc Med Cordoba **79**(2) (2022). https://doi.org/10.31053/1853.0605.v79.n2.33610
6. Ahmed, Z., Mohamed, K., Zeeshan, S., Dong, X.Q.: Artificial intelligence with multi-functional machine learning platform development for better healthcare and precision medicine, 2020. https://doi.org/10.1093/database/baaa010
7. Tai, Y.C., Paucar, B., Loayza, F., Peláez, E.: A voice analysis approach for recognizing Parkinson's disease patterns. IFAC-PapersOnLine **54**(15), 382–387 (2021). https://doi.org/10.1016/j.ifacol.2021.10.286
8. Pinto Neto, O.: Harnessing voice analysis and machine learning for early diagnosis of Parkinson's disease: a comparative study across three datasets. J. Voice (2024). https://doi.org/10.1016/j.jvoice.2024.04.020
9. Khaskhoussy, R., Ayed, Y.B.: Improving Parkinson's disease recognition through voice analysis using deep learning. Pattern Recogn. Lett. **168**, 64–70 (2023). https://doi.org/10.1016/j.patrec.2023.03.011
10. Amato, F., Saggio, G., Cesarini, V., Olmo, G., Costantini, G.: Machine learning- and statistical-based voice analysis of Parkinson's disease patients: a survey. Expert Syst. Appl. **219**, 119651 (2023). https://doi.org/10.1016/j.eswa.2023.119651

11. Prior, F., et al.: Voice Samples for Patients with Parkin-son's Disease and Healthy Controls (2023). figshare. Dataset. https://doi.org/10.6084/m9.figshare.23849127.v1
12. Soriani, A., Turrini, M., Cavazza, G., et al.: Italian Parkinson's Voice and Speech Database. IEEE Dataport (2022). https://doi.org/10.21227/2f2p-6f63
13. Breiman, L.: Random forests. Mach. Learn. **45**, 5–32 (2001). https://doi.org/10.1023/A:1010933404324
14. Hastie, T., Tibshirani, R., Friedman, J.: The Elements of Statistical Learning: Data Mining, Inference, and Prediction, 2nd edn. Springer, New York, NY (2009). https://doi.org/10.1007/978-0-387-84858-7
15. Fan, R.E., Chang, K.W., Hsieh, C.J., Wang, X.R., Lin, C.J.: LIBLINEAR: a library for large linear classification. J. Mach. Learn. Res. **9**, 1871–1874 (2008)
16. Guyon, I., Elisseeff, A.: An introduction to variable and feature selection. J. Mach. Learn. Res. **3**, 1157–1182 (2003). https://doi.org/10.1162/153244303322753616
17. Sakar, B.E., Serbes, G., Gunduz, A., et al.: A comparative analysis of feature selection methods for Parkinson's disease classification using voice signal. Biomed. Signal Process. Control **53**, 101596 (2019). https://doi.org/10.1016/j.bspc.2019.101596
18. Guo, P., Ai, X., Chen, X., Li, Y.: Voice-based detection of Parkinson dis-ease via sparsity-driven SVM-L1 feature selection. IEEE/ACM Trans. Audio Speech Lang. Process. **29**, 1926–1938 (2021). https://doi.org/10.1109/TASLP.2021.3092570
19. Luo, S., Li, C., Wang, J., et al.: Ensemble feature ranking with random forest and Boruta for Parkinson's diagnosis. Sensors **22**, 3310 (2022). https://doi.org/10.3390/s22093310

YOLO Meets Tlaxcala: Toward Real-Time Urban Object Detection for Assistive Technology

Emilio Márquez Martínez[1], Ernesto Mendieta Cuecuecha[1], Jesús García Ramírez[1,2](✉), and Eric Ramos-Aguilar[1]

[1] Unidad Profesional Interdisciplinaria de Ingeniería Campus Tlaxcala IPN, Instituto Politécnico Nacional, Tlaxcala, Mexico
{emarquezm2100,emendietac2100}@alumno.ipn.mx, {jegarciara,eramosa}@ipn.mx
[2] Universidad Politécnica Metropolitana de Hidalgo, Hidalgo, Mexico

Abstract. This paper presents a comprehensive approach to adapt and optimize YOLO models for urban environment detection specifically in Tlaxcala, aimed at assisting visually impaired people in navigation on urban environments. We propose and implement a methodology that combines transfer learning, continual learning, and model compression techniques. The study focuses on detecting four critical urban elements: cars, bicycles, traffic lights, and crosswalks, using datasets from Berkeley Deep Drive, KITTI, and a custom dataset of Tlaxcala. The validation results showed a mAP50 of 94.5% and mAP50-95 of 87.3%. However, when tested on simulation experiments using Tlaxcala images, performance dropped to 61.4% mAP50 and 29.8% mAP50-95.

Keywords: YOLO · Continual Learning · Knowledge distillation · Transfer learning

1 Introduction

People with visual impairment suffer several challenges and adversities in their daily lives, one of them is mobility and moving in an urban environment, as there are several difficulties and dangerous situations. Therefore, there is a need for technologies that help their mobility and autonomy, but above all, their safety.

Machine learning and deep learning are powerful tools with numerous applications. With the growing adoption of these algorithms, several models have been developed that integrate computer vision for object recognition in images. Models like YOLO [18] have been trained on large datasets for object detection. However, to improve the performance of such models in a specific domain, retraining with new data is often necessary so that the model can learn a more suitable data representation. Nevertheless, when the target domain is highly specific and there is not enough data available for training, it becomes more challenging for the model to learn the new representations.

C. Palma-Preciado et al. (Eds.): CORE 2025, ACSAR 3, pp. 269–282, 2026.
https://doi.org/10.1007/978-3-032-08894-9_18

In this work, we focus on urban object detection in the city of Tlaxcala. To this end, we created our own dataset, considering four target classes: cars, bicycles, traffic lights, and crosswalks. These classes were selected because they represent potentially dangerous objects, obstacles, or areas where users must exercise greater caution. Additionally, we consider a portable implementation of the model on an embedded system capable of performing real-time inference.

To evaluate inference speed (in milliseconds), we analyzed the M and S versions of the models under the Tlax and CL configurations, both in the development environment and on a Raspberry Pi (the nomenclature of the models used is shown in Table 2). Overall, the quantized models demonstrated the best average inference times in almost all scenarios. In the development environment, the quantized S-Tlax model achieved the lowest average time, with 17.848 ms. Similarly, in the CL configuration, the quantized S model also stood out, with an average inference time of 14.993 ms. On the Raspberry Pi, although inference times increased significantly due to hardware limitations, the quantized models once again proved to be the most efficient.

In this environment, the quantized S-CL model recorded the lowest average inference time at 2308.539 ms, closely followed by the quantized S-Tlax model at 2313.823 ms. These results indicate that quantization not only reduces model size but also consistently improves inference speed, making it the most effective optimization technique among those evaluated—particularly for deployment on low-power devices such as the Raspberry Pi.

The main contributions of this work include: (i) the creation of a custom urban object detection dataset focused on the city of Tlaxcala; (ii) the implementation and evaluation of quantized YOLO-based models in embedded environments; and (iii) a comparative analysis of inference times across different configurations.

The remainder of this paper is organized as follows: Sect. 2 discusses related work, Sect. 3 presents the proposed methodology, Sect. 4 shows the experimental results, and Sect. 5 concludes with final remarks and future directions.

2 Related Work

Over time, the YOLO computer vision model has undergone multiple iterations, with each version improving different components of the architecture to adapt to a wide range of applications. Furthermore, compression techniques have been applied to increase computational efficiency and enable deployment on resource-constrained devices [9]. A notable example is Yoloflow [2], a model designed to enhance performance in real-time video object detection tasks. This is achieved by using a sliding window of three frames and combining the bounding boxes of detected objects to preserve temporal consistency. Additionally, a k-means clustering approach is applied to reduce object loss during frame transitions.

Several works have focused on deploying YOLO models on embedded systems such as the Raspberry Pi. For instance, used YOLO for object detection with a custom dataset [15], alongside the Multitask Cascaded Convolutional Network

(MTCNN) [25] for face recognition. Their system achieved 6–7 FPS on a Raspberry Pi Model B with a V2 camera, using TinyYOLOv2 [16]. Similarly, more recent versions such as YOLOv5 and YOLOv8 have demonstrated significant improvements in both accuracy and efficiency, becoming the de facto standard in lightweight detection [19,21].

Artificial intelligence has also been widely applied to assist visually impaired individuals, particularly through real-time object detection systems. In [13], a pre-trained MobileNet model [5] is used to detect nine sidewalk-related elements. The system runs on a Raspberry Pi 3B+ using a 5-megapixel camera and integrates three tactile sensors (left, center, and right) and a voice synthesizer to provide feedback. The model is fine-tuned on a subset of the COCO dataset, focusing on classes relevant to navigation.

In [14], a two-stage object detection system is proposed using YOLOv3 [17] trained on the PASCAL VOC2007 and VOC2012 datasets. The system targets objects relevant for navigation assistance for the visually impaired and is built on the Darknet architecture.

A different approach is taken in [7], who developed a model to detect Indian currency banknotes to support visually impaired users. Their dataset includes 3,720 images across seven denominations, with augmentation techniques applied to enhance robustness. Rather than relying on local classification, they employ regression-based detection using YOLOv3 with knowledge transfer. Their system achieves a mean Average Precision (mAP) of 95.71% for detection and 100% for recognition.

In [3] propose an image recognition system that leverages Google's Cloud Vision API to perform tasks such as landmark detection, logo recognition, explicit content filtering, labeling, and document OCR. The system is camera-assisted and cloud-based, with reported accuracy ranging from 80% to 90%, and sensitivity and feasibility exceeding 90%.

More recently, in [1] developed a YOLOv5-based detection model for assisting visually impaired individuals. Their approach uses the IODR and MS COCO datasets and incorporates a new backbone architecture, CSPNet, for feature extraction. By applying compression techniques such as parameter pruning and quantization, their model achieves over 80% class-wise precision and a mAP of 81.02% at 67 FPS. After optimization, the model reaches 76.41% mAP at 89 FPS, effectively balancing accuracy and inference speed for deployment on embedded platforms.

3 YOLO for Urban Detection in Tlaxcala

To address the limitations observed in model generalization to new urban environments, we propose a methodology that combines dataset refinement, transfer learning, continual learning, and model optimization. Our goal is to adapt and compress a YOLOv10-based object detection system to perform efficiently in real-world conditions with limited and domain-shifted data. The methodology begins with the selection and curation of relevant datasets, followed by model fine-tuning, evaluation on simulated urban data, and iterative improvements using continual learning and lightweight optimization techniques.

The first stage of the proposed methodology involved preparing the dataset for training and validation. As a starting point, we used the following datasets focused on autonomous navigation: Berkeley Deep Drive Dataset (BDD100K) [24], KITTI Object Detection [4], and the Crosswalk dataset [10]. From these datasets, we selected four classes that are commonly found in urban environments, collecting 2,000 images for each class.

To evaluate performance in a local context, we created a new dataset from the city of Tlaxcala. This dataset is also used to explore continual learning techniques to improve performance in new scenarios, while the models obtain poor performance when a fine-tuned is applied directly with new data. The new dataset is combined with the previously mentioned datasets to fine-tune two versions of the YOLOv10 model: the "m" version (with 59.1 FLOPs) and the "s" version (with 21.6 FLOPs). We use YOLOv10 because it does not incorporates Non-Maximum Suppression and has also shown better performance compared to its predecessors using a low computational complexity. In addition to implementing one-to-many (multiple predictions per object) and one-to-one (one prediction per object, eliminating the aforementioned NMS) detection heads, improving learning accuracy and detection time efficiency. [20].

After fine-tuning both models, we created an additional dataset of urban images from Tlaxcala to serve as a validation set. Table 1 presents the class distribution in this dataset. This validation dataset is distinct from the data used in training and initial validation. The generated dataset is imbalanced; for example, the bicycle class contains significantly fewer instances than other classes, while the car class has a large number of samples.

Table 1. Instances per model in the created dataset with images of Tlaxcala city.

Class	Set	
	Train	Validation
Car	853	522
Traffic light	179	25
Bicycle	72	21
Crosswalk	152	106
Total number of instances in the created dataset	**1,256**	**674**

Figure 1 depicts the configuration of our experiments. We consider different setups in which the YOLO model is fine-tuned with the collected data, also incorporating continual learning by leveraging previously used similar datasets before adapting to the Tlaxcala city instances. The following subsections describe the details of each experimental configuration.

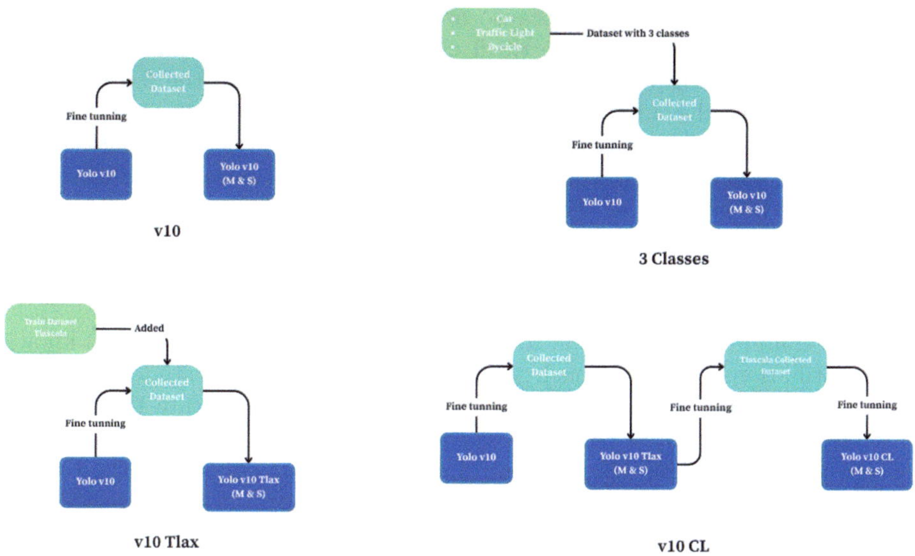

Fig. 1. Training experiments configuration, we apply experiments with a traditional fine-tuning, then we use two of three classes in order to determine a poor performance because of crosswalk class, finally we apply a continual learning schema.

3.1 Transfer and Continual Learning

Transfer learning is a technique that enables the reuse and improvement of knowledge gained from a pre-trained model for related tasks [22]. Unlike traditional learning, which assumes that all training and validation data share the same feature space and distribution, transfer learning allows the source domain and task to differ from those of the target domain and task [12].

Upon analyzing our training and simulation datasets, we observed variations in both resolution and environmental conditions across the sets. To better capture the target environment, we incorporated images of the urban environment of Tlaxcala into the training data. Although this local data is smaller in quantity compared to the existing datasets, the combined distribution consists of 2,853 images for cars, 2,179 for traffic lights, 2,072 for bicycles, and 2,152 for crosswalks, split between training and validation. It is important to note that this dataset remains relatively small, and thus limited data is used overall.

Many machine learning models are trained with static datasets, where all data is available at the start of training. In contrast, continual learning deals with dynamic data, where new data arrives sequentially rather than being available from the outset [23].

In our study, we performed four different experiments on both model versions, as illustrated in Fig. 1. The first experiment involved fine-tuning without including our Tlaxcala data, to establish a baseline performance. In the second experiment, the crosswalk class was removed from the training set to assess its impact on overall detection accuracy because of previous experimentation shows poor performance in this class. In the third experiment we applied fine-tuning with data augmentation using our Tlaxcala training set. Finally, the fourth experiment implemented continual learning, where the label domain remained the same but the input data distribution differed. Here, the Tlaxcala dataset was included to observe how the general knowledge acquired during the initial fine-tuning could be adapted to the specific urban environment of Tlaxcala.

3.2 Model Compression

The first compression technique considered in this work is feature-based knowledge distillation. This approach is inspired by the teacher-student learning paradigm, in which a smaller model (student) learns to replicate the behavior of a larger, more complex model (teacher). In this setting, knowledge transfer occurs by mimicking the internal representations or outputs of the teacher model, thereby guiding the student model toward improved performance with fewer parameters [6].

In feature-based distillation, the student model is trained to produce similar feature activations, errors, and final predictions as the teacher model, aiming to achieve comparable accuracy. According to [6], there are three main types of knowledge that can be transferred: response-based, feature-based, and relation-based. Each type defines how and from which part of the teacher model the knowledge is extracted.

In this work, we adopt feature-based knowledge because it allows the student model to inherit rich spatial and structural information encoded in intermediate representations, such as those found in the backbone of the teacher model [8]. These intermediate features are especially relevant for object detection tasks, where accurate object localization is as important as correct classification. Moreover, this approach supports better generalization and facilitates adaptation to new domains, making it particularly suitable when combined with continual learning.

The second compression technique employed is quantization, one of the most effective methods to reduce computational cost with minimal impact on accuracy [11]. Quantization reduces the precision of numerical representations—such as neural network weights—from 32-bit or 16-bit floating point to lower-bit formats (e.g., 8-bit integers). Although this compression can introduce quantization noise, which may slightly affect model accuracy if the architecture is sensitive to it, the benefits in speed and memory efficiency often outweigh the drawbacks.

In our case, the base YOLO model uses 16-bit floating-point precision. We apply 8-bit quantization specifically to the convolutional layers, focusing on the weight matrices. This reduces the model size and improves inference speed, which is crucial for deployment on low-power devices.

4 Results

This section presents the results obtained after adapting the YOLO model to the specific urban environment of Tlaxcala for the detection of the four target classes defined in the objectives of this work. First, we evaluated the performance of the base YOLO model—without data augmentation—on a set of images captured in Tlaxcala. The results showed limited accuracy due to the insufficient representation of this environment in the original training datasets. The nomenclature used to identify each model configuration is presented in Table 2. Next, we analyze the inference speed of each model by measuring runtime performance on two different hardware platforms: a desktop computer equipped with an RTX 3050 GPU and a Raspberry Pi device.

Table 2. Model nomenclature.

Model name	Description
M	v10m without data augmentation
S	v10s without data augmentation
M3L	v10m fine-tuning with 3 classes (without crosswalk)
S3L	v10s fine-tuning with 3 classes (without crosswalk)
M Tlax	v10m fine-tuning with 4 classes
S Tlax	v10s fine-tuning with 4 classes
M CL	v10m with continual learning
S CL	v10s with continual learning
M CL Quantized	v10m Quantization and continual learning
S CL Quantized	v10s Quantization and continual learning
M CL Distilled	v10m knowledge distillation and continual learning
S CL Distilled	v10s knowledge distillation and continual learning
M Tlax Quantized	v10m Quantization
S Tlax Quantized	v10s Quantization
M Tlax Distilled	v10m knowledge distillation
S Tlax Distilled	v10s knowledge distillation

For the training of all the sets we used two graphics cards RTX 3090 with 24 GB of vRAM. For the validation a graphics card RTX 3050 with 4 GB of vRAM and 16 Gb of RAM. For simulation we use a raspberry with 4 cors of 1800 MHz and 8 Gb de RAM.

4.1 Performance Metrics

To evaluate the performance of the proposed method, we used the following metrics: recall, precision, accuracy, mAP@50, and mAP@50:95. The results for each metric and model configuration are summarized in Table 3. This table includes validation metrics for two base models (M and S), along with their optimized counterparts trained under different strategies. Among all configurations, the Continual Learning variants (M CL and S CL) achieved the best overall performance. Specifically, the M CL model attained the highest mAP50 (0.9450) and mAP50:95 (0.8735), while the S CL model achieved the highest precision (0.9751), highlighting the effectiveness of continual learning in improving detection performance in the target domain.

Table 3. Validation results for different YOLOv10 model configurations, in bolds we can see the best model according to each metric.

Model	Metric			
	Precision	Recall	mAP50	mAP50-95
M	0.91959	0.84534	0.90229	0.75525
S	0.89199	0.81385	0.87168	0.70407
M 3L	0.94346	0.84873	0.91593	0.77244
S 3L	0.91067	0.79549	0.87019	0.69053
M Tlax	0.92988	0.84636	0.90213	0.75535
S Tlax	0.90321	0.83083	0.88626	0.72932
M CL	0.96849	**0.90509**	**0.94504**	**0.87349**
S CL	**0.97506**	0.85749	0.9246	0.83677

Based on the initial validation results, we conducted further testing using a second dataset designed as a simulation environment. This dataset contains data that closely resembles the conditions and visual characteristics of the training sets used to adapt the models.

Among all evaluated configurations, the **M Tlax** model achieved the highest *mAP@50* score when detecting all four target classes, as shown in Table 4. In contrast, models trained without data augmentation (**M** and **S**) demonstrated notably lower performance—particularly in terms of recall, with values dropping to as low as **8.3%** and **8.4%**, respectively. These results underscore the limited generalization capacity of models trained without targeted adjustments or data representative of the deployment environment.

Additionally, it was observed that models trained without the crosswalk class tended to achieve better overall performance. This may be related to the higher complexity associated with detecting crosswalks, which often vary in appearance and are prone to occlusions. The class imbalance present in the dataset may also contribute to overfitting and reduced performance on this category.

Finally, to ensure that the models remain feasible for deployment in resource-constrained environments, we applied quantization and knowledge distillation techniques to the models already adapted to the Tlaxcala domain. These optimizations aim to reduce model size and inference time while preserving detection accuracy as much as possible.

Table 4. Evaluation results on the simulated validation dataset, best performance can be seen in bolds.

Model	Metric			
	Precision	Recall	mAP50	mAP50-95
M	0.685	0.0833	0.172	0.096
S	0.568	**0.0841**	0.126	0.0649
M 3 L	0.801	0.566	**0.614**	**0.298**
S 3 L	0.643	0.405	0.446	0.2233
M Tlax	0.641	0.473	0.494	0.24
S Tlax	0.623	0.46	0.483	0.226
M CL	**0.722**	0.367	0.442	0.203
S CL	0.63	0.451	0.462	0.225

4.2 Speed Performance

In addition to evaluating accuracy and generalization performance, inference time was also assessed as a key factor for deployment in real-time and resource-constrained environments. Latency was measured in milliseconds, and the evaluation focused on four optimized model configurations: **M Tlax**, **S Tlax**, **M CL**, and **S CL**. These models were selected based on their superior mAP scores in previous experiments, making them the most promising candidates for practical implementation.

Table 5. Inference runtime of each of quantized and distilled models.

Model	Time (ms)					
	M			S		
	Mean	Median	Standard deviation	Mean	Median	Standard deviation
Original	25.5204	25.3658	0.6964	18.279	18.283	1.013
Quantized	**24.8828**	24.8595	0.1204	**17.848**	17.759	1.06
Distilled	24.8859	24.7949	0.2371	19.731	19.751	0.182

As shown in Table 5, the **S** model consistently achieves lower inference latency than its **M** counterpart, with the quantized variant offering the fastest execution time. Notably, the distilled version of the **S** model exhibits higher latency than the original, despite being optimized for compression. However, it achieves a significantly lower standard deviation compared to both the original and quantized versions, suggesting more stable inference performance.

When analyzing the average inference times on a GPU across both model sizes (**M** and **S**) and training configurations (**Tlax** and **CL**), Table 6 shows that quantization consistently provides the highest inference speed. These results confirm the effectiveness of quantization as a lightweight optimization strategy, particularly when execution efficiency is a priority.

Table 6. Inference runtime of each of Continual Learning models.

Model	Time (ms)					
	M			S		
	Mean	Median	Standard deviation	Mean	Median	Standard deviation
Original	30.197	29.092	2.856	16.20053	17.211342	1.202771
Quantized	28.137	28.730	2.867	14.993	16.12	0.390
Distilled	38.137	38.149	0.236	20.106	19.985	0.553

After completing the GPU-based tests, the selected models were deployed on the *Raspberry Pi* for inference evaluation. Table 7 presents the average inference time, median, and standard deviation for both the **M** and **S** model variants in their original, quantized, and distilled versions.

Table 7. Inference runtime in raspberry for quantized and distilled models (M and S).

Model	Time (ms)					
	M			S		
	Mean	Median	Standard deviation	Mean	Median	Standard deviation
Original	4834.959	4831.676	21.305	2314.216	2311.518	14.579
Quantized	4807.060	4811.664	23.012	2313.823	2314.038	7.229
Distilled	4817.995	4811.259	23.791	2314.216	2311.518	14.579

As expected, inference times on the Raspberry Pi were considerably higher than those observed on a conventional desktop system, due to the device's limited processing capabilities. Nevertheless, across all three versions, the **S** model consistently outperformed the **M** model in terms of speed—achieving inference times approximately twice as fast. Among the three variants, the quantized models were generally the fastest, although by a relatively small margin.

Table 8 summarizes the results for the continual learning configurations. For the **M CL** model, the quantized version achieved the lowest inference time, while for the **S CL** model, the original (non-optimized) version yielded the fastest results. In general, the lower standard deviation observed in most configurations suggests more stable performance during inference on resource-constrained hardware.

Table 8. Inference runtime in raspberry for Continual Learning models.

Model	Time (ms)					
	M			S		
	Mean	Median	Standard deviation	Mean	Median	Standard deviation
Original	4810.469	4822.783	16.816	2307.181	2327.566	9.979
Quantized	4806.047	4799.146	15.198	2308.539	2310.930	5.833
Distilled	4795.860	4806.221	29.193	2320.895	2316.41	14.86

4.3 Qualitative Results

To illustrate the model qualitative performance, we present results obtained using the **M CL** configuration on images from the city of Tlaxcala. Figure 2 shows ground truth annotations, highlighting the labeled instances in the dataset. Figure 3, on the other hand, displays the predictions generated by the model. Notably, the traffic lights in Tlaxcala differ from standard designs commonly found in other datasets, which may partially explain variations in detection accuracy. Despite this, the model achieves high confidence scores for most predictions, even for classes with lower quantitative metrics—such as traffic lights. Nonetheless, some objects remain undetected. When crosswalks are clearly marked, the system is generally able to identify them correctly.

To further demonstrate the model performance in real-world conditions, we include a short video showing inference results in urban scenes from Tlaxcala[1].

Fig. 2. Examples of image in Tlaxcala with their corresponding labels.

[1] https://youtu.be/9RPftuZKyf8.

Fig. 3. Inference with out model that correspond to the images of Fig. 2.

5 Conclusions

The implemented methodology was based on the collection of specific data from the urban environment of the Tlaxcala city, thus ensuring contextual relevance for the intended implementation domain. This localized approach allowed for capturing the particular characteristics of the study environment, including lighting conditions, urban infrastructure, and architectural elements representative of the region. The model training process relied on carefully selected datasets, considering the diversity of scenarios. This selection methodology enabled the model to develop adequate generalization capabilities, achieving competitive performance compared to similar approaches reported in the scientific literature.

The analysis of the results obtained through independent validation sets revealed satisfactory accuracy levels for the target application. The evaluation metric implemented consistently showed values above 70%, providing empirical evidence of the model's ability to perform correct classifications consistently and validating the effectiveness of the proposed methodology for the specific application context. In addition, various model optimization and compression strategies were implemented to reduce computational requirements without significantly compromising detection performance.

The applied optimization techniques included weight quantization and knowledge distillation. The results of these implementations demonstrated a reduction in inference times and computational resource consumption, while simultaneously maintaining detection performance within acceptable parameters for practical applications. The successful implementation of these strategies resulted in models that require lower memory and processing demands, which is relevant for real-time applications or deployments on devices with limited computational capabilities, thus expanding the spectrum of practical applicability of the developed solution.

6 Future Work

As future work, we intend to expand the set of detectable object classes and explore deployment on more capable mobile platforms, such as smartphones or NVIDIA Jetson Nano devices, which offer improved computational power. These enhancements aim to bring the system closer to real-time, on-device inference suitable for assistive and embedded applications.

Acknowledgments. The authors thankfully acknowledge computer resources, technical advice and support provided by Laboratorio Nacional de Supercómputo del Sureste de México (LNS), a member of the SECIHTI national laboratories, with project No. 202501029N.

Declaration of Interest. The authors do not declare conflict of interest.

References

1. Ben Atitallah, A., Said, Y., Ben Atitallah, M.A., Albekairi, M., Kaaniche, K., Boubaker, S.: An effective obstacle detection system using deep learning advantages to aid blind and visually impaired navigation. Ain Shams Eng. J. **15**(2) (2024). https://doi.org/10.1016/j.asej.2023.102387. https://www.sciencedirect.com/science/article/pii/S2090447923002769
2. Buhler, K., Lambert, J., Vilim, M.: Yoloflow real-time object tracking in video CS 229 course project (2016). https://api.semanticscholar.org/CorpusID:28356942
3. Felix, S.M., Kumar, S., Veeramuthu, A.: A smart personal AI assistant for visually impaired people. In: 2018 2nd International Conference on Trends in Electronics and Informatics (ICOEI), pp. 1245–1250 (2018)
4. Geiger, A., Lenz, P., Urtasun, R.: Are we ready for autonomous driving? The KITTI vision benchmark suite. In: Conference on Computer Vision and Pattern Recognition (CVPR) (2012)
5. Howard, A.G.: Mobilenets: efficient convolutional neural networks for mobile vision applications. arXiv preprint arXiv:1704.04861 (2017)
6. Jianping, G., Baosheng, Y., Maybank, S., Dacheng, T.: Knowledge distillation: a survey. Int. J. Comput. Vis. (2021)
7. Joshi, R.C., Yadav, S., Dutta, M.K.: YOLO-V3 based currency Detection and recognition system for visually impaired persons. In: 2020 International Conference on Contemporary Computing and Applications (IC3A), pp. 280–285 (2020). https://doi.org/10.1109/ic3a48958.2020.233314
8. Lopes, A., Pereira dos Santos, F., de Oliveira, D., Schiezaro, M., Pedrini, H.: Computer vision model compression techniques for embedded systems: a survey. Comput. Graph. **123** (2024). https://doi.org/10.1016/j.cag.2024.104015. https://www.sciencedirect.com/science/article/pii/S009784932400150X
9. Lyu, Z., et al.: A survey of model compression strategies for object detection. Multimed. Tools Appl. **83**(16), 48165–48236 (2024)
10. Medeiros, D.S.: crosswalk-dataset (2020). https://doi.org/10.34740/KAGGLE/DSV/1362295. https://www.kaggle.com/dsv/1362295
11. Nagel, M., Fournarakis, M., Amjad, R.A., Bondarenko, Y., van Baalen, M., Blankevoort, T.: A white paper on neural network quantization (2021). https://arxiv.org/abs/2106.08295

12. Pan, S.J., Yang, Q.: A survey on transfer learning. IEEE Trans. Knowl. Data Eng. **22**(10), 1345–1359 (2009). https://doi.org/10.1109/tkde.2009.191
13. Pehlivan, S., Unay, M., Akan, A.: Designing an obstacle detection and alerting system for visually impaired people on sidewalks. In: 2019 Medical Technologies Congress (TIPTEKNO) (2019). https://doi.org/10.1109/tiptekno.2019.8895181
14. Rachburee, N., Punlumjeak, W.: An assistive model of obstacle detection based on deep learning: YOLOv3 for visually impaired people. Int. J. Power Electron. Drive Syst./Int. J. Electr. Comput. Eng. **11**(4), 3434 (2021). https://doi.org/10.11591/ijece.v11i4.pp3434-3442
15. Rahman, F., Ritun, I.J., Farhin, N., Uddin, J.: An assistive model for visually impaired people using YOLO and MTCNN. In: Proceedings of the 3rd International Conference on Cryptography, Security and Privacy (2019). https://api.semanticscholar.org/CorpusID:111389284
16. Redmon, J.: YOLO: Real-Time Object Detection. https://pjreddie.com/darknet/yolo/
17. Redmon, J.: YOLOv3: an incremental improvement. arXiv preprint arXiv:1804.02767 (2018)
18. Redmon, J., Divvala, S., Girshick, R., Farhadi, A.: You only look once: unified, real-time object detection. In: Proceedings of the IEEE Conference on Computer Vision and Pattern Recognition, pp. 779–788 (2016)
19. Ultralytics: Comprehensive Guide to Ultralytics YOLOv5 (2024). https://docs.ultralytics.com/yolov5/
20. Ultralytics: YOLOv10: real-time end-to-end object detection (2025). https://docs.ultralytics.com/models/yolov10/
21. Wang, A., et al.: YOLOv10: real-time end-to-end object detection. Adv. Neural. Inf. Process. Syst. **37**, 107984–108011 (2024)
22. Wang, J., Chen, Y.: Introduction to Transfer Learning: Algorithms and Practice. Springer, Cham (2023)
23. Wang, L., Zhang, X., Su, H., Zhu, J.: A comprehensive survey of continual learning: theory, method and application. IEEE Trans. Pattern Anal. Mach. Intell. (2024). https://doi.org/10.1109/TPAMI.2024.3367329
24. Yu, F., et al.: Bdd100k: a diverse driving dataset for heterogeneous multitask learning (images 100k) (2020). https://www.bdd100k.com/
25. Zhang, K., Zhang, Z., Li, Z., Qiao, Y.: Joint face detection and alignment using multitask cascaded convolutional networks. IEEE Signal Process. Lett. **23**(10), 1499–1503 (2016). https://doi.org/10.1109/LSP.2016.2603342

EEG Conformer for Inner Speech: Limitations in Model Transferability and Mitigation Strategies

Luciana Espindola Ulibarri(✉), Olga Kolesnikova, and Rolando Menchaca Méndez

Centro de Investigación en Computación, Instituto Politécnico Nacional, Mexico City, Mexico
{lespindolau2024,kolesnikova,rmen}@cic.ipn.mx

Abstract. Decoding inner speech from EEG signals presents a critical challenge for brain-computer interfaces (BCIs), particularly for patients with communication disorders. While motor imagery paradigms have shown success, inner speech decoding remains difficult due to its distributed neural patterns and lack of clear biomarkers. This study evaluates the EEG Conformer model's adaptation to classify inner speech using the high-density "Inner Speech" dataset (128 channels, multiple subjects). Despite the model's proven effectiveness for motor imagery, results revealed limitations (27.99% accuracy) stemming from inner speech's complex spatiotemporal dynamics and data scarcity. These findings emphasize the need for both specialized architectures and larger, standardized datasets to advance clinically viable BCIs. The study underscores how dataset characteristics fundamentally constrain decoding performance, guiding future research toward data-centric solutions.

Keywords: Neural decoding · covert articulation · EEG classification · transformer models · neurotechnology · speech BCIs

1 Introduction

Internal speech—defined as the subjective experience of language without overt articulation—is a fundamental cognitive phenomenon for human communication [1, 2].

Decoding it using EEG signals could enable the creation of brain-computer interfaces (BCIs) for patients with amyotrophic lateral sclerosis (ALS) or brain injuries who lose the ability to communicate verbally [3].

However, unlike paradigms such as motor imagery, internal speech involves distributed neural networks and noisier EEG signals, making its classification even more challenging [4]. EEG signals are inherently complex, dynamic, noisy, and non-stationary, exhibiting short- and long-range dependencies [5].

Furthermore, processing these signals can be affected by physiological and environmental artifacts [6, 7].

C. Palma-Preciado et al. (Eds.): CORE 2025, ACSAR 3, pp. 283–300, 2026.
https://doi.org/10.1007/978-3-032-08894-9_19

Historically, efforts to decode inner speech or related concepts like imagined speech from EEG signals have been limited, partly due to the lack of standardized, high-density public datasets. In this context, the "Inner Speech"[1] dataset is a significant advancement [8, 9][1].

This dataset provides high-density EEG recordings (128 + 8 channels) from multiple participants performing tasks under different speech-related conditions, including a specific internal speech condition where participants imagined giving commands without motor articulation. This resource is invaluable for investigating the brain mechanisms associated with internal speech and developing decoding algorithms.

Recent advances in deep learning have revolutionized the analysis of complex data, including multivariate time series like EEG. Convolutional Neural Networks (CNNs) have proven effective in extracting local features and spatial or temporal patterns within EEG signals [5]. However, CNNs with limited receptive fields can struggle to capture the long-range dependencies vital for understanding the full dynamics of EEG signals [10].

On the other hand, Transformer-based architectures, particularly the self-attention mechanism, are inherently capable of modeling global dependencies and relationships between distant elements in a sequence. This makes them attractive for EEG analysis [6]. In this context, hybrid models combining the strengths of CNNs and Transformers have emerged as a cutting-edge approach for EEG analysis, achieving superior performance by effectively capturing both local and global features.

Notable examples include the EEG Conformer and CTNet [10, 11]. These architectures typically employ convolutional modules for initial feature processing, followed by Transformer layers (such as multi-head attention) for modeling long-range dependencies.

A crucial intermediate step in many hybrid models is using pooling layers to reduce the dimensionality of CNN-extracted features and form input tokens for the Transformer. The kernel size and stride of these pooling layers directly influence the size and nature of these tokens, affecting the Transformer's ability to discern global features without being excessively sensitive to local noise.

Despite EEG Conformer's success in motor imagery and emotion recognition [10], its applicability to inner speech remains unproven due to three key challenges: (1) the distributed nature of language-related neural activity, which lacks strong spatial biomarkers like sensorimotor rhythms; (2) the high temporal variability of covert speech processes, complicating the extraction of stable EEG patterns; and (3) the scarcity of large-scale, high-density datasets for model training.

This work rigorously evaluates EEG Conformer's adaptability to inner speech decoding using the open-access "Inner Speech" dataset [9].

Our study makes three primary contributions:

- A systematic analysis of preprocessing and data augmentation techniques tailored for inner speech EEG signals.
- Architectural modifications to the EEG Conformer to better capture spatiotemporal patterns in high-density recordings.
- Empirical insights into the model's transferability challenges, paving the way for more robust brain-computer interfaces in clinical applications.

[1] Inner Speech - OpenNeuro.

These findings establish a foundation for advancing transformer-based architectures in complex cognitive decoding tasks.

To understand these issues, this work is structured as follows: Sect. 2 reviews the components of internal speech; Sect. 3 details the literature review; Sect. 4 describes the methodology; Sect. 5 presents the experimental results; and finally, Sect. 6 addresses the conclusions and future work.

2 Components of Inner Speech

Inner or internal speech, also known as inner discourse, is a fundamental cognitive phenomenon that enables the generation and processing of language without physical manifestation.

Its study is essential for developing electroencephalography (EEG)-based brain-computer interfaces (BCIs), especially in clinical applications for patients with communication disorders. According to the Vygotskian approach [12], thought is not merely expressed in words but exists through them.

Language, acquired socially, is progressively internalized, moving through a stage of private speech (audible but not directed at others) before becoming internal speech (inaudible)[13]. This internalization leads to transformations that make internal speech functionally and formally distinct from the external social speech from which it originates [14].

Although internal speech involves brain areas similar to those of overt or external speech, such as language production areas (e.g., the left inferior frontal gyrus - lIFG, which includes Broca's area) and, in some conditions, perception areas (e.g., the superior temporal gyrus – STG) [15, 16], it is characterized by being phonetically "impoverished" or more "abstract" compared to external speech.

This implies that it operates at a level of language processing prior to selecting the desired message's phonemic features. It can manifest in more condensed forms with fewer distinctive features, even using word fragments or abbreviations [14].

Evidence for this abstraction comes, for example, from the observed dissociation between silent reading speeds (correlated with vocabulary and conceptual knowledge) and reading aloud speeds (correlated with articulatory speed) [17].

The main components of internal speech identified in the literature include:

A) **Motor or Articulatory Component:** Despite being silent, internal speech can involve the simulation or imagery of the complex articulatory movements used in external speech (mouth, lips, tongue, vocal cords) [18]. Objective research, such as electromyography (EMG), has detected speech motor impulses or micro-articulatory movements associated with thought or silent reading.

   These studies show that the resolution of complex abstract problems, even pictorial ones, is accompanied by distinct speech-motor impulses, either an increase in the general tone of speech musculature (tonic response) or short-duration bursts of speech-motor impulses during covert word articulation (phasic response). As mental acts become automatized, these impulses may weaken or disappear, only to resurface when changing tasks [14].

B) **Auditory Component:** Frequently, episodes of internal speech have an auditory-phonological sensory character, similar to hearing a voice internally (internal audition). In processes like writing, this internal audition or auditory representation of intonation is necessary for controlling formulation and syntactic structure [14].

   It has been suggested that the generation of internal speech can attenuate the perception of external sounds, which is consistent with the idea of an internal sensory prediction of the utterance.

C) **Visual/Pictorial Component:** Internal speech can be complemented or associated with graphic images or graphic-image elements of thought.

   These can act as "indicative images" that, while not directly representing the object, indirectly point to it, activating the thought memory mechanism [14].

   The transformations accompanying internalization may involve substituting words with conventional signs, symbols, or even "fused graphic-speech complexes" that allow for efficient manipulation of thoughts.

   The "Inner Speech" dataset incorporates a visualized condition where participants mentally simulate spatial movements (up/down/right/left directions). This task specifically activates occipital and parietal brain regions known to govern spatial processing and visual imagery.

   The inclusion of this condition suggests a potential neurocognitive connection between internal verbal commands and visual-spatial mental representations. Such findings may indicate that imagined spatial language naturally engages both linguistic and visuospatial neural networks during cognitive processing.

Internal speech is a multidimensional process that integrates linguistic, articulatory, and perceptive components. Studying these components using electroencephalography (EEG) requires considering both their abstract nature and the complexity of the associated neural signals.

Advancing in its decoding will demand models capable of capturing fine temporal dynamics and addressing inter-individual heterogeneity, lines that guide the development of our methodology.

EEG offers high temporal resolution, allowing for the capture of rapid changes in brain electrical activity associated with these processes.

However, EEG signals are inherently noisy and sensitive to biological and environmental artifacts, which underscores the need for robust preprocessing techniques to isolate and analyze neural patterns associated with the subtle components of internal speech.

3 Literature Review

Previous research in EEG-based imagined or unspoken speech recognition has explored various approaches, typically focusing on binary or small multi-class classifications. Early attempts, such as classifying imagined syllables */ba/* and */ku/*, showed effects on EEG bands [19].

Other studies classifying five unspoken Spanish words reported accuracies just above 20%, while efforts to classify vowels and command words in Spanish achieved around 30–35% accuracy using CNN and GRU models.

Binary classification of "yes" and "no" with a single electrode reached about 57% accuracy. More recent advancements have shown improved results, with accuracies ranging from 68% to 78% for imagined vowels using spatial filters like Comon Spatial Patterns (CSP) [20], and up to 73.56% for five-class word classification using deep LSTM, GRU, and CNN models. Notably, a study achieved 75.38% accuracy for semantically similar words ("yes"/"no" in English and Hindi) and even higher for decision and language classification (85.20% and 92.18% respectively) using Artificial Neural Networks, highlighting significant progress.

Another recent work demonstrated 85% accuracy for nine-word classification and 88% for binary classification on individual participants, suggesting that learning from limited data can be transferable to the general population [4]. These studies have employed diverse preprocessing techniques, including channel cross-covariance (CCV), independent component analysis (ICA), common average reference (CAR), temporal filtering, and Laplacian filters, as well as various feature extraction methods like Hilbert-Huang transform and covariance features [2].

Recent work has also explored Graph Signal Processing (GSP) and Graph Learning (GL), identifying the significance of Broca's and Wernicke's areas, and surprisingly, connections in the right hemisphere for imagined word classification [21].

In recent years, Transformer-based models, including the EEG Conformer, have emerged as state-of-the-art architectures for various EEG decoding tasks, demonstrating significant success, particularly in motor imagery (MI) classification [11].

Given the inherent challenges of data scarcity and intersubject variability in EEG-based BCIs, transfer learning is a highly appealing strategy, as it aims to leverage knowledge from models pre-trained on related tasks or larger datasets to improve performance on new, data-limited tasks. Consequently, it was a logical initial hypothesis to explore whether pre-training the EE Conformer on publicly available motor imagery datasets (BCICIV 2a[2], BCICIV 2b and SEED[3]) could enhance its performance in inner speech classification.

The rationale was based on the perceived cognitive overlap between motor imagery and inner speech, both being forms of internal mental simulation, and the proven efficacy of the EEG Conformer in motor imagery contexts.

However, despite this promising premise, our recent comparative experiments, as detailed in our preliminary findings, have revealed a critical and unexpected phenomenon: the direct application of transfer learning from existing motor imagery datasets and emotions to inner speech decoding using the EEG Conformer resulted in what is commonly termed "negative transfer".

4 Methodology

This study focused on decoding inner speech from EEG signals using the EEG Conformer model. The methodology encompassed several key steps (see Fig. 1): selection of the "Inner Speech" dataset, preprocessing to enhance signal quality, data augmentation to address dataset scarcity, and analysis of the augmented dataset's spectral characteristics.

[2] BCI Competition IV.

[3] SEED Dataset.

Additionally, modifications were made to the EEG Conformer architecture to adapt it to the specific temporal and spatial dimensions of the preprocessed data. These adaptations included adjustments to the pooling layer and spatial convolution kernel to optimize the model's performance for the task.

The following sections detail each of these steps, providing a comprehensive overview of the experimental pipeline.

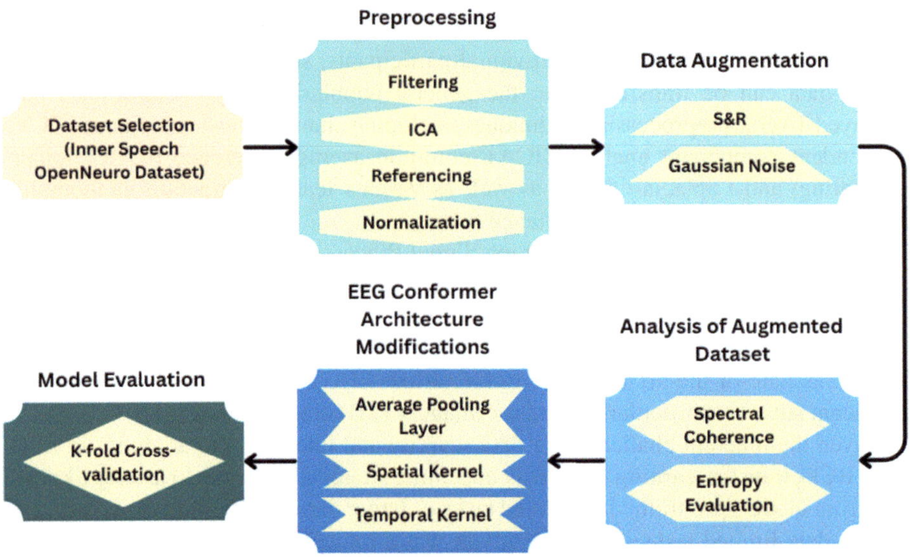

Fig. 1. Methodological pipeline for EEG-based inner speech decoding. The workflow includes selection and preprocessing of the "Inner Speech" dataset (filtering, ICA, normalization), data augmentation via Gaussian noise and segmentation-reconstruction (S&R), spectral analysis of augmented signals, and adaptations to the EEG Conformer architecture (pooling layer and spatial and temporal kernel adjustments). The hybrid CNN-Transformer model was optimized to capture spatiotemporal features of covert speech.

4.1 Dataset

This study utilized the "Inner Speech" open-access dataset, also referred to as "Thinking out loud, an open-access EEG-based BCI dataset for inner speech recognition" [9]. This dataset is publicly available through the OpenNeuro repository, and was specifically designed to advance the understanding of brain mechanisms related to inner speech and aid in the development of Brain-Computer Interfaces (BCIs).

Participants: The dataset comprises EEG recordings from ten healthy, right-handed participants (four females, six males). Their mean age was 34 years (standard deviation = 10 years). All participants were native Spanish speakers and reported no prior BCI experience, neurological, hearing, or speech disorders. Each individual participated in approximately two hours of recording sessions.

Data Acquisition System: Electroencephalography (EEG) and external physiological data (EOG, EMG) were acquired using a BioSemi ActiveTwo high-resolution biopotential measuring system. The system employed 128 active EEG channels and 8 external active EOG/EMG channels, totaling 136 channels, with a 24-bit resolution. The signals were sampled at a high frequency of 1024 Hz. Before each recording session, the impedance of all electrodes was carefully checked to be less than 40 Ω.

During acquisition, a digital 208 Hz low-pass filter was applied, but no high-pass filter was used. The recordings were saved as continuous.bdf files, which included all EEG/EXG data and tagged events.

The 8 external channels included electrodes for referencing (EXG1, EXG2 on earlobes), horizontal eye movement (EXG3, EXG4 on temples), vertical eye movement (EXG5, EXG6 above/below right eye), and mouth movement (EXG7, EXG8 on orbicularis oris). The latter were used to control for no movement during the inner speech and visualization conditions.

Experimental Protocol and Conditions: The study was conducted in an electrically shielded room, with participants seated comfortably in front of a computer screen displaying visual cues. The experimental protocol included three distinct mental conditions to explore speech-related brain activities:

- *Inner Speech:* In this primary condition, participants were instructed to imagine their own voice giving a direct command to a computer, repeatedly vocalizing a specific word until a visual cue changed color. Explicit instructions were given to avoid focusing on articulatory gestures, remain as still as possible, and not move their mouth or tongue. No rhythmic cues were provided to encourage natural imagination.
- *Pronounced Speech:* Participants repeatedly pronounced aloud the word corresponding to a visual cue, simulating a direct command to a computer. This condition aimed to identify motor regions involved in overt pronunciation that might also be activated during inner speech.
- *Visualized condition:* Given the visual and spatial nature of the chosen words, participants were asked to mentally concentrate on moving a circle on the screen in the direction indicated by a visual cue. This condition was included to identify activity related to spatial thinking, whose main neural centers are typically located in the occipital and parietal regions.

Each trial in the protocol had a fixed duration of 4.5 s and followed a specific structure:

- It began with a 0.5-s concentration interval, during which a white circle appeared for gaze fixation.
- This was followed by a 0.5-s cue interval (at $t = 0.5$ s), where a white triangle indicated the command.
- At $t = 1$ s, the triangle disappeared, marking the start of a 2.5-s action interval, during which the participant performed the mental task (inner speech, overt speech, or visualization).
- At $t = 3.5$ s, the white circle turned blue, initiating a 1-s relaxation interval.
- The trial concluded at $t = 4.5$ s when the blue circle vanished, followed by a variable rest interval (between 1.5 and 2 s) before the next trial.

Raw Data Volume: The dataset collectively contains over 9 h of continuous EEG recordings, accumulating more than 5600 trials across all conditions and participants. Specifically, for the inner speech condition, 2236 trials were acquired.

The number of trials contributed by each participant varied, with each individual performing between 475 and 570 trials in total across the sessions. The raw data files (in.bdf format) captured the complete session recordings for all 136 channels, with a mean duration of 1554 s per recording [9].

It is important to acknowledge certain considerations and limitations related to the dataset´s collection. Since all participants were naïve BCI users, there is an inherent challenge in ensuring that the mental activity precisely matched the intended task, and individual interpretations of instructions might have varied across subjects.

Furthermore, the absence of rhythmic cues during acquisition could lead to natural variations in the timing of imagination across trials, a phenomenon also expected in real-world BCI applications. Despite these complexities, the "Inner Speech" dataset remains a valuable public resource for advancing research in this intricate domain.

4.2 Preprocessing

The preprocessing pipeline combined steps from the original "Thinking Out Loud" dataset with adaptations for the EEG Conformer model. Below, we detail the workflow in two phases: initial preprocessing (following the original dataset protocol) and Conformer-specific refinements.

Initial Preprocessing

1. *Signal Acquisition*
   - Raw EEG data were recorded at 1024 Hz using a 136-channel BioSemi system (128 EEG + 8 auxiliary EOG/EMG electrodes).
2. *Re-referencing and Filtering*
   - Re-referencing: Data were re-referenced to the average of mastoid electrodes (*EXG1–EXG2*) to mitigate common-mode noise.
   - Bandpass filtering: A zero-phase FIR filter (0.5–100 Hz) removed low-frequency drifts and high-frequency noise.
   - Notch filtering: A 50 Hz notch filter attenuated line interference.
3. *Downsampling and Epoching*
   - Downsampling: Data were decimated to 256 Hz to reduce computational load while preserving relevant spectral features.
   - Epoching: Continuous data were segmented into 4.5 s trials, time-locked to stimulus onset.
4. *Artifact Removal*
   - Ocular artifacts: Independent Component Analysis (ICA) identified and removed components correlated with blinks/eye movements (using EOG channels *EXG3–EXG6*).

- Muscle artifacts: Trials with EMG activity (*EXG7–EXG8* power exceeding *μ + 3σ* of baseline) were excluded (2.5% of trials).

EEG Conformer-Specific Adaptations

For compatibility with the EEG Conformer architecture, additional preprocessing was performed:

- *Temporal Trimming:* Trials were trimmed to 3 s (768 samples at 256 Hz), retaining only the visual stimulus (0.5 s) and action (2.5 s) intervals to focus on active inner speech.
- *Normalization:* Per-channel Z-score normalization was applied to mitigate inter-subject and inter-electrode variability:

$$x_{norm} = \frac{x - \mu_{channel}}{\sigma_{channel}} \tag{1}$$

where $\mu_{channel}$ and $\sigma_{channel}$ are the mean and standard deviation of each channel. This reduced amplitude distribution skewness from − 0.04 to − 0.01 and kurtosis from 317.44 to 0.08.

The pipeline balanced noise reduction with feature preservation (spectral coherence). Trimming and normalization optimized input uniformity for the EEG Conformer's hybrid CNN-Transformer architecture.

4.3 Data Augmentation Methods

To enhance the limited training data while maintaining evaluation integrity, we implemented two distinct augmentation approaches exclusively during the 5-fold cross-validation training phases. Both methods operated on the 80% training portion of each fold, leaving the 20% test data completely untouched to prevent any evaluation bias.

The first method, *Segmentation & Reconstruction (S&R)*, carefully preserved the temporal structure of EEG signals while creating new synthetic samples. Each 3-s trial was divided into four consecutive, non-overlapping segments of equal duration.

These segments were then recombined under strict conditions: segments could only be combined with others from the same class and had to maintain their original temporal sequence. This approach generated new trials that preserved the fundamental characteristics of each command while introducing natural variability in the signal patterns.

For the second approach, *Gaussian Noise Injection*, we added carefully calibrated random noise to the original signals. The noise level was precisely controlled to maintain a 20dB signal-to-noise ratio, ensuring the augmented signals remained physiologically plausible while introducing valuable variability. This method proved particularly effective at making the model more robust to the natural noise present in EEG recordings.

Both augmentation methods doubled the size of the training data in each fold, expanding **from 1,661** original samples **to 3,322** augmented samples. While S&R created new signal combinations that helped the model learn more diverse temporal patterns, Gaussian noise injection improved the model's resilience to signal variability.

Importantly, neither method was applied to the test sets, ensuring our evaluation metrics reflected true model performance on authentic, unaltered data.

The S&R method's strict class-matching and sequence-preserving rules ensured the augmented data maintained meaningful physiological patterns, while the Gaussian noise approach provided a more straightforward way to increase data diversity.

Together, these complementary strategies significantly enhanced our model's training without compromising the validity of our evaluation process.

4.4 Characteristics of the Preprocessed and Augmented Dataset

The preprocessed dataset exhibited distinct spectral patterns across different inner speech commands. As shown in Fig. 2, spectral analysis revealed class-specific variations in theta (4–8 Hz) and alpha (8–12 Hz) band power. The *"arriba"* (up) command showed the highest theta power ($2.8 \times 10^{-}12$ μV2/Hz), while *"derecha"* (right) displayed peak alpha power ($3.2 \times 10^{-}12$ μV2/Hz), consistent with attention and inhibition processes during linguistic processing.

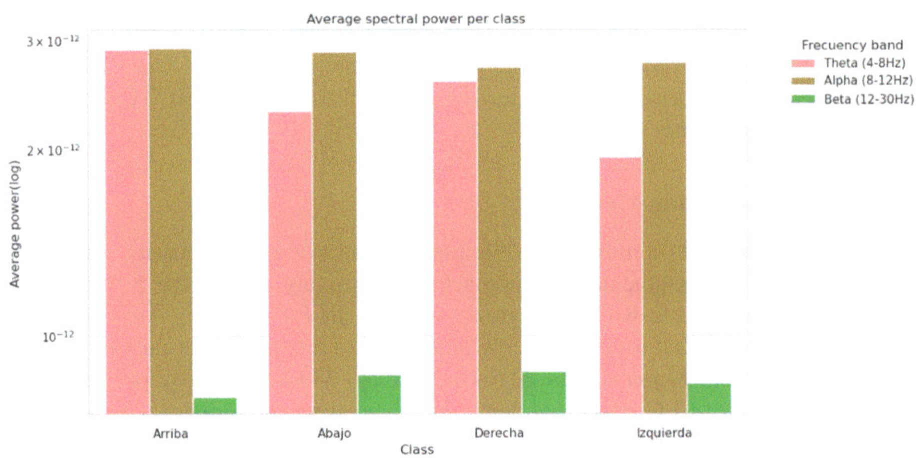

Fig. 2. Spectral power distribution across inner speech commands, showing dominant theta (4–8 Hz) and alpha (8–12 Hz) band activity. *"Arriba"* (up) exhibits highest theta power (linked to attention), while *"derecha"* (right) shows peak alpha power (associated with inhibitory processes).

The two augmentation methods produced markedly different effects on signal properties.

Gaussian noise injection maintained **excellent spectral coherence** (theta: 0.993 ± 0.005; alpha: 0.998 ± 0.002) with **minimal entropy change** ($\Delta = 0.031 \pm 0.019$), demonstrating its signal-preserving quality.

In contrast, **segmentation and reconstruction** significantly **reduced coherence** (theta: -0.012 ± 0.113; alpha: -0.014 ± 0.154) while **increasing entropy** by 0.717 ± 0.562, indicating **greater signal alteration**. This clear divergence in impact guided our selective application of augmentation methods.

As illustrated in Fig. 3, Gaussian noise preserved the amplitude distribution's statistical properties, maintaining near-zero skewness (-0.01) and low kurtosis (0.08).

This confirmed the method's ability to expand the dataset without distorting its fundamental characteristics. The spectral power distributions remained stable across all classes after this augmentation.

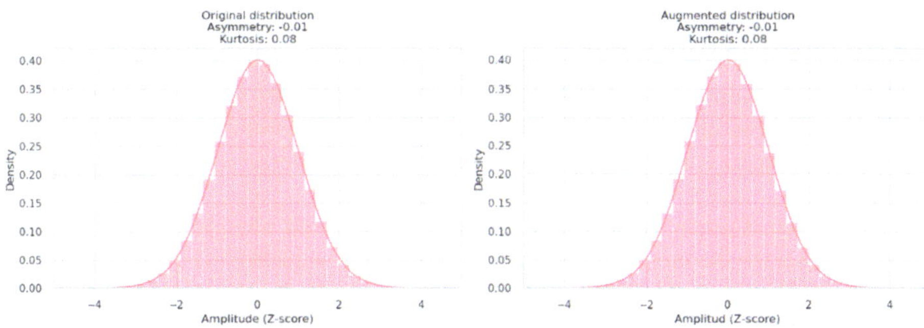

Fig. 3. Amplitude distribution comparison pre- and post-Gaussian noise augmentation (SNR = 20 dB), demonstrating preservation of original signal characteristics (skewness = -0.01, kurtosis = 0.08).

The preprocessed data maintained clear physiological patterns despite the augmentation. Theta power, associated with sustained attention, showed consistent patterns across commands, while alpha power variations reflected class-specific cognitive demands. These preserved features ensured the augmented dataset remained biologically meaningful while providing sufficient diversity for robust model training.

The combination of careful preprocessing and controlled augmentation resulted in a dataset that balanced physiological validity with expanded training opportunities.

The spectral and statistical metrics confirmed that while both augmentation methods increased data volume, Gaussian noise better preserved the signal characteristics critical for accurate inner speech classification.

4.5 EEG Conformer Architecture: Original Design and Modifications for the 'Inner Speech' Dataset

Original Design

We employed the EEG Conformer model as the base architecture to address the task of classifying EEG signals associated with internal speech. This model combines the strengths of convolutional neural networks (CNNs) and attention-based Transformers to capture local features and global dependencies in EEG signals. The EEG Conformer architecture follows an end-to-end process for classifying EEG trials as shown in Fig. 4. It consists of three main components: a convolutional module, a Transformer encoder module (based on self-attention), and a final classifier (based on prior information).

The convolutional module encodes low-level spatiotemporal information within the EEG trial. It is inspired by previous architectures like EEGNet. It decomposes the two-dimensional convolution operator into one-dimensional components, temporal convolution, and spatial convolution, in addition to introducing depthwise convolution. This module processes standardized EEG data and considers the temporal continuity of sampled signals and the functional interconnectivity between electrode channels. The first temporal convolution layer uses filters to capture information associated with different frequency ranges. The subsequent depthwise convolution is used for spatial filtering, facilitating the learning of representations of interactions between channels [11].

The convolutional module in the EEG Conformer learns low-level local features through one-dimensional temporal and spatial convolution layers. Specifically, the first layer performs temporal convolution, while the second layer acts as a spatial filter. An average pooling layer along the temporal dimension follows these convolution layers. This three-layer convolutional module generates a higher-level temporal sequence representation.

Next, a Transformer encoder employs a multi-head self-attention (MHA) mechanism to emphasize the most critical features within this sequence. The attention mechanism aims to emulate the human brain's behavior of selectively focusing on significant elements, and self-attention can intrinsically evaluate global dependencies in long sequences. The self-attention module extracts global correlation within the global temporal features. Finally, a compact classifier, composed of fully connected layers, generates the decoding results [10].

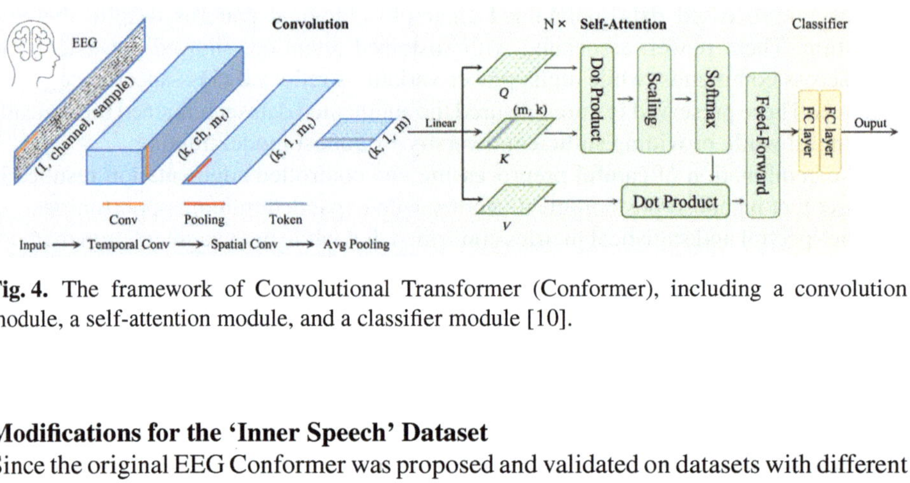

Fig. 4. The framework of Convolutional Transformer (Conformer), including a convolution module, a self-attention module, and a classifier module [10].

Modifications for the 'Inner Speech' Dataset

Since the original EEG Conformer was proposed and validated on datasets with different dimensional characteristics (e.g., 22 or 3 channels and different durations/samples), it was necessary to adapt the architecture to effectively process signals with the specific characteristics of our dataset (128 channels, 768 samples per trial at 256 Hz).

Modifications to the Average Pooling Layer:

The original EEG conformer architecture has a convolution module with the two-dimensional convolution operator separated into two one-dimensional temporal and spatial convolution layers.

The first layer has k kernels of size (1,25) with a stride of (1,1), which means the convolution is performed over the time dimension.

The second layer keeps k kernels of size (ch, 1) with a stride of (1,1), where ch equals the number of electrode channels of EEG data. Subsequently, batch normalization is adopted to boost the training process and alleviate overfitting.

They used exponential linear units (ELUs) as the activation function for nonlinearity following.

The original architecture includes a temporal average pooling layer after the initial convolutions to reduce dimensionality and define the "tokens" for the Transformer.

The kernel size and stride in the original implementation are (1,75) and (1,15), respectively.

However, maintaining these values might not be optimal with an input sequential length of 768 samples.

Therefore, the average pooling layer was adapted to a kernel size of (1,64) and a stride of (1,16). This choice was made to adapt the temporal aggregation operation to the new input signal length (768 samples).

The (1,64) kernel groups local features over 64-sample windows, and the (1,16) stride determines the displacement between windows, influencing overlap and the length of the output sequence (see Table 1).

Table 1. Network architecture of the tailored Convolutional Module

Layer	In	*Out*	Kernel	Stride
Temporal Conv	1	k	(1,25)	(1,1)
Spatial Conv	k	k	(ch,1)	(1,1)
Avg Pooling	k	k	(1,64)	(1,16)
Rearrange	(k, 1, m) → (m, k)			

The length of the output sequence (number of tokens fed into the Transformer module) is determined by the following pooling formula:

$$L_{out} = \left\lceil \frac{L_{in} - kernel}{stride} \right\rceil + 1 \tag{2}$$

where:

L_{in}= 768 (input temporal samples for 3 s at 256 Hz), kernel = 64 (pooling window size) and stride = 16 (pooling step).

Substituting in (2):

$$L_{out} = \left\lceil \frac{768 - 64}{16} \right\rceil + 1 = \frac{704}{16} + 1 = 44 + 1 = 45 \tag{3}$$

The average pooling layer transforms the input temporal signal (768 samples) into a sequence of 45 tokens, each representing a compressed temporal segment. This sequence of 45 tokens represents the 3-s signal in a form suitable for processing by the Transformer's self-attention mechanism. Adjusting these pooling hyperparameters is crucial for balancing dimensionality reduction and preserving relevant temporal information for the Transformer module.

Adaptation to the Spatial Convolution Kernel:

The preprocessed "Inner Speech" dataset has 128 EEG channels, a higher number than some datasets used for the original EEG Conformer design. The second layer of the convolutional module performs a spatial or depthwise convolution with a kernel whose size depends on the number of input channels.

To correctly process the interactions between the 128 channels, the kernel size of this layer was adjusted to (128,1) instead of smaller sizes (like 22 or 3) that would correspond to datasets with fewer channels. This adaptation is fundamental for the convolutional module to learn spatial representations across all available channels.

These adaptations in the average pooling layer and in the spatial convolution kernel are essential to allow the EEG Conformer to effectively process the preprocessed internal speech signals, generating appropriate representations for the classification task.

Other network hyperparameters (such as the number of filters, the number of Transformer layers, etc.) can also be subject to adjustment during model optimization.

However, the specific spatial and temporal dimensions of the input data used directly dictate the modifications to temporal pooling and the spatial convolution kernel.

4.6 Model Evaluation Protocol

The model training preserved several hyperparameters from the original EEG Conformer implementation to maintain architectural consistency.

The **Adam optimizer** was used with identical momentum terms (**β_1 = 0.9, β_2 = 0.999**) and an initial **learning rate of 0.001**. These values were kept unchanged as they had demonstrated optimal convergence in the motor imagery tasks described in the foundational paper.

The categorical **cross-entropy loss function** was preserved as it effectively handles multi-class classification tasks.

Training proceeded for **2,000 epochs with early stopping monitoring validation loss**. The **dropout rate of 0.5** was maintained for both spatial filters and dense layers, following the original regularization strategy. This approach prevented overfitting while allowing sufficient model capacity for the inner speech classification task.

The evaluation used **5-fold cross-validation** with strict separation between training and test sets. All augmentation techniques were exclusively applied to training data, ensuring unbiased performance estimation. This configuration balanced computational efficiency with the need for robust model assessment given our limited sample size.

The training protocol maintained the original paper's core optimization approach while adapting specific parameters to our inner speech decoding requirements.

This hybrid strategy allowed direct comparison with prior results while addressing the unique challenges of our task. The complete hyperparameter set reflected careful consideration of both architectural inheritance and dataset-specific needs.

5 Results

This work addressed the complex task of classifying EEG signals corresponding to internal speech, using a portion of the "Inner Speech" dataset, focusing on the internal speech condition, and segmenting the signals into 3-s excerpts.

We employed a variant of the EEG Conformer architecture—a hybrid model combining convolutional (CNN) modules and Transformers, designed to capture local features and global dependencies in EEG signals. In this study, we used this architecture with a specific modification: the kernel of the average pooling layer was changed to (1,64) with a stride of (1,16).

This pooling configuration directly influences the length of the sequence ("token size") fed into the Transformer and can affect the model's ability to learn patterns at different temporal scales. Corresponding adjustments were made to the channel-related dimensions handled by the model's initial convolutional module.

It is important to note that, apart from the specific configuration of this average pooling layer and the dimensional adjustments associated with the channels, the rest of the architecture's hyperparameters and the training process used in this particular study remained unchanged.

As shown in Table 2, the original data achieved an average accuracy of 27.02% across folds, establishing the baseline performance.

The S&R augmentation yielded inconsistent results, with an average accuracy of 26.49% and substantial variability between folds (ranging from 23.86% to 28.92%). While it produced the highest single-fold accuracy (28.92% in fold 5), it also showed the poorest performance in fold 4 (23.86%), indicating unreliable effectiveness.

This variability aligns with spectral coherence metrics (Sect. 4.2), which revealed that S&R's segmentation approach significantly disrupted signal properties (Theta coherence: -0.012 ± 0.113).

In comparison, Gaussian noise demonstrated more stable improvements, achieving a 27.99% average accuracy with consistent gains across all folds while better preserving physiological signal characteristics (Theta coherence: 0.993 ± 0.005).

Table 2. Model performance across augmentation methods

k	Original data Test Accuracy (%)	With data augmentation S&R Test Accuracy (%)	With data augmentation Gaussian Noise Test Accuracy (%)
1	28.61	25.96	29.09
2	23.86	27.71	25.30
3	25.78	26.02	26.75
4	27.71	23.86	28.67
5	29.16	28.92	30.12
Average	**27.02**	**26.49**	**27.99**

These results underscore several critical limitations. First, while data augmentation can expand training sets, its effectiveness depends on maintaining physiological plausibility. Second, the EEG Conformer's performance remained near chance levels (25% for four classes), suggesting fundamental challenges in decoding inner speech patterns.

This may stem from the model's difficulty in capturing fine-grained temporal dynamics or the inherent noisiness of EEG signals during covert speech. The pooling strategy (kernel = 64, stride = 16) may require optimization to handle these temporal patterns better.

The near-chance classification performance (~27%) suggests that inner speech decoding may require fundamentally different approaches compared to traditional EEG paradigms. Three understudied factors could explain these limitations: First, the neurophysiological correlates of inner speech might be more susceptible to intersubject variability than motor imagery, as suggested by the high variance in cross-validation folds (e.g., 23.86% to 29.16% for original data). Second, the linguistic nature of the task (4-word classification) may introduce confounds from semantic processing networks that overlap with articulation areas, diluting discriminative features.

Alternative methodologies not explored here—such as Riemannian geometry-based feature extraction (shown to outperform deep learning in small EEG datasets) or explicit modeling of articulatory kinematics through latent variables—could bypass some limitations of end-to-end architectures. Furthermore, the observed theta-band coherence preservation with Gaussian noise (0.993 ± 0.005) implies that phase consistency in low frequencies may be more critical for inner speech than currently acknowledged, warranting frequency-specific augmentation strategies.

6 Conclusions and Future Work

The EEG Conformer's limited performance (27.99% accuracy) on inner speech classification reveals fundamental challenges: the model's motor imagery origins may be inadequate for covert speech's distributed neural patterns, and current datasets remain too small for transformer-based architectures.

While Gaussian noise augmentation showed promise (preserving spectral coherence better than S&R), results confirm inner speech decoding requires paradigm-specific solutions.

Three key directions emerge from this study:

- **Architecture Optimization**: Systematic exploration of temporal pooling configurations and attention mechanisms tailored for inner speech's unique spatiotemporal patterns.
- **Advanced Augmentation**: Development of physiologically grounded augmentation techniques that preserve linguistic-related spectral features while expanding dataset diversity.
- **Multimodal Integration**: Incorporation of the visualized condition data as auxiliary inputs to potentially enhance pure inner speech decoding through shared neural correlates.

These improvements should be validated on larger-scale inner speech datasets to overcome current data scarcity limitations.

Acknowledgements. This research was funded in part by the "Secretaría de Ciencia, Humanidades, Tecnología e Innovación" (Secihti) of Mexico and the "Instituto Politécnico Nacional" under grants SIP 20253428 and 20253468.

Conflict of Interest. The authors declare no competing interests.

References

1. Lee, Y.E., Lee, S.H., Kim, S.H., Lee, S.W.: Towards voice reconstruction from EEG during imagined speech. In: Proc. 37th AAAI Conf. Artif. Intell. AAAI 2023, vol. 37, pp. 6030–6038 (2023). https://doi.org/10.1609/aaai.v37i5.25745
2. Lopez-Bernal, D., Balderas, D., Ponce, P., Molina, A.: A state-of-the-art review of EEG-based imagined speech decoding. Front. Hum. Neurosci. **16**(April), 1–14 (2022). https://doi.org/10.3389/fnhum.2022.867281
3. Gu, X., et al.: EEG-based brain-computer interfaces (BCIs): a survey of recent studies on signal sensing technologies and computational intelligence approaches and their applications. IEEE/ACM Trans. Comput. Biol. Bioinforma. **18**(5), 1645–1666 (2021). https://doi.org/10.1109/TCBB.2021.3052811
4. Vorontsova, D., et al.: Silent EEG-speech recognition using convolutional and recurrent neural network with 85% accuracy of 9 words classification. Sensors **21**(20), 1–19 (2021). https://doi.org/10.3390/s21206744
5. Sharma, A., et al.: EEG classification for visual brain decoding with spatio-temporal and transformer based paradigms. https://doi.org/10.1145/3702250.3702286
6. Vafaei, E.: Transformers in EEG analysis : a review of architectures and applications in motor imagery, seizure, and emotion classification (2025)
7. Gour, N., et al.: Transformers for autonomous recognition of psychiatric dysfunction via raw and imbalanced EEG signals. Brain Inform. (2023). https://doi.org/10.1186/s40708-023-00201-y
8. Nieto, N.: Inner Speech. https://openneuro.org/datasets/ds003626/versions/2.1.2
9. Nieto, N., Peterson, V., Rufiner, H.L., Kamienkowski, J.E., Spies, R.: Thinking out loud, an open-access EEG-based BCI dataset for inner speech recognition. Sci. Data **9**(1) (2022). https://doi.org/10.1038/s41597-022-01147-2
10. Song, Y., Member, G.S., Zheng, Q.: EEG conformer: convolutional transformer for EEG decoding and visualization. IEEE Trans. Neural Syst. Rehabil. Eng. **31**, 710–719 (2023). https://doi.org/10.1109/TNSRE.2022.3230250
11. Zhao, W., Jiang, X., Zhang, B., Xiao, S., Weng, S.: CTNet : a convolutional transformer network for EEG - based motor imagery classification. Sci. Rep., pp. 1–22 (2024). https://doi.org/10.1038/s41598-024-71118-7
12. Luria, L., Vigotsky: Psicología y pedagogía, 5th ed. AKAL, España (1986)
13. Vigotsky, L.S.: Pensamiento y lenguaje. Ediciones Quinto Sol, México (1988)
14. Sokolov, A.N.: Inner Speech and Thought, A plenum/. Moscow, USSR: Plenum Press, London (1975)
15. Langland-Hassan, P.: Inner speech. Wiley Interdiscip. Rev. Cogn. Sci. **12**(2), 1–18 (2021). https://doi.org/10.1002/wcs.1544
16. Fernyhough, C., Alderson-Day, B.: Inner speech: development, cognitive functions, phenomenology, and neurobiology. Psychol. Bull. **141**(5), 931–965 (2015)
17. Fernyhough, C., Borghi, A.M.: Inner speech as language process and cognitive tool. Trends Cogn. Sci. **27**(12), 1180–1193 (2023). https://doi.org/10.1016/j.tics.2023.08.014

18. Gregory, D.: Inner speech: new voices. Anal. (United Kingdom) **80**(1), 164–173 (2020). https://doi.org/10.1093/ANALYS/ANZ096
19. Balaji, A. et al.: EEG-based classification of bilingual unspoken speech using ANN. In: Proc. Annu. Int. Conf. IEEE Eng. Med. Biol. Soc. EMBS, pp. 1022–1025 (2017). https://doi.org/10.1109/EMBC.2017.8037000
20. Agarwal, P., Kumar, S.: Electroencephalography-based imagined speech recognition using deep long short-term memory network. ETRI J. **44**(4), 672–685 (2022). https://doi.org/10.4218/etrij.2021-0118
21. Einizade, A., Mozafari, M., Jalilpour, S., Bagheri, S., Hajipour Sardouie, S.: Neural decoding of imagined speech from EEG signals using the fusion of graph signal processing and graph learning techniques. Neurosci. Inform. **2**(3), 100091 (2022). https://doi.org/10.1016/j.neuri.2022.100091

Analysis of Conversations in Adults Using Multimodal Data Processing

Carolina Naomi Alvarez-Peralta(✉), Janet Badillo-Tecuapacho, Eric Ramos-Aguilar, Daniel Sánchez-Ruiz, and Ricardo Ramos-Aguilar

Instituto Politécnico Nacional, UPIIT, Tlaxcala, Mexico
{calvarezp2101,jbadillot2100}@alumno.ipn.mx,
{eramosa,dsanchezro,rramosa}@ipn.mx

Abstract. This study performs emotion classification in older adults through the analysis of multimodal conversations that integrate data from three modalities: text, audio, and video. This approach is essential in contexts where communication plays a central role, as it enables a more accurate and empathetic interpretation of emotions. During the development process, Natural Language Processing, Computer Vision, and Audio Signal Processing techniques were employed to extract relevant features from each modality. Based on these features, three classification models were built and evaluated: a Multilayer Perceptron (MLP), a Support Vector Machine (SVM), and Random Forests (RF). The models were assessed using the F1-score metric, achieving competitive results exceeding 90%. Beyond the numerical performance, this work highlights the importance of multimodal integration for understanding the complexities of human interaction in aging populations. The analysis aims to contribute to the development of more effective systems for emotion detection, with potential applications in healthcare, social support, and human-computer interaction.

Keywords: Emotion Analysis · Natural Language Processing Techniques · Multimodal Data Analysis · Older Adults

1 Introduction

In Mexico, individuals aged 60 and over are considered older adults. According to the 2022 National Survey of Occupation and Employment, this population reached nearly 18 million, representing 14% of the total population [1]. Similarly, the World Health Organization (WHO) estimates that there were approximately 1 billion people aged 60 and over worldwide in 2020, a figure expected to rise to 1.4 billion by 2030 about one in six people globally [2]. In Mexico, this trend reflects a rapid demographic transition: for every 100 children under 15, there are 48 older adults, emphasizing the urgency of addressing their specific needs through inclusive technologies [3].

Older adults often face discrimination, social isolation, and communication barriers, which hinder accurate recognition of their emotional states and increase

C. Palma-Preciado et al. (Eds.): CORE 2025, ACSAR 3, pp. 301–318, 2026.
https://doi.org/10.1007/978-3-032-08894-9_20

their vulnerability [4]. Previous research has shown that the induction of negative emotions can cause immediate physiological changes (such as transient impairment of endothelial function), with potentially more severe consequences in older populations [5].

Moreover, the particularities of their verbal and non-verbal communication make it difficult to accurately identify the emotions they experience. A specific challenge is that expressions through speech, gestures, and posture may not be as coherent or fluid as those of younger individuals, making it harder for a system or even a robot to understand the intentions of older adults based on information from a single modality [6].

Emotions are multifaceted psychological phenomena that influence human relationships and interactions, and significantly affect individuals' behavior. Recognizing emotions during communication is essential for sustaining meaningful conversations. Emotion recognition based on a single modality, such as facial expressions or voice, is often difficult and inaccurate [7,8]. Therefore, multimodal emotion recognition [9] has been developed to overcome these limitations, aiming to improve the reliability of emotion identification systems by incorporating data from multiple modalities such as facial expressions, spoken language, and textual content.

This type of recognition has driven the development of adaptive systems that respond to users' emotional states and have proven useful in education and healthcare. [10]. Therefore, digital technologies are needed to support the emotional well-being of older adults [11], enabling the early detection of signs of depression or social isolation, with the aim of implementing personalized strategies to enhance their quality of life. Such systems can be applied in nursing homes, home-based medical care, or psychological support platforms.

This work proposes a model for classifying emotions in older adults through multimodal conversations, integrating Natural Language Processing (NLP), Computer Vision, and Audio Signal Processing techniques to analyze verbal and non-verbal cues. The proposed technology could be implemented in virtual assistants or deployed in care settings such as nursing homes and hospitals, aiming to detect emotional states more accurately. Such integration would enable early interventions and facilitate more personalized and empathetic care, thereby contributing to the emotional well being and communicative engagement of older adults.

The remainder of this work is organized as follows: Sect. 1, presents related work on emotion recognition. Section 2, describes the proposed methodology, including data processing and model implementation. Section 3, reports the experimental results. Section 4, discusses the comparative performance of the models. Finally, Sect. 5 concludes the study and outlines future directions.

2 Related Work

Emotion analysis is an advanced branch of sentiment analysis that focuses on identifying and classifying specific emotions expressed in text, images, or human interactions. This field has become increasingly relevant in areas such as social media, mental health, marketing, and human-computer interaction systems. Psychological models, such as Ekman's six basic emotions and appraisal-based dimensional models, are commonly used to support classification [12,13].

Emotion analysis can be conducted on text, images, or audio. In text, methods include keyword- and lexicon-based approaches, traditional machine learning, and hybrid deep learning models (e.g., CNN, Bi-GRU combined with SVM), achieving accuracy rates above 80% [14–16]. For image-based analysis, deep neural networks incorporating stimuli such as color, objects, and facial features enhance emotion recognition [17,18]. However, text-based detection is challenged by language ambiguity and the absence of non-verbal cues, while image analysis faces subjectivity and stimulus variability [13,17,18].

Multimodal sentiment analysis has gained importance for enabling richer and more contextual understanding of emotions [19]. Various studies have employed unimodal and multimodal approaches. For example, [20] applied deep learning to detect depression in older adults via projective drawings, achieving accuracies between 92% and 98%. In [21], a multitask framework integrates sentiment and emotion analysis using contextual and multimodal data via GRUs, demonstrating performance improvements through joint learning.

Dialogue-based approaches, such as [22], highlight the role of conversational history in recognizing emotions and intentions. Similarly, [23] integrates text, audio, and video via GRUs, using GloVe embeddings and visual/audio features like facial expressions and speech rhythm. Other works, such as [24], leverage cross-modal attention with pretrained models like BERT and RoBERTa, achieving improved precision, recall, and F1-score.

Feature fusion with attention mechanisms has also proven effective. [25] combines recurrent neural networks with cross-attention to emphasize relevant conversational features, while [26] proposes attention-based fusion of facial and speech features for enhanced multimodal emotion detection.

The state of the art analysis in this study was conducted during the year 2024, focusing on relevant previous works available up to that time. The review prioritized studies specifically centered on emotion analysis in older adult populations, given the particular communication characteristics of this group. Additionally, many of the most recent models are still in experimental phases, with computational requirements and datasets that exceed the scope of the present study. However, as a future research direction, a broader comparison with state of the art models is proposed, including modern architectures such as VideoBERT, LXMERT, or MME-Transformer.

Overall, the reviewed literature demonstrates that multimodal sentiment analysis continues to evolve as a key tool for the in-depth understanding of human emotions. Although challenges remain particularly concerning the unequal contribution of each modality recent advances such as the integration of pretrained models, the use of attention mechanisms, and efficient feature fusion have led to significant improvements in model performance. These studies not only highlight the potential of the multimodal approach in general contexts, but also emphasize its applicability to specific populations such as older adults, paving the way for more accurate, adaptive, and context-sensitive emotional analysis solutions.

3 Methodology

This chapter describes the methodology followed for the development of the multimodal emotion classification model using audio, text, and video data. The approach is structured into three main phases: preprocessing, data analysis, and model development with evaluation. Figure 1 illustrates the overall methodology adopted in this project, providing a structured overview of the key stages and their interconnections. The following sections detail each phase, outlining the techniques and tools employed throughout the process.

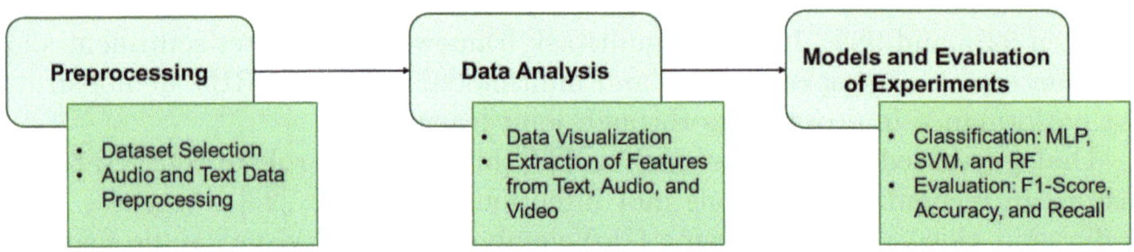

Fig. 1. Methodology for Multimodal Conversation Analysis.

3.1 Dataset

This study utilizes the dataset named **ElderReact**, a multimodal English-language dataset designed to study emotional responses in elderly individuals. It contains 1,323 video clips from a total of 46 participants, of whom 26 are female and 20 are male. Each video clip is annotated with six basic emotions (Anger, Disgust, Fear, Happiness, Sadness, Surprise) and valence [27]. Figure 2 displays some example frames from the dataset.

For data collection, participants were exposed to various audiovisual stimuli designed to evoke specific emotions. These stimuli included content such as video games, recorded social events, or viral challenges. After viewing the stimulus, both their spontaneous reactions (audio, video, and facial expressions) and their verbal responses to questions related to their opinions or emotional experiences regarding the observed content were recorded. This procedure allowed for obtaining natural and diverse samples of emotional expression in older adults within a controlled and structured context.

Fig. 2. ElderReact: A Multimodal Dataset.

The older adult population is particularly difficult to recruit for emotion recognition studies due to their reluctance to participate in audiovisual recordings and the presence of stricter ethical requirements. Recording older adults requires controlled environments, informed consent, and privacy protection, which further restricts the sample size. Moreover, there are very few public datasets with videos of older adults expressing emotions, which makes a sample of even 46 individuals a relevant contribution to the field.

The design of the study prioritized obtaining annotated samples per individual. Each participant contributed multiple video clips, which compensates for the small sample size by allowing an analysis of emotional expressions with intra-individual variability.

Inclusion criteria:

- Aged 60 or older (focused on the older adult population).
- Ability to provide informed consent.
- Willingness to be video recorded while expressing basic emotions.

Exclusion criteria:

- Younger than 60 years old.
- Refusal to participate in audiovisual recordings.

Although the limited size of the dataset may restrict the generalization of results to the entire older adult population, this limitation is mitigated by the fact that each clip was obtained under controlled conditions and with an emphasis on intra-individual emotional variability. The present work establishes methodological foundations for future research with larger samples.

Each video clip is annotated with six basic emotions (Anger, Disgust, Fear, Happiness, Sadness, Surprise) and valence [27]. Figure 2 displays some example frames from the dataset.

These six emotions are used because they correspond to the universally recognized basic emotions. This selection is based on the work of psychologists such as Paul Ekman and Daniel Goleman, who identified these emotions as universal and present across all cultures: Happiness, Surprise, Fear, Disgust, Anger, and Sadness. It is worth noting that these emotions are expressed and recognized in a similar way by people of different cultures and ages. Due to their well defined nature and their clear manifestation through facial expressions and physiological responses, these emotions are particularly useful for developing and validating computational models of emotion recognition [28–30].

3.2 Dataset Preprocessing

During the preprocessing stage, various tasks were performed on both the audio data and the textual transcriptions. These tasks included noise reduction in the audio signals as well as text normalization, transforming the text into its canonical form by removing punctuation marks such as commas, periods, and apostrophes. Figure 3 visually summarizes this workflow applied to the dataset.

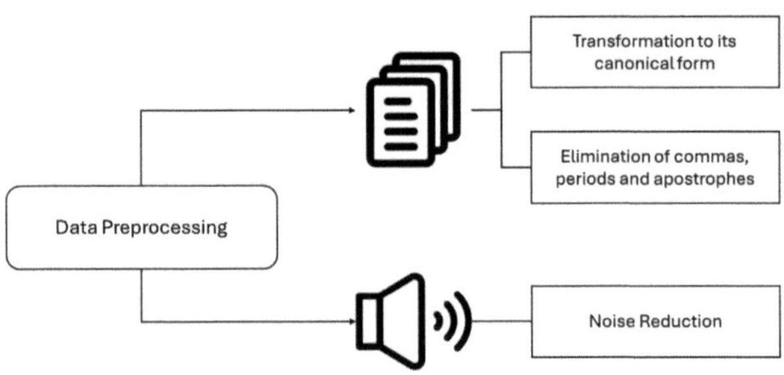

Fig. 3. Preprocessing of Text and Audio Data.

Based on the original data, audio modality features were extracted. To this end, the videos were converted into individual audio files. Subsequently, these audio files underwent a cleaning process using noise reduction techniques, employing the NoiseReduce tool, which implements a spectral noise subtraction approach. This process aimed to enhance the most relevant segments of the audio content, particularly those where the subjects were speaking.

To improve the quality of audio in the analyzed multimodal conversations, a technique based on spectral noise gating was used. This method involves estimating a noise profile from silent segments of the audio (where no speech is present) and subtracting it from the rest of the signal in the frequency domain, which significantly reduces background noise without noticeably affecting the speech signal [31]. The procedure involves applying a Fast Fourier Transform (FFT) to obtain the signal spectrum, estimating the noise spectrum, and then subtracting this component from the total spectrum. The audio signal is then reconstructed using the Inverse Fourier Transform (IFFT) [32].

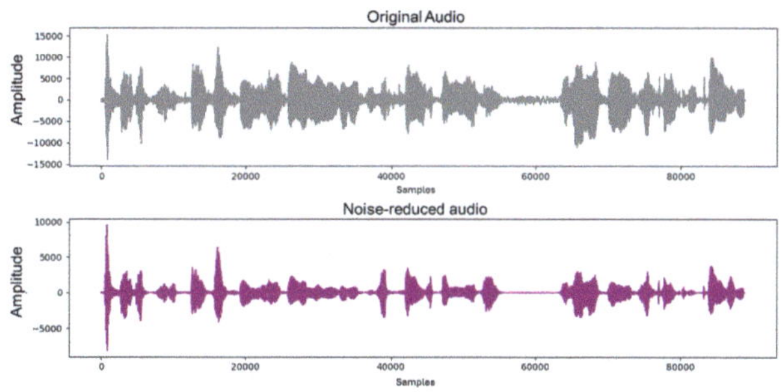

Fig. 4. Audio File Visualization Pre- and Post-Noise Reduction.

Figure 4 displays two waveforms: the original audio signal (top) and the signal resulting from noise reduction processing (bottom).

The primary objective of this process was to enhance the main speaker's voice, as the original videos captured not only their voice but also external sounds such as the interviewer's voice and noises from the audiovisual content shown to the elderly participants.

Despite the noise reduction, the overall structure of the speech signal is preserved. Segments containing significant vocal content were neither removed nor drastically altered. This indicates that no important information was lost; rather, background noise was reduced, thereby facilitating subsequent analysis.

Subsequently, an Automatic Speech Recognition (ASR) tool was applied, enabling the conversion of human speech into written text. This step aimed to transcribe the audio content, thereby facilitating the textual representation of each individual's utterances in the video clips.

With the complete transcriptions for each videoclip, standardization was performed. This step involved normalizing words to their canonical forms and removing unnecessary characters such as punctuation marks (commas, periods, apostrophes, among others), thus facilitating automated analysis.

For the text cleaning process, the transcriptions obtained in this stage were used. Punctuation marks such as commas and periods were removed, aiming to facilitate subsequent processing, especially for tokenization tasks. The original transcriptions did not contain exclamation marks or other explicit intonation markers, so no additional cleaning was necessary in that regard.

Finally, the respective emotional labels were assigned to each videoclip. As previously described, the dataset contains annotations for six distinct emotions, and in many cases, multiple emotions are present within the same videoclip (Table 1). Due to this multilabel nature, the problem was reformulated as a multilabel classification task, which involved transforming the annotations from a binary to a decimal representation.

Table 1. Emotion Labels Assigned to Each Instance.

Name	Anger	Disgust	Fear	Happiness	Sadness	Surprise	Emotion
gta2_43	1	1	0	1	0	1	53
play_road_redemp_14	0	0	0	1	0	1	5

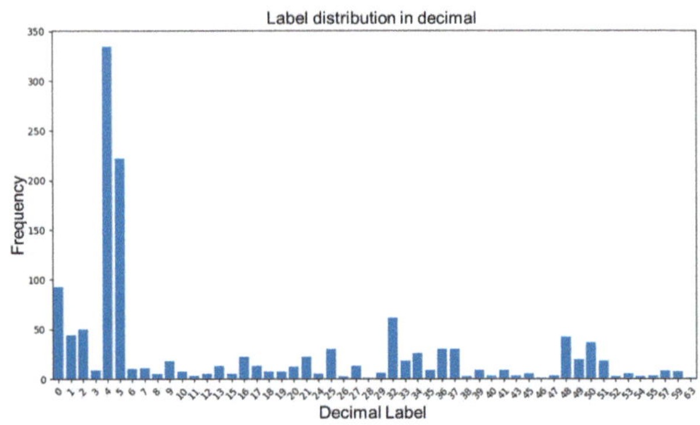

Fig. 5. Distribution of label values represented in decimal form.

As shown in Fig. 5, the distribution of each emotion and their combinations within the dataset is depicted. This graph corresponds to the histogram of decimal labels, representing the frequency of occurrence of emotion combinations. The histogram reveals multiple peaks, indicating that emotions rarely occur in isolation and commonly co-occur with others.

The most frequent combinations reach approximately 150 instances and correspond to emotions that typically coexist, such as happiness and surprise, and anger and disgust. Conversely, the least frequent combinations, with fewer than 50 occurrences, reflect less common emotional associations, such as sadness and fear.

This distribution suggests that the emotional responses of the elderly in the analyzed interactions are predominantly multicomponent, meaning they are not limited to a single emotion but involve more complex emotional sets.

In total, 62 distinct labels (excluding label 0) are identified, resulting from all possible combinations of the six basic emotions considered: surprise (1), sadness (2), happiness (4), fear (8), disgust (16), and anger (32). Each combination is represented by the sum of the individual values associated with each emotion, allowing multiple simultaneous emotions to be encoded into a single decimal label. For example, label 5 represents the combination of happiness (4) + surprise (1).

Although all possible emotion combinations are encoded and preserved through the decimal labeling process, the histogram shows a clear imbalance in their distribution. Specifically, combinations that include the emotion "fear" are among the least frequent. This is not due to a filtering artifact, but rather reflects the natural rarity of fear-related expressions in the dataset. As shown in Fig. 5, combinations that include fear generally appear fewer than 50 times, suggesting that fear occurs in less expressive contexts or is expressed less frequently in the video stimuli shown to older participants.

3.3 Data Analysis and Visualization

During this stage, the primary focus was on exploring the textual data derived from the audio transcriptions, aiming to identify linguistic patterns associated with different emotions. NLP techniques were applied to extract the most frequent words linked to each emotional class. Subsequently, this information was visualized using word clouds (see Fig. 6) to facilitate visual inspection of predominant terms.

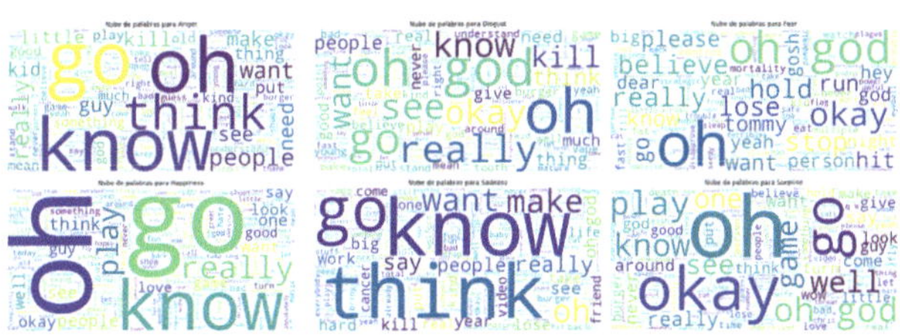

Fig. 6. Emotion-Specific Word Clouds.

Figure 6 presents the word clouds by emotion. It was observed that terms such as "know", "go", "oh", "think", "okay", "really", and "god" are common across all emotions, suggesting that they are not representative of any specific emotion but rather part of everyday language. In contrast, each emotion exhibited distinctive words: anger included terms like "kill", "need", and "make", associated with aggressive content; disgust featured "infection", "tooth", and "garbage", related to unpleasant experiences; fear stood out with "death", "accident", and "run", reflecting threat or danger; happiness was linked to "love", "fun", and "win"; sadness to "hard", "life", and "friend", related to loss or personal relationships; and surprise to "wow", "game", and "turn", evoking unexpected events.

This analysis is supported by previous research. For example, in the case of happiness, it has been documented that certain words and mental associations are linked to the concept of well-being, which explains the presence of terms such as "family", "success", or "friendship" in joyful contexts [33]. For emotions such as surprise, anger, disgust, fear, and other negative emotions, various studies have employed lexical analysis to identify characteristic linguistic patterns in emotionally charged messages, demonstrating the usefulness of this type of textual representation for understanding different emotional categories [34]. This preliminary data analysis was essential to assess possible class imbalances and to lay the groundwork for the design and training of emotional classification models, considering both individual labels and emotion combinations.

3.4 Feature Extraction

Subsequently, three processes were implemented to obtain embeddings and vector representations for the text, audio, and video modalities, using specialized pre-trained models: BERT for text, WavLM for audio, and MediaPipe for video.

For the textual modality, tokenized transcripts were processed using the bert-base-uncased architecture, and the vector corresponding to the [CLS] token was extracted, which represents a semantic compression of each sentence. The resulting vectors are 769-dimensional, as illustrated in Table 2.

Table 2. Example of a Text Embedding Vector.

ID_text	Embedding_0	...	Embedding_768	Label
50_50_104	−0.01669	...	0.01562	2

For the audio modality, the signals were normalized to 16 kHz and then processed using the pretrained WavLM model along with the Wav2Vec2 Feature Extractor to convert the acoustic signals into 512-dimensional vectors, capturing acoustic, phonetic, and semantic aspects of the voice (Table 3).

Table 3. Example of an Audio Embedding Vector.

ID_Audio	Embedding_0	...	Embedding_511	Label
50_50_104	−0.0196	...	0.0169	2

For the visual modality, facial features were extracted from videos using MediaPipe FaceMesh [35], identifying key landmarks such as eyebrows, eyes, forehead, nose, and mouth. These points were selected for their relevance to facial movement, as they tend to show significant variation in emotional expressions. Euclidean distances representative of emotional expressions were calculated from these points and averaged per video to obtain vectors with homogeneous dimensions (see Fig. 7 and Table 4).

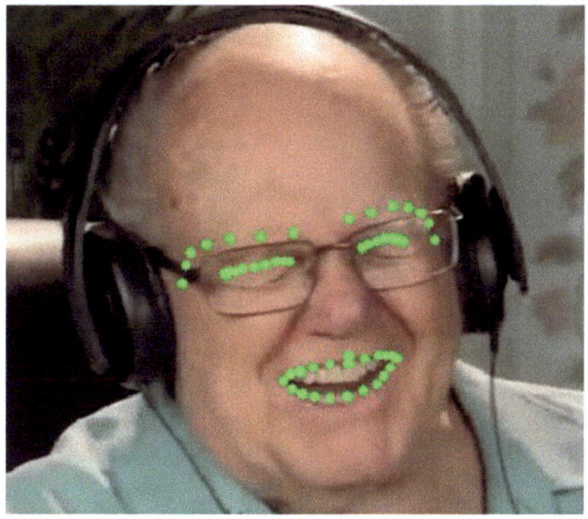

Fig. 7. Facial Landmark Detection Using MediaPipe.

Table 4. Facial Feature Measurements Extracted from a Sample.

ID_Video	forehead_left_distance	...	cheek_right_distance	Label
50_50_104	0.5179	...	0.4352	2

Finally, for multimodal information fusion, a strategy based on the concatenation of embeddings (text and audio) and the feature vector (video) was chosen. While this technique does not introduce architectural novelty in terms of complex fusion model design, its selection aligned with the objectives of the present work, as it allows for the direct and efficient integration of different modalities, maintaining lower computational complexity and facilitating model training. This approach leverages the latent representations generated by each pretrained model, preserving the richness of each modality with minimal computational overhead.

4 Results

Prior to model training, the t-SNE (t-Distributed Stochastic Neighbor Embedding) technique was applied to analyze the distribution of the multimodal data in the latent space. This allowed us to project the embeddings and feature vectors into a two-dimensional space to facilitate visualization. As shown in Fig. 8, the embeddings and feature vectors do not exhibit clearly defined clusters corresponding to the different emotional labels. This dispersion indicates the absence of evident separation prior to training and suggests that the model will not be biased or influenced by pre-existing patterns in the initial data representation.

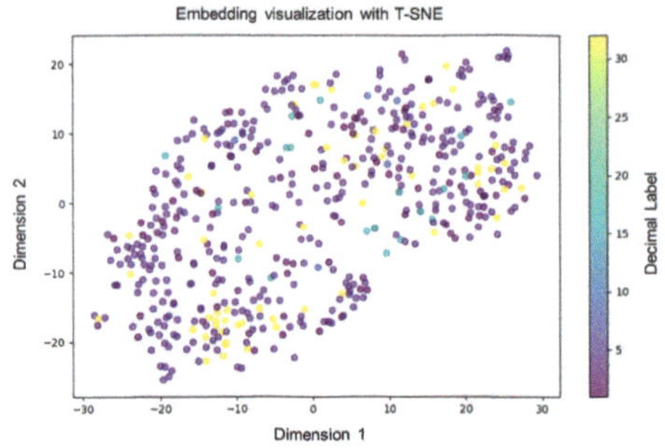

Fig. 8. Visualization of Embeddings Using t-SNE.

Although a significant imbalance was identified in the class distribution within the dataset which posed a major challenge for the models performance by favoring majority classes, techniques such as oversampling or undersampling were not applied. These approaches carry risks, such as generating synthetic data that may not accurately reflect the real expressions of older adults, or reducing the size of the training set, potentially compromising the representativeness of the models.

Instead, one of the experiments employed an internal class balancing function, specifically, the class_weight='balanced' parameter in the Random Forest classifier. This technique automatically adjusts the weights of each class during training without altering the original data.

Each model was initially trained using the entire available dataset, with a total of 1,287 features, taking into account the text and audio embeddings, as well as the mean vector from the video data, after applying normalization with the StandardScaler tool from the scikit-learn library. This technique standardizes the data so that all features have a mean of zero and a standard deviation of one, ensuring that both the embedding vectors and the feature vector are on the same scale. This normalization is crucial for optimizing the performance of many machine learning algorithms.

Subsequently, model evaluation focused exclusively on a set of basic emotions: Surprise, Sadness, Happiness, Fear, Disgust, and Anger. These emotions were selected for their universal nature, according to Paul Ekman's theory [7], which allows for a clearer and more coherent interpretation of the results, as well as reducing the ambiguity associated with complex or nuanced emotions.

To ensure robust and generalizable evaluation, all models were validated using 5-fold cross-validation. This method guarantees that samples of each emotion are present in each fold, allowing for a more reliable estimation of model performance and reducing the risk of overfitting.

At the end of each training, a confusion matrix was used to evaluate the performance of each model. From this, key metrics such as precision, recall, F1-score, and support were calculated for each emotional class.

4.1 Multilayer Perceptron

A Multilayer Perceptron (MLP) was used, defined as an MLP classifier with two hidden layers containing 10 and 5 neurons, respectively. The ReLU activation function and the Adam optimizer were also employed.

Overall, the results show high performance across all classes. However, there is slight variability: emotions such as Happiness (label 4) and Anger (label 32) achieved high F1-scores, while others like Fear (label 8) had lower scores due to the very few instances labeled with that emotion. The results are presented in Table 5.

Table 5. Evaluation Metrics by Class Using MLP.

Label	Accuracy	Recall	F1-Score	Support
1	1.00	0.82	0.90	44
2	0.98	0.94	0.96	50
4	0.99	0.99	0.99	334
8	1.00	0.60	0.75	5
16	1.00	0.86	0.93	22
32	1.00	0.95	0.97	61

4.2 Support Vector Machine

A Support Vector Machine (SVM) model was used with a fifth-degree polynomial kernel and a C value of 1.

In this experiment, the results obtained using this model are presented in Table 6. These results reflect an interesting behavior of the model: despite being trained on the entire dataset, it was able to correctly identify several emotions. For instance, label 4 (Happiness) achieved a recall of 1.00, indicating that the model was able to recognize all true instances of this emotion in the test set.

Table 6. SVM Experiment Results: Evaluation Using Polynomial Kernel.

Label	Accuracy	Recall	F1-Score	Support
1	1.00	0.41	0.58	44
2	1.00	0.48	0.65	50
4	0.77	1.00	0.87	334
8	1.00	0.40	0.57	5
16	1.00	0.41	0.58	22
32	1.00	0.44	0.61	61

However, for most of the other emotions, recall was low (between 0.40 and 0.48), indicating that the model failed to classify several instances as true positives. Despite this, precision scores were high (1.00 in almost all classes), suggesting that the model mostly labels instances correctly.

4.3 Random Forest

For the development of the Random Forest (RF) model, the following parameters were set: the number of trees was fixed at 100, a reasonable and commonly used value, as increasing the number of trees can improve model performance up to a certain point. Additionally, the maximum depth of each tree was limited to 10 levels.

The class_weight='balanced' parameter was used, which automatically adjusts the weight of each class based on its inverse frequency. This allows underrepresented classes to have a greater influence during training, reducing the model's bias toward majority classes.

The results indicate that the model exhibits very favorable average performance across all target classes, regardless of their frequency (Table 7). In particular, Class 4—the most frequent in the dataset—achieved an F1-score of 0.91 and a recall of 0.85, reflecting a good balance between precision and recall.

Table 7. Evaluation Metrics for Individual Labels Using Random Forests.

Label	Accuracy	Recall	F1-Score	Support
1	0.95	0.91	0.93	44
2	0.86	0.88	0.87	50
4	0.98	0.85	0.91	334
8	1.00	1.00	1.00	5
16	1.00	0.91	0.95	22
32	0.97	0.92	0.94	61

5 Discussion

This study analyzed the performance of three machine learning models in the task of emotion classification using a combination of modalities: audio, text, and video. The evaluation was conducted using the F1-score metric, and it was observed that the Random Forest model achieved the best overall and per-class results, outperforming both the MLP and SVM models (Table 8).

Table 8. Comparison of F1-Score by Emotion Across MLP, SVM, and RF Models.

Emotion	Label	MLP	SVM	RF
Surprise	1	0.90	0.58	**0.93**
Sadness	2	**0.96**	0.65	0.87
Happiness	4	**0.99**	0.87	0.91
Fear	8	0.75	0.57	**1.00**
Disgust	16	0.93	0.58	**0.95**
Anger	32	**0.97**	0.61	0.94

The MLP model demonstrated high overall performance, with F1-scores exceeding 74% across all classes. It performed particularly well in classifying emotions such as Happiness and Anger but showed a slight decrease in performance for low-frequency emotions like Fear, which can be attributed to the scarcity of instances in this class.

On the other hand, the SVM model exhibited a different behavior. It achieved very high precision values (1.00 in most classes) but low recall values (ranging between 0.40 and 0.48 for most emotions), suggesting it was highly conservative in its classifications and failed to label many instances as positive. This behavior indicates that the model is able to recognize specific patterns but struggles to generalize for underrepresented classes.

Finally, the Random Forest model achieved a balanced performance across all classes, including minority ones. Emotions such as Fear, despite having very few instances, reached an F1-score of 1.00. This demonstrates that the model was capable of learning even under imbalanced conditions. This result was made possible by using the class_weight='balanced' parameter, which adjusts class weights during training. This adjustment reduced the bias toward majority classes and improved recognition of less frequent emotions.

Traditional statistical tests, such as the calculation of p-values or confidence intervals, were not performed. Instead, the performance of the classifiers (SVM, Random Forest, and MLP) was evaluated using widely adopted metrics such as accuracy, F1-score, and the confusion matrix. These metrics effectively assess model performance in terms of predictive capability and the trade-off between precision and recall.

The results obtained in this study are generally competitive with previous works such as ElderReact [27], which used models like Naive Bayes, SVM, and XGBoost to detect emotions in older adults. For example, ElderReact achieved an F1-score of 0.70 for Happiness using SVM, whereas our approach reached 0.87 with the same model and 0.91 with Random Forest. Overall, the best-performing model in this work outperformed previous results by a notable margin.

These findings demonstrate that the use of multimodal data and balancing strategies has a significant impact on model performance, making them more accurate and generalizable.

One of the main limitations of this study was the small size and imbalance of the dataset. This was largely due to the scarcity of research focused on the older adult population, which makes it difficult to access public databases that adequately represent their communicative particularities. Unlike other populations, communication in older adults is often influenced by factors such as cognitive decline, hearing loss, reduced facial mobility, and other age-related conditions.

These factors complicate both data collection and annotation. As a result, the present study was limited to using a small corpus, which may affect the generalizability of the results. However, this limitation also highlights the importance of continuing to generate resources and studies focused on this age group, in order to promote the development of more representative models.

As future work, we recommend expanding the dataset in both size and diversity, which would allow for training more robust and representative models.

6 Conclusion

The results obtained in this study show that the Random Forest model was the most competitive, achieving a balanced performance in terms of recall and F1-score in the classification of pure emotions. In particular, it stood out in classifying emotions such as Happiness and Anger, reaching F1-scores above 90%, and maintained notable performance even for minority classes like Fear, thanks to the use of the class_weight='balanced' parameter, which helped mitigate class imbalance.

The model's results stand out compared to those reported in previous studies such as ElderReact, where the highest F1-score was 0.71 with XGBoost, while this work achieved values above 0.87 with MLP and 0.91 with Random Forest, highlighting the importance of using multimodal data.

The main objective of this work was not to propose a new architecture or a novel fusion strategy, but rather to evaluate the performance of classical models using multimodal features by integrating audio, text, and video signals in an underrepresented population such as older adults. An innovative architecture was not introduced; however, as future work, we plan to explore more complex fusion architectures and deep neural networks, comparing them with the models used in this study.

These findings reinforce the relevance of emotional analysis in older adults, a population group that can greatly benefit from automated tools for monitoring emotional well-being. Accurate emotion classification can support healthcare institutions in the early detection of potential mental health issues or critical mood states, laying the groundwork for personalized care.

Although the results obtained represent significant progress compared to what has been reported in the literature, practical implementation requires more complex testing, as well as the management of ethical and administrative aspects such as obtaining consent and permissions.

As future work, we propose the development of a real-time system that integrates this multimodal classification for use in clinical or assisted-living environments. Additionally, exploring data augmentation techniques would be valuable to address the limitations posed by the low frequency of some emotions.

Acknowledgments. No acknowledgments to declare.

Conflicts of Interest. The authors declare no conflict of interest.

References

1. United Nations. International day of older persons (2022). https://www.inegi.org.mx/contenidos/saladeprensa/aproposito/2018.pdf
2. World Health Organization (WHO). Mental health of older adults (2023). Accessed 15 July 2025
3. INEGI. Statistics on the occasion of the international day of older persons (October 1). Press release No. 547/21 (2021)
4. National Council to Prevent Discrimination. Discrimination against older adults (2023). https://www.conapred.org.mx/wp-content/uploads/2024/02/FT_Mayores_Noviembre2023.pdf
5. Sumner, J.A., et al.: Negative emotion induction and endothelial function in older adults. J. Am. Heart Assoc. **12**(14), e032698 (2023)
6. Hoffman, P., Loginova, E., Russell, A.: Poor coherence in older people's speech is explained by impaired semantic and executive processes. eLife, **7**, e38907 (2018)
7. Ekman, P.: The face of the 7 emotions (2022). https://edpyn.com/blog-coaching/paul-ekman-rostro-emociones/. EDPyN Coaching School | Coaching Training
8. Cordero, J., Aguilar, J.: Multimodal emotion recognition in an intelligent environment based on chronicles. J. Name 525–541 (2016)
9. Kumari, A.K., Uppunda, A.: Multiclass sentiment classification using skip-gram embeddings with support vector machine stochastic gradient descent (SVM-SGD). Ann. Comput. Sci. Ser. **17**(2), 234–242 (2019)
10. Anderson, G.F., Hussey, P.S.: Population aging: a comparison among industrialized countries. Health Aff. **19**(3), 191–203 (2000)
11. Thomas, A., Waibel, A.: Emotion-aware human-computer interfaces. In: ITRW on Speech and Emotion (2000)
12. Soleymani, M., Garcia, D., Jou, B., Schuller, B., Chang, S.-F., Pantic, M.: A survey of multimodal sentiment analysis. Image Vis. Comput. **65**, 3–14 (2017). Multimodal Sentiment Analysis and Mining in the Wild
13. Schouten, K., Frasincar, F.: Survey on aspect-level sentiment analysis. IEEE Trans. Knowl. Data Eng. **28**(3), 813–830 (2016)
14. Medhat, W., Hassan, A., Korashy, H.: Sentiment analysis algorithms and applications: a survey. Ain Shams Eng. J. **5**(4), 1093–1113 (2014)
15. Birjali, M., Kasri, M., Beni-Hssane, A.: A comprehensive survey on sentiment analysis: approaches, challenges and trends. Knowl.-Based Syst. **226**, 107134 (2021)
16. Mäntylä, M.V., Graziotin, D., Kuutila, M.: The evolution of sentiment analysis–a review of research topics, venues, and top cited papers. Comput. Sci. Rev. **27**, 16–32 (2018)
17. Wnkhade, M., Rao, A., Kulkarni, C.: A survey on sentiment analysis methods, applications, and challenges. Artif. Intell. Rev. **55**, 5731–5780 (2022)
18. Yang, J., Li, J., Wang, X., Ding, Y., Gao, X.: Stimuli-aware visual emotion analysis. IEEE Trans. Image Process. **30**, 7432–7445 (2021)

19. Hu, R., et al.: Multichannel cross-modal fusion network for multimodal sentiment analysis considering language information enhancement. IEEE Trans. Industr. Inf. **20**(7), 9814–9824 (2024)
20. Kim, K.Y., Yang, Y., Kim, M., Kim, J., Parque Ji, S.: Early depression prediction in WZT drawing images based on deep learning. Expert Syst. (2024). First Published: July 24, 2024
21. Chauhan, D.S., et al.: Sentiment and emotion help sarcasm? A multi-task learning framework for multi-modal sarcasm, sentiment and emotion analysis. In: Proceedings of the Annual Meeting of the Association for Computational Linguistics, pp. 4351–4360 (2020)
22. Liu, R., et al.: Emotion and intent joint understanding in multimodal conversation: a benchmarking dataset (2024)
23. Shenoy, A., Sardana, A.: Multilogue-net: a context-aware RNN for multi-modal emotion detection and sentiment analysis in conversation. In: Challenge-HML, ACL 2020, pp. 19–28 (2020)
24. Wang, D., Liu, S., Wang, Q., Tian, Y., He, L., Gao, X.: Cross-modal enhancement network for multimodal sentiment analysis. IEEE Trans. Multimed. **25**, 4909–4921 (2023)
25. Huddar, M.G., Sannakki, S.S., Rajpurohit, V.S.: Attention-based multi-modal sentiment analysis and emotion detection in conversation using rnn. Int. J. Interact. Multimed. Artif. Intell. **6**(6), 112–121 (2021)
26. Mamieva, D., et al.: Multimodal emotion detection via attention-based fusion of extracted facial and speech features. Sensors **23**(12), 5475 (2023)
27. Ma, K., Wang, X., Yang, X., Zhang, M., Girard, J.M., Morency, L.-P.: Elderreact: a multimodal dataset for recognizing emotional response in aging adults. In: Proceedings of the 2019 International Conference on Multimodal Interaction, ICMI 2019, pp. 349–357. Association for Computing Machinery, New York (2019)
28. Corbalán, A.S.: Types of basic or primary emotions (2021). Published on MentSalud
29. Colombo, D.: The 6 basic emotions: How to use them with intelligence (2021). Published on LinkedIn
30. Montañés, M.C.: Psychology of emotion: the emotional process. Technical report, Department of Basic Psychology, University of Valencia (2005). http://www.uv.es/~choliz
31. Boll, S.F.: Suppression of acoustic noise in speech using spectral subtraction. IEEE Trans. Acoust. Speech Signal Process. **27**(2), 113–120 (1979)
32. Weiss, M.D., Deller, E.R.: DSP System Design: Complexity Reduced Implementation. CRC Press (2012)
33. Shin, J.E., Suh, E.M., Eom, K., Kim, H.S.: What does "happiness" prompt in your mind? Culture, word choice, and experienced happiness. Asian J. Soc. Psychol. (2022)
34. Alkaabi, N., Zaki, N., Ismail, H., Khan, M.: Detecting emotions behind the screen. ResearchGate (2022)
35. Mediapipe for dummies (n.d.). https://www.assemblyai.com/blog/mediapipe-for-dummies. Accessed 30 Apr 2025

Application of Natural Language Processing Techniques for the Classification and Recommendation of University-Level Mathematical Content

María Fernanda León-Pluma(✉), Estefanía Fernanda Vázquez-Osorno, Daniel Sánchez-Ruiz, Eric Ramos-Aguilar, and Jesús García-Ramírez

Unidad Profesional Interdisciplinaria en Ingeniería Campus Tlaxcala, Instituto Politécnico Nacional (IPN), Tlaxcala de Xicohténcatl, Tlaxcala, Mexico
{mleonp2100,evazquezo2101}@alumno.ipn.mx,
{dsanchezro,eramosa,jegarciara}@ipn.mx

Abstract. This paper presents a methodology for generating personalized educational recommendations in the field of university-level mathematics, using Natural Language Processing techniques and Transformer-based models. First, an English-language dataset is preprocessed and translated into Spanish using the `deep-translator` library, aiming to adapt the system for a Spanish-speaking audience. Subsequently, a pre-trained Transformer model is fine-tuned and tailored to the educational-mathematical domain. The quality of the generated content is evaluated using metrics such as accuracy and TransQuest, achieving an accuracy score of 0.96 and an average TransQuest score of 0.456. These results demonstrate that the system is effective in terms of coherence, relevance, and linguistic adequacy. This approach aims to promote autonomous learning, improve the understanding of mathematical concepts, and support personalized teaching in virtual or hybrid learning environments.

Keywords: Natural Language Processing · Conversational Agent · Educational Recommendations · Text Generators

1 Introduction

In recent years, the use of intelligent technologies in education has optimized teaching and academic management processes [1,2]. Among these, chatbots have proven to be effective tools for providing immediate and personalized assistance, enhancing student motivation, performance, and autonomy [2,3].

Beyond handling administrative queries, some conversational systems have been employed to offer micro-explanations and individualized feedback through Natural Language Processing (NLP) and machine learning techniques [4]. However, there are still limitations in their application to subjects such as mathematics, where adaptive and timely responses are required [5].

This work presents a methodology for generating personalized educational recommendations in university-level mathematics, using NLP techniques, semantic analysis, and generative models. The proposed approach includes phases such

C. Palma-Preciado et al. (Eds.): CORE 2025, ACSAR 3, pp. 319–334, 2026.
https://doi.org/10.1007/978-3-032-08894-9_21

as data translation and preprocessing, model fine-tuning, recommendation generation, and semantic and linguistic evaluation. The goal is to support instructors and reinforce the understanding of key content in subjects such as calculus.

The remainder of this work is organized as follows: in Sect. 2, the Related ork section reviews studies on dialogue systems and educational recommendation. In Sect. 3, the Methodology section describes the proposed approach and its phases. Section 4, Experiments and Results, presents the evaluations carried out, including a practical case. Finally, Sect. 5, the Conclusions section, discusses the findings and presents closing remarks.

2 Literature Review

Several studies have explored the application of NLP in the educational domain. The potential of chatbots in relation to their integration with teaching practices is highlighted in [6], which synthesizes implementation evidence and challenges in personalized learning, identifying where AI tools and conversational agents can fit within instructional ecosystems. Regarding the automatic resolution of math problems, [7] shows that certain NLP models can recommend solving strategies based on problem variable extraction without necessarily performing deep mathematical reasoning, relying instead on structural patterns in problem statements.

Educational recommender systems (ERS) have evolved to adapt to students progress and context, yet face challenges due to diverse learning styles and pedagogical objectives—particularly in culturally and linguistically diverse environments [8,9]. ERS are intelligent tools that suggest learning content tailored to a learner's needs, interests, and progress. They typically employ content-based filtering, collaborative filtering, matrix factorization, or hybrid approaches to improve recommendation accuracy [10,11]. In education, ERS recommend resources such as textbooks, videos, exercises, and personalized learning paths [12], and they play an increasing role in personalized learning supported by policies in countries like the UK and US [6]. However, integrating ERS with chatbots and NLP-based conversational agents—particularly for Spanish-language mathematics content—remains largely unexplored.

Advanced NLP-based metrics such as BERTScore and TransQuest have proven effective for evaluating the quality of automatically generated or translated texts. BERTScore computes semantic similarity using contextual embeddings from Transformers, while TransQuest is an open-source framework for translation quality estimation that employs cross-lingual Transformer-based architectures to predict translation quality without requiring a reference sentence [13]. Although these tools have been applied in general NLP evaluation, their application in specialized domains—such as Spanish-language educational mathematics—remains limited, leaving room for further exploration [14].

In the Latin American context, [15] demonstrates the feasibility of developing educational chatbots by combining NLP with algorithms such as SVM, decision trees, random forests, and BERT variants for intent classification in Spanish. Similarly, [16] presents a BERT-based multi-tier question answering system capable of retrieving and ranking academic answers from heterogeneous sources, outperforming TF-IDF + logistic regression baselines.

This project proposes an educational recommendation system in mathematics for Spanish-speaking university students, combining machine translation, fine-tuning of Transformer-based models, and evaluation using semantic metrics such as BERTScore and TransQuest. Unlike previous work, it aims to improve the understanding of mathematical reasoning, adapt to non-English-speaking contexts, and enhance the precision of recommendations in virtual autonomous learning environments.

3 Methodology

This section describes the methodology used to develop the personalized educational recommendation system in the field of mathematics, specifically focused on the subject of calculus. The approach is based on the use of NLP techniques to analyze and interpret mathematical content, with the goal of generating useful and relevant recommendations for students.

The development process includes data collection and preparation, text preprocessing, NLP model training, recommendation generation, model implementation, and, finally, system testing and validation. Figure 1 presents the general methodology followed throughout the project.

The following sections detail the key stages of this methodology, from data acquisition to the evaluation of the proposed system.

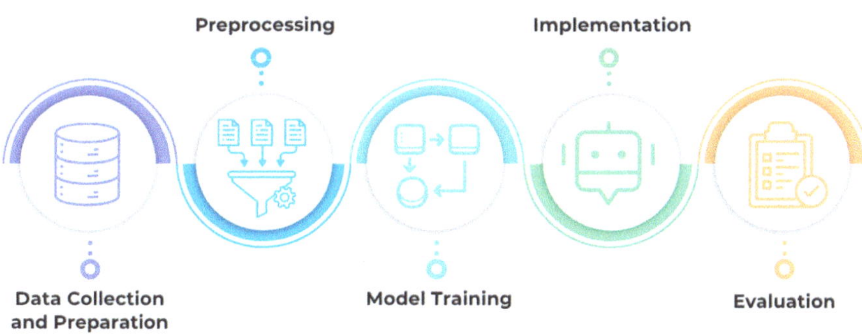

Fig. 1. Methodological proposal for a personalized mathematical recommender system.

3.1 Data Collection and Preparation

For data collection and preparation, the following dataset was used:

- **Math QA:** This dataset contains 50,000 math problems along with their corresponding solutions, generated using GPT-4. The problems are organized into 25 main topics and 25 subtopics per main topic. Each topic-subtopic combination includes approximately 80 problems, offering a wide variety of exercises categorized by area of knowledge [17].

The structure and content of the dataset can be better understood through concrete examples, as shown in Table 1. It includes two representative records from the `math50k.zip` dataset, illustrating how the relevant fields are organized.

Table 1. Representative examples from the dataset`math50k.zip`

topic	sub_topic	question	answer
Algebra	Linear equations	If 2x + 3 = 7, what is the value of x?	Subtracting 3: 2x = 4; dividing by 2: x = 2
Geometry	Areas and perimeters	What is the area of a circle with radius 3 cm?	Using A = pi r squared: A = pi * 9 = approximately 28.27 cm^2

Once the structure of the dataset was defined, the thematic distribution of the questions was analyzed. Figure 2 shows a bar chart with the number of questions per topic, which made it possible to identify the most represented mathematical areas in the corpus and to adjust the model's focus accordingly.

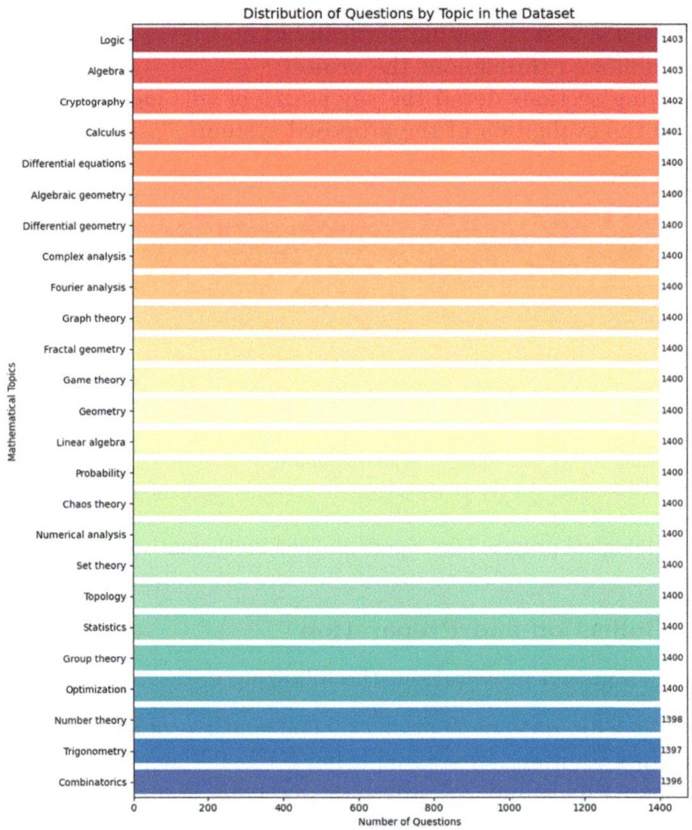

Fig. 2. Distribution of questions by topic.

As shown, the dataset includes approximately 1,400 questions for each of the 25 topics, ensuring a balanced distribution. This uniformity was intentionally preserved in the dataset design to provide equal representation of all covered areas during model training and evaluation.

3.2 Data Preprocessing

The Hugging Face datasets library was used to load the data, which was then converted into pandas DataFrames to facilitate manipulation.

An initial exploration was conducted to understand the total number of records, the overall structure of the dataset, and the topic distribution. From the 25 topics available in the original dataset, 13 were selected based on their relevance to the focus of the project: Trigonometry, Optimization, Differential Geometry, Calculus, Probability, Linear Algebra, Differential Equations, Geometry, Statistics, Set Theory, Numerical Analysis, Algebra, and Logic. This selection was based on the fact that these subjects are commonly part of university curricula in science, engineering, and mathematics programs, and are therefore considered representative of general mathematical knowledge in that academic context.

To ensure the quality of the translated dataset, an exhaustive text cleaning and correction process was carried out. First, the CSV file was loaded and unnecessary columns such as `sub_topic` were removed to retain only the relevant information. Then, text normalization functions were applied, including standardizing capitalization and correcting common errors introduced during automatic translation. Generic or noisy phrases that did not add meaningful content were also removed.

To improve spelling accuracy, the `SpellChecker` library for Spanish was used [18]. This tool detected misspelled words in the dataset's questions. Using an external corrections file, only useful suggestions were filtered, those where the original word was not recognized by the spell checker and the suggestion belonged to the valid vocabulary of the language. These corrections were applied using optimized regular expressions, ensuring precise replacements without affecting other parts of the text.

3.3 Automatic Translation

To perform the automatic translation of the dataset, we used the `deep_translator` Python library, which offers a straightforward interface to various translation engines, including Google Translate. This service is based on neural machine translation models [19], which use Transformer-based architectures trained on large multilingual corpora. Unlike traditional statistical systems, Google's NMT models are better at capturing the semantic context of sentences and maintaining coherence at the paragraph level. This capability was crucial for preserving the original meaning of the questions and explanations during the translation from English to Spanish.

3.4 Semantic Evaluation of Translations

To evaluate the semantic quality of the translations, the `Mono TransQuest` model was used, based on the multilingual `xlm-roberta` architecture. This model estimates the semantic similarity between pairs of sentences without the need for human references [13].

This model was applied to the `question` and `explanation` fields of the translated dataset. The results were then analyzed to assess the consistency and semantic fidelity of the translations.

Unlike traditional metrics such as BLEU, which focus on surface-level lexical overlap, TransQuest estimates the semantic similarity between sentence pairs without the need for human reference translations, making it particularly suitable for evaluating specialized educational content where multiple valid phrasings may exist. This was a key reason for its selection in our study, as our dataset contains mathematical problems whose correct translation may vary in wording while preserving meaning.

Finally, the resulting dataset was prepared for use in fine-tuning the model. To this end, the key columns from the translated and corrected file—topic, question, and explanation—were selected. These were structured into a list of dictionaries with the fields `prompt` and `completion`, in JSON format and encoded in UTF-8.

3.5 Training and Integration of Classification and Generation Models

To build a system capable of assisting in solving mathematical problems, two complementary models were trained: one for thematic classification of questions and another for generating pedagogical explanations. Both were later functionally integrated within an automated workflow.

In the first phase, a classification model based on the `DistilBert` tokenizer was trained and organized using a custom class `MathQuestionDataset`, enabling structured handling within Hugging Face's `Trainer`. Common strategies such as early stopping were applied during training to improve generalization. Additionally, a visualization system was implemented to monitor loss during training, allowing detailed performance analysis.

In the second phase, a generative model was trained using `DeepSeekR1-DistillLlama-8B`, optimized with the `Unsloth` framework. The *Low-Rank Adaptation* (LoRA) technique was applied to reduce memory usage without compromising performance, following recent recommendations [20,21]. The model was fine-tuned with problem-explanation pairs, using customized instructions to guide text generation in a teaching style. As with the BERT-based classification model, a visualization system was implemented to analyze model behavior during training and evaluate its performance in detail.

Finally, both models were integrated into an automated workflow. When a user submits a question, it is thematically classified by `DistilBERT`. The resulting category is incorporated as part of a *prompt* that feeds the generative model

`DeepSeek`, allowing the generated response to be contextualized according to the problem type (see Fig. 3).

[Clase: Cálculo]
Pregunta: ¿Cómo resuelvo un polinomio?

Fig. 3. Sample of the contextualization of the *prompt* for response generation.

This integrated design promotes clear, relevant, and topic-tailored responses, offering an effective pedagogical solution for math assistance.

3.6 Model Implementation

To validate the combined behavior of the classification and generation models prior to final deployment, a functional visualization was created using the `Gradio` tool, which allows building lightweight web interfaces for machine learning models. This visualization served as an exploratory prototype to evaluate the sequential interaction between the two components: the model responsible for classifying the questions, and the generative model, which produces detailed explanations based on the predicted category. This stage was key for verifying the coherence of the data flow and the proper formatting of the prompt.

Once the flow was validated through Gradio, the development of a functional prototype in the form of a Telegram bot was carried out. It was designed to interact directly with users through a question-and-answer system. This choice was made to ensure an accessible, cross-platform, and low-cost interface. Additionally, Telegram's instant messaging facilitates a natural, asynchronous, and student-centered interaction.

It is important to highlight that all commands, messages, and variables were adapted to Spanish, as the system is intended for Spanish-speaking students. This linguistic adaptation ensures that the interaction feels intuitive and contextually appropriate for the target audience.

The implementation of the classification model was carried out using the `Trainer` class from the `transformers` library. During fine-tuning, key hyperparameters were defined to improve generalization and optimize model performance. A weight decay of `0.05` was applied as a form of *L2 regularization*, helping to reduce overfitting by penalizing large weights. The learning rate was initialized at `2e-5`, a standard value for fine-tuning transformer models, and it was adjusted dynamically throughout training via a learning rate scheduler. Furthermore, the training was guided by the metric `eval_loss`, with the flag `greater_is_better=False`, meaning that the model checkpoint with the lowest validation loss was selected as the best model for deployment.

Subsequently, the database was set up, establishing the required tables:

- **usuarios:** Records the users who interact with the bot.
- **respuestas_usuarios:** Stores the answers given by users, including whether they were correct or not.

- **estadisticas_usuarios:** Stores individual statistics (total number of questions, correct answers, mistakes, and success rate).
- **respuestas:** Detailed record of answers by subject.

All table names and their fields are defined in Spanish to maintain consistency with the language of interaction and the educational focus on Spanish-speaking users.

The Telegram client, in this context, refers to the software component that communicates directly with the Telegram API to send and receive messages. This client was implemented using the `Telethon` library, which facilitates the management of sessions, messages, and events. Through this client, the bot can interpret and respond to various commands that enhance the user experience, such as:

- /**inicio:** Starts a new user session and displays the available commands.
- /**pregunta:** Sends a random question selected from the database.
- /**estadísticas:** Displays the user's personal statistics, including visual charts.
- /**modelo:** Allows the user to send a text to be analyzed by the trained classification model.

Note that all bot commands are also presented in Spanish to ensure clarity and alignment with the user's native language.

The message processing distinguishes between answers to questions—comparing the user's response with the correct one through text normalization and updating the corresponding statistics—and analytical texts, which are processed by the trained model, providing the predicted class and associated confidence level.

Robust error handling is implemented for both database connection and inference processing, using structured `Try/except` blocks to catch and log exceptions at every critical operation. For database interactions, the system ensures proper closure of connections and cursors in finally blocks, preventing resource leaks. User registration, question retrieval, and statistics generation each include dedicated error messages for both console logs and Telegram bot responses. In inference processing, errors are caught during tokenization and model prediction, returning descriptive alerts to the user without interrupting the bot's execution. This approach prevents crashes, facilitates debugging, and maintains a consistent user experience in production.

4 Experiments and Results

This section presents the results obtained throughout the implementation of the proposed system. It covers various aspects of the experimental process, including the semantic evaluation of the automatic translations of the dataset, the performance of the BERT-based classification model, the thematic categorization of educational content, and the generation of explanations using language models.

Each subsection describes the experiments conducted, the metrics used, and the most relevant findings, aiming to validate the effectiveness of the proposed approach.

4.1 Results of the Semantic Evaluation

After applying the MonoTransQuest model, based on the xlm-roberta architecture, semantic similarity scores were obtained for each pair of original English sentences and their corresponding Spanish translations.

The results show an average score of **0.456** for the question field and **0.453** for the explanation field. The corresponding medians are **0.437** and **0.441**, respectively. These results suggest that the translations maintain a generally acceptable level of semantic equivalence. The inclusion of descriptive statistics such as mean, median, and 95% confidence intervals helps characterize the overall behavior of the distributions.

Figures 4 and 5 illustrate the distributions of similarity scores, normalized with kernel density estimation (KDE). A 95% confidence interval is visualized as a shaded region around the mean, and vertical lines mark both the mean and median values.

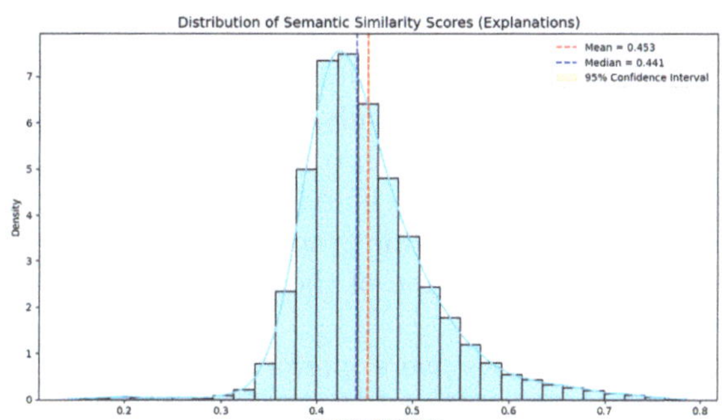

Fig. 4. Distribution of semantic similarity scores for the translated explanations.

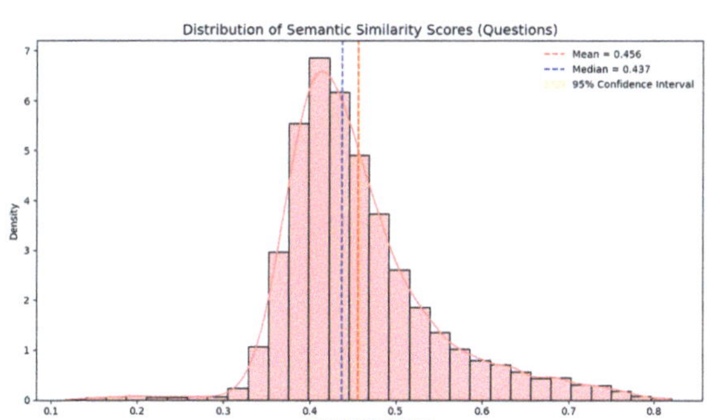

Fig. 5. Distribution of semantic similarity scores for the translated questions.

Both distributions are relatively symmetric, with most scores concentrated between 0.4 and 0.6. This indicates that the translations generally maintain a stable and coherent semantic alignment between the original and translated texts. The narrow confidence intervals and close proximity between the mean and median values reinforce the consistency and reliability of the translation process, making the dataset suitable for downstream tasks such as classification and explanation generation.

4.2 Evaluation of the BERT Classification Model

The evaluation of the BERT-based classification model was conducted using a comprehensive approach that combined quantitative metrics with qualitative analysis. First, the *accuracy* metric was employed as the primary criterion, as it directly measures the percentage of correct predictions out of the total examples evaluated. This metric was calculated on a hold-out validation set containing 20% of the available data, ensuring that the evaluation was performed on data unseen during training.

From a qualitative perspective, the internal structure of the representations learned by BERT was analyzed. Specifically, the output vectors from the model's final layer, known as *embeddings*, were extracted and subjected to dimensionality reduction using Principal Component Analysis (PCA) to project these vectors onto a two-dimensional space. This graphical representation facilitated the examination of the spatial distribution of thematic classes in the model's latent space.

Additionally, manual reviews were performed on selected representative examples from each class to verify whether the projections aligned with the semantic content of the questions. This procedure was particularly useful for identifying borderline cases or ambiguities that might explain confusion between categories.

Finally, the loss curve during training iterations was visualized, as shown in Fig. 6. This graph allowed monitoring the model's performance evolution over time and provided visual evidence of the convergence process. The observed decreasing trend in the loss was a key indicator of effective parameter optimization.

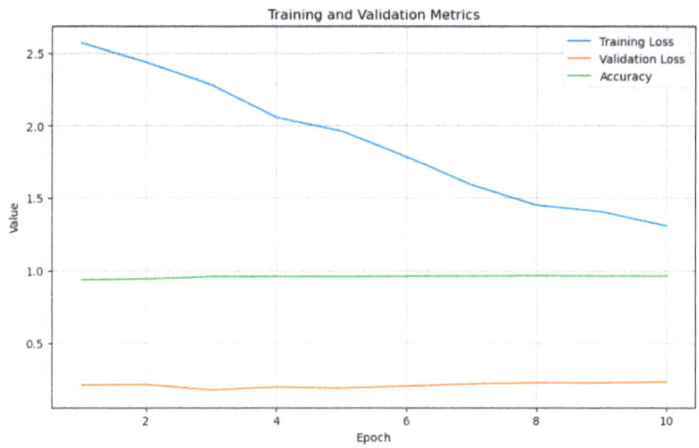

Fig. 6. Loss evolution during training of the BERT classification model.

4.3 Thematic Classification

For the automatic classification of mathematical problems, a model based on DistilBERT was trained to identify the main topic of a given question. The goal is that, upon receiving a text input, the model assigns the appropriate thematic category (such as linear algebra, statistics, differential geometry, among others).

The model was evaluated using the accuracy metric. As a complementary qualitative analysis, PCA was applied to visualize the output vectors generated by the model. This allowed us to observe how the model internally organizes semantic representations (Fig. 7).

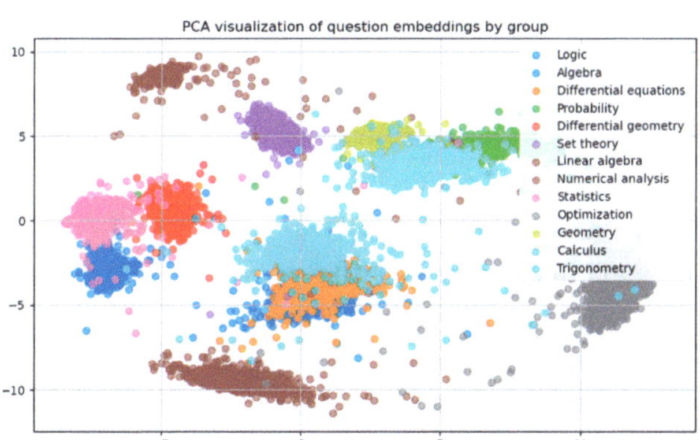

Fig. 7. Two-dimensional visualization of the embeddings generated by BERT using PCA.

The visualization shows clearly formed clusters differentiated by topic, which supports the model's ability to learn meaningful semantic structures within the mathematical domain. However, some overlapping regions were observed, especially between probability and statistics, due to their conceptual closeness.

This classification module is fundamental because the detected topic activates the recommendation mechanism that guides the selection of problem-solving strategies. Therefore, thematic classification acts as the initial filter in the response generation process.

4.4 Training Results of the DeepSeek Model

During the training of the `DeepSeekR1-DistillLlama-8B` model, a monitoring system was implemented to visualize the loss evolution in real time, facilitating the tracking of the process and the detection of potential signs of overfitting.

Figure 8 shows a decreasing trend in the loss function, indicating a progressive convergence toward an optimal solution. This behavior suggests that the model was able to properly adapt to the dataset without overtraining.

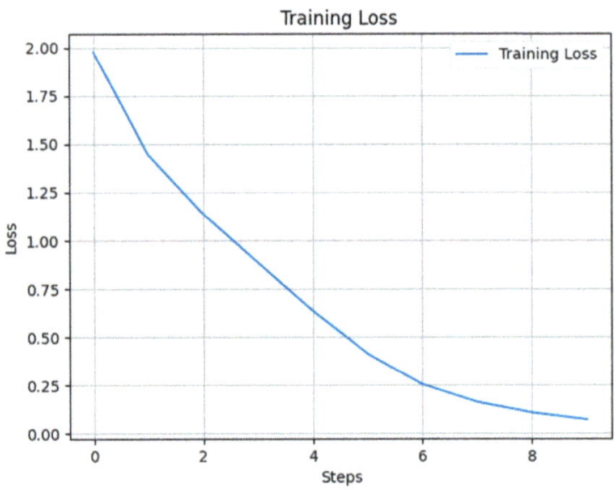

Fig. 8. Loss evolution during the training of the text generation model.

4.5 Text Generation Model Results

The goal of the model is to produce responses that not only provide the final result but also explain the reasoning necessary to reach it, in a clear, didactic manner adapted to the type of problem.

Example of Text Generation. As part of the qualitative evaluation, the model was asked to answer questions related to integrals. Table 2 presents a sample of the generated responses, along with their corresponding evaluation scores using TransQuest and BERTScore. These metrics allow for an assessment of semantic similarity and linguistic quality, highlighting differences in relevance and precision among model outputs.

Table 2. Evaluation of text generation using TransQuest and BERTScore (*Evaluación de la generación de texto usando TransQuest y BERTScore*)

Prompt	Generated Text	TransQuest	BERTScore
¿Qué es la integral? (What is the integral?)	*La integral es una operación fundamental en el cálculo que permite encontrar el área bajo una curva dado intervalo en el plano x-y.* (The integral is a fundamental operation in calculus that allows finding the area under a curve over a given interval in the x-y plane.)	0.7295	**Precision:** 0.8555 **Recall:** 0.9118 **F1:** 0.8828
¿Qué es la integral? (What is the integral?)	*La derivada es el reversa de la integral y es utilizada para hallar la velocidad derivada de un movimiento.* (The derivative is the reverse of the integral and is used to find the rate of change of motion.)	0.4019	**Precision:** 0.7435 **Recall:** 0.7822 **F1:** 0.7624
¿Qué es la integral? (What is the integral?)	*La integral es una operación que relaciona las polineses con sus derivadas.* (The integral is an operation that relates polynomials to their derivatives.)	0.2489	**Precision:** 0.6154 **Recall:** 0.6287 **F1:** 0.6220

4.6 Functional Prototype

All components were integrated into a functional prototype accessible through a Telegram bot. This interface allows users to interact with the system via simple commands, submit questions, and receive immediate responses.

The interaction flow involves the following steps:

- Classify the submitted question using the BERT model to identify the type of problem and the corresponding subject area.
- Query the database to select previously solved similar problems and extract statistics related to the student's performance, such as the number of attempts, accuracy rate by category, and temporal evolution of their performance.
- Generate a personalized explanation based on the detected topic, using a generative model that adapts the level of detail according to the user's history.

As illustrated in Fig. 9, the Telegram bot identifies the topic of the question and generates an appropriate explanation using the integrated models.

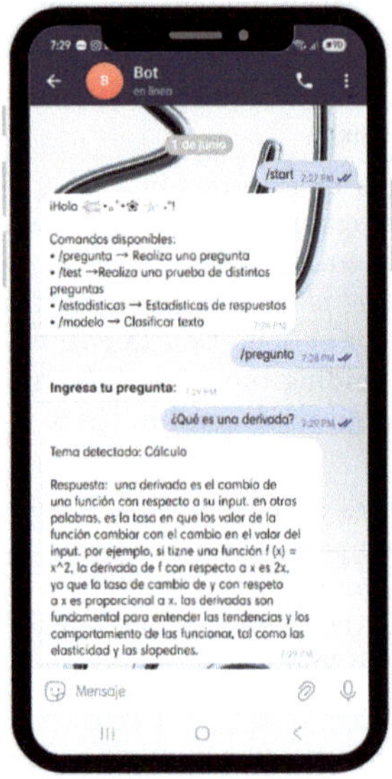

Fig. 9. Telegram bot identifying the topic and generating an explanation for a math question.

The system not only responds to submitted questions but also automatically logs user interactions, enabling the construction of a progressive learning profile. This tracking functionality is essential for identifying strengths, weaknesses, and patterns in the student's progress.

5 Conclusion

This work presented a comprehensive approach to support mathematics learning through natural language processing techniques. By combining classification and generation models, a system was built capable of interpreting questions, assigning them to specific topics, and generating explanatory answers in a conversational environment.

The results obtained show that the generated answers adequately preserve meaning, even in cases with minor grammatical errors. Thematic integration in the prompts proved useful for improving the coherence of the responses.

However, key areas for improvement were identified. Full integration of the models still faces technical limitations, and the evaluation has only been conducted in controlled environments. To strengthen the validity of the results, it is necessary to implement trials with real students to collect qualitative data on the system's pedagogical usefulness and its impact on learning.

6 Future Work

In future versions, the following is proposed:

- Integrate more advanced models such as `GPT-4` or `Gemini` to enhance text generation.
- Incorporate complementary metrics, such as `BLEU`, `ROUGE`, `METEOR`, or others adapted to educational evaluation.
- Generate or use natively created Spanish datasets focused on academic university content.
- Explore adaptation mechanisms based on the student's profile, such as question history or educational level.

Acknowledgements. The authors thank the Unidad Profesional Interdisciplinaria de Ingeniería Campus Tlaxcala of the Instituto Politécnico Nacional for its support in the preparation of this work.

Conflict of Interest. The authors declare that they have no competing interests to declare that are relevant to the content of this article.

References

1. Muñoz, C., González, D.: Los chatbots como herramienta de apoyo para la orientación universitaria. Edutec **87**, 1–15 (2024)
2. Fernández, M.M.: Chatbots: Apoyo en la educación/chatbots: Support in education (n.d.)
3. Al Ka'bi, A.: Proposed artificial intelligence algorithm and deep learning techniques for development of higher education. Int. J. Intell. Netw. **4**, 68–73 (2023)
4. Álava, L.D.: Revisión sistemática de la literatura de los sistemas de recomendación de contenidos educativos. Informática y Sistemas: Revista de Tecnologías de la Informática y las Comunicaciones **4**(2), 21–26 (2021)
5. Ulloa, L.H.A., et al.: Deserción y reprobación en cálculo diferencial, un estudio cualitativo en el instituto tecnológico de chihuahua. Estudios y Perspectivas Revista Científica y Académica **4**(1), 2063–2096 (2024)
6. Zhang, L., Basham, J.: Chatbots in education: a systematic review. J. Educ. Technol. Dev. Exchange **13**(1), 1–15 (2020)
7. Patel, H., Prajapati, H., Gohil, R.: A review on educational recommender systems. Int. J. Comput. Appl. **183**(38), 1–6 (2021)
8. García, E., Delgado, A.: Recommender systems for education: state of the art and trends. J. Educ. Technol. **5**(2), 115–129 (2009)
9. Manouselis, N., Drachsler, H., Verbert, K., Duval, E.: Recommender systems in technology enhanced learning. In: SpringerBriefs in Computer Science, pp. 1–22 (2010)
10. Moreira, D., et al.: Análisis del estado actual de procesamiento de lenguaje natural. Revista Ibérica de Sistemas e Tecnologias de Informação **E42**, 126–136 (2021)
11. Bertossi, V., Romero, L., Gutiérrez, M.d.l.M.: Sistemas recomendadores para el desarrollo de objetos de aprendizaje para educación en ingenierías: una revisión sistemática. Revista de Educación a Distancia (RED) **24**, 77 (2024)

12. Grant , P., Basye, D.: Personalized learning: a guide for engaging students with technology. International Society for Technology in Education (2014)
13. Ranasinghe, T., Orasan, C., Mitkov, R.: Transquest: translation quality estimation with cross-lingual transformers. In: Proceedings of the 58th Annual Meeting of the Association for Computational Linguistics (ACL) (2020). https://arxiv.org/abs/2011.01536
14. Yuan, W., Neubig, G., Liu, P.: Bartscore: evaluating generated text as text generation. In: Ranzato, M., Beygelzimer, A., Dauphin, Y., Liang, P., Vaughan, J.W. (eds.) Advances in Neural Information Processing Systems, vol. 34, pp. 27 263–27 277. Curran Associates, Inc. (2021)
15. Lecona, M., et al.: Chatbots educativos: Aplicaciones de pln y aprendizaje automático. In: Congreso Internacional de Tecnologías en Educación (2023)
16. Rana, U., Kaur, S.: Eaglebot: a BERT-based chatbot for education. In: Proceedings of the 12th International Conference on Educational Data Mining, pp. 546–551 (2019)
17. Li, G., Hammoud, H.A.A.K., Itani, H., Khizbullin, D., Ghanem, B.: Camel: communicative agents for "mind" exploration of large scale language model society (2023)
18. P. Developers: Pyspellchecker: Pure python spell checking (2024). https://pypi.org/project/pyspellchecker/, Último acceso: mayo de 2025
19. Wu, Y., et al.: Google's neural machine translation system: bridging the gap between human and machine translation. arXiv preprint arXiv:1609.08144 (2016)
20. Hu, E.J., et al.: Lora: low-rank adaptation of large language models. arXiv preprint arXiv:2106.09685 (2021)
21. U. Team: Unsloth: Fast and memory-efficient fine-tuning of LLMs (2024). https://github.com/unslothai/unsloth

Enhancing English–Urdu Machine Translation Using Transfer Learning

Fida Ullah, M. Tayyab Zamir, M. Ahmad, Irina Gelbukh, Grigori Sidorov, and Edgardo Manuel Felipe Riverón(✉)

Instituto Politécnico Nacional (IPN), Centro de Investigación en Computación (CIC), Av. Juan de Dios Batiz, s/n, 07320 Mexico City, Mexico
{Fullah-2022,Edgardo}@cic.ipn.mx

Abstract. The process of automatically converting the text from one language to another natural language is Machine Translation. Urdu is a language that is spoken in Pakistan and in some part of India, Afghanistan, and Middle East. Only 5 to 10% people can understand English language. They are not able to get latest knowledge in this digital globe. That's why, this study explores the development of English to Urdu and Urdu to English machine translation system using transfer learning-based approaches. The research aims to address the language barrier that limits access to information for Urdu speakers by leveraging the FB mBART-50 model, a state-of-the-art multilingual sequence-to-sequence model. Through extensive evaluation, the FB mBART-50 model demonstrated significant improvements over previous models, achieving maximum BLEU score from the combined data is approximately 0.867 for English to Urdu translation and 0.669 BLEU score for Urdu to English translation. Despite some challenges with pronoun accuracy and lexical repetition, the model consistently produced contextually appropriate and semantically accurate translations. This study highlights the potential of deep/transfer learning methods to enhance machine translation quality, suggesting that with further improvements and optimizations, these methods can facilitate seamless communication in multilingual environments.

Keywords: Machine Translation · Natural Language Processing · Transformers · Low Resource Language

1 Introduction

English is an international language that preserves a large amount of literature and scientific knowledge etc. There is a large population all over the world who can't understand the English language [1]. Urdu language is spoken in Pakistan and in some part of India, Afghanistan and the Middle East. Only 5 to 10% of people can understand the English language. [2–4] They cannot get the latest knowledge and remove communication hurdles worldwide [5]. The world has become a global village because of World Wide Web, social media and international businesses. For convenient communication, the language barrier must be covered by translating one natural language to another natural language with or without human interference [6]. A process by which a machine can translate

C. Palma-Preciado et al. (Eds.): CORE 2025, ACSAR 3, pp. 335–346, 2026.
https://doi.org/10.1007/978-3-032-08894-9_22

from source language sentences to target language sentences accurately without losing its semantics by using some computer software [7]. MT used computer resources to translate important content of high-resource English language to low-resource Urdu language to overcome the language barrier [8]. There are many Urdu speakers, around 104 million, worldwide, but there are a few public domain machine translation tools like Google, Babylon, SDL Translator and Bing Translator for the Urdu language. According to our research, few available online systems do not support the Urdu language like SYSTRAN Translator, PROMT Translator, BabelFish, LogoMedia, InterTran and WorldLingo. Table 1. Presents examples of English sentences and their translation in Urdu language using Bing and google translator.

Table 1. Here are few examples of English sentences, translate in Urdu on Google and Bing Translator.

Sentence	Bing Translator	Google Translator
It's raining cats and dogs.	بلیوں اور کتوں کی بارش ہو رہی ہے۔	یہ بلیاں اور کتے برس رہے ہیں۔
She is walking on air.	وہ ہوا میں چل رہا ہے.	وہ ہوا پر چل رہی ہے۔
He's pulling your leg.	وہ آپ کی ٹانگ کھینچ رہا ہے.	اس نے آپ کا ٹانگ کھینچ رکھی ہے۔
Tomorrow early morning first I go to morning walk.	کل صبح سویرے سب سے پہلے میں صبح کی چہل قدمی کے لیے جاتا ہوں۔	کل صبح سب سے پہلے میں مارننگ واک پر جاتا ہوں۔
I am full.	میں بھرا ہوا ہوں	میں بھرا ہوا ہوں.

There are different types of challenges that researchers may face in MT, which we have to overcome to generate an accurate and context-aware machine translation system. In bilingual translation, it isn't easy to translate such words with different meanings in different contexts. Translation divergence is a common obstacle in MT between bilingual translational models. It occurs when the lexical and syntactical same text of the source language (English) cannot accurately translate into a similar text of the target language (Urdu) [9]. Word-by-word phrase translation is another obstacle in idiomatic and proverb text. In English, adjectives and nouns generally lack gender associations. In contrast, Urdu attributes gender to both adjectives and nouns. Urdu follows Subject-Object-Verb word order, whereas English follows Subject–Verb–Object. When the position of the subject interchange in English sentences, the meaning of the sentence will change, but in the Urdu language, there is no change in the meaning of the sentence [10].

For many decades now, researchers have been working to improve machine translation. Machine translation's primary value lies in its capacity to break down linguistic barriers. Moreover 100 million people in Pakistan, India, Afghanistan, and the Middle East are fluent in Urdu, Pakistan's national language. The ordinary Urdu speaker has a hard time interacting with individuals from other countries due to the low English literacy rate. Use a computer program to translate phrases precisely and idiomatically from English to Urdu and Urdu to English [11–13].

1.1 Contributions

This study makes several key contributions to the field of machine translation, particularly for low-resource language pairs such as English–Urdu and Urdu–English. First, we developed an effective machine translation system for both English–Urdu and Urdu–English directions and built an evaluation platform to assess the execution and performance of various NLP methodologies. Second, we applied the FB mBART-50 model to this low-resource language pair, demonstrating its adaptability and effectiveness, while identifying the challenges associated with transfer learning in bilingual translation. Third, our approach achieved superior translation performance compared to traditional models, as measured by evaluation metrics such as BLEU and NIST. Additionally, we highlighted critical issues such as pronoun accuracy and lexical repetition, providing insights to guide future improvement efforts. Finally, our study demonstrates the model's potential for enhancing multilingual communication and improving access to information across diverse linguistic contexts.

2 Literature Review

In this research [14], a novel Linguistics Knowledge-Driven Multi-Task (LKMT) model was developed to enhance Urdu to English neural machine translation (NMT) by embedding linguistic features such as part-of-speech (POS) and dependency parsing (DEP). The model was trained on a dataset of over 5.4 million Urdu sentences and achieved notable improvements in translation accuracy, evidenced by BLEU score increases of 1.97 points for Urdu to English and 2.42 points for English to Urdu. These enhancements underscore the potential of integrating linguistic knowledge to address translation challenges for low-resource languages like Urdu.

This study [15] makes a valuable contribution to machine translation by focusing on the unique challenges of translating low-resource languages. Utilizing a transformer-based neural network model, the research addresses specific linguistic complexities in Urdu-to-English translation. Unlike much prior work on translation for resource-rich languages, this study applies deep learning techniques to less commonly translated languages. The model was trained on four datasets UMC005, Tanzil, The Wire, and PIB covering religious and news content, achieving an impressive BLEU score of 23.9. This score reflects the model's accuracy in producing precise and contextually relevant translations.

In this paper [16], the authors develop a deep learning model for sentiment analysis of Urdu text, with a focus on the challenges arising from the language's complex morphology and script. Given the limited resources available for Urdu sentiment analysis, they compiled a dataset of 25,000 Urdu reviews, partly translated from IMDB data. Two models, CNN and LSTM, were trained to classify sentiment at the sentence level. The LSTM model outperformed CNN, achieving 96% accuracy and a 91% F1 score, demonstrating superior effectiveness for Urdu sentiment analysis compared to traditional methods. In this paper [17], they work on to develop a model to solve the translation issue from Roman Urdu to the English language.

It's a challenging situation that Roman Urdu language does not follow any specific grammatical pattern and no specific rule for spellings. That's why we used rule-based translation and prepared the grammatical rules to accomplish the process of language translation in a tagger. We entered a Roman Urdu sentence which gave the best possible translation in the English language. Transtech work best and translate more accurately than Google translator and have an average 0.45 BLUE score.

In another research [18], the authors proposed a multilingual machine translator which is capable to translate from English to Urdu and Hindi language which is based on translation Rules-Based approach along with artificial neural network model. Artificial neural network is suitable for this translation system because of its efficient ability to learn by examples and pattern matching. By using machine translation evaluation methods, the translation results of this model are evaluated and conclude that this translation model works very well on the trained bilingual dictionaries and translation rules along with higher accuracy.

This paper [19], builds on existing work in machine translation by addressing the challenges specific to English-Urdu translation, a low-resource language pair with distinct syntactic and semantic features. Previous methods, including statistical and traditional neural machine translation models such as LSTM and GRU, have struggled with Urdu's complex grammar and cultural nuances.

Recognizing these limitations, recent advancements have leaned towards hybrid models that combine multiple neural network architectures, aiming to capitalize on both sequential and spatial data processing. This study advances this approach by integrating LSTM and GRU models with CNNs to improve feature extraction, coupled with transfer learning using FastText embeddings to enhance semantic and syntactic accuracy. Employing evaluation metrics like BLEU, TER, and METEOR, the study demonstrates how hybrid models surpass the performance of individual neural architectures, setting a new standard for English-to-Urdu translation accuracy.

In another research study [20], author worked on a domain specific language translation model to translate English to Urdu language based on Religious, General, Technological and Biomedical domains by using Statistical and Neural Machine Translation. Domain dependent data is used to train the system. MT produces wrong results if the testing domain data differ from the training domain data. To enhance the performance multiple experiments are attempted. The proposed system translates source language to target language efficiently based on the domain to which the word is related and has an average 0.6029 n-gram blue score.

This study [21], addresses the ongoing challenge of low-resource language translation, specifically focusing on Urdu-English translation. Traditional neural machine translation (NMT) methods, such as CNN and CNN-ADL models, have demonstrated limitations in capturing the complex linguistic structures inherent in Urdu, a morphologically rich language. To improve upon these limitations, recent studies have explored the use of fully convolutional neural networks (FConv-NN) due to their efficiency in handling longer sequences and their potential for capturing local dependencies within sentences. Building on this, the authors developed an FConv-NN encoder-decoder model with an integrated attention mechanism, designed to better manage Urdu syntax and semantics. Evaluated on an Urdu-English parallel corpus containing 10,000 sentences from diverse sources like news, sports, and movie dialogues, the model was tested against conventional CNN-based models. The FConv-NN model outperformed prior methods, achieving a BLEU score of 40.22, a substantial improvement over the 21.80 BLEU score of the standard CNN model. This result underscores the effectiveness of fully convolutional architectures in enhancing translation accuracy for under-resourced language pairs.

3 Methodology and Techniques

The proposed model for machine translation between English and Urdu involves the following steps: collecting data, preparing the data for analysis, converting words into numerical representations, transforming these numerical representations back into words, and ultimately translating the content into the desired language. Figure 1 illustrates the methodology workflow.

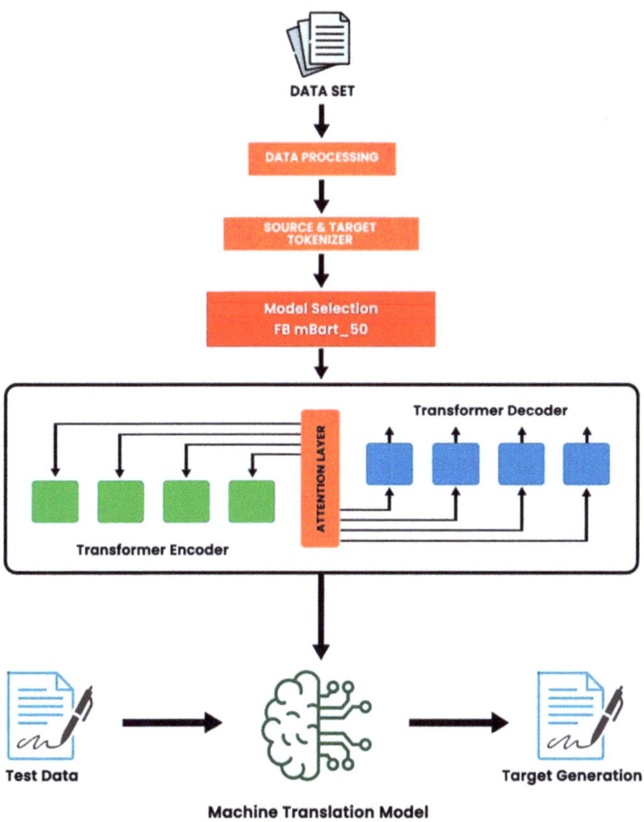

Fig. 1. English to Urdu Machine Translation Methodology Diagram

3.1 Data Collection

We collected data from the Emille corpus [20], distributed by ELRA (European Language Resource Association) and UMC005 for the bilingual translational model. The detail description of dataset is shown in Table 2. The Emille corpus is a written and spoken collection of analyzed, parallel and monolingual corpus. It is the combination of educational, social, legal and health etc related multi domain dataset in 14th South Asian languages and is distributed by ELRA (European Language Resource Association). UMC005 English-Urdu is a parallel corpus that is made of English and Urdu aligned sentence pairs, which are employed for statistical machine translation experiments. This corpus contains texts from the Quran, Bible, and Penn Treebank. The compilation of this dataset is done by the European Language Resource Association (ELRA) and UMC005.

Table 2. Dataset Description

Languages	Words	Tokens	Unique Words
English	1437074	1532948	7113
Urdu	1582430	1967119	7410

3.2 Data Preprocessing

Dataset preprocessing for Urdu to English and English to Urdu translation involves several key steps. Initially, the data is cleaned to remove noise such as HTML tags and special characters, followed by tokenization into words or sub words. Normalization techniques are then applied, including lowercase conversion and punctuation removal, stop words, which have minimal semantic value, are eliminated to enhance the model's focus on meaningful content. The text is structured in such a way that it consists of sentences or phrases which are required to be language-specific. All of these preprocessing is done through MBart50TokenizerFast.

3.3 Tokenization

Tokenization converts input text into a sequence of tokens, which are numerical representations that the model can process. The input text is split into smaller units called tokens by using MBart50TokenizerFast from the transformers library by Hugging Face, which can be subwords, words or characters. Every token is associated with a distinctive integer ID which is derived from a predetermined vocabulary that is specific to the

MBart model. This model has tokens for several languages. Special tokens such as the start-of-sequence and the end-of-sequence, are added to the sequence to help the model identify the beginning and end of the input. Attention masks are generated to indicate which tokens should be attended to by the model, helping manage padded sequences during batch processing. This process transforms the text into a numerical format the model can understand and use for tasks like translation.

3.4 Data Encoder

In an English to Urdu machine translation system, the data encoder is a vital part that is responsible for converting input English sentences into a format that can be understood and processed by the translation model. The process starts with the tokenizer setting a source language token, like “en_XX” for English language. The tokenizer is then splitting the text into smaller units called tokens and converting these tokens into unique IDs which are in numeric form. These IDs are transformed into PyTorch tensors which include both token IDs and attention masks. The attention masks help the model turn its focus on the relevant tokens. This encoded input, already in a numerical format, is now sent to the MBart model for language translation detail shown in Fig. 2.

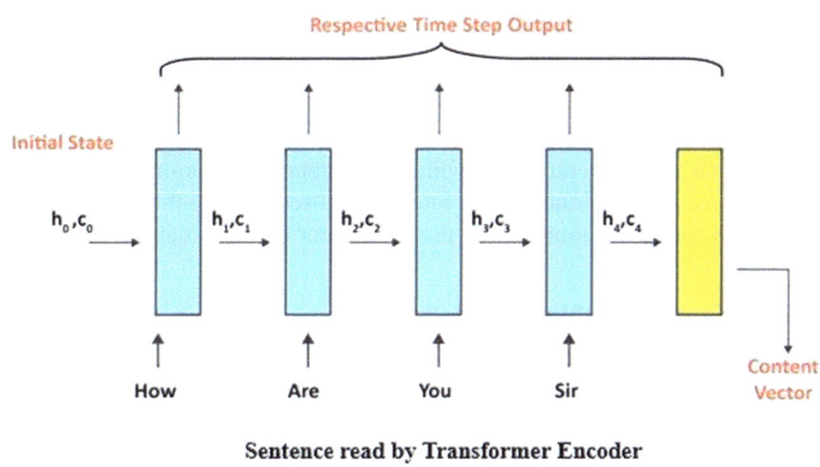

Fig. 2. Sentence read by Encoder

3.5 Decoding and Generating the Output

A decoder in a machine translation model converts the encoded representation of the input text into the target language text. The decoder starts by tokenizing English text into a sequence of tokens by using MBart tokenizer. The next step is that the tokenized text is fed into the MBart model, which then produces a sequence of tokens that signify the translated text in Urdu. This generated sequence is decoded back into human-readable Urdu text using the tokenizer's batch_decode‘ method, which converts the sequence of tokens into a string of Urdu text. In this case, English is used as the source language, the English text is encoded, the model generates the translated tokens, and finally, decoding these tokens into Urdu text is done to complete the translation process from English to Urdu.

4 Results

In this section, the results and discussion of the translation model are presented, which is accurate and efficient in translating routes between English and Urdu. The translation outcomes are analyzed in detail, expressing the strengths and limitations of the model. As a result, the implications of these findings are explored, with suggestions for potential improvements in future research and applications in the field of machine translation. Analysis of the relationship between the machine-made translations and the human-translated reference texts gives us the means to evaluate the machine translation system performance. For this assessment, i use the BLEU and NIST score as the benchmark metric to determine the quality of the translations. The BLEU score is a metric that compares the machine-generated text with the reference translation by examining the precision of n-grams in the output. The more BLEU scores a machine translation gets, the better its translation, demonstrating that it is closer to the human translations.

4.1 Urdu to English Machine Translation

This section presents the test results of the Urdu-to-English machine translation. The accuracy of translation and the speed of data processing are first highlighted, followed by key performance metrics such as BLEU, NIST, WER (Word Error Rate), Precision, Recall, F-measure, and Accuracy. The talk gives the strengths and weaknesses of the model. Table 3 provides a detailed comparison between the predicted and reference outputs, while Table 4 presents detailed evaluation metrics for 10 test cases, each corresponding to one sentence translation. Each row in the table represents the scores computed for a single Urdu-to-English sentence pair.

Table 3. Comparison of predicted output with reference output

Urdu Text	Reference English	Machine Translation	Observation
اسے لیموں اور سیب پسند ہ نی۔	she likes lemons and apples.	He likes lemons and apples.	Gender misinterpretation (She → He)
کیا وہ فٹ بال کے میدان م نی جانا پسند کرے گا؟	would he like to go the football field?	Would he like to go to the football field?	Accurate
آپ کا سب سے کم پسندیدہ جانور پرندہ ہ۔	your least favorite animal is the bird.	Your least favorite animal is the bird.	Accurate
آپ کو لیموں اور لیموں پسند ہ نی۔	you like limes and lemons.	You like lemons and lemons.	Repetition error (limes → lemons)
لیموں آپ کا سب سے پسندیدہ پھل ہے، لیکن نارن .ج اس کا سب سے کم پسندیدہ پھل ہ۔	the lemon is your least favorite fruit, but the orange is his least favorite.	Lemon is your favorite bean, but orange is his least favorite bean.	Semantic error (fruit → bean)
کیلیفورنیا کبھی کبھی نوم .ب کے دوران ہلکا ہوتا ہے، اور یہ اپریل م نی کبھی مصروف نہ نی ہوتا ہ۔	california is sometimes mild during november, and it is never busy in april.	California is sometimes mild during November, and it's never busy in April.	Accurate

Table 4. Several evaluation metrics values

Test case	BLEU Score	NIST Score	WER Score	Precision	Recall	F-Measure	Accuracy
1	0.66874	1.858	0.200	0.800	0.800	0.800	0.800
2	0.354948	2.113	0.444	0.750	0.667	0.706	0.667
3	0.532946	1.988	0.375	0.714	0.625	0.667	0.625
4	9.30E-155	1.393	0.400	0.600	0.600	0.600	0.600
5	0.27821	1.951	0.438	0.700	0.583	0.636	0.583
6	0.246898	2.118	0.467	0.667	0.571	0.615	0.571
7	0.430125	1.693	0.429	0.667	0.571	0.615	0.571

(continued)

Table 4. (*continued*)

Test case	BLEU Score	NIST Score	WER Score	Precision	Recall	F-Measure	Accuracy
8	2.93E-78	1.663	0.667	0.636	0.500	0.560	0.500
9	6.60E-155	1.847	0.600	0.583	0.500	0.538	0.500
10	0.364093	1.411	0.500	0.667	0.500	0.571	0.500

Overall, the model demonstrates strong performance in simpler sentence structures, achieving a BLEU score as high as 0.66874 and precision, recall and F1 measure values up to 0.800, indicating high reliability. However, certain sentences reveal semantic mismatches, such as incorrect word substitution ("fruit" translated as "bean") or gender misidentification ("she" translated as "he"). These errors highlight areas where the model requires refinement, particularly in lexical disambiguation and contextual awareness.

The graphical summary in Fig. 3 illustrates the performance of the model across various evaluation metrics. Although some variations are visible between test cases, the model generally shows promising translation capabilities, suggesting its potential for real-world Urdu-to-English translation tasks.

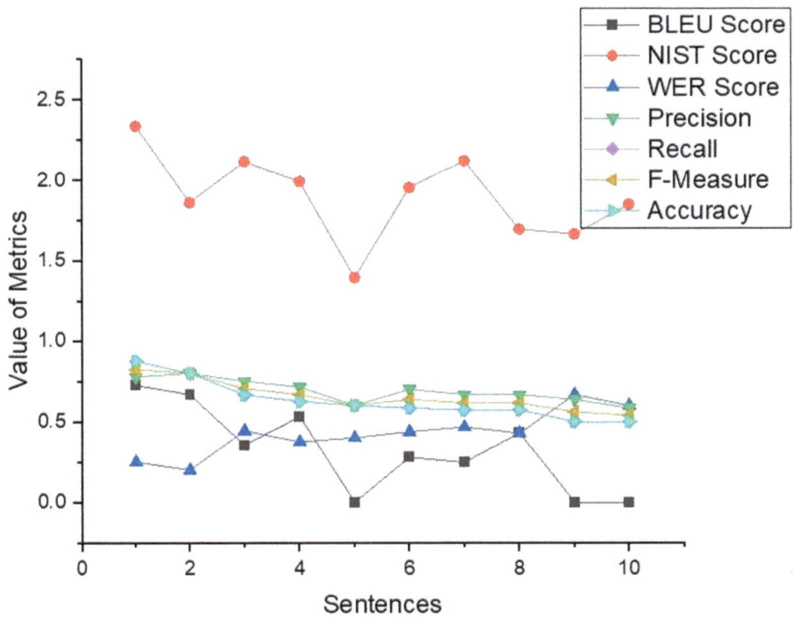

Fig. 3. Performance comparison of different evaluation metrics for Urdu to English translation

5 Conclusion

The research effectively addresses the language barrier that limits access to information for Urdu speakers by leveraging the FB mBART-50 model, a state-of-the-art multilingual sequence-to-sequence model. An extensive evaluation of the FB mBART-50 model for both Urdu-to-English and English-to-Urdu machine translation demonstrates significant advancements in translation quality compared to previous models, including LSTM, BiLSTM, encoder-decoder, and GRU. The model's superior performance is evident through various evaluation metrics, including BLEU and NIST scores, precision, recall, and accuracy, achieving a maximum BLEU score of approximately 0.867 and highest NIST score is 3.646 for English to Urdu translation and achieving 0.669 BLUE score and highest NIST score recorded is 2.398, reflecting a good ability to capture detailed translation features for Urdu to English translation.

Acknowledgments. The work was done with partial support from the Mexican Government through the grant A1-S-47854 of CONACYT, Mexico, grants 20241816, 20241819, and 20240951 of the Secretaría de Investigación y Posgrado of the Instituto Politécnico Nacional, Mexico. The authors thank the CONACYT for the computing resources provided through the Plataforma de Aprendizaje Profundo para Tecnologías del Lenguaje of the Laboratorio de Supercómputo of the INAOE, Mexico, and acknowledge the support of Microsoft through the Microsoft Latin America PhD Award.

Conflicts of Interest. The authors declare no conflicts of interest.

References

1. Okpor, M.D.: Machine translation approaches: issues and challenges. Int. J. Comput. Sci. Issues (IJCSI) **11**(5), 159 (2014)
2. Ullah, F., Ahmad, M., Zamir, M.T., Arif, M., Riverón, E.M., Gelbukh, A.: EDU-NER- 2025: named entity recognition in Urdu educational texts using XLM-RoBERTa with X (formerly Twitter). arXiv preprint: arXiv:2504.18142 (2025)
3. Ullah, F., Ullah, I., Kolesnikova, O.: Urdu named entity recognition with attention Bi-LSTM-CRF model. In: Mexican International Conference on Artificial Intelligence, pp. 3–17. Springer, Cham (2022)
4. Ullah, F., Gelbukh, A., Zamir, M.T., Riverón, E.M., Sidorov, G.: Enhancement of named entity recognition in low-resource languages with data augmentation and BERT models: a case study on Urdu. Computers **13**(10), 258 (2024)
5. Ahmed, T., Alvi, S.: English to Urdu translation system. Manuscript, University of Karachi (2002)
6. Akeel, M., Mishra, R.: ANN and rule based method for English to Arabic machine translation. Int. Arab J. Inf. Technol. **11**(4), 396–405 (2014)
7. Tufano, M., Watson, C., Bavota, G., Di Penta, M., White, M., Poshyvanyk, D.: An empirical study on learning bug-fixing patches in the wild via neural machine translation. ACM Trans. Softw. Eng. Methodol. **28**(4), 1–29 (2019)
8. Malik, A.A., Habib, A.: Urdu to English machine translation using bilingual evaluation understudy. Int. J. Comput. Appl. **82**(7) (2013)
9. Khan, S., Mir, U., Shreem, S.S., Alamri, S.: Translation divergence patterns handling in English to Urdu machine translation. Int. J. Artif. Intell. Tools **27**(05), 1850017 (2018)

10. Jindal, S., Goyal, V., Bhullar, J.S.: English to Punjabi statistical machine translation using Moses (Corpus Based). J. Stat. Manag. Syst. **21**(4), 553–560 (2018)
11. Ali, S.A., Khan, S., Perveen, H., Muzzamil, R., Malik, M., Khalid, F.: Urdu language translator using deep neural network. Indian J. Sci. Technol. **10**(40), 1–7 (2017)
12. Andrabi, S.A., Wahid, A.: [Retracted] machine translation system using deep learning for English to Urdu. Comput. Intell. Neurosci. **2022**(1), 7873012 (2022)
13. Ullah, Z., Alam, M.F., Ihsan, W.: Juxtaposing Urdu to English captions of Facebook/metaverse: a neural machine translation study. Global Lang. Rev. **VII**, 55–66 (2022)
14. Ul Hassan, M.N., et al.: LKMT: Linguistics knowledge-driven multi-task neural machine translation for Urdu and English. Comput., Mater. Continua **81**(1) (2024)
15. Safder, I., et al.: Transforming language translation: a deep learning approach to Urdu-English translation. J. Ambient. Intell. Humaniz. Comput. **15**(10), 3651–3662 (2024)
16. Ahmed, N., Amin, R., Aldabbas, H., Saeed, M., Bilal, M., Song, H.: A novel approach for sentiment analysis of a low resource language using deep learning Models. ACM Trans. Asian Low-Resour. Lang. Inf. Process. (2024)
17. Masroor, H., Saeed, M., Feroz, M., Ahsan, K., Islam, K.: Transtech: development of a novel translator for Roman Urdu to English. Heliyon 5(5) (2019)
18. Khan, S.N., Usman, I.: A model for English to Urdu and Hindi machine translation system using translation rules and artificial neural network. Int. Arab J. Inf. Technol. **16**(1), 125–131 (2019)
19. Adrees, M., et al.: A hybrid technique for English to Urdu machine translation using transfer learning. In: Intelligent Systems Conference, pp. 65–77. Springer, Cham (2024)
20. Abdul-Rauf, S., Abida, S., Zahra, S., Parvez, D., Bashir, J.: On the exploration of English to Urdu machine translation. In: Proceedings of the 1st Joint Workshop on Spoken Language Technologies for Under-Resourced Languages (SLTU) and Collaboration and Computing for Under-Resourced Languages (CCURL), pp. 285–293 (2020)
21. Israr, H., Shahzad, M.K., Anwar, S.: Improved Urdu-English neural machine translation with a fully convolutional neural network encoder. Int. J. Math. Eng. Manag. Sci. **9**(5) (2024)

Authorship Attribution in a Scientific Papers by Syntactic and Semantic Textual Representations

Carlos Pérez Guarneros[1], Cecilia Reyes-Peña[1,2](✉), Jesús García-Ramírez[1,2], and Silvia Sánchez-Márquez[1]

[1] Unidad Profesional Interdisciplinaria de Ingeniería Campus Tlaxcala IPN, Tlaxcala, Mexico
{creyespe,jegarciara,ssanchezma}@ipn.mx

[2] Universidad Poltécnica Metropolitana de Hidalgo, Hidalgo, Mexico

Abstract. Authorship Attribution is a well-established task in computational linguistics, involving the identification of the likely author of a given text based on linguistic and stylistic features. This work explores a hybrid approach to authorship attribution by constructing a feature vector that integrates both syntactic and semantic information from scientific texts. The experimental setup focuses on evaluating the effectiveness of these features in distinguishing authorship across of three curated corpora of scientific documents. We employ computationally lightweight classification models (as logistic regression) in order to assess the discriminative power of the features themselves, rather than relying on the complexity of the classifier. Our results indicate that the enriched feature representation achieves accuracy levels ranging from 0.85 to 0.96, aligning with or exceeding benchmarks reported in the literature. These findings underscore the viability of combining manual feature engineering with pre-trained language models and traditional machine learning algorithms for authorship attribution. Furthermore, the approach offers a compelling alternative to deep learning-based pipelines, especially in scenarios where computational resources are limited.

Keywords: Authorship Attribution · Semantic Representation · Syntactic Feature Extraction

1 Introduction

Authorship Attribution (AA) in scientific texts has historically been a central concern in academic integrity and bibliometric analysis. With the exponential growth in the number of scientific publications and the increasing availability of open-access databases such as arXiv and PubMed, the need for automatic and scalable methods to verify document authorship has become more pressing. Reliable authorship verification contributes directly to maintaining the integrity and credibility of scholarly communication systems [6].

C. Palma-Preciado et al. (Eds.): CORE 2025, ACSAR 3, pp. 347–357, 2026.
https://doi.org/10.1007/978-3-032-08894-9_23

AA can be formally defined as a classification task in which, given an input text, the goal is to determine which author from a predefined set is the most likely source, based on stylistic and linguistic evidence [5]. In the era of Natural Language Processing (NLP) driven by machine learning, this task has increasingly relied on the identification of latent patterns within texts through semantic representations [9,12]. However, current trends in NLP often prioritize contextualized distributed representations (as those produced by transformer-based language models) at the expense of incorporating manually engineered linguistic features, such as syntactic structure or grammatical patterns.

While these end-to-end approaches offer efficiency and performance gains in many contexts, they may also introduce biases and lead to reduced interpretability, particularly when applied to tasks requiring fine-grained linguistic analysis. In this context, the exclusive reliance on deep neural architectures can reduce the importance of textual signals that could otherwise contribute to authorship characterization.

In this study, we propose a computational approach to authorship identification in English-language scientific texts. We leverage supervised classification models informed by a robust set of stylometric features, encompassing both syntactic and semantic information. Our evaluation focuses on a multi-author, multi-topic corpus, assessing the predictive power of these features in distinguishing writing styles across different scientific authors.

2 Literature Review

AA is a classical task within Natural Language Processing (NLP) and stylometry that has undergone significant evolution in recent years, particularly with the emergence of neural network models and contextualized language representations. Below, we highlight some of the most representative advances in the field.

In [2], the authors propose a model named ADHOMINEM (Attention-based Deep Hierarchical Convolutional Siamese Bidirectional Recurrent Neural Network Model) for authorship verification in Amazon reviews. This model extends the previous Hierarchical Recurrent Siamese Network (HRSN) approach and achieves an accuracy of 85.3%, demonstrating greater discriminative power compared to systems based solely on stylometric features. The study also notes that error rates increase significantly in particularly challenging scenarios, such as *same author/similar topics* and *different authors/same topic*.

The 2022 PAN competition on authorship verification[1] introduced a dataset comprising emails, essays, text messages, and business memos, derived from the Aston 100 Idiolects Corpus in English[2]. The most effective approaches in the competition [8] employed siamese networks with graph-based text representations, incorporating Part-of-Speech (POS) tag embeddings [4].

[1] https://pan.webis.de/clef22/pan22-web/author-identification.html.

[2] https://fold.aston.ac.uk/handle/123456789/17.

In the domain of journalistic texts, [1] proposed a hybrid authorship attribution model that combines TF-IDF-based feature extraction with classifiers such as Logistic Regression, Random Forest, Multilayer Perceptron, and XGBoost. Among these, XGBoost achieved the highest accuracy (70.8%). Meanwhile, for the task of problem-solving within the context of the PISA 2012 dataset, Random Forest trained on TF-IDF features delivered the best predictive performance [12].

Specifically, regarding authorship verification in scientific texts, several studies have explored the applicability of various feature types. Wu et al. [11] emphasize that while simple features such as average sentence or word length provide some useful cues, they are insufficient on their own, as they fail to capture deeper syntactic and semantic information. This underscores the relevance of manual feature extraction as a complementary strategy.

Finally, Suman et al. [10] developed a Capsule Convolutional Neural Network (Capsule CNN) for AA in scientific abstracts, achieving an accuracy of 79.31%. This approach demonstrates the potential of specialized neural architectures, although performance remains dependent on the domain and text structure.

3 Methodology

This section outlines the dataset construction process, taking into account the relationships between authors and their respective publications. It then details the analytical methods applied for lexical and semantic feature extraction. Finally, it presents the evaluation phase, in which metrics such as precision, accuracy, and F1-score were computed to quantitatively assess each model's performance in the specified task.

3.1 Dataset Construction

The data used in this study were obtained from the arXiv Dataset [3], which comprises 2,643,168 abstracts of scientific articles covering a wide range of topics, including physics, mathematics, computer science, quantitative biology, and statistics. This dataset is structured with well-defined sections such as titles, authors, categories, and abstracts, along with additional metadata such as a unique identifier for each article.

For the purpose of authorship identification proposed in this work, we focus exclusively on abstracts written by a single author, in order to better capture individual writing styles and avoid ambiguity introduced by multi-author collaboration. Consequently, a subset of the original dataset was filtered to retain only single-author documents, ensuring more accurate attribution of stylistic features.

Three datasets were constructed based on varying numbers of authors and documents per author:

- Dataset A300_P45: Contains 300 authors, each with 45 abstracts, totaling 13,500 abstracts.

- Dataset A140_P60: Includes 140 authors, each associated with 60 abstracts, totaling 8,400 abstracts.
- Dataset A35_P100: Comprises 35 authors, each contributing 100 abstracts, totaling 3,500 abstracts.

It is important to note that the number of authors in each dataset represents the maximum possible under the constraint that each article must be written by a single author. Additionally, the number of documents per author was balanced in each dataset to ensure class uniformity, which is crucial for fair and robust evaluation of classification models.

3.2 Data Visualization

The goal of applying t-Distributed Stochastic Neighbor Embedding (t-SNE) [7] in this work is to reduce the dimensionality of the numerical representations of scientific articles in order to visualize how texts cluster according to their authorship. This visualization aids in selecting classification models that are better suited to the inherent structure of the data.

Starting from the 20 previously extracted features, such as embeddings or text-based vectors, t-SNE projects these high-dimensional data points into a low-dimensional space, preserving, as much as possible, the local proximity relationships between points. This visualization enables us to assess whether articles written by the same author tend to form coherent groups or clusters, which would suggest that the features capture stylistic or thematic patterns unique to each author.

Additionally, this analysis facilitates the identification of overlaps or similarities between the writing styles of different authors, as well as the quality and discriminative power of the selected features.

In order to examine the spatial distribution of articles and verify the presence of natural clusters by author, we applied the t-SNE algorithm to reduce the dimensionality of the combined feature vectors—including TF-IDF, SciBERT embeddings, and linguistic features extracted with spaCy—into a two-dimensional space. The resulting visualization corresponds to a sample of five authors selected from the A35_P100 dataset (see Fig. 1), it shows that the points—each representing an individual article—tend to form well-defined clusters by author. Notably, authors such as A.G. Ramm and Amelia Carolina Sparavigna exhibit compact and clearly separated groups, indicating that their writing styles are captured by the model as highly distinctive.

In contrast, authors like ALICE Collaboration and Ali Mostafazadeh also show clustered patterns, albeit with a higher degree of dispersion, suggesting greater variability in their abstracts. The ATLAS Collaboration appears as the most dispersed and overlapping class, particularly with ALICE, which may reflect stylistic or thematic similarities between their texts, as both are part of large-scale scientific collaborations in the field of particle physics.

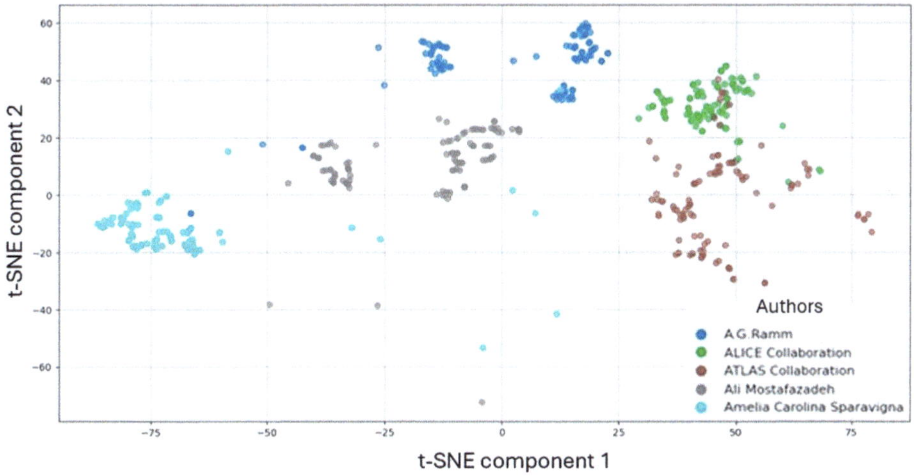

Fig. 1. t-SNE visualization of combined features (TF-IDF, SciBERT, spaCy) for 5 authors from the A35_P100 dataset. Each point represents a paper each color an author.

This visualization provides empirical support that the feature representations are capable of capturing author which reinforces the validity of the feature engineering process and the classification performance reported in later sections.

3.3 Data Pre-processing

The objective of the pre-processing stage is to remove irrelevant or noisy information and convert the raw text into a more uniform format. This step enhances the effectiveness of the authorship identification model by facilitating subsequent analysis. Specifically, URLs were removed, whitespace was normalized, and line breaks were eliminated.

Three main techniques were used for language representation and analysis are: SciBERT, TF-IDF, and spaCy. Each of these methods performs a distinct set of internal pre-processing steps that impact how the text is handled. Below, we summarize the key operations carried out by each technique, including lowercasing, tokenization, stopword removal, punctuation handling, lemmatization, and sentence segmentation:

- **SciBERT** converts text to lowercase, applies advanced tokenization based on the WordPiece model, and treats punctuation marks as separate tokens. However, it does not perform stopword removal, lemmatization, or sentence segmentation.
- **TF-IDF** also lowercases the text and uses basic regular-expression-based tokenization. By default, it does not remove stopwords, although this functionality was manually added in the model pipeline. Punctuation is removed, but no lemmatization or sentence segmentation is applied.

- **spaCy** does not lowercase text by default, but it uses advanced tokenization. It retains punctuation in the text and performs both lemmatization and sentence segmentation. Stopwords are not removed by default.

3.4 Feature Extraction

The syntactic features comprise a total of 45 dimensions, derived from various structural and lexical aspects of the text. First, Part-of-Speech (POS) tags are considered for seven specific categories: `NOUN`, `VERB`, `ADJ`, `ADV`, `NUM`, `PRON`, and `AUX`. Additionally, statistical elements such as the count of punctuation marks defined in `string.punctuation` are included, contributing 32 additional values.

Six lexical features are also integrated: average sentence length, total number of sentences, count of specific functional words, number of parenthetical expressions, and the frequency of numerical expressions followed by measurement units. These components collectively form a 45-dimensional syntactic feature vector.

This syntactic representation is then combined with numerical and semantic features:

- **TF-IDF** generates a 500-dimensional vector, adapted to the restricted length of abstracts. The vocabulary is limited to the most relevant terms in the corpus. The proposed TF-IDF conversion by SciKit-Learn was used to generate the numerical vectors.
- **SciBERT embeddings** are derived by segmenting each abstract using SciBERT's tokenizer and feeding it into the deep neural model. The final vector is obtained by averaging the token representations across the text. As with all BERT-based models, each token is represented by a **768-dimensional vector**, resulting in a semantic embedding of the same size.

All feature vectors are normalized to a [0, 1] range to ensure compatibility across representations. The final concatenated feature vector thus has a dimensionality of 1,312, composed of 45 syntactic, 500 TF-IDF, and 768 SciBERT-based semantic features.

3.5 Model Train and Evaluation

To address the authorship identification task, a classification approach was adopted. Given the high dimensionality of the feature vectors, the selected models were chosen for their robustness and relatively low computational cost.

The models employed include: Logistic Regression, Convolutional Neural Network (CNN), Multilayer Perceptron (MLP), Gated Recurrent Unit (GRU), Support Vector Machine (SVM), and two variants of Naïve Bayes classifiers: `MultinomialNB` and `GaussianNB`. Although originally designed for binary classification, Logistic Regression was adapted to the multi-class scenario using the One-vs-Rest (OvR) strategy. In this configuration, one binary classifier is trained for each author, determining whether or not a given abstract belongs to them.

All three datasets were split into training (80%) and testing (20%) subsets to train and evaluate the models.

The architecture of the MLP model consists of a single fully connected hidden layer with 256 neurons, using the ReLU activation function. For the CNN, the input data was reshaped to fit the requirements of a one-dimensional convolutional network (`Conv1D`), adding an additional channel dimension. After the convolutional layers, the output is flattened and passed through a fully connected dense layer with 128 neurons, followed by a softmax activation function for multi-class classification. In the case of the GRU, the model was trained over 10 epochs using the Adam optimizer and cross entropy as the loss function, suitable for multi-class classification. The performance of the models were evaluated using standard classification metrics: accuracy, recall, and F1-score, providing a comprehensive view of each model effectiveness in correctly attributing authorship.

4 Results and Discussion

To evaluate the impact of the extracted features, various combinations of feature extraction techniques were tested on the A300_P45 dataset. The aim was to assess how different linguistic and semantic representations affect model performance. In our experiments, we used 80% of the data for training and 20% for testing the models. In all the tables presented, we report the testing values for the used evaluation metrics.

As shown in Table 1, the combination of SciBERT embeddings, TF-IDF vectors, and linguistic features (CL) consistently outperformed the other configurations across all metrics (accuracy, precision, and F1-score). This result confirms that integrating syntactic and semantic information significantly enhances the discriminative power of the representation. Table 1 illustrates that using SciBERT embeddings alone yields solid performance (accuracy = 0.8159), which improves when combined with TF-IDF (0.8444) or linguistic features (0.8107).

The best overall accuracy of 0.8563 was achieved when all three representations were used in conjunction, highlighting the complementary nature of these feature types. In contrast, using only TF-IDF or TF-IDF combined with linguistic features yielded significantly lower performance, demonstrating that while surface-level statistical features are useful, they are insufficient on their own for capturing stylistic nuances in scientific writing.

A deeper analysis of model performance across datasets is presented in Table 2. This comparison spans six classification models applied to the three proposed datasets (A300_P45, A140_P60, and A35_P100), evaluating accuracy, precision, and F1-score. In all experiments, we used the default hyperparameters provided by the libraries (Scikit-Learn an Pytorch), as they have shown good performance according to the literature.

In the **A300_P45** dataset, where each of the 300 authors contributes 45 documents, Logistic Regression achieves the highest performance, followed closely by SVM. Deep learning models like CNN and GRU perform slightly worse, likely

Table 1. Results of Feature Extraction using different Models.

Model	Accuracy	Precision	F1-score
SCIBERT+ TFIDF+CL	**0.8563**	**0.8685**	**0.8547**
SCIBERT+TFIDF	0.8444	0.8562	0.8416
SCIBERT	0.8159	0.8280	0.8145
SCIBERT+CL	0.8107	0.8241	0.8093
TFIDF+LC	0.6396	0.6636	0.6390
TFIDF	0.6170	0.6431	0.6185

Table 2. Evaluation of six proposed models using all datasets

Dataset	Model	Accuracy	Precision	F1-score
A300_P45	Logistic Regression	**0.8563**	**0.8685**	**0.8547**
	SVM	0.8467	0.8609	0.8460
	MLP	0.8226	0.8341	0.8193
	CNN	0.7993	0.8197	0.7947
	GRU	0.7704	0.7863	0.7677
	Naïve Bayes	0.7659	0.7778	0.7616
A140_P60	Logistic Regression	**0.9042**	**0.9106**	**0.9035**
	SVM	0.8946	0.9037	0.8951
	MLP	0.8673	0.8749	0.8653
	CNN	0.8798	0.8890	0.8780
	GRU	0.8548	0.8620	0.8528
	Naïve Bayes	0.8208	0.8332	0.8185
A35_P100	Logistic Regression	**0.9629**	**0.9658**	**0.9630**
	SVM	**0.9629**	0.9639	0.9628
	MLP	0.9600	0.9615	0.9598
	CNN	0.9586	0.9610	0.9587
	GRU	**0.9629**	0.9647	0.9628
	Naïve Bayes	0.9157	0.9258	0.9148

due to their greater capacity requirements and the relatively limited number of examples per class. Naïve Bayes classifiers showed the lowest scores, suggesting their strong assumptions about feature independence may not hold in this complex, high-dimensional space.

In contrast, the **A140_P60** dataset—with more authors but fewer documents per author—showed an improvement in overall performance. Logistic Regression again achieved the best results (accuracy = 0.9042), with SVM in close second. This suggests that reducing the number of samples per author did not impair model performance, and may even facilitate better author separation, possibly due to a more diverse range of writing styles.

The **A35_P100** dataset, which includes only 35 authors but with 100 documents each, produced the highest performance across the board. Most models, including CNN and MLP, achieved accuracies above 0.95. Notably, Logistic Regression, SVM, and GRU all attained an accuracy of 0.9629, indicating that having a larger number of samples per class greatly improves classification reliability, even for simpler models. These results emphasize the importance of data volume per author in capturing stylistic consistency. The experiments demonstrate that:

- Combining semantic (SciBERT), lexical (TF-IDF), and syntactic (linguistic features) representations leads to the best classification results.
- Simpler models such as Logistic Regression and SVM consistently outperform more complex neural architectures in limited-data scenarios.
- Increasing the number of documents per author yields clear performance gains, supporting the idea that stylometric features benefit from larger, more consistent writing samples.

These findings validate the proposed approach and provide insight into the trade-offs between feature richness, model complexity, and data distribution in authorship attribution tasks.

5 Conclusions

This study successfully developed an effective and robust system for authorship attribution in scientific article abstracts by integrating advanced techniques from natural language processing (NLP), machine learning, and deep learning. The proposed approach focuses on capturing stylistic and linguistic nuances by combining multiple text representation strategies: statistical features (TF-IDF), contextual embeddings (SciBERT), and syntactic linguistic features derived from grammatical analysis using spaCy.

The joint representation strategy proved to be a key factor in enhancing model performance. Experimental results showed that while individual techniques such as TF-IDF or SciBERT embeddings alone achieved respectable performance, their combination—especially when enriched with linguistic features—significantly improved classification accuracy. The highest performance (accuracy = 0.8563) was achieved when all three types of representations were integrated, confirming the hypothesis that these features provide complementary information critical for identifying subtle stylistic patterns in scientific writing.

All models were evaluated across three distinct datasets. These were designed to simulate varying scenarios in terms of the number of authors and articles per author. Results indicated a clear correlation between the number of samples per author and classification performance. Specifically, the A35_P100 dataset—characterized by a small number of authors with many documents each—yielded the highest accuracy scores (above 96%) across almost all models, including the simpler logistic regression classifier. This suggests that having more textual data per author allows the model to more effectively learn individual stylistic traits, thereby reducing classification ambiguity. In contrast, while more complex models such as CNN and GRU did not outperform logistic regression, they exhibited competitive performance in richer data scenarios, indicating potential for further improvement with larger datasets.

These findings underscore that combining heterogeneous representations into a single enriched feature vector provides a more holistic view of an author writing style, substantially enhancing the model predictive capability. The proposed methodology demonstrates strong effectiveness for authorship attribution in scientific texts, confirming its value for applications such as plagiarism detection, academic style analysis, authorship verification in collaborative research, and automated editorial review support.

Moreover, due to its modular and adaptable architecture, the system has potential for extension to other textual domains, such as technical documentation, policy papers, and specialized literature, thus broadening its applicability in real-world NLP tasks.

Acknowledgments. The authors thankfully acknowledge computer resources, technical advice and support provided by Laboratorio Nacional de Supercómputo del Sureste de México (LNS), a member of the CONAHCYT national laboratories, with project No. 202301003N. Cecilia Reyes-Peña acknowledges to Consejo de Ciencia, Tecnología e Innovación de Hidalgo for the support provided in the program *"Becas para Posgrados de Excelencia, Maestría y Doctorado"*.

References

1. Abbas, S., et al.: Active learning for news article's authorship identification. IEEE Access **11**, 98415–98426 (2023). https://doi.org/10.1109/ACCESS.2023.3310813
2. Boenninghoff, B., Rupprecht, C., Rathgeb, C., Busch, C., Kolossa, D.: Explainable deep learning for text-based authorship attribution. Digit. Investig. **28**, S30–S38 (2019)
3. Clement, C.B., Bierbaum, M., O'Keeffe, K.P., Alemi, A.A.: On the use of arXiv as a dataset (2019)
4. Embarcadero-Ruiz, D., Gómez-Adorno, H., Embarcadero-Ruiz, A., Sierra, G.: Graph-based Siamese network for authorship verification. Mathematics **10**(2), 277 (2022)
5. He, X., Lashkari, A.H., Vombatkere, N., Sharma, D.P.: Authorship attribution methods, challenges, and future research directions: a comprehensive survey. Information **15**(3) (2024). https://doi.org/10.3390/info15030131. https://www.mdpi.com/2078-2489/15/3/131
6. Huang, B., Chen, C., Shu, K.: SIGKDD Explor. Newsl. 21–43 (2025). https://doi.org/10.1145/3715073.3715076
7. Van der Maaten, L., Hinton, G.: Visualizing data using t-SNE. J. Mach. Learn. Res. **9**(11) (2008)

8. Stamatatos, E., et al.: Overview of the authorship verification task at pan 2022. In: CEUR Workshop Proceedings, vol. 3180, pp. 2301–2313 (2022). https://ceur-ws.org/Vol-3180/, 2021 Copyright for this paper by its authors. Use permitted under Creative Commons License Attribution 4.0 International (CC BY 4.0). Proceedings of the Working Notes of CLEF 2022 - Conference and Labs of the Evaluation Forum, CLEF; Conference date: 05-09-2022 Through 08-09-2022
9. Suman, C., Saha, S., Bhattacharyya, P.: Authorship attribution of scientific abstracts. In: 2022 26th International Conference on Pattern Recognition (ICPR), pp. 1522–1528. IEEE (2022)
10. Suman, C., Saha, S., Bhattacharyya, P.: Authorship attribution of scientific abstracts. In: 2022 26th International Conference on Pattern Recognition (ICPR), pp. 1522–1528 (2022). https://doi.org/10.1109/ICPR56361.2022.9956343
11. Wu, H., Zhang, Z., Wu, Q.: Exploring syntactic and semantic features for authorship attribution. Appl. Soft Comput. **111**, 107815 (2021). https://doi.org/10.1016/j.asoc.2021.107815. https://www.sciencedirect.com/science/article/pii/S1568494621007365
12. Zhou, J., Ye, Z., Zhang, S., Geng, Z., Han, N., Yang, T.: Investigating response behavior through TF-IDF and Word2vec text analysis: a case study of PISA 2012 problem-solving process data. Heliyon **10**(16) (2024)

Author Index

A
Ahmad, M. 335
Alaniz, Omar Sánchez 187
Alarcón-Paredes, Antonio 80, 202
Alvarez-Peralta, Carolina Naomi 301
Antonio, Alarcón-Paredes 226

B
Badillo-Tecuapacho, Janet 301
Baeza-García, Cynthia 64

C
Cabrera Navarrete, Emmanuel Angel 149
Cajica-Maceda, Lourdes Beatriz 215
Carbajal-Hernández, José 64
Castro, Roberto Marquez 245
Cedillo-Hernandez, Manuel 121
Cervantes, José Luis Sánchez 97, 245
Córdova-Manzo, J. F. 258
Cornelio, Yáñez-Márquez 226
Cortes, Miguel Ángel Vejar 187
Cuecuecha, Ernesto Mendieta 269

D
Díaz Cortès, Gabriela Berenice 149
Díaz Cortés, Gabriela Berenice 168
Díaz, Jorge Ernesto González 245
Díaz-Rodríguez, Carlos Adolfo 121
Diaz-Sanguino, Oscar A. 35
Domínguez Zacarías, Galileo 168

E
Espindola Ulibarri, Luciana 283

F
Figueroa-González, Josué 35
Fuentes Cruz, Gorgonio 168

G
Gante-Díaz, Saulo Abraham 3
Gárate-Cahuantzi, Zaida Adriana 215
García-Díaz, Jesús 215
García-Ramírez, Jesús 319, 347
Gelbukh, Irina 335
Gerardo, Acevedo-Sánchez 226
Gómez-Acosta, J. A. 258
González-Baldovinos, Diana 64
González-Beltrán, Beatriz A. 35
Guarneros, Carlos Pérez 347
Guerrero-Estrada, Areli-Yesareth 136
Guzmán-Bonilla, Brenda I. 48
Guzmán-Guzmán, Iris P. 80

H
Hernández, Giner Alor 97
Hernández-Jiménez, A. 258

K
Kolesnikova, Olga 283

L
León-Pluma, María Fernanda 319

M
Mañón Juárez, J. Brandon 18
Martínez, Emilio Márquez 269
Martínez-Guerrero, Emmanuel 3
Mazahua, Lisbeth Rodríguez 97
Mazahua, Nidia Rodríguez 97
Menchaca Méndez, Rolando 283
Merino-Pérez, María J. 48
Minor-Martínez, A. 258
Montiel-Pérez, Jesús Yaljá 3
Mora-Guerrero, León S. 80
Mora-Sánchez, Juan 64

C. Palma-Preciado et al. (Eds.): CORE 2025, ACSAR 3, pp. 359–360, 2026.
https://doi.org/10.1007/978-3-032-08894-9

N
Nieto, Yara Anahí Jiménez 245

O
Olvera-Martínez, Luis Ángel 121
Óscar, Camacho-Nieto 226
Otero-Martínez, J. A. 258

P
Parada, Adolfo Rodríguez 245

Q
Quezada, L. F. 136

R
Ramírez, Jesús Emmanuel Brizuela 187
Ramírez, Jesús García 269
Ramírez, Salvador Ávila 187
Ramos-Aguilar, Eric 48, 269, 301, 319
Ramos-Aguilar, Ricardo 48, 301
Reyes-Peña, Cecilia 347
Ricárdez Vázquez, Eusebio 18
Riverón, Edgardo Manuel Felipe 335
Rodríguez-Peña, A. 258
Rosales, Carlos Andrés Morales 97
Ruíz, Abel Romero 187

S
Saavedra-Benavides, Jorge 3
Salgado Rivera, Rodolfo 202
Sánchez López, Zoila 168
Sánchez-Fernández, Luis 64
Sanchez-Garcia, Juan Carlos 121
Sánchez-Márquez, Silvia 347
Sánchez-Ruiz, Daniel 48, 301, 319
Sidorov, Grigori 335
Sun, Guo-Hua 3, 136

U
Ullah, Fida 335

V
Valerio-Trigueros, Karen Alejandra 121
Vázquez-Osorno, Estefanía Fernanda 319
Ventura Molina, Elias Jesús 202

Y
Yañez Marquez, Cornelio 202

Z
Zamir, M. Tayyab 335
Zamora Zamora, Jorge Emmanuel 202

MIX
Papier aus verantwortungsvollen Quellen
Paper from responsible sources
FSC® C105338

If you have any concerns about our products,
you can contact us on
ProductSafety@springernature.com

In case Publisher is established outside the EU,
the EU authorized representative is:
Springer Nature Customer Service Center GmbH
Europaplatz 3, 69115 Heidelberg, Germany

Printed by Libri Plureos GmbH
in Hamburg, Germany